BASIC LAW
FOR THE
ALLIED HEALTH
PROFESSIONS

—— The Jones and Bartlett Series in Health Sciences ——

Michael L. Cowdrey, J.D.

Melinda Drew, R.N., J.D.

BASIC LAW FOR THE ALLIED HEALTH PROFESSIONS

SECOND EDITION

JONES AND BARTLETT PUBLISHERS
BOSTON   **LONDON**

Editorial, Sales, and Customer Service Offices
Jones and Bartlett Publishers
One Exeter Plaza
Boston, MA 02116
617-859-3900
800-832-0034

Jones and Bartlett Publishers International
7 Melrose Terrace
London W6 7RL
England

Library of Congress Cataloging-in-Publication Data

Cowdrey, Michael L., 1944-
    Basic law for the allied health professions / Michael L. Cowdrey
and Melinda Drew. -- 2nd ed.
        p.   cm.
    Includes bibliographical references and index.
    ISBN 0-86720-710-8
    1. Allied health personnel--Legal status, laws, etc.--United
States.   2. Medical personnel--Malpractice--united States.
I. Drew, Melinda.   II. Title.
KF2914.C69 1995
344.73'041--dc20
[347.30441]   94-38115
                                                                                      CIP

Acquisitions Editor: Jan Wall
Production Editor: Judy Songdahl
Manufacturing Buyer: Dana L. Cerrito
Editorial Production and Typesetting: TKM Productions
Cover Design: Lina Haddad
Printing and Binding: Malloy Lithographing

Printed in the United States of America
99 98 97 96 95   10 9 8 7 6 5 4 3 2 1

DEDICATION

This book is dedicated to my wife and children,
who, through their continued support, many hours of typing,
examples and suggestions, and personal sacrifice,
made this a labor of love.

Michael L. Cowdrey
(from the first edition)

The second edition of this book is dedicated to my mother,
to my sister, Kate, and to Jeff, with gratitude for his
love and support in this, as in all things.

Melinda Drew
(for the second edition)

CONTENTS

PREFACE

The updating of these materials and the revisions for this second edition were done by Melinda Drew, a nurse-attorney in Boston, Massachusetts. Ms. Drew has a professional background as a psychiatric nurse specializing, for many years, in the treatment of substance abusers, as well as experience as an attorney since 1987. In addition to her private practice of law, Ms. Drew is an adjunct faculty member in the Paralegal Studies program at Suffolk University and Fisher College in Boston.

The second edition of this text remains faithful to Michael L. Cowdrey's original format while, at the same time, updating and revising the relevant law to reflect the changes of the past decade.

While every attempt has been made to ensure that the law discussed is current, the reader must keep in mind that the law varies from state to state and is constantly changing. Therefore, a concept that is accurate for one state may not be for another. Moreover, what is accurate and relevant today can be outdated tomorrow. If you need up-to-date information on any concept discussed in this book, you should check with an attorney in your state to find out whether the information is still valid. Similarly, the forms provided in this book are general in nature and may not fit your specific circumstances. Any form you wish to use should be reviewed and carefully tailored to your particular circumstances. Again, the advice of an attorney in your state is recommended.

Melinda Drew
October, 1994

Preface to the First Edition

This book addresses the legal concerns and questions of individuals who work in a health care setting. The text uses simple, straightforward language and draws on specific cases and statutes from diverse health fields, including medical and dental assisting, dentistry, radiological technology, nursing, chiropractics, and medical record keeping. The generalized concepts of the law and the illustrations given can be applied to any of the allied health professions.

The text employs numerous learning aids: a glossary of key terms, review questions and examples, AMA-style medical forms, suggested letters, and model processed forms. Questions and examples following each chapter directly relate to the material contained in that chapter and are generalized to allow the reader to adapt them to his or her particular profession.

This broad survey of legal concepts relevant to the health professions is based on my many years of lecturing to undergraduates and practitioners in these professions. While practicing radiological technology for fifteen years, including ten years as a medical assistant in a private office, I became acutely aware of the many pitfalls attendant to medical assisting. Subsequently, I taught medical assisting, including both front- and back-office procedures, at Southern California College of Medical and Dental Careers and Saddleback Community College in Mission Viejo, California. As an attorney since 1975, I have become well aware of the pressing need for a simple, straightforward text on the law as it relates to the allied health professions and have given numerous lectures on this topic for medical assistants through the American Association of Medical Assistants (AAMA). This text represents an expansion of a lecture that has been approved for continuing educational units in California for Certified Medical Assistant.

The usual conclusion for a preface is an exhaustive list of all those persons who supported and assisted the author in writing the text. Trusting that my wife, family, and professional colleagues know who they are, I do wish to acknowledge the students whose questions and examples demonstrated to me the necessity for this text. In addition, I wish to give special acknowledgment to Adrian Perenon, senior editor for Wadsworth Health Sciences, whose initial and continued enthusiasm and assistance have made this text possible.

Michael L. Cowdrey

CHAPTER ONE

INTRODUCTION TO THE LAW

STATUTES OR CODES
    Case Law and Common Law

MALPRACTICE

THE PLAINTIFF

THE PROSECUTOR

THE DEFENDANT

THE CAUSE OF ACTION

CONTRACT LAW

TORT LAW

CRIMINAL LAW

ADMINISTRATIVE LAW
    Violation of a Regulation
    Conduct Under a Criminal Statute
      Methadone treatment
      Food and Drug Administration
      Licensing regulations

EXAMPLES/QUESTIONS/
PROJECTS

Key Terms

consideration	defendant	felony
premeditated	theory	mayhem
malpractice	assert	burglary
failure to act	negligence	robbery
liability	contract	fraud
plaintiff	imply	embezzlement
alleged	implied contract	trust
heir	trespass	arson
guardian	infraction	murder
ad litem	misdemeanor	rape
litigation	tort	

Laws are nothing more than a set of rules or principles that command or restrain us from doing certain things. Historically, the law has been derived from court rulings, federal and state constitutions, legislation, and custom. The law has also been divided into various categories and subcategories. For example, laws dealing with the transfer of land or its use have been classified as *real property law*. Laws dealing with the obligation of one person to perform an act for another person on receipt of some type of **consideration** fall into the category of *contract law*. Laws dealing with injury to one person by another person traditionally are the concern of *tort law*. Laws dealing with the formation of a **trust** or with overseeing the distribution of a person's estate on his or her death most commonly fall within the area of *probate law*.

In addition to classification by subject matter, the law has also been classified as public or private. *Public law* most commonly deals with the state, either by itself or in its relations with individual persons. For example, constitutional law deals with a person's right of free speech, right to privacy, and so on. Administrative law deals with rules and regulations governing a person's conduct as set down by a bureaucratic agency. The federal Food and Drug Administration, local zoning departments that govern the operation of a business or its locale, worker's compensation appeals boards or their equivalents, and state and federal licensing boards that govern a person's practice or profession are examples of such bureaucratic agencies. Criminal law and criminal procedure likewise fall into the category of public law and govern or restrict our conduct or the conduct of a law-enforcement agency in prosecuting a case.

Private laws are a set of rules that govern conduct between two individual persons or groups of persons. These laws also establish an individual's right to be compensated or otherwise made whole by the individual who caused the person harm. These laws are briefly discussed later in this chapter under the categories of tort law, contract law, real property law, and probate law.

Within the various areas of law that have been mentioned, the law is also divided into two basic parts. *Substantive law* is that part of the law that creates rights and obligations. *Procedural*, or *adjective, law* provides a method of enforcing and protecting such rights and obligations.

If you feel dismayed or confused at this point, you are not alone—even jurists and legal scholars do not fully agree on a comprehensive definition of the term *law*. Suffice it to say that for the majority of this text we will be dealing with only a very few areas of the law.

The following chapters discuss various areas of the law and provide a breakdown of elements within a particular set of laws or rules. Examples are presented, and each set of facts is analyzed as it applies to a particular area of the law or an element of that area. Based on the assumption that the student reading this text has very little knowledge of the law and its terms, basic, concise definitions can be found in a glossary at the back of the book.[1] Ex-

---

[1]Glossary terms will appear in **boldface** type throughout the book.

amples of completed forms used in practice are given, along with an explanation of the purpose and use of each form.

In the remainder of this chapter, definitions of major terms are provided as a foundation for the discussion presented in this book.

STATUTES OR CODES

Statutes—also termed *codes* in some jurisdictions—are rules or regulations set down in printed form by a legislative branch of the government. Federal statutes are established by the Congress, whereas state statutes are established by the various state legislatures.

Case law and Common law

Case law is generally used to refer to the written opinions of appellate courts on specific issues arising from litigation. That is, if two or more parties have a dispute that results in a lawsuit, the trial court decides the factual questions raised by the case and then applies the appropriate law to the facts. Once the trial is over, either party that feels the trial court applied the wrong law or legal standard may appeal to a higher level court (appellate court) concerning that question of law. Once the appellate court makes its decision and writes an opinion on the specific issue or issues appealed, that opinion is case law.

Common law expresses the view that the law is an evolving body of doctrine decided by judges in cases brought before them. Such decisions then become established as precedents for future cases that rest on similar facts and are interpreted according to the same reasoning. Over time, as these established principles are tested and adapted to meet new situations as presented by new cases, the common law changes.

Some areas of the law are governed entirely by case law while other areas are governed in part by case law and in part by statute, or governed by statutes as interpreted by the courts. That is, often the legislature enacts a statute prohibiting certain kinds of activities or behavior. However, whether a particular action or type of behavior violates the statute must be determined by the courts. Death penalty cases are good examples of this principle. The majority of states have a statute that dictates that the punishment for premeditated murder is death. Should a person be found guilty of premeditated murder in one of these states, he or she would be sentenced to die in the manner and form prescribed by the state. Such manner might take the form of hanging, death by lethal injection, death by the gas chamber, and so on. However, the facts of certain cases in many states have led the U.S. Supreme Court to overturn the state statute because it conflicted with some other fundamental principles of law or with the person's protected constitutional rights. For example, a state statute that prescribed that a person found guilty of premeditated murder would be put to death by starvation would undoubtedly be overturned by the Supreme Court because it was in conflict with the constitutional protection against cruel and unusual punishment.

MALPRACTICE

In modern times, the term **malpractice** has been somewhat overgeneralized to every area of the law dealing with the alleged misconduct of a professional person. Originally, the term dealt only with the allied health professions. However, it has been expanded to encompass legal malpractice, accountant's malpractice, real estate broker's malpractice, architect's malpractice, and, generally, any misconduct of a professional person that occurs within that person's field of expertise.

Malpractice itself is defined as "any professional misconduct, unreasonable lack of skill or fidelity in professional or fiduciary duties, evil practice or illegal or immoral conduct" (*Black's Law Dictionary*, 1979).

Analysis of the definition indicates that the misconduct or unreasonable lack of skill must be within the profession of the person committing the act or omission. Thus, malpractice can only be associated with an act or **failure** (omission) **to act** by a person who pursues a profession and makes his or her living therefrom. The pursuit of a profession means that the professional person, in carrying out his or her duties, makes decisions based on his or her judgment in light of the facts or circumstances presented by a particular patient or case. To illustrate, let us look at the difference between the work performed by a professional person and that performed by a worker on an assembly line. On a traditional assembly line, a worker does the same job day in and day out—for example, putting a particular nut on a particular bolt or welding part A to part B. In contrast, the professional person has many duties associated with his or her profession, routinely making judgments relating to those duties. Although guided by some set of standards, he or she carries out those duties differently from patient to patient or from case to case depending on the circumstances encountered.

Further analysis of the definition of malpractice indicates that the misconduct must fall within that person's professional dealings with another person. In other words, a medical assistant, nurse, physician, dentist, or other professional person would not necessarily be guilty of malpractice for causing injury to another person as a result of an automobile collision as long as the automobile collision occurred outside the professional relationship with the individual injured. Even though the medical assistant, physician, dentist, or other professional may be liable to the injured party, **liability** would not be assessed on the grounds of malpractice.

However, an ambulance driver on an emergency call may be guilty of malpractice and liable to a patient riding in the ambulance who sustains injuries as a result of a collision between the ambulance and another car. This is only because the ambulance driver is acting within the course and scope of his or her profession in transporting the patient.

These two simplified examples are only meant for illustration, since in both instances the medical assistant or physician or the ambulance driver could possibly be held responsible for any individual's injuries on other grounds, including ordinary negligence.

THE PLAINTIFF

The **plaintiff** in a lawsuit is the person bringing the action or asserting a claimed right. The term *plaintiff* should not necessarily be associated with the term *patient*. Most commonly, the plaintiff is the patient who brings an action against the professional person for **alleged** malpractice. However, the plaintiff may also be the spouse, heir, or legal representative of the patient. For example, the husband or **heir** of a former patient may file a lawsuit against a physician for alleged misconduct that caused the patient's death.

Also, the law generally does not recognize the ability of a minor child or an incompetent person to bring an action or file a lawsuit on his or her own behalf. Thus, a dentist or dental assistant who negligently performs dental work on a minor child or an incompetent person may be sued by a child's parent or by a guardian appointed by the court to represent a child or an incompetent person Such a guardian, called a guardian **ad litem,** is an adult who prosecutes or defends a suit on behalf of a minor child or an incompetent person.

Finally, the professional person could file a lawsuit against a patient, thus becoming a plaintiff in the **litigation.** For example, a physician, dentist, hospital, or similar institution may file a lawsuit against a patient to collect fees for professional services rendered.

In all cases where a person is the plaintiff in a lawsuit, the lawsuit is based on a civil remedy. In other words, the lawsuit is brought by one individual person or group of persons against another individual person or group of persons.

THE PROSECUTOR

The prosecutor is somewhat similar to the plaintiff in a civil lawsuit. However, this term is used exclusively in dealing with areas of public law. The prosecutor is the person bringing the action on behalf of the public at large. This person may be the district attorney, the U.S. prosecuting attorney, the attorney general, or another authorized member of an enforcing agency that acts on the public's behalf. The term *prosecutor* is commonly associated with criminal proceedings. Because the prosecutor is acting on the public's behalf, he or she is also much like the guardian ad litem who sues or defends on behalf of a minor or incompetent person in a civil lawsuit.

THE DEFENDANT

The **defendant** to an action is the person being sued or prosecuted. He or she is known as the defendant, whether the lawsuit is based on a violation of a public law or on a violation of a private type of statute. Thus, the professional person being sued by an individual for injuries allegedly caused by the professional's misconduct is the defendant to the lawsuit. He or she is also the defendant when being prosecuted by an authorized agent of the people. Thus, a medical assistant, nurse, or physician is also the defendant when he or she is being prosecuted by the district attorney for criminal misconduct.

THE CAUSE OF ACTION

The cause or type of action brought against the defendant to a lawsuit is the **theory** on which liability for the alleged misconduct is being **asserted** against the defendant. Most, if not all, jurisdictions, whether state or federal, allow for the assertion of more than one theory of liability against the defendant. Thus, an obstetrician who refuses to deliver a patient's baby after being paid by the patient to perform that service may be sued for his or her breach of promise. The theory on which liability could be asserted against the doctor would be based on the principles of contract law. The doctor may also be sued on the principles and theories of tort law for abandonment of the patient in refusing to deliver the baby if such abandonment occurs at or near the time of the scheduled delivery.

In addition to the various theories of civil liability that may be asserted by an individual against the professional for alleged misconduct, the state or federal government may prosecute the same individual for the alleged misconduct if it is a violation of some criminal law. However, criminal prosecution for such alleged misconduct would be a separate proceeding from the civil lawsuit. For example, a nurse could be criminally prosecuted for murder, under certain circumstances, for disconnecting a critical life-support system of a patient. In addition, that nurse could be sued by that patient's heirs or representative for any damages under tort law for bringing about or aiding in the patient's death. The nurse would be prosecuted by the district attorney or some other authorized agent acting on behalf of the particular state. This criminal proceeding would be tried separately from the civil lawsuit brought by the patient's heirs or representative. The theories on which the prosecutor might base his or her case include murder, voluntary or involuntary manslaughter, or negligent homicide in causing the patient's death.

The heirs or representative of the patient would undoubtedly base their civil lawsuit on theories of **negligence**, intentional misconduct, and/or breach of a contractual obligation owed by the nurse to the patient, which breach brought about the patient's death.

CONTRACT LAW

It is sufficient at this time to define a **contract** as a promise made in exchange for a promise. The promise may be an actual promise in exchange for another person's actual promise. For example, John may say to Mary, "I promise to pay you ten dollars if you promise to sell me your roller skates." When Mary agrees to sell the roller skates, the contract is formed. Thereafter, should John not give Mary the money, she could sue him for breaching the contract. Conversely, John could sue Mary if she failed to deliver the roller skates to him.

The promise can also be made by implication. For example, when a patient goes into a doctor's office for an examination or treatment, the patient **implies** a promise to pay for the services rendered. Conversely, the doctor implies a promise to render professional services to the patient. If the patient fails to pay for the services after they have been rendered, the doctor may sue the patient for payment of his or her bill, asserting that the patient has breached the **implied contract**. The patient may likewise sue the doctor for breaching their implied contract in the event that the doctor fails to provide sufficient or adequate treatment. Remember, too, that the doctor may also be sued under the principles of tort law for providing inadequate treatment or treatment that is below the standard of care of the profession.

TORT LAW

Tort law deals with a legal wrong that is committed by one person on the person or property of another and is based not on public laws or any contractual obligation. Rather, a lawsuit in tort is a private suit between the parties involved. It is a civil matter as opposed to a criminal matter; it is brought by one individual or entity against another for relief, such as compensation for an injury or a court order requiring the defendant to stop committing the wrongful act.

For example, the legal wrong committed may be a direct invasion or violation of some legal right of the individual. The violation may be an invasion of the person's right to privacy, a negligent infliction of an injury, or trespassing that causes damage to that person's property.

It may also be an infraction of some public duty by which some special damage may attach to an injured individual. For example, a person fails to stop his or her automobile at a stop sign: this would be a violation of a public law.

As a result of this violation, an automobile collision occurs with another vehicle, causing that driver to be injured. The medical bills incurred for treatment by the injured driver constitute that driver's *special damage.* This special damage is incurred and caused by the infraction of the other driver, whose public duty it was to stop at the stop sign.

Finally, the violation of some private obligation by which damage is sustained by the individual falls under the category of tort law. The wrong committed—whether by an act or by a failure to act where there is a duty to do so—is classified as a civil wrong as opposed to a criminal wrong. A more detailed analysis of tort law and its elements will be provided in subsequent chapters.

CRIMINAL LAW

The statutes or codes that form the basis of this area of the law fall under the general category of public law previously discussed. More specifically, the statutes and codes that define criminal activity carry the imposition of penalties. Most commonly, the penalty imposed is that of incarceration (jail or prison) or activity restriction in the form of probation. Also, many statutes allow the court to impose a fine of some dollar amount on the defendant to the action. This may be in addition to or in lieu of a jail sentence. For example, the court may give the defendant the option of either paying a twenty-five dollar fine or spending two days in jail as punishment for violating a traffic law.

Criminal laws are also categorized as either infractions, misdemeanors, or felonies. **Infractions** are minor violations, most commonly associated with traffic laws. However, many states have now adopted the principle that minor drug violations, such as the possession of a small amount of marijuana, are to be included as minor criminal infractions. Infractions commonly carry the penalty of payment of a fine by the defendant for his or her violation.

Misdemeanors are criminal acts that carry the penalty of fine, jail, or probation. The amount of time that the defendant may be required to serve in jail generally does not exceed one year. An example of a misdemeanor in the state of California is the possession of a hypodermic syringe or needle by an unauthorized person. This may include a medical assistant or an allied health professional other than a physician where such possession is outside the treatment facility. An individual found guilty of this type of statutory criminal activity may be incarcerated for a period not to exceed six months for each alleged violation.

A **felony** is a major criminal activity, The old English common law felonies included **murder, rape, mayhem, burglary, robbery,** and **arson.** Felonious activities have been expanded to include narcotic sales, **fraud, embezzlement,** and many others. The penalty for a felony conviction is usually incarceration in a penal institution for a period exceeding one year. In addition, for certain types of felonious conduct, the court may impose a fine. The court may also require the defendant to make restitution to an injured individual in cases of fraud, embezzlement, or similar offenses.

ADMINISTRATIVE LAW

Administrative law falls under the category of public law. The major difference from criminal law is that the activities defined are in the form of regulations, set by an administrative or bureaucratic agency.

Violation of a regulation

Violation of a regulation generally carries with it the imposition of a penalty in the form of a restricting or restraining of the professional's right to practice. For example, the federal regulating agency governing a facility's right to compensation under the Medicare or Medicaid programs is the Department of Health and Human Services. The department sets up certain guidelines that the facility must follow if it is to be compensated by the government for treatment rendered to patients in such programs. Included in the guidelines are the method of record keeping, the charges allowed for certain types of treatment, and the government's right to inspect the records of the facility on reasonable demand. In the event that the facility does not follow the established guidelines, the government may then restrict that facility from participating in the government's funded programs. This penalty may be withdrawn on the facility's demonstration of compliance as outlined in the specific regulation.

Conduct under a criminal statute

Within the area of administrative law are also included regulations defining criminal conduct and providing for criminal prosecution. Often a state legislature or the congress will effectively put into law a broadly worded statute or code restricting certain types of conduct. The task of defining such conduct is then given to the appropriate administrative agency. For example, statutes dealing with drugs and narcotics and their distribution are broadly defined in terms depicting the conduct restricted, not the specific drug or narcotic. The definition of the type of drug related to the restricted conduct is then left to a federal agency such as the Food and Drug Administration. Application and prosecution in this area can be seen in numerous cases. Two such examples follow.

Methadone treatment

The federal government, by statute, restricted the prescription of methadone in the treatment of heroin addicts to physicians whose practice was recognized as a methadone treatment facility. The definition of a methadone treatment facility was then left to the administrative agencies which, in turn, developed regulations that explain what a methadone treatment facility is, as well as set forth many other criteria to be met. The regulations further provide that if the persons responsible for administering or dispensing narcotic drugs for narcotic addict treatment fail to abide by all of the regulation's requirements, criminal prosecution may be instituted against him or her.

Food and Drug Administration

The federal Food and Drug Administration has broad powers, including the power to enforce its decisions, under such federal statutes as the Fair Packaging and Labelling Act, the Federal Food, Drug, and Cosmetic Act, and the Public Health Service Act. Among other things, the Food and Drug Administration has the power to require warning labels on products. If a manufacturer fails to comply with an order of the Food and Drug Administration to include a warning label on its product, the Commissioner of the Food and Drug Administration may bring criminal prosecution under the Federal Food, Drug, and Cosmetic Act. In such a case, the regulations also state what notice must be given to the manufacturer and that the manufacturer must be given an opportunity to present information in its defense and to show cause why prosecution should not be recommended to a United States attorney.

Licensing regulations

Further regulation of the professional's conduct is found in the various rules set by the regulating agencies governing the health professional's license and right to practice. State legislatures have granted the power to various state licensing agencies to regulate the practice of professionals, including dentists, doctors, chiropractors, orthodontists, osteopaths, registered nurses, laboratory technicians, radiological technologists (X-ray technicians), and many others. All of the state licensing agencies have set certain rules that cover the educational requirements for becoming licensed and the criteria for licensing examinations. More importantly, the states have set guidelines relating to the conduct, including the moral conduct of the individual in obtaining or maintaining his or her license. Thus, the regulating agency may revoke or suspend a professional's license to practice because of immoral or illicit conduct, even though that conduct may not be criminal or fall within the category of professional misconduct.

EXAMPLES / QUESTIONS / PROJECTS

1. *Jane is applying to the state licensing agency for a registered nurse's license. Jane was previously found guilty in a criminal proceeding for sex offenses involving minor children. Will she be granted the license?*

> **Answer:** Probably not, since Jane's prior conduct involved acts that are considered immoral by most state regulating agencies.

2. *Mark is a medical assistant who accidentally uses the wrong solution to clean a patient's open wound. The patient sustains only minor injuries, however, as a result of his mistake. May Mark's conduct be considered an act of malpractice?*

> **Answer:** Yes. It makes little difference that the injury sustained was only minor. Mark was acting as a professional in cleaning the patient's wound, and he undoubtedly breached the standard of care owing to the patient by not checking to make sure that the solution was the proper one to use. His conduct in not checking was negligent.

3. *Joe is a dental assistant who accidentally causes a patient's gum to be lacerated by a dental instrument while he is helping his employer. May Joe's conduct be considered an act of dental malpractice?*

> **Answer:** Yes. Joe was acting as a professional at the time of the patient's injury. If the patient can demonstrate that Joe was not careful, as he should have been, his conduct will be judged negligent.

4. *Deborah is a medical assistant/receptionist for Dr. Smith. Mr. Bradley, one of the doctor's patients is injured when he attempts to sit down in the waiting-room chair and the chair collapses. Can Deborah be charged with malpractice?*

> **Answer:** Deborah can be charged with negligent conduct for failing to routinely look for broken waiting-room chairs. This is one of the routine duties associated with the medical assistant who performs front-office duties for the doctor or for another treatment facility. However, Deborah cannot be charged with negligent conduct if she can demonstrate that she did check for broken chairs on a routine basis. Also, she cannot be found guilty of any misconduct or professional negligence if the chair collapses because Mr. Bradley weighs 450 pounds. (See the section on professional negligence, misfeasance, malfeasance, and nonfeasance in Chapter 3 for more information on this topic.)

Chapter Two

THE CONTRACT

FORMAL CONTRACT
  Condition Precedent
  Abandonment of Patient
IMPLIED CONTRACT

FORMATION OF THE CONTRACT
  Principle or Detrimental Reliance
  Limitations of Contractual Duties
EXAMPLES/QUESTIONS/PROJECTS

Key Terms

formal contract

express contract
condition precedent

detrimental reliance

Common sense would dictate that the professional person owes a duty of care to a patient under his or her treatment. The question is, How does the duty arise, and, once established, does it ever end? Most commonly, the duty of care owing to a patient is established under the principles of contract law.

FORMAL CONTRACT

As described in Chapter 1 in the example of John and Mary's buy-sell agreement for her roller skates, a physician, dentist, or other practitioner may be held to a duty of examining and/or rendering treatment to a patient under a **formal contract** or **express contract.** An example of this is to be found in prepaid health plans, in which the practitioner's services have been formally contracted in advance by the patient. In this case, the patient subscribes to the service by a prepayment of money.

A premium paid to an insurance company gives the patient a list of subscribing physicians to the service. In some states, private clinics formally contract with patients to examine and/or render treatment based on the patient's payment of monthly dues for the services.

Formal contracts are also commonly made between orthodontists and their patients—typically, where periodic orthodontic treatment is required to accomplish the desired result, as in cases dealing with the application of braces to straighten a patient's teeth. Based on the length of time required, the contract also sets out the method of payment. Generally, the contract requires payment to be made on a monthly basis until the full amount has been paid for services rendered.

Condition precedent

The contract itself establishes the duty to examine and/or treat the patient. However, in cases dealing with prepaid services, the duty to examine and/or treat is predicated on prepayment of money for the services. In contractual terms, this prepayment is called a **condition precedent,** which must be met before the duty to perform arises. Should the patient fail to pay the premium under the contract, the dentist, doctor, or other professional would not owe a duty to perform professional services under the terms of the contract. However, as will be seen, the doctor, dentist, clinic, institution, or other professional operating under the formal contract may nevertheless be obligated to continue treatment that has been undertaken even though the patient fails to pay the monthly premium.

Where the patient has paid the prepayment premium, he or she can maintain an action against the physician, dentist, or other professional based on a breach of the contractual obligation for refusal to render services. Most commonly, the only cause of action the patient can maintain is based on the breach of the contractual obligation. As mentioned in subsequent chapters dealing with the breach of duty and with damages, the patient may be restricted in the amount of money he or she may receive as compensation for the refusal to provide professional services based on this legal theory.

Abandonment of patient

However, as in the case of the orthodontist's contract with the patient, once treatment has been undertaken, the patient might also be able to sue the orthodontist or other contracting professional under theories of tort law. The most common theory asserted is that of *abandonment of patient*.[1] This theory can be asserted in the lawsuit in addition to the theory of breach of the contractual obligation should the orthodontist, dentist, physician, clinic, or institution refuse to render further services.

IMPLIED CONTRACT

More commonly, the contractual duty to render professional services to a patient arises by implication. This type of contract has been termed the *implied-in-fact contract.* Generally, the patients come into the doctor's office, whereupon they are greeted by the receptionist. They may then be asked to fill out a general information form giving a brief history of their chief complaint. Next they are told that they should be seated and that the doctor will be along shortly. The doctor, by the acts of the receptionist, implies a promise to examine and/or treat the patient. Conversely, the patient implies the agreement to pay for the services. The contract arises from these facts alone. There is no formal promise in exchange for another promise within the definition of an implied-in-fact contract.

As will be more fully discussed in the sections dealing with breach of the duty of care and standard of care, the doctor or other professional implies an agreement to render professional care conformable to the standards set by the profession. However a question often presented is, how much may the doctor or other professional charge for the services rendered?

Under the prepayment contract for professional services, the patient is charged only the monthly premium for all services, plus, perhaps, a small fee (usually in the $2.00 to $10.00 range) per visit. Thus, a patient obtaining medical care under a prepayment system most often is not aware of the actual cost of the care. For a patient who is paying the physician directly for medical care, the law allows the doctor to charge a reasonable value for his or her services. Again, the definition of the term *reasonable* is established by standards of custom for the type of service rendered. It is based on the geographic area of the doctor, dentist, or other professional's practice. In other words, the court will look at the types of service rendered by the professional to the patient and

---

[1]See also Chapter 3

the amount charged for these services. The court will then compare this amount to the amount charged by other physicians or similar professionals within the local geographic area for similar professional services. The court will also take into consideration the doctor's expertise when assessing the reasonableness of his or her charges.

FORMATION OF THE CONTRACT

The formal oral contract is established when both parties have formally promised to be bound. Thus, when one party offers to do something in exchange for the other party's agreement to do something, the contract is formed by the acceptance of the offer. For example, where Mary offers to sell John the roller skates for ten dollars, the contract is formed when John accepts the offer by his agreement (promise) to pay the ten dollars.

Certain formal contracts will not be enforced if made verbally. For example, the common law and most state statutes require that contracts for personal services that will take longer than one year to be performed must be in writing.

The duty of the physician or other professional, then, begins with the formation of the contractual obligation. In the case of a formal written contract, the duty begins when the written agreement has been signed by the doctor (or his or her authorized representative) and the patient. In the case of prepaid insurance plans or similar allied health plans, the duty to render professional services begins when the condition precedent (prepayment of money) has been met by the patient. However, problems become apparent when dealing with the implied-in-fact contract, as the following section makes clear.

Principle of detrimental reliance

Physicians, dentists, chiropractors, osteopaths, and other professionals are not obligated to examine or render treatment to anyone who comes into their office unless there is an express contractual obligation to render such services. However, the common law principle of **detrimental reliance** has long been asserted in establishing a contractual relationship. This principle maintains that, when a person relies to his or her detriment in thinking that the other party will agree to become obligated, this reliance is sufficient to establish the contractual obligation. The following simplified example illustrates this principle.

A phone call is received from frantic Mrs. Davis late on a Friday afternoon when the doctor and her assistants are preparing to close the office. Mrs. Davis tells the medical assistant that her son has just fallen off his bicycle and is bleeding badly. The medical assistant tells Mrs. Davis to bring her son into the doctor's office immediately. Mrs. Davis then puts her son into the family car and drives to the doctor's office.

En route, Mrs. Davis passes two emergency clinics, an emergency treatment hospital, and three other doctors' offices. All of these facilities and doctors offices would have treated her son for his injuries.

Mrs. Davis finally arrives at the doctor's office, whereupon she is greeted by the medical assistant. Never having been to this doctor before, she is requested to pay for the examination and treatment before the doctor will render care to the injured boy. At this point, she tells the medical assistant that she has not brought any money or her checkbook. She explains that the medical assistant she spoke to over the phone did not mention anything about prepayment in the initial telephone conversation. The medical assistant/receptionist responds with a gratuitous smile, her apologies and the statement that payment for the initial visit is "office policy." Accordingly, the doctor does not see Mrs. Davis's son.

Thereafter, Mrs. Davis's son suffers irreparable injuries caused by the delay in receiving treatment elsewhere. In her presentation to the jury, Mrs. Davis maintains that her son could have been treated at the other facilities that she passed en route to the doctor's office. However, on the advice given her by the medical assistant to bring the injured boy into the office immediately, Mrs. Davis relied to her son's detriment.

On conclusion of the case, the judge instructs the jury that the doctor would have a contractual obligation to render care to the injured boy if they found in fact that Mrs. Davis relied to her son's detriment. Further, if a contractual duty to render care was found, the jury could then consider awarding damages for breach of that duty and abandonment of patient.

In the preceding example, you be the judge. In most jurisdictions and with most juries, liability would probably be assessed against the doctor based on a contractual obligation to render care to Mrs. Davis's son. The duty to render care arose as a combination of the initial telephone conversation and the reliance of Mrs. Davis on the doctor's treating her son. In addition, note that it was the doctor's failure to act, rather than her negligent or unprofessional action, that gave rise to her liability. Also, the doctor's obligation arose from the representation made by her medical assistant and not from the doctor herself. Liability would be imposed because the medical assistant was acting as the doctor's authorized agent, both at the time of the initial telephone conversation and at the time that the assistant refused to allow the injured boy to be seen based on the office policy of prepayment. These two important principles will be discussed in detail in subsequent chapters.

Limitations of contractual duties

In all cases dealing with a contractual obligation to perform, the duty to perform is restricted to that specified under the terms and conditions of the contract. In cases dealing with prepaid insurance or similar medical plans, the duty to render examinations and/or treatment for any and all ailments is only predicated on the patient's prepayment of a premium. However, in the cases dealing with an informal or implied contract, the physician, dentist, or other professional is obligated to render services only for the ailment for which the patient is being treated.

For example, Mr. Nguyen is being treated by Dr. Gold for a broken arm. During the course of treatment, Mr. Nguyen suffers chest pains while at home. He goes to Dr. Gold and requests treatment for his chest pains, but Dr. Gold refuses to treat him because Mr. Nguyen has failed to pay his bill for treatment of the broken arm. Would Dr. Gold be liable to Mr. Nguyen for breach of his contractual duty to render treatment? The answer to this question is no. The only duty, contractual or otherwise, owing to Mr. Nguyen by Dr. Gold is for treatment of Mr. Nguyen's broken arm. There is no contract to extend services for the treatment of another ailment.

EXAMPLES / QUESTIONS / PROJECTS

1. *Maria is the front-office receptionist and medical assistant for Dr. Ruiz. Mr. Samuels is being treated for a broken arm. During the course of treatment, Maria tells Mr. Samuels that Dr. Ruiz refuses to render further medical care for the broken arm because Mr. Samuels has not paid his bills for past services. Is that refusal to render further care a breach of any contractual obligation owed by Dr. Ruiz to Mr. Samuels?*

   Answer: Yes. The contract probably arose as an implied-in-fact contract when Dr. Ruiz undertook to render treatment for the broken arm. However, Mr. Samuels has breached the contract by not paying his bill. This gives the doctor a legal excuse for not performing further services. But the doctor must give the patient adequate notice of his intent to cease further performance under the contract. In addition, the doctor must give the patient reasonable time to secure the services of another physician.

2. *Mr. Samuels merely walks into Dr. Ruiz's office and requests to see the doctor. He explains to the medical assistant/receptionist that he has been having chest pains. The medical assistant tells Mr. Samuels to be seated and then checks with Dr. Ruiz to ascertain whether the doctor will see Mr. Samuels. Dr. Ruiz indicates that he will not examine Mr. Samuels. May Dr. Ruiz be held liable by Mr. Samuels for breach of contract?*

Answer: No. Merely telling Mr. Samuels to be seated is not an expression by the medical assistant that Dr. Ruiz will render an examination or treatment. Moreover, Mr. Samuels cannot demonstrate that he relied to his detriment by not seeking medical attention elsewhere because neither the medical assistant nor the doctor stated, or implied by act, that Dr. Ruiz would perform the requested services.

3. *Dorothy is a patient of Dr. Marlow, who is a very fine orthodontist. Dr. Marlow has applied braces to Dorothy's teeth for the purpose of straightening them. The overall treatment, to obtain the desired results, will take approximately eighteen months. Dorothy tells Dr. Marlow that she will pay him the requested fee in monthly installments until the total amount is paid. Thereafter, Dorothy fails to pay. Dr. Marlow then brings a lawsuit against Dorothy based on breach of their contractual obligation. He indicates that the breach was occasioned by Dorothy's failure to pay monthly installments. May he collect?*

   Answer: The answer to this question is no in those states requiring that a contract to perform personal services that take longer than one year to complete must be in writing. In this situation, the express contract between Dorothy and Dr. Marlow is only verbal. Therefore, the doctor would be barred from collecting based on the express contract. However, most states recognize that he can collect a reasonable fee for the services he has already provided to Dorothy.

4. *John is an eight-year-old boy who is treated by Dr. Rogers for a broken arm. John's parents fail to pay John's medical bill for the services rendered. May Dr. Rogers maintain an action for breach of contract against the parents for failure to pay?*

   Answer: Yes. In all states, the parents or legal guardian of a minor child are obligated to provide that child with the necessities of life, including medical treatment. The minor child is not legally competent to enter into and be bound to a contract. However, the parents, by authorizing medical treatment, create an implied-in-fact contract to pay for medical services rendered to the child.

CHAPTER THREE

NEGLIGENCE AND THE STANDARD OF CARE

LEGAL DUTY
    Abandonment of Patient
    Standard of Care
TERMINATION OF DUTY
    Worse Position or State
    Cure or Arrest of Ailment
    Reasonable Time
    Giving the Patient Notice
BREACH OF DUTY AND
STANDARD OF CARE
    Follow-Up Care

Errors In Judgment
    Test for Determining Malpractice
PROFESSIONAL
NEGLIGENCE
    Custom and Practice
    Due Care and Warning
BREACH OF
CONTRACTUAL DUTY
EXAMPLES/QUESTIONS/
PROJECTS

Key Terms

Good Samaritan laws	proximately	misfeasance
standard of care	per se	malfeasance
bona fide	tort law	nonfeasance

This chapter begins the subject of **tort law.** Tort law is a civil wrong as opposed to a criminal wrong. It is conduct separate and distinct from that of a contractual obligation. This and following chapters will discuss the elements of tort law as it applies to the allied health professional in his or her dealings with patients.

LEGAL DUTY

Legal duty comprises two general types. The first is the duty of a person to use ordinary care in activities from which a harm might reasonably be anticipated, An example of this is the duty of the medical assistant or nurse to check the type and dosage of a medication before giving the medication to a patient. The medical assistant's or nurse's duty of care owed to the patient is breached when he or she administers the wrong medication without checking the doctor's prescription. Should the patient sustain an injury as a result of being administered the wrong medication, the medical assistant or nurse would be liable to the patient for damages.

The second type of legal duty arises where there is an affirmative duty to act. This only occurs where a person occupies a particular relationship to another individual. An example of a failure, or omission, to act where there is an affirmative duty to act is to be found in the case of a lifeguard on a public beach who refuses to go to the rescue of a drowning person. The lifeguard is paid by public tax dollars to save drowning persons. When the lifeguard fails or refuses to take affirmative action, he or she has breached his or her legal duty owed to the drowning victim.

Another example of legal duty arises in cases where cardiopulmonary resuscitation (CPR) is begun on one individual by another. Most jurisdictions recognize that such administration of CPR gives rise to a legal duty to continue until: the patient is revived; the patient is pronounced dead by a physician or authorized medical personnel; the person administering CPR is relieved by authorized medical personnel; or the person is no longer physically able to continue CPR. The person administering CPR breaches his or her legal duty to continue when he or she merely stops administering CPR. This is a failure to act where there is a legal duty to continue.

Abandonment of patient

Still another example of a failure to act where there is an affirmative legal duty to act occurs in abandonment of patient cases. In these situations, the doctor or other professional has undertaken to render treatment to the patient but fails to continue treatment, thereby leaving the patient in a perilous position. Cases dealing with abandonment of patient vary widely in their circumstances, from a refusal to continue treatment because of the patient's nonpayment for services to a refusal to give the patient follow-up care after a surgical procedure.

If a doctor or other health care professional has agreed to provide only emergency treatment, he or she may want to ensure that the patient understands this and understands the need to seek another provider for evaluation and follow up care, if needed. A sample form for the patient to sign indicating understanding that medical care given (or about to be given) will be limited solely to emergency care is given in Illustration 3.1.

These cases should not be confused with cases involving the rendering of first aid, in which the defense of the **Good Samaritan laws** may be asserted by the doctor, nurse, or other professional to protect him or her from the duty of rendering follow-up care.

Standard of care

A more abstract example of a failure to act constituting a breach of duty is seen in cases where the practitioner fails to follow a **standard of care** established by professional guidelines within the particular profession—for example, where the medical assistant or nurse fails to clean an open wound that later becomes infected. If the established professional practice would be to clean the wound, failure may be considered tantamount to malpractice as an omission of the

---

Date: _____

Time: _____ a.m. p.m.

I acknowledge that the medical care which (was) (is about to be) furnished to (*name of patient*) by Dr. (was) (will be) limited solely to emergency treatment. I understand that it will be necessary to select another physician and make immediate arrangements with that physician for a complete diagnosis and continuation of treatment.

Witness _____

Signed _____
(patient or person
authorized to
consent for patient)

*If the physician has agreed to provide only emergency treatment, the execution of this form before or immediately after treatment would be valuable as evidence against any later claim that the physician abandoned the patient by failing to continue treatment.

ILLUSTRATION 3.1 ACKNOWLEDGMENT OF EMERGENCY TREATMENT (REPRINTED WITH PERMISSION OF THE AMERICAN MEDICAL ASSOCIATION, *MEDICOLEGAL FORMS WITH LEGAL ANALYSIS,* COPYRIGHT 1991, AMERICAN MEDICAL ASSOCIATION)

legal duty. The standard of care associated with the examination and/or treatment of patients within any given profession is established by guidelines set by the profession itself. Any variation from the guidelines would be a failure to properly act where there is a duty to perform services within those guidelines.

Confusion has long existed among legal scholars attempting to assert the "true" theory on which the legal duty is founded—whether a person acted in a negligent or improper manner as compared with a failure to act in a proper manner. Suffice it to say, for the purpose of this text, that it makes little difference.

TERMINATION OF DUTY

As the preceding discussion of cardiopulmonary resuscitation (CPR) makes clear, most jurisdictions recognize that administration of CPR gives rise to a legal duty owing to the victim. This duty terminates only when one of the four previously mentioned conditions is met: the patient is revived; the patient dies; the person administering CPR is relieved; or the person administering CPR is unable to continue.

Worse position or state

In addition, excluding for the moment the Good Samaritan laws, the common law recognizes the principle that a person rendering first aid cannot leave the victim in a worse position or state after beginning to render aid. For example, a doctor, medical assistant, nurse, or other professional beginning to render first aid to a victim of an automobile accident may be held liable if he or she leaves the victim in a worse state after rendering aid. If ambulance personnel leave the scene of an accident because the medical assistant, nurse, or other professional rendering aid states that he or she will transport the patient to the hospital, the professional will be liable to the victim if he or she fails to continue treatment, including transportation to the hospital. This, of course, presupposes that the victim is left in a more perilous state by the person rendering aid.

Cure or arrest of ailment

When a patient is being treated for an ailment, the duty to render treatment ends when the patient is cured of that ailment. When the ailment for which treatment is being rendered becomes stationary or otherwise controlled, the duty to continue treatment may likewise end. However, the law recognizes the doctor's, dentist's, or other professional's right to terminate the contractual relationship before the patient's cure. Caution should be exercised before terminating such a relationship with a patient at any time before the cure of the ailment for which treatment is being rendered.

Reasonable time

The patient must be given notice of the intent by the doctor, physical therapist, or other professional of the professional's intent to cease rendering further treatment. In addition, the patient must be given ample opportunity to secure the services of another professional before the actual duty to cease rendering further treatment ends. Again, this ample opportunity has been interpreted by the courts as being *reasonable time* for the patient to secure treatment elsewhere. As preceding discussions of reasonableness suggest, the term is based at least in part on the geographic area in which the treatment has been rendered. In addition, consideration is given to the particular ailment for which treatment has been sought and the type of treatment. Finally, the obligation to treat the patient may not be terminated for discriminatory reasons based on constitutionally protected rights such as race, national origin, or religious beliefs.

Giving the patient notice

Most commonly, the treating doctor, dentist, or other medical practitioner desires to terminate his or her obligation to continue treatment because the patient has not paid the bill for past services rendered. The professional may also desire to terminate the obligation to continue when the patient refuses to follow prescribed orders. In these situations, the patient is breaching the contract previously established. This breach gives the treating physician, dentist, or other professional the right to terminate the contractual obligation to continue rendering aid or services. In terminating the professional relationship with a patient, the following procedural steps are recommended.

Give the patient formal written notice of the intent to terminate the professional relationship. Notice may be given in letter format and sent to the patient by registered or certified mail with a return receipt requested from the post office. The letter should contain the reason for the termination—for example, the patient's continued refusal to pay his or her bill, failure to keep appointments, or other ways of frustrating the doctor's recommended treatment regimen. Finally, the letter should contain a statement to the effect that the relationship will be terminated at some specific time in the future. This time of termination must be based on the ability of the patient to obtain similar services for the particular ailment in question. As previously stated, this ample or reasonable time will depend on the treatment, availability of other physicians or professionals who can render such treatment, and the geographic area and distance involved in obtaining the needed treatment. An example of a simple letter of termination is given in Illustration 3.2.

```
┌─────────────────────────────────────────────────────────────┐
│                                    Date: _____         │
│                                                               │
│  Dear _____:                                             │
│  I find it necessary to inform you that I am withdrawing      │
│  from further profes-                                         │
│  sional attendance upon you because you have persisted in     │
│  refusing to follow                                           │
│  my medical advice and treatment. Since your condition        │
│  requires medical atten-                                      │
│  tion, I suggest that you place yourself under the care of    │
│  another physician with-                                      │
│  out delay. If you desire, I shall be available to attend you │
│  for a reasonable time                                        │
│  after you receive this letter, but in no event for more      │
│  than___days.                                                 │
│                                                               │
│  This should give you ample time to select a physician of     │
│  your choice from the                                         │
│  many competent practitioners in this city. With your         │
│  authorization, I will make                                   │
│  available to this physician your case history and            │
│  information regarding the                                     │
│  diagnosis and treatment you have received from me.           │
│                                                               │
│                                         Very truly yours,     │
│                                                               │
│                                    _____, M.D.         │
│                                                               │
└─────────────────────────────────────────────────────────────┘
```

ILLUSTRATION 3.2 LETTER OF WITHDRAWAL FROM A CASE (REPRINTED WITH PERMISSION OF THE AMERICAN MEDICAL ASSOCIATION, *MEDICOLEGAL FORMS WITH LEGAL ANALYSIS,* COPYRIGHT 1991, AMERICAN MEDICAL ASSOCIATION)

BREACH OF DUTY AND STANDARD OF CARE

The standard of care within a particular profession was discussed in a previous section. That standard of care is determined by examination of a particular profession and its members. Educational background, years of experience, expertise, and the geographic location within which they practice are also considered in judging the professional conduct of particular individual members. The standard of care is most commonly associated with a duty of care owed to the patient in his or her examination and/or treatment. The standard of care has also been associated with a test as to whether or not a particular act or omission is tantamount to malpractice. The common law has termed this the *reasonable person test*.

The reasonable person test evolved as a doctrine of law through custom based on fairness. It is an overly broad and generalized test associated with or used to establish guidelines for certain types of conduct. Simply stated, conduct that would be attributed to a reasonable person or from which a reasonable person would refrain establishes a guideline for such conduct. Should an individual act in a manner different from the established, generalized guidelines, this individual's conduct would be termed *unreasonable*. Unreasonable conduct has for a long time been associated with negligent conduct, which may impose on an individual liability and damages.

This test is subject to several practical qualifications. For example, certain types of persons engaging in certain types of activities are required to exercise a higher degree of care than others under the same conditions or circumstances. Thus, an orthopedic surgeon will owe a patient a higher standard or degree of care than a general practitioner when the treatment involves injuries that fall within the orthopedist's area of expertise. Similarly, a registered nurse will be held to a higher standard of care than a medical assistant in carrying out duties at the direction of a physician in a private office; a periodontist will be held to a higher standard of care than a dentist in caring for a patient with gum disease; and an orthopedic specialist in the field of chiropractic will be held to a higher degree of care than a general chiropractor.

Consideration will also be given to the particular individual's experience within his or her field of expertise. Thus, a medical assistant with many years of experience working in a very active treating facility will be held to a higher standard of care than a medical assistant who has fewer years of experience or is employed by a physician with a small or limited practice.

In considering the appropriate standard of care, some courts consider the geographic location of the professional's practice. For example, formerly, the standard of care was commonly held to be higher in densely populated metropolitan areas than in rural areas because treatment facilities and diagnostic equipment available in metropolitan areas are generally superior. Thus, in jurisdictions where geographic location is considered as one factor in determining the appropriate standard of care, the professional must exercise the degree of skill or care usually found among other members in good standing of his or her profession in that general locality.[1] However, in other jurisdictions, courts apply in all cases a general national standard,[2] especially in cases involving medical specialists.[3]

In essence, then, the standard of conduct can be described as "good medical practice," that is, the standard of practice that is customary and usual in the profession.[4] This change in the standard of care is largely due to the establishment of vast communication resources, including computer hookups, which enable health care personnel to obtain accurate diagnostic information even in rural areas. Also, many professionals are required under the terms of their licenses to participate periodically in continuing education programs. Thus the standard of care as it relates to different geographic areas has become somewhat standardized throughout the United States.

---

[1]*Sinz v. Owens*, 33 Cal. 2d 749, 205 P. 2d 3 (1949).

[2]*Brune v. Belinkoff*, 354 Mass. 102, 235 N.E. 2d 793 (1968).

[3]*Hines v. St. Paul Fire & Marine Ins. Co.*, 365 So. 2d 537 (La. App. 1978).

[4]*Hirn v. Edgewater Hospital*, 86 Ill. App. 3d 939, 408 N.E. 3d 970 (1980)

Follow-up care

The Supreme Court of Nebraska made the following comments in the case of *Stohlman v. Davis et al.* regarding breach of the standard of care owing to a patient. This case deals with a surgeon who performed surgery on a patient and then referred follow-up care to another, less experienced doctor—a referral that resulted in injury to the patient.

It may be said that the relations between physicians and patients are personal and highly confidential, and on engaging a physician to treat his case the patient impliedly engages him to attend throughout that illness, or until his services are dispensed with. The patient places himself in the hands of the physician and surgeon and therefore relies on the judgment or knowledge of the physician or surgeon. When a surgeon performs an operation, not only must he use reasonable care and skill in its performance, but also, in subsequent treatment of the case, it is his duty to give the patient such attention after an operation as the necessity of the case demands, in the absence of any special agreement limiting the service or reasonable notice to the patient.

It is also to be remembered in this connection that the facts in the record disclose that the defendant (doctor), by his excellent preparation and for thirty-odd years of successful practice, had acquired peculiar qualifications and *special knowledge* of the subject of the surgery. In short, his employment by the plaintiff was in fact, if not in name, the employment of a specialist or an expert in surgery. It would seem in view of the nature of his employment and the circumstances and conditions of his patient, as shown by the record in this case, that to substitute for himself another physician of but three or four years' experience in the practice without any notice to or agreement with the patient involved or those representing him would not only be a clear violation of duty but, in effect, to utterly abandon the case.[5]

Errors in Judgement

It has been said that "physicians and surgeons are not required to possess the highest knowledge or experience, but the test is the degree of skill and diligence which other physicians in the same general neighborhood and the same general line of practice ordinarily have and practice."[6] It should be noted that a mere error in judgment for which an injury is suffered by a patient may not necessarily be considered malpractice for a breach of standard of care. Malpractice consists of a negligent or unskillful performance by a medical assistant, nurse, physician, or other professional of the duties that devolve and are

---

[5]*Stohlman v. Davis*, 117 Neb. 178, 220 N.W. 247 (1928)

[6]*McDaniel v. Wolcott*, 115 Neb. 675, 214 N.W. 296 (1927)

incumbent on him or her. Where a health professional exercises ordinary care and skill, in keeping with recognized and approved methods, he or she is not liable for the results of a mere mistake of judgment. The law imposes a duty on a medical practitioner to base any professional decision on skill and careful study in consideration of a particular case. However, when the decision depends on the exercise of judgment, the law may only require that the judgment be **bona fide.** In this regard, the law requires that a professional maintain the integrity of the profession by keeping up-to-date on new treatment methods, drugs, appliances, and so on. Thus, as previously noted, courts are increasingly moving away from basing their evaluation of the appropriate standard of care on a locality rule and are moving toward the application of a national standard.

Test for determining malpractice

A simplified test may be used by the medical assistant, nurse, doctor, or other member of the health team in ascertaining whether an act of malpractice has been committed by asking the following question: Would everyone else in the professional community have acted or failed to act as did the professional in this particular situation? If the answer is yes, there is probably no breach of the standard of care tantamount to malpractice in the particular case. However, if the answer to the question is no, meaning that other professionals in the same field would have acted differently, then a breach of the standard of care probably exists.

PROFESSIONAL NEGLIGENCE

Negligence has been characterized as "not the act itself, but the fact which defines the character of the act and makes it a legal wrong;...it is the absence of care in the performance of an act."[7]

> Negligence is either the omission of a person to do something which an ordinarily prudent person would have done under given circumstances or the doing of something which an ordinarily prudent person would not have done under such circumstances. It is not absolute or to be measured in all classes in accordance with some precise standard but always relates to some circumstance of time, place, and person.[8]

Various states have defined the term *professional negligence.* For example, the California statute states:

---

[7]*Stephenson v. Southern Pacific Co.*, 102 C. 143 (1894)

[8]*Fouch v. Warner*, 99 C.A. 557, 279 P. 183 (1929)

"Professional negligence" means a negligent act or omission to act by a health care provider in the rendering of professional services, which act or omission is the proximate cause of a personal injury or wrongful death, provided that services are within the scope of services for which the provider is licensed and which are not within any restriction imposed by the licensing agency or licensed hospital.[9]

As the first definition suggests, for negligence to exist the alleged wrongdoer must owe a duty to another person or group of persons. This duty, which must be adhered to, represents one of the four basic elements on which an individual can maintain an action within the confines of tort law.

Negligence consists of a breach of that duty by either an affirmative act or a failure to act by the wrongdoer. This breach must also cause injury or damages by the wrongdoer, either actually or **proximately.** Under common law, such conduct has been termed **misfeasance, malfeasance,** or **nonfeasance.**

The distinction between nonfeasance, misfeasance, and malfeasance is often of great importance in determining a person's liability to third persons. *Nonfeasance* means the total failure to enter into the performance of some distinct duty or undertaking that one has agreed to perform. *Misfeasance* means the improper performance of an act that one might otherwise lawfully perform—in other words, the performance of one's duty in such a manner as to infringe on the rights and privileges of others. *Malfeasance* is the doing of an act that one ought not to do at all.

Custom and practice

Custom and practice may be evidence for establishing the standard of care owing to a patient. However, such custom, though relevant, is not necessarily conclusive evidence. For example, a patient sues a hospital for damages, alleging malpractice. The patient/plaintiff alleges that the hospital was negligent because a Kelly clamp, a six-inch metal instrument, was left in the patient's abdomen following an operation. The superintendent of the hospital testifies that, before and after surgery, hospitals generally maintain a count of sponges and needles but not of other instruments. Although this testimony is relevant to the issue of standard of care, it does not dispel the inference of negligence of the hospital and its operating room staff for not fulfilling its duty of care to the patient by counting instruments.

One of the tests often used to determine whether or not an act is negligent is the foreseeability of harm. Although the hospital custom of not counting instruments in the preceding example is asserted as establishing a standard of care, the law imposes a duty of care owing to the patient that requires the

---

[9]C.C.P. 340.5 (2).

hospital to count such instruments. This duty is based on the reasonable foreseeability that an instrument might be left in the patient's abdomen following surgery.

Due care and warning

Professional negligence may also be asserted when the examination or treatment is not performed with the care or skill required by the circumstances. Where the circumstances require careful preparation, failure in this respect constitutes negligent conduct. Also, failure to give appropriate warning before certain acts are performed may be tantamount to negligence. For example, the physician who fails to warn a patient of the potential side effects of a drug may be held negligent for his or her failure to warn. What constitutes due care under a given set of circumstances must ordinarily be decided by the court or jury.

Where the evidence establishes a violation of clearly defined statutes or ordinances, responsibility may be fixed without proof of failure to exercise due care. The lack of an excuse or justification for the violation may demonstrate that an act or omission was negligent **per se,** or negligence as a matter of law.

BREACH OF CONTRACTUAL DUTY

As previously mentioned, the patient may base his or her lawsuit on several theories, In addition to theories of tort law, the patient may base the lawsuit on the professional's breach of a contractual duty to render treatment. Rarely are cases based on this theory, however, when treatment has been rendered to the patient in a negligent manner, since the damages that may be recovered by the patient are severely limited. In lawsuits based on negligence, the patient is allowed recovery for pain and suffering associated with his or her injury in addition to all out-of-pocket expenses. When the lawsuit is based on breach of a contractual duty to render treatment, the patient is allowed only reimbursement for out-of-pocket expenses in obtaining similar treatment. Therefore, very few medical or dental malpractice cases are based on the breach of a contractual obligation.

EXAMPLES / QUESTIONS / PROJECTS

1. *Nancy is a medical assistant who fails to stop and render aid to a victim of an automobile accident. Is Nancy guilty of negligent conduct?*

Answer: No. Unless an affirmative duty to act has been established, Nancy is not guilty of negligence for failing to render aid to the victim. She is not even obligated to report the accident to the police.

2. *Nancy stops at the scene of an automobile accident. She sees that the victim is bleeding profusely and requires medical attention. She does not render aid but tells the victim that she will go to get help. No one else stops to aid the victim. Is Nancy guilty of failing to perform the promised act if she fails to get help?*

Answer: No. Even though she promised the victim she would get help, the victim was not left in any worse or more perilous position than when Nancy found him. Nor was there any contractual obligation on the part of Nancy, since the facts do not suggest that the patient offered to pay Nancy for help.

3. *Deborah is a highly experienced medical assistant who holds a valid first aid certificate issued by the American Red Cross. Deborah renders emergency first aid to the victim of an automobile accident. The first aid treatment includes applying a tourniquet to the victim's leg, which is not sanctioned as authorized first aid treatment. However, this is the only method that Deborah can use to save the victim's life. Application of the tourniquet causes cell death to the victim's lower leg, which later causes gangrene to set in. Ultimately, the victim's lower leg is amputated because of the gangrenous condition. Is Deborah liable to the victim for causing gangrene and the ultimate necessity of amputation?*

Answer: Probably not. Although the procedure of applying the tourniquet was not sanctioned first aid treatment, the victim would have died had the tourniquet not been applied. The Good Samaritan laws would almost certainly protect Deborah from liability in this situation, especially since she saved the victim's life.

4. *Mike is a dental assistant. Part of his duties include taking X-ray films of patients' teeth. Mr. Johnson sustains an injury when Mike accidentally pushes the X-ray tube against Mr. Johnson's jaw. Is Mike's conduct negligent in breaching a standard or duty of care owing to the patient?*

Answer: Possibly. Mike would be held liable for breaching the standard of care owing to the patient if it can be shown that injury to the patient was reasonably foreseeable. The fact that Mike knew that the X-ray tube occasionally moved, causing it to strike patients, suggests negligent conduct on his part. Mike should have been more careful in aligning the tube to the patient's face. However, Mike would not be held to have breached a duty of care owing to the patient if he could demonstrate that he did nothing different than any other dental assistant would have done. This would be especially true if it could be shown that it was not foreseeable that the X-ray tube would move against the patient with such force as to cause an injury.

5. *Sally, a medical assistant in charge of sending out patient billing, accidentally sends John Wilson's statement to Harry Fujimura. Harry is a banker from whom John is trying to obtain a loan. Harry accidentally opens the envelope and reads the bill without initially realizing it to be the wrong statement. The bill is quite sizable, and Harry turns John down for the loan. Is the medical assistant's conduct tantamount to a breach of care owing to John?*

> **Answer:** Probably. It is the duty of the medical assistant to ensure that all correct names and addresses are properly recorded on the appropriate patient's ledger card, medical chart, or other record. To check and double-check that the correct bill has been sent to the correct patient is a duty that the medical assistant owes to every patient to whom she sends a bill. However, if the assistant could demonstrate that the mere inadvertence of sending the wrong bill was an error that anyone could have made, she would escape liability based on breach of the duty of care. This would be especially true if she could demonstrate that she did nothing different in billing procedures than any other medical assistant would have done in her position. Further, that John would be turned down for the loan might not be considered a foreseeable injury.

6. *David is a registered nurse who works in Dr. Harris's office. David improperly dresses a patient's wound with a gauze bandage. However, David can demonstrate that other medical assistants in the geographic community would have used the same type of dressing and technique in bandaging the patient's wound. Is David guilty of breaching a duty of care owing to the patient?*

> **Answer:** The answer to this question is probably yes. As a registered nurse, David is held to a high standard of care in treating patients. The test of whether or not David's conduct was tantamount to negligence for a breach of the duty of care would be based on whether other registered nurses would have bandaged the wound in the same manner, not on what a medical assistant with less educational background or experience would have done.

CHAPTER FOUR

CAUSATION

ACTUAL CAUSE

PROXIMATE CAUSE
    Determining Initial Cause
    Ascertaining Consequences
    Intervening Forces (Acts)
    Foreseeability of Injury

CONCURRENT CAUSATION
    "Deeper Pockets" Doctrine

EXAMPLES/QUESTIONS/
PROJECTS

Key Terms

statutory	doctrine	percentage-of-fault
restatement of torts	causation	execute
jury	joint and several liability	judgment
judge		"deeper pockets' doctrine

Thus far we've been dealing with conduct that constitutes negligence and the duty to refrain from such conduct as it relates to a person or a group of persons. This chapter deals with the relationship between negligent conduct and injury caused by such conduct.

ACTUAL CAUSE

There is little problem in determining causation in cases in which the negligent conduct of a particular person directly causes injury to another person. Thus, where John hits Sam and breaks Sam's nose, the act of John striking Sam is the *actual cause* of Sam's injury. Where the injury complained of is a reaction to improper medication being administered by a particular medical assistant, nurse, or doctor, the act of administering the improper medication is the actual cause of the patient's injury—assuming that the act of administering the wrong medication falls below the standard of care owed to the patient, as previously discussed. Where a medical assistant uses acid instead of an antiseptic to clean an open wound, thereby causing the patient an additional injury, such an act is the actual cause of the injury. Likewise, a person who negligently causes his or her automobile to collide with an automobile driven by another person is the actual cause of that other person's injury. *Actual causation* refers to the active cause that results in injury due to the negligent performance of some act or the failure to act.

PROXIMATE CAUSE

Often cases deal with injuries suffered by a person as a result of a number of contributing factors. In these situations, the law has imposed that the breach of duty must be the *proximate cause* of the plaintiff's injury. The **statutory** language of the California code defining professional negligence uses this specific language. The proximate cause is also termed the *legal cause* in the **Restatement of Torts** followed in some states. Basically, the doctrine of cause, like negligence, has been held to be a question of fact for the **judge** or **jury** to decide.

The **doctrine** of proximate cause means, in its simplest form, that "consequences which follow from the original wrong in unbroken sequence, without an intervening sufficient independent cause are natural and proximate and for these the original wrongdoer is responsible." [1] There must be an unbroken connection—a continuous sequence—between the wrongful act and the injury; that is, there must be a succession of events so linked together as to constitute the person's injury.

Thus, odd as it may seem, in a situation where person *A* negligently injures person *B* and *B* is taken to the hospital where a physician commits

---

[1] *Merril v. Los Angeles Gas & Electric Co.*, 158 C. 499 (1910).

malpractice on B, A can be held liable to B for the damages caused by the malpractice as well as for the original injury because the malpractice arose out of the original injury. That is, if A had not injured B, B would not have gone to the hospital and would not have been further injured by the physician's malpractice. Of course, B can also sue the physician for the harm caused by the physician's malpractice.

For an oversimplified example of proximate cause, consider the following. Car 1 is stopped at a traffic light at the foot of a hill. Behind Car 1, stopped on the hill, are Cars 2, 3, and 4. The driver of Car 5, speeding up on the other side of the hill, cannot see the cars stopped on the downward side. Therefore, Car 5 proceeds over the hill and slams into Car 4. Car 4 strikes Car 3 which hits Car 2 which then runs into Car 1, causing a back injury to the driver of Car 1. The actual physical cause of injury to the driver of Car 1 is the fact that Car 2 ran into Car 1. However, the proximate or legal cause is Car 5 striking Car 4.

Determining initial cause

As the simplified example of Cars 1 through 5 suggests, the first element necessary for the patient to demonstrate proximate cause is the *initial cause in fact*. The patient/plaintiff must demonstrate that the medical assistant, doctor, nurse, or other professional's negligence contributed in some way to his or her injury. The primary test for establishing the causal link is to ask, "*But for* the defendant's negligence or wrongful conduct, would the injury have been sustained?" For example, *but for* the doctor's negligent misdiagnosis of the plaintiff's ailment, would surgery have had to be performed on the patient by another physician? If the answer is no, the proximate cause is established, making the initial physician liable for the patient's injury. If the answer is yes, that the patient would have sustained the unnecessary surgery anyway, the initial physician would not be liable for the patient's injuries.

Ascertaining consequences

In some states, courts have held that the person guilty of negligence should be held responsible for all the consequences of his or her negligent conduct where such consequences could have been ascertained by reasonable diligence. This may be viewed as another application of the foreseeability of harm or risk doctrine previously discussed. Thus, the health professional's negligent conduct may not be the sole cause of the patient's injury. Suffice it to say that the mere fact that it is a cause is enough to constitute liability for the whole injury sustained by the patient. However, the prevailing view in most states is that the foreseeability is immaterial; that is, a person is liable for the consequences that follow in an unbroken sequence from his or her negligent act, whether or not such consequences are anticipated.

Intervening forces (acts)

Numerous are the cases in which the patient's injury is caused by more than one person. When the negligent conduct of the professional is the stimulus for some other negligent conduct that causes the harm, there is no break in the chain of **causation,** and the original wrongdoer may be held liable.

The subsequent conduct is termed a *dependent intervening act.* The initial wrongdoer cannot escape liability for the patient's injury by labeling the subsequent conduct a superseding cause.

However, an *independent intervening act* may break the chain of causation. This occurs when, subsequent to the original professional's negligent conduct, an independent intervening act occurs that actively operates to produce the patient's injury. For example, the physician would not be held liable for a patient's death in misdiagnosing a terminal ailment if the patient died as a result of an independent automobile accident. However, the same physician might be held liable as a proximate cause of the patient's death if the patient became so distraught that he or she committed suicide—especially if the doctor told the patient that he or she was terminally ill and that the illness would produce a painful death.

Foreseeability of injury

The foreseeability required is of the potential risk of harm or injury, not of the particular intervening act. Thus, a health professional may be held liable where his or her conduct is a substantial factor in bringing about the patient's injury or death. The test is not whether the professional did foresee, or by the exercise of ordinary care should have foreseen, the specific consequence that occurred. The test is whether the specific consequence or result was reasonably foreseeable. Bringing this into focus demonstrates the foreseeability required is of the risk of harm, not the particular intervening act.

For example, Dr. Smith prescribes an antihistamine for Mr. Drayhill, his patient. The doctor fails to warn Mr. Drayhill to refrain from consuming alcoholic beverages while taking the antihistamine (the combination could cause extreme drowsiness). Mr. Drayhill takes the medicine and consumes two cans of beer. Thereafter he sustains an injury while operating a power lawnmower. Neither the antihistamine nor the beer by itself would have caused Mr. Drayhill's injury. The states following the minority view would consider Dr. Smith's failure to instruct Mr. Drayhill not to consume alcohol after taking the antihistamine to be a substantial factor regarding the injury sustained. It would not be a defense for the doctor to assert Mr. Drayhill's consumption of the beer to be a superseding cause. It is the foreseeability of risk that Mr. Drayhill could consume beer after taking the medicine that would cause drowsiness and result in an injury to Mr. Drayhill.

The ordinarily prudent person would have little difficulty accepting that the doctor in the first example in the preceding section could not have foreseen an automobile accident causing the patient's death. However, the doctor would have substantial difficulty demonstrating to the ordinarily prudent person the nonforeseeability of the patient's suicide following the doctor's description of a painful and horrible death from a disease that the patient did not have.

CONCURRENT CAUSATION

More than one person may be negligent in causing a patient's total injury. Therefore, the law recognizes that more than one person may be held liable for the injury. This has been termed the doctrine of **joint and several liability**. When separate and distinct negligent acts by different parties contribute to cause the injury, each is said to be a proximate cause, and the plaintiff may recover damages in full from one or all. For example, in the case of an instrument left inside the patient's abdomen following surgery, the nurse, surgical technician, and/or hospital personnel may be held liable for not properly counting the instruments. In addition, the general surgeon may be held jointly and/or separately liable for failing in his or her responsibility to make sure that all such instruments have not been left in the patient's abdomen.

"Deeper pockets" doctrine

In cases such as the preceding one, the plaintiff sues both the general surgeon and the surgical technician or nurses, alleging negligent conduct on each and all their parts. After successfully demonstrating malpractice, the patient may collect damages from the doctor, the scrub nurse, the circulating nurse, the hospital, or from all of them, to the full extent of the jury verdict. This is true even though the jury may have assessed negligent conduct on each individual party on a **percentage-of-fault** basis. Obviously, the patient would seek recovery for the full extent of his or her damages from the person or institution from which it would be easiest to collect.

When the successful plaintiff **executes** or otherwise collects on the **judgment** against one of the joint-party defendants, that party can then seek contributions from the other codefendants based on the percentage of negligence assessed against each of them for causing the plaintiff's injury. This avenue of collecting—where the plaintiff, in obtaining judgment against multiple parties, seeks collection from the party with the most money or from his or her insurance company—has sometimes been termed the **"deeper pockets" doctrine**.

Consider the following example. After an extensive examination, Dr. Renaldi tells Mr. Stone that he is suffering from an illness that will require surgical amputation of his left leg. Not being an orthopedic surgeon, Dr. Renaldi refers Mr. Stone to Dr. Costello for the operation. He also sends Dr. Costello X-rays of Mr. Stone's left leg. However, Dr. Renaldi's radiological technologist (X-ray technician) mislabels the X-ray, indicating that the film shows the patient's right leg instead of the left.

Dr. Costello concurs with Dr. Renaldi that surgical amputation is necessary. Thereafter, Dr. Costello has Mr. Stone admitted to the local hospital, where the surgery is performed. Dr. Costello, relying on Dr. Renaldi's X-rays, proceeds to amputate the right leg.

Following the surgery, Mr. Stone discovers that the wrong leg has been amputated and files suit against both Dr. Renaldi and Dr. Costello for malpractice. His argument to the jury is that Dr. Renaldi, through the act of his radiological technologist, was negligent in mislabeling the X-ray film that Dr. Costello relied on during surgery. Further, Dr. Renaldi could have reasonably foreseen that Dr. Costello would rely on the X-ray examination and amputate the wrong leg as depicted on the mislabeled film. Thus, Dr. Renaldi's negligent conduct was a substantial factor in causing the wrong leg to be amputated, This act was the initial proximate cause of Mr. Stone's overall injury.

In addition, Mr. Stone argues to the jury that Dr. Costello was negligent in his own right in not double-checking to make sure that the proper leg was being amputated.

Following this argument, the jury returns the verdict in favor of Mr. Stone in the amount of $1,000,000. The jury also finds that the negligent conduct of Dr. Renaldi was a 50 percent contributing or substantial factor in causing Mr. Stone's injury and that the failure of Dr. Costello to double-check that the proper leg was being amputated was also a 50 percent contributing factor. Following the jury verdict, Mr. Stone discovers that Dr. Renaldi is not covered by medical malpractice insurance but that Dr. Costello is covered. Noting Dr. Costello's "deeper pockets," based on his insurance coverage, Mr. Stone then executes the judgment against Dr. Costello, and Dr. Costello's insurance company pays Mr. Stone the full $1,000,000. Thereafter, the insurance company may seek a 50 percent contribution from Dr. Renaldi. This action may entail the filing of a separate lawsuit by the insurance company for collection based on the original judgment in favor of Mr. Stone and the 50 percent comparative causation assessed against Dr. Renaldi as established by the jury verdict.

Had the X-ray that Dr. Costello relied on been taken by a radiological technologist at the hospital who was not Dr. Renaldi's agent, Dr. Renaldi could have asserted a complete defense to any liability assessed against him. In that situation, Dr. Renaldi could properly have asserted that the mislabeling of the X-ray film by the hospital technologist was an independent intervening act that broke the chain of proximate causation leading to the wrong leg of Mr. Stone being amputated. Further, Dr. Renaldi could have properly asserted as a defense that he could not have foreseen that the X-ray film might be mislabeled and relied on by Dr. Costello in performing the surgery.

EXAMPLES / QUESTIONS / PROJECTS

1. *Carl is a medical assistant who works for Dr. Jensen. Dr. Jensen tells Carl to give a patient an antibiotic injection for treatment of the patient's infection. Carl draws a syringe of medication that he believes to be the one prescribed. However, he fails to double-check the vial of medication. As it turns out, Carl gives the patient sleeping medication. On the way home, the patient sustains injuries as a result of an automobile collision she is involved in because she fell asleep while driving her car. Is Carl liable to the patient under any legal theory for the injuries sustained as a result of the automobile collision?*

   Answer: Yes. Carl is not the actual cause of the patient's injury. He is not negligent in driving the patient's vehicle and thereby causing her injury. However, he can be considered the actual, causative force that results in the patient's falling asleep while driving her vehicle. This actual, causative force can be traced, step by step, back to the negligent conduct of Carl, who did not double-check to make sure that he was administering the proper medication. Thus, Carl's negligence would be assessed as the proximate cause of the patient's injury.

2. *What would be the difference in the preceding example if Carl were to give the patient sterile water instead of the antibiotic, and the patient were to fall asleep while driving her automobile?*

   Answer: Although Carl was negligent in not checking to make sure that he was giving the proper medication when he gave the patient the injection of sterile water, the jury or judge would undoubtedly not assess liability against Carl unless it could be clearly and convincingly demonstrated that the sterile water injection somehow caused the patient to fall asleep while driving her vehicle. However, although sterile water in and of itself is not known to have propensities for causing drowsiness, the plaintiff's attorney could argue that the drowsiness was a result of the infection. Had Carl given the patient the antibiotic, the infection would have subsided rather than increased to the point that it caused the patient's drowsiness. This assumes, of course, that the plaintiff could prove that the antibiotic could have controlled the infection so quickly.

   Cases have also held a doctor or an assistant liable for failing to warn a patient of the adverse effects of certain medications that have been administered or prescribed, especially where such medications might cause drowsiness. Where the patient is involved in an automobile collision or other type of accident and sustains injury because he or she falls asleep while driving or engaging in some other activity, and the drowsiness is a result of taking prescribed medication, the physician and/or his or her assistant may be said to be the proximate cause of such injury for failing to warn the patient of the potential side effects.

CHAPTER FIVE

DOCTRINE OF
RESPONDEAT SUPERIOR

Key Terms

agency	employee	tortious
vicarious	ostensible agent	independent contractor
	writ	

Respondeat superior literally means "let the master answer." This doctrine, sometimes referred to as the doctrine of **agency,** means that a master is liable in certain cases for the wrongful acts of his servants. Today the doctrine has been expanded to include liability assessed against a principal for the acts of his or her agents. It has also been referred to as the doctrine of **vicarious** liability. Thus, a physician who employs medical assistants, nurses, or other paramedical personnel will be held vicariously liable for their torts (wrongs) committed in the course and scope of their employment by the physician. The physician may also be held liable for torts committed by hospital nurses or other paramedical employees when the physician performs a service for a patient in a supervisory capacity during the course of treatment. For example, in the case mentioned in the previous chapter, the surgeon as well as the surgical personnel was held liable for leaving a foreign object in a patient's abdomen following surgery.

The case law that developed in the 1940s and the 1950s expanded the principle of agency law to include the "borrowed servant" rule. This rule was applied in a number of states to place vicarious liability on the physician for the acts of nonemployee medical assistants. The courts termed that a private physician performing surgery in a hospital was the "captain of the ship" because he or she had the right of control over other professional paramedical personnel. Thus, under the "borrowed servant" rule, vicarious liability has even been imposed on a surgeon for negligent conduct committed by another professional such as an anesthesiologist.

HISTORY OF THE DOCTRINE

The doctrine of *respondeat superior* came about in feudal England when masters or landlords maintained large family estates. The master or landlord had many peasant servants who worked for room and board and a mere pittance, all provided by the master. The master held the vast wealth; the peasant servant was very poor.

During this time, much of the law consisted of **writs,** which were proclamations of law set down by the king or queen of England. Each writ was very specific in its terminology and application of the king's or queen's wishes or mandates. If a person violated the law, the sheriff would issue a writ of enforcement. One such writ required the payment of money damages to a person injured by another person's intentional conduct. Initiation of the doctrine came about as represented in the following example.

Case example

Master Charles and Master James were two adjoining landowners. One day, Master Charles hit Master James in the nose over a dispute concerning land boundaries. Master James then sought damages for his broken nose, claiming that the act of battery was intentional and unprovoked. A writ was issued by the sheriff against Master Charles, and Master Charles, being very wealthy, was forced to pay.

Of course, Master Charles was very upset at having to pay Master James. Being a clever as well as vindictive person, Master Charles decided to send one of his peasant servants over to James estate to punch Master James in the nose. In this way, Master Charles was able to get his revenge, whereas Master James could only seek recovery for damages from a penniless peasant. Such restrictions in the law led to similar conduct by other landowners. More often than not, attacks on estates and their landlords were made by penniless servants at their master's direction. In the face of the impossibility of collecting damages, the doctrine of *respondeat superior* came into being. The intent of the doctrine was that the master should answer for the acts of his servants. The initial rationale for invoking the doctrine was that the servant was a mere extension of the master's arm. The intentional conduct of the servant was under the master's instruction and direction. Therefore, it was reasoned, the master should not be allowed to escape liability or otherwise benefit from the wrong being committed by his servants.

Over time, the doctrine slowly evolved to include liability assessed against a master for the *negligent* acts of his servants. However, the negligent conduct of the servants had to occur in the course and scope of doing something for the master and had to be authorized by the master.

Employer liability

The doctrine of *respondeat superior* ultimately came to include liability assessed against an employer for the negligent acts of his or her **employees.** Again, the negligent conduct of the employee had to occur within the course and scope of his or her employment duties.

For a long time, many employers escaped liability by merely asserting that the negligent conduct of the employee fell outside the actual authority to act on behalf of his or her employer. After all, what employer in his or her right mind would authorize an employee to perform negligent acts that would injure someone? For years, the courts had little difficulty applying the doctrine of respondeat superior to the acts of the servant committed at the direction of the master. Now the application of the doctrine to negligent conduct became a perplexing task for the courts and was made on virtually a case-by-case basis.

For example, doctors escaped liability when, in their absence, a medical assistant or office nurse rendered special emergency treatment to a patient and negligently caused the patient injury. The defense the doctor asserted was generally based on two propositions: (1) the nurse or assistant lacked actual authority to render aid in the doctor's absence and (2) neither an express nor an implied contractual relationship existed between the patient and the doctor. These successful defenses, like that of the master before the inception of the doctrine of *respondeat superior* often left the patient with the inability to collect damages from a less well-paid medical assistant or nurse.

Determining liability

The courts ultimately decided that the inability of the patient to collect damages for his or her injury was grossly unfair, and they began to uphold assertions of liability against the doctor. The courts rationalized that the doctor practiced a unique trade or profession. Further, the doctor profited from the employment of his or her medical assistant or nurse. Often the doctor charged the patient for services rendered by the medical assistant or nurse in the doctor's absence from the office. Therefore, it was totally inconsistent for the doctor to argue that the services performed by the medical assistant or nurse in the doctor's absence were outside the authority of his or her employment. In their decisions, the courts decided that the nurse or medical assistant had apparent authority, thus becoming the **ostensible agent** of the doctor to act in rendering aid or treatment to the patient in the doctor's absence. Thus, when the nurse or medical assistant gives the appearance of performing services on behalf of the doctor/employer, liability rests with the doctor/employer for the negligent conduct of the nurse or medical assistant who causes a patient injury. Liability is often based on the fact that the doctor/employer places the nurse, medical assistant, dental assistant, or other professional in a position that gives them the apparent authority to act on behalf of the physician.

INDEPENDENT CONTRACTORS

In modern professional health care services, **independent contractors** are becoming increasingly prevalent. However, an employer is not ordinarily liable for the negligence or other tortious conduct of an independent contractor or an independent contractor's employees.

For example, many radiologists contract with the hospital to perform X-ray services on behalf of the hospital. Radiological technologists (X-ray technicians) or other personnel are paid their salaries by the radiologist or radiology department. The radiologist rents floor space in the hospital for the X-ray department, and bills patients independently of the hospital for X-ray examinations and/or treatment. Thus, the X-ray department is an independent contractor separate from the hospital.

Likewise, clinics, physical therapy departments, respiratory therapy departments, anesthesiologists, and emergency-room physicians often maintain the same type of independent contractor status within the hospital. However, such an arrangement does not mean the hospital can escape liability to a patient injured as a result of the negligence of a radiological technologist in performing a professional service. Under the "borrowed servant" doctrine, a general surgeon has been held liable for the negligent conduct of an anesthesiologist in causing injury to a patient during surgery. The "borrowed servant" doctrine may be applied in many situations to enable the patient to recover damages from the hospital for injuries sustained as a result of negligent conduct by independent contracting facilities or services within the hospital.

Vicarious liability

The more prevalent view in holding a hospital liable for a patient's injury, however, has been the application of the theory of vicarious liability based on the ostensible agency of the treating facility or service to act on behalf of the hospital. The underlying rationale in refusing to allow a hospital to escape liability for a patient's injury where such injury actually occurs as a result of the negligent act of some alleged independent contractor seems to be based on the hospital's allowing this contractor to practice within the confines of the facility.

Further, the hospital generally claims to be a full diagnostic and treatment facility. Thus, the public expects a broad range of services to be provided by the hospital. The hospital would be deceiving the public if it were to escape liability for a patient's injury by merely subcontracting out various services with other persons. In turn, the radiologist could contract out liability to the radiological technologist, and so on until every professional was an independent contractor and no one could be held liable except the person who actually committed the negligent act that caused the patient's injury.

Based on public policy, the law generally has refused to punish the injured patient by interfering with his or her ability to collect damages against the hospital or treating facility. Most patient care is performed by aides, assistants, or technicians whose financial ability to pay for the patient's injury falls far below the ability of the hospital or the doctor deemed to be the "captain of the ship." Note, however, that the defense of charitable immunity might be raised by a hospital. While charitable immunity originally relieved a charitable institution from tort liability in order to protect the charitable entity's assets, most jurisdictions have now rejected the doctrine. In some jurisdictions, charitable immunity may partially protect a charitable institution from liability. In Massachusetts, for example, there is a ceiling of $20,000 (not including interest and costs) on a plaintiff's recovery for torts arising out of "any activity carried on to accomplish directly the charitable purposes of such corporation."[1]

Substandard professional care

The courts have also reasoned that the employment of an employee or independent contractor may in and of itself amount to a negligent act. This occurs where the employer has reason to believe that the employee or independent

[1]M.G.L. chapter 231, section 85K

contractor's general professional conduct falls below that of the recognized standard of care. The California courts have gone even further by imposing liability on a hospital for the sole negligent conduct of a doctor who caused an injury to a patient while that patient was in the hospital. The rationale for the decision was based on the level of expertise of the hospital's personnel, which included board member physicians who should have been able to recognize professional care that fell below recognized standards. Thus, the California law imposes as a standard of care owing to a patient the duty of a hospital and its personnel to police its own staff physicians. Further, the law requires that the hospital terminate staff privileges to any physician whose professional conduct in the examination and/or treatment of patients falls below recognized standards.

EXAMPLES / QUESTIONS / PROJECTS

1. *Emily is a medical assistant who works for Dr. Harris. She is paid a salary and works defined hours. One day, in Dr. Harris's absence, Emily gives a patient, at the patient's request, two tablets that she thinks to be aspirin. The patient sustains a violent reaction to the undefined medication. Is Dr. Harris liable for Emily's act in giving the patient the medication?*

    Answer: Yes. Emily is acting in her official capacity as a medical assistant on behalf of Dr. Harris when she gives the patient the medication. For this reason, the doctrine of *respondeat superior* could be invoked by the patient in establishing liability against Dr. Harris. The patient believes Emily has the authority to do all things attendant to her job, including giving the patient the requested medication.

2. *One day, a neighbor at home asks Emily, who works as a medical assistant for Dr. Harris, what can be done for a headache. Emily responds that Dr. Harris always prescribes two aspirins and proceeds to give the neighbor two aspirins, which the neighbor takes. Unknown to Emily and the neighbor, the neighbor is suffering from an ulcer, which becomes inflamed because of the aspirin. Is Dr. Harris liable for Emily's conduct?*

    Answer: No. In this situation, Emily is acting on her own. It makes little difference that she indicates what Dr. Harris usually prescribes for a headache. She has neither the actual authority nor the apparent authority to act on behalf of Dr. Harris when she gives the neighbor the aspirin.

3. *Henry is a medical assistant employed by Dr. Lopez. One of his routine duties is to make bank deposits of money received in the office on behalf of Dr. Lopez. On the way to the bank, Henry causes an injury to the driver of another car when he fails to stop his car at a stop sign, causing it to collide with the other vehicle. Who is liable?*

> **Answer:** Both Henry and Dr. Lopez are liable to the injured victim. Dr. Lopez would be held liable because Henry is acting under her authority and on her behalf at the time of the accident. It makes no difference that the injury was sustained as a result of an automobile accident rather than some professional misconduct (malpractice) on Henry's part.

Chapter Six

DOCTRINE OF *RES IPSA LOQUITUR*

invoke ispa
The dat res ispa

Key Terms

atrophy   negligence   plaintiff
absolute liability   prima facie

The doctrine of *res ipsa loquitur* (literally, "the thing speaks for itself") is invoked where a person's injury would not have occurred without negligent conduct on the part of the defendant. Application of this doctrine relieves the plaintiff from the necessity of proving the specific acts of negligence that caused him or her injury. To invoke the doctrine, the **plaintiff** must demonstrate that the injury complained of arises out of circumstances over which the defendant had control. Further, the injury must be one that does not ordinarily occur when due care is used—that is, in the absence of **negligence.**

EVOLUTION OF THE DOCTRINE

Before the application of the doctrine of *res ipsa loquitur*, the plaintiff was obligated to demonstrate that a specific defendant had a duty owing to the plaintiff to refrain from conduct that would cause the plaintiff injury. The plaintiff also had to adequately demonstrate (1) that the defendant, by some negligent conduct, had breached the affirmative duty owed to the plaintiff and (2) that the negligent conduct, whether act or failure (omission) to act, in some way caused the plaintiff's injury. Until these three factors of liability were demonstrated, the plaintiff was prevented from arguing to the jury any damages that he or she may have suffered as a result of the injury. Thus, unless the plaintiff could demonstrate that his or her injury was caused by some particular negligent conduct by some particular defendant, the plaintiff was barred from recovery of damages for his or her injuries. The application of the doctrine is illustrated by the following example.

Case example

One day, Mr. Smith is walking down the street. As he passes Mr. Roberts's warehouse, he is hit and injured by a barrel of nails that falls from a loading platform. It is apparent that the barrel either was pushed off the loading platform by Mr. Roberts or one of his employees or fell because it was improperly placed on the loading platform by Mr. Roberts or one of his employees. But Mr. Smith is not certain which particular person was negligent.

There is no question that Mr. Roberts and his employees owe a duty to others to refrain from conduct that would cause a barrel to fall and injure a person walking by the warehouse. Likewise, there is no question that the barrel actually caused Mr. Smith's injuries. The dilemma Mr. Smith faces is his inability to demonstrate negligence against Mr. Roberts or any particular employee. Further, Mr. Smith is unable to demonstrate which specific method of conduct caused the barrel of nails to fall and cause his injury. For these reasons, Mr. Smith would have been unable to maintain a lawsuit against Mr. Roberts before the application of the doctrine of *res ipsa loquitur*. Plaintiffs were often barred from recovering damages for their severe injuries merely because they did not see a particular defendant cause their injuries. For this reason, the courts leaned toward the rights of the plaintiff and began to assess liability based on the doctrine.

Shifting the burden of proof

In the case described in the preceding section, the court's rationale in holding in favor of Mr. Smith in his lawsuit against Mr. Roberts would be based on the following circumstances. First, the instrumentality, the barrel that caused Mr. Smith's injury, was in the exclusive control of Mr. Roberts or his employees. Second, Mr. Smith's injury could not have occurred without some negligent conduct on the part of Mr. Roberts or his employees. Accordingly, the court would shift the burden of proving the absence of negligence to the defendant. In the event that Mr. Roberts could not demonstrate that Mr. Smith's injury occurred as a result of someone other than Mr. Roberts's or his employee's negligent conduct, Mr. Roberts would be held liable.

It should noted that the doctrine of *res ipsa loquitur* does not in and of itself establish the liability of the defendant. But the plaintiff's ability to apply the doctrine to his or her case places the burden of demonstrating the absence of negligent conduct on a particular defendant.

APPLICATION OF THE DOCTRINE TO THE ALLIED HEALTH PROFESSIONS

Cases against physicians, surgeons, dentists, and other professionals in which the doctrine has been invoked are generally divided into two classes. The first group comprises cases in which the merits of a diagnosis and/or treatment are called into question. In this class of cases, the doctrine has been held inapplicable on the grounds that health professionals are not liable for an error in judgment where there was no negligence or for an honest mistake. Failure to effect a cure does not raise a presumption of negligence. A physician cannot guarantee a cure.

The second class of cases involves charges that the professional was negligent and failed to use reasonable care while performing the diagnostic examination or treatment. No question is raised as to the competency or skill of the defendant. The majority of cases in this class generally concern the special situation where a surgeon, nurse, or some other chargeable personnel has left sponges or instruments used during surgery inside the patient's body. In these situations, the doctrine of *res ipsa loquitur* is usually applied.

The doctrine has also been invoked in cases dealing with burns suffered as a result of diathermy or similar types of heat treatment. In these cases, there are three necessary elements. First, the defendant physician, nurse, physical therapist, or similar professional has control over the method of treatment. Second, there is no need to consider scientific evidence or to make a judgment. A reasonably prudent person could adequately understand from the act or injury itself that someone was negligent. Finally, the injury is one that would not occur *but for* the defendant's negligence.

Case example: *Ybarra v. Spangard*

An interesting application of the doctrine of *res ipsa loquitur* was made by the California Supreme Court in the case of *Ybarra v. Spangard*.[1] In this case, an action was brought by Mr. Joseph Ybarra against Dr. Spangard and others for injuries resulting from allegedly improper treatment by physicians and nurses. The following set of circumstances gave rise to the action.

Mr. Ybarra consulted Dr. Tilley, who diagnosed Mr. Ybarra's ailment as appendicitis. Dr. Tilley then made arrangements for an appendectomy to be performed by Dr. Spangard at a hospital owned and managed by Dr. Swift. All three doctors were subsequently named as defendants in the case.

Mr. Ybarra entered the hospital, was given an injection, and later was awakened by Dr. Tilley and Dr. Spangard. He was then wheeled into the operating room by a nurse. He was adjusted on the surgical table for the operation by the anesthesiologist, who pulled his body to the front end of the table. Mr. Ybarra indicated that the anesthesiologist had placed him against two hard objects at the top of his shoulders, about an inch below his neck. He was then given anesthetic, and he lost consciousness. He awoke early the following morning in his hospital room attended by a special nurse named Thompson (who was subsequently named as a defendant in the case) and another nurse (who was not named as a defendant).

Mr. Ybarra testified that before the operation he never had any pain or injury to his right arm or shoulder. However, when he awakened, he felt sharp pain about halfway between the neck and the point of the right shoulder. He complained to the nurse and then to Dr. Tilley, who gave him diathermy treatments while he remained in the hospital. The pain did not cease but instead spread to his lower arm. After his release from the hospital, the condition grew worse; he was unable to rotate or lift his arm and developed paralysis and **atrophy** of the muscles. He received further treatment from Dr. Tilley and then returned to work wearing his arm in a splint on the advice of Dr. Spangard.

Position of the defendants

The defendants took the position that the plaintiff's condition was in fact the result of an injury. There was no way to show that the acts of any particular defendant or any particular instrumentality were the cause. They attacked Mr. Ybarra's action as an attempt to fix liability *en masse* on various defendants,

---

[1] 93 Cal. App. 2d 43, 208 P. 2d 445 (1949)

some of whom were not responsible for the acts of others. They further argued the failure of Mr. Ybarra to show which defendant had control of the instrumentalities that may have been involved.

The defendants' main defense was briefly stated in two propositions. First, there are several defendants, and there is a division of responsibility in the use of an instrumentality causing the injury. The injury might have resulted from the separate act of one of a number of persons. Accordingly, the rule of *res ipsa loquitur* cannot be invoked against any of them. Second, where instrumentalities are involved and no single instrumentality or person is shown to have caused the injury, the doctrine does not apply.

Rationale of the court

The California Supreme Court decided that the case conformed to the reason and spirit of the doctrine more fully, perhaps, than any other. The court reasoned that

> a passenger sitting awake in a railroad car at the time of a collision, the pedestrian walking along the street and struck by a falling object or debris of an explosion, are surely not more entitled to an explanation than the unconscious patient on the operating-room table. Viewed from this aspect, it is difficult to see how the Doctrine could, with any justification, be restricted in its statement as to become inapplicable to a patient who admits himself to care and custody of doctors and nurses, is rendered unconscious, and receives some injury from instrumentalities used in his treatment. Without the aid of the Doctrine a patient who receives permanent injuries of serious character, obviously the result of someone's negligence, would be entirely unable to recover unless the doctors and nurses and attendants voluntarily disclose the identity of the negligent person and the facts establishing liability. If this were the state of the law of negligence, the courts, to avoid gross injustice, would be forced to invoke the principles of **absolute liability,** irrespective of negligence, in actions by persons suffering injuries during the course of treatment under anesthesia.
>
> Further, the condition that the injury must not have been due to the plaintiff's voluntary action is, of course, fully satisfied under the evidence produced in the case. The same is true of the condition that the accident must have been one which ordinarily does not occur unless someone was negligent.

The court went on to state that the problem was not one of negligence in treatment but one of distinct injury to a healthy part of the body not the subject of treatment and not within the area of the operation. The decision in California makes it clear that circumstances that point to negligence call on the defendants to explain the unusual result.

Liability of the defendants

As previously mentioned, the defendants argued that the plaintiff had not shown that the injury was caused by an instrumentality under a defendant's control, nor had he shown that any one of the defendants or their employees had exclusive control over any particular instumentality. Defendants asserted that some of them were not the employees of other defendants and thus did not stand in any permanent relationship from which liability for wrongful conduct would follow. In view of the nature of the injury and the number of defendants performing different functions, they could not all be liable for the wrong. However, the court indicated its concern that in a modern hospital a patient is quite likely to come under the care of a number of persons in different types of contractual and other relationships with each other.

In the case of Mr. Ybarra, it appeared that Dr. Swift, Dr. Spangard, and Dr. Tilley were physicians and surgeons commonly placed in the legal category of independent contractors. The anesthesiologist and defendant Thompson, a special nurse, were employees of Dr. Swift and not of the other doctors. However, the court did not believe that either the number or the relationship of the defendants alone determined whether the doctrine of *res ipsa loquitur* applied. Every defendant in whose custody the patient was placed for any period of time was bound to exercise ordinary care to see that no unnecessary harm came to him, and each was liable for failure in this regard. Any defendant who negligently injured him, and any defendant charged with his care who so neglected him as to allow injury to occur, would be considered liable. The defendant employers would be liable for the negligence of their employees, and the doctor in charge of the operation would be liable for the negligence of those who became his temporary servants for the purpose of assisting him in the operation.

The court further pointed out at trial that consistent with the principles of agency and independent contractor status, one or more defendants would be found liable and others absolved. However, this should not preclude the application of the rule of *res ipsa loquitur*. Control at one time or another of one or more of the vicarious agencies or instrumentalities that might have harmed the plaintiff was in the hands of every defendant or his employees or temporary servants. The court thought that this placed on the defendants the burden of initial explanation. Mr. Ybarra was rendered unconscious for the purpose of undergoing surgical treatment by the defendants. Therefore, it was manifestly unreasonable for defendants to insist that Mr. Ybarra identify any one of them as the person who did the allegedly negligent act that caused him injury.

If the court were to accept the contention of the defendants in such cases, compensation would rarely be allowed to patients injured while unconscious. A hospital conducts a highly integrated system of activities, with many persons contributing their efforts. For example, there may be preparation for surgery by nurses and interns who are employees of the hospital; administration of an anesthetic by a doctor who may be an employee of the hospital, an employee of the operating surgeon, or an independent contractor; performance of an operation by a surgeon and by assistants who may be the surgeon's employees, employees of the hospital, or independent contractors; and post-surgical care by the surgeon, a hospital physician, and nurses. The fact that the patient is placed in the care of large numbers of health professionals is not good reason for denying the patient all reasonable opportunity to recover damages for negligent harm.

General application of the doctrine

The court did not undertake to state the extent to which the reasoning of the *Ybarra* case might be applied to other situations in which the doctrine of *res ipsa loquitur* is invoked. The court merely held that, where a plaintiff receives unusual injuries while unconscious in the course of medical treatment, all those defendants who had any control over his or her body or the instrumentality that might have caused the injury may be properly called on to answer to the charge of negligence by giving an explanation of their conduct. The *Ybarra* decision has also been followed in other states.

The doctrine of *res ipsa loquitur* has no application where the alleged negligence consists of a failure of the doctor, dentist, or other professional in matters peculiarly within the knowledge of members of his or her profession. However, the rule requiring expert testimony does not apply when the relevant facts are such that no medical knowledge is needed to arrive at a solution.

For example, the lay person on a jury is as competent as the expert to say that reasonable care has not been exercised when sponges, instruments, or other foreign objects are allowed to remain inside the patient following surgery. Even in cases where it has been demonstrated by expert testimony that it is an approved medical practice to delegate to a nurse the duty to count sponges or instruments, a jury is well justified in assessing negligence against the surgeon who closes the incision without checking the nurse's count. The surgeon has an independent duty to see that nothing is left inside the patient that does not belong there. He or she is negligent in relying exclusively on the scrub nurse or the circulating nurse, who may in turn be negligent in not accounting for all the sponges or instruments following surgery. Also, as seen in the *Ybarra* case, no expert interpretation is needed when the injury is done to a portion of the patient's body outside the scope of the operation being performed.

But the doctrine of *res ipsa loquitur* is not confined to cases dealing with surgery. Most commonly, the doctrine is invoked in surgery patient cases because the patient is unaware of who actually caused him or her the injury. However, the doctrine may be properly used or invoked where the patient has sustained any damages as a result of injury to his or her person, reputation, fame, or character. The patient need only show that such injury would not have occurred without someone's negligent conduct and that the conduct or instrumentality causing the injury was within the exclusive control of some particular person or group of persons.

Implications of the doctrine's application

Much legal confusion has arisen regarding the implications of the application of *res ipsa loquitur*. The plaintiff is permitted to establish a **prima facie** case of negligence at trial when the doctrine is invoked merely by proving the existence of the injury. Thus, the plaintiff can establish negligence merely by proving the existence of the injury itself without needing to prove the existence of specific negligent acts or omissions causing that injury by any one or all defendants in the case. The burden of producing evidence demonstrating the absence of negligent conduct by any specific defendant then shifts to the defendant or defendants themselves. Therefore, the doctrine of *res ipsa loquitur* has been restricted to issues of negligence involving standards of reasonable conduct required of reasonable people and has not involved standards of professional capacity or professional judgment. When the issues involved are those of technical competence of the physician, dentist, or other professional, the injured patient must overcome the presumption that the physician, dentist, or other professional acted competently, skillfully, or within the appropriate standard of care by providing affirmative proof of specific acts of negligence.

Trial strategy

The ability of a plaintiff to invoke the doctrine of *res ipsa loquitur* at trial overcomes the myriad burdens involved in establishing negligence. Most often, one or more of the defendants are unable to prove that the plaintiff's injury was not caused by their negligent conduct. Accordingly, plaintiffs are left only with needing to demonstrate that they suffered an injury as a result of someone's negligence and to set forth the nature and extent of their damages.

EXAMPLES / QUESTIONS / PROJECTS

Mr. Bailey is a patient of Dr. Cheng. Dr. Cheng employs many medical assistants and front-office personnel in his practice. Mr. Bailey routinely pays for office examinations and treatment at the time such treatment is rendered. He always pays in cash and obtains a receipt for payment of his bill from Dr. Cheng's front-office assistant. He never receives any itemized statement from Dr. Cheng's office because of his promptness in paying for services.

One day, Mr. Bailey attempts to buy a new automobile. Checking his credit, the bank learns that he has an account with Dr. Cheng that has been turned over to a collection agency and written off as a bad debt by both Dr. Cheng and the collection agency. No further explanation is given to Mr. Bailey regarding this credit report. Because of the bad credit rating, Mr. Bailey is turned down for the loan. Does Mr. Bailey have any remedy against Dr. Cheng or his office staff?

Answer: The essential question in this case is: Who was actually negligent in turning a paid-up account over to a collection agency? Obviously, someone in Dr. Cheng's office. In fact, more than one of Dr. Cheng's office assistants could have been at fault, with one assistant failing to post payment to Mr. Bailey's ledger card and another assistant improperly turning over to the collection agency what he or she thought to be a delinquent account. Mr. Bailey could undoubtedly bring a lawsuit against Dr. Cheng based on the doctrine of *respondeat superior* for the negligent conduct of his assistants. This would probably be the safest route to take, since Dr. Cheng would be in a better financial situation than his assistants to pay for any damages resulting from Mr. Bailey's inability to obtain credit.

However, the more important question is whether or not Mr. Bailey would have to demonstrate that some negligent conduct on the part of Dr. Cheng's assistants was the actual or proximate cause for his being turned down for the loan. Mr. Bailey would have a strong argument in this example for applying the doctrine of *res ipsa loquitur.* After all, the medical assistants could reasonably foresee that turning a patient's bill over to a collection agency would adversely affect that patient's credit. Common knowledge dictates that people with bad credit are unable to obtain important loans. More significant is the fact that Mr. Bailey paid for every examination and treatment in cash and obtained a receipt from Dr. Cheng's office. Therefore, his account would not have been turned over to a collection agency without someone's negligence. Accordingly, Mr. Bailey may be able to apply the doctrine of *res ipsa loquitur* in this case. If successful, he would only need to argue to the judge or jury hearing the case the extent of his damages as a result of the negligent conduct causing him injury.

CHAPTER SEVEN

DAMAGES AND REMEDIES

Key Terms

quantum merit	neurosis	consortium
unconscionable	amenable	derivative
vindicate	abstain	verification
	propensity	

This chapter deals with various aspects of a plaintiff/patient's injuries sustained as a result of the defendant's negligent conduct. *Damages* are generally associated with compensation (money) awarded to the injured plaintiff, whereas the term *remedy* is generally associated with something other than monetary compensation which the plaintiff may obtain through his or her lawsuit. This chapter discusses both forms of legal recovery and their sometimes apparent overlap.

SPECIFIC PERFORMANCE

The remedy of *specific performance*, which is rarely invoked in cases dealing with the medical or allied health professions, is based on the principles of contract law. The application of the doctrine requires one party to live up to his or her contractual promise. Remember the buy-sell agreement between John and Mary in which John promised to pay ten dollars and Mary agreed to sell her roller skates to John? John's request for damages for Mary's failure to live up to her agreement would be based on the doctrine of specific performance. In other words, the court would require Mary to give John the "specific" roller skates that John paid for.

If, for some reason, Mary did not have the "specific" roller skates in question, John could sue Mary for the money it would take to purchase a similar pair of roller skates, even if a similar pair cost twenty-five dollars.

With few exceptions, the practice of the healing arts is a personal service rendered to a patient. The courts have been very reluctant to enforce contracts involving personal services, even though an established standard of care may be associated with a particular examination or treatment. The underlying rationale is that enforcement would require involuntary servitude of the person rendering the service. Further, the courts have no way of monitoring the services to determine that the services performed are exactly those contracted for by the patient.

However, the doctrine can be invoked in some instances. Many physicians, physical therapists, chiropractors, and other professionals currently prescribe and sell or dispense orthopedic appliances or devices such as orthopedic back swings used in the treatment of spinal problems. The patient contracts with the health professional to purchase the device at some specified price. Should the therapist or physician refuse to sell the equipment at the agreed upon price, the patient could maintain an action for specific performance.

At first glance, one might surmise that the doctor, therapist, or other allied health professional is basing his or her action on the doctrine of specific performance when he or she sues the patient for fees for professional services rendered. In theory, this sounds correct. However, courts have ruled that the item being sued for under the doctrine of specific performance must be unique and readily identifiable. Since money is not unique in substance, an action could not be maintained for specific performance. Rather, the litigation would be a generalized suit for money damages.

The back swing, in contrast, is unique and readily identifiable, even though no one specific back swing is being sought. The courts feel that a dollar is merely a dollar, whereas a specific type of back swing is unique.

For example, suppose that the therapist agrees to sell a particular type of back swing to a patient for $150. Subsequently, the therapist discovers that the swing will actually cost him $250 and so refuses to sell the back swing to the patient for the agreed-upon price. Further, assume that the patient is not able to purchase this or any similar back swing from any other source. If the patient were left with a suit for money damages as the only remedy, he or she would only be able to obtain the $150 paid to the therapist. Therefore, the court will probably take the position that the therapist must specifically perform the contract between the parties because of the unavailability of a similar piece of equipment for the amount contracted for. Specific performance is a remedy, not a damage for which a plaintiff requests and receives some sum of money.

RESCISSION AND RESTITUTION

In *rescission,* one party to the law suit indicates to the other party his or her *intent* to undo their contractual agreement. The purpose is to return the parties to the position they were in before the contract was made. Although often coupled with a lawsuit for restitution, rescission is an act between the parties.

In contrast, *restitution* is the *act* of restoring the parties to their original position before forming the contract and is most commonly associated with a lawsuit. Generally, the rescinding party brings an action to force the other contracting party to restore whatever consideration was given to him or her by the rescinding party. This consideration may be in the form of money or in the form of some specific piece of property.

For example, suppose the physical therapist in the preceding example agrees to sell a particular type of back swing to the patient for $150. The patient pays the therapist the money and thereafter discovers that the swing he purchased was not the swing he ordered. He then indicates to the therapist that he will not accept the delivery of the particular back swing because it is not the one he ordered. In addition, he requests that the therapist return the $150. When the therapist refuses to return the money, the patient files an action with the court based on restitution.

Note that, in this example, the act of rescission is the patient's refusal to accept the back swing from the therapist. The action filed with the court is a request for the court to force the therapist to return the patient's money.

Rescission and restitution should not be confused with the doctrine of specific performance. The doctrine of specific performance is an action to enforce adherence to one party's contractual obligation to the other. The purpose of rescission and restitution, in contrast, is to undo the contractual obligations of each of the parties and to restore them to their original bargaining position just before the contract was made. Both specific performance and rescission and restitution are remedies enforceable by the courts. In none of those cases is the remedy considered a matter of damages due, since the plaintiff is requesting the court either to enforce or to undo the contract.

INSURANCE REVIEW OF CLAIMS

The doctor may sue a patient for the patient's breach of his or her contractual agreement to pay for professional services rendered. This situation was discussed previously in the section on contract law. Most commonly, charges are accrued by the patient once the professional services have been rendered. It is common knowledge that professional services are expensive. However, patients seldom know in advance the amount of each service for which they are being charged.

The establishment of a reasonable fee for a particular type of service is based on the type of service, the expertise of the health care provider, and the geographic location of his or her practice. The common-law principle in the establishment of fees has often been termed **quantum merit**—"as much as he or she deserves." This is a promise on the part of the patient/defendant to pay the professional/plaintiff as much as he or she deserves for his or her labor. As one physician put it, charges are based on what the traffic will bear.

In assessing what is considered to be a reasonable fee, the courts most commonly look to what other similar health providers in the local area charge for similar services. Unless the fees charged are totally **unconscionable,** the courts rarely side with a disgruntled patient whose only defense for nonpayment is the feeling that the charges are excessive.

However, the workers' compensation laws in some states provide an affirmative defense for an insurance company or employer to assert that the fees for services rendered are unreasonable. In addition, the workers' compensation laws provide an affirmative defense for the insurance company or employer to assert that the treatment rendered is unnecessary to cure or otherwise relieve the employee of injuries sustained as a result of a work-related accident. These defenses are discussed in more detail in the chapter on workers' compensation.

The allied health professions are currently faced with the prevalence of medical or dental health insurance. Insurance companies have used the vast resources of computers to establish a reasonable basis for fees charged by health care providers for particular services. Many such providers have undoubtedly encountered scrutinized review of their bills by the peer review committee of an insurance company.

The peer review committee reviews the claim for fees submitted by the health care provider and compares these fees with fees charged by similar health care providers for the same services. In addition, the peer review committee often makes its own determination concerning whether such services were reasonably necessary to cure the patient of his or her ailment. More commonly than not, the insurance company rejects some portion of the provider's fee based on the recommendation of the peer review committee.

The review and rejection by the insurance carrier of some portion of the patient's bill under the contract of insurance may formulate a defense for the patient in a lawsuit brought by the health care provider for payment of the patient's bill. However, the courts have taken the position that the peer review committee's actions are self-serving in their attempt to save the insurance company money. Accordingly, many courts have rejected the committee's findings when asserted as a defense by a patient for not paying a bill. The courts merely look to the peer review committee's finding as another fact or piece of evidence in determining whether the health care provider's fees charged are reasonable and customary within the geographic area.

At this point, one must remember that the contract for payment of fees and provider services is between the patient and the health care provider, not between the health care provider and the insurance company. Consequently, the patient is solely responsible to the provider (doctor, dentist, or other allied health professional) for his or her bill.

NOMINAL DAMAGES

There are three basic kinds of damages in tort law: *nominal damages, compensatory damages,* and *punitive damages.* Nominal damages consist of a small sum of money awarded to a plaintiff for the purpose of **vindicating** his or her rights and preventing the defendant from acquiring rights to proceed against the plaintiff in a subsequent action. In addition, the awarding of nominal damages generally carries with it an award to the plaintiff for incurred costs in bringing the lawsuit. These costs may include the fee paid to the court for filing the lawsuit, sums expended in retaining the services of an expert witness to testify on behalf of the plaintiff at trial, and other related out-of-pocket expenses attendant to bringing the action. Costs ordinarily do not include fees paid to an attorney to prosecute the action on behalf of the plaintiff, although there are some circumstances under which a specific statute (law) may require the defendant to pay the prevailing plaintiff's attorneys' fees.

Some courts and jurisdictions have viewed the awarding of nominal damages as a mere sham and not a true representation of the case or the patient's right of recovery. For example, the jury may find that the health care provider's conduct in examining and/or treating the patient fell below the standard of care and was therefore negligent. However, finding that the patient sustained no damage as a result of negligence, the jury may then award the patient/plaintiff the sum of one dollar. With the nominal jury award, the court then allows the plaintiff to recover all costs expended in bringing the lawsuit against the professional. These costs may amount to several thousand dollars.

Many juries have expressed sympathy toward the patient/plaintiff in basing their assessment of liability and awarding nominal damages. However, many courts have overturned such verdicts. The rationale of the court is that such a verdict is not derived from the facts of the case but rather from the extraneous feelings of the jurors. More importantly, the rendering of such a verdict eliminates the professional's possible right in a subsequent lawsuit to seek damages against the patient/plaintiff for malicious prosecution or abuse of process.

COMPENSATORY DAMAGES

The second type of damages allowed in tort law is compensatory damages. Awarded to an injured patient/plaintiff, such compensation is intended to represent the closest possible dollar equivalent of the loss or harm suffered as a result of injuries sustained by the patient due to the negligent conduct of the health care provider. These damages are intended to restore the patient to his or her position prior to the negligent act that caused the injury. They take the form of compensation to the patient for all his or her incurred losses from the time of the injury to the time of trial. They also include all reasonably expected losses that may be incurred in the future from the time of trial to the patient's death. The losses are broken down into the factors or categories discussed in the following sections.

Special damages

Special damages are incurred losses that may be readily identified and proved. Typically, they are incurred between the time of the negligent act that causes the injury and the time of trial. Medical expenses incurred to relieve or cure the patient/plaintiff from the effects of an injury constitute one such loss. Loss of wages sustained because of the patient/plaintiff's inability to work are also presented to the jury, generally in the form of **verification.** For example, a patient's employer may tell the jury that the patient/plaintiff was employed prior to the injury, earned the sum of ten dollars per hour, and worked forty hours per week. Due to the injuries sustained, the patient/plaintiff was unable to work for a period of six months, thus incurring a wage loss of $9,600 ($10 per hour × 40 hours per week × 4 weeks per month × 6 months).

Medical bills and testimony from various subsequent treating physicians and other health care providers are received into evidence, demonstrating the injury, the need for treatment, and the amount of loss or charges incurred for such treatment. The patient may have been required to hire a nurse to provide home medical care. Testimony that this care was necessary, along with the amount charged for the professional service, may likewise be admitted into evidence as an element of the patient's special damages.

In addition to these factors, the patient may have been required to employ the services of a maid, cook, or other person to do household chores because of the patient's incapacity. The fact that these services were needed and the amounts such services cost the patient may also be admitted into evidence as an element of the patient's special damages. Special orthopedic appliances may be included, including those used in the home or automobile, and bills for such appliances or devices would be presented to the jury.

Based on this evidence, the health care provider would be obligated to reimburse the injured patient/plaintiff for all special damages incurred for the necessities of life and directly related to the injury and the patient's inability to perform. The only apparent criterion for the jury to use in allowing or disallowing claimed special damages is whether such expenses were reasonably or necessarily incurred by the patient/plaintiff as a result of his or her injury.

For example, a jury might disallow a patient's claim that he employed a gardener to mow his lawn weekly when the evidence demonstrates that the patient employed the gardener on a continuous basis before the injury. Or the jury might disallow the patient's claim that it was necessary to employ a housekeeper to do domestic chores when the patient's injury did not preclude her from doing such chores. Of course, these are all matters for jury consideration. As such, each claim turns on the facts of the case.

General damages

The term *general damages* is a broad expression, an abstract in form, that covers a number of items claimed as special damages. General damages include compensation to an injured person for past pain, suffering, and inconvenience as well as estimates of compensation for future pain and suffering, including future medical expenses, loss of earning capacity, permanent disability and disfigurement, and estimated cost of other established special future damages, such as the necessity for the employment of domestic help and repair and/or replacement of orthopedic appliances or devices. These elements of a patient's claimed loss are most often based on expert testimony that such losses will be incurred in the future.

Much debate has taken place over the awarding of general damages. Often the defendant feels that the verdict is excessive, whereas the plaintiff feels that the verdict is inadequate. When either party feels aggrieved by the jury verdict, a posttrial motion is generally made to the court to increase or decrease the jury award. This posttrial motion is called *remittitur* when the request is for the court to reduce the jury's award and *addititur* when the request is to increase the jury award. The legal standard on which the court gauges the verdict for remittitur is premised on what the court believes the maximum jury verdict could have been. The legal standard on which the court gauges the verdict for addititur is premised on the minimum amount the jury could have reasonably awarded. An excellent example of the court's assessment and discussion of the plaintiff's claimed damages is provided in the nonmedical malpractice case of *Anderson v. Sears, Roebuck and Co.*[1] The following is a summary of the case.

Helen Britton, a young child, was severely burned when her home was completely consumed by fire. The fire was triggered by a heater that was negligently manufactured by Sears, Roebuck and Co. Following a jury trial, the jury awarded Miss Britton $2,000,000 in damages, whereupon Sears, Roebuck and Co. asked the court for remittitur (reduction in the award) of the verdict. The trial court concluded that the amount of the award was justified, whereupon Sears, Roebuck and Co. appealed the decision to a higher court. The appellate court, reviewing the records of the trial court and citing various other cases, upheld the trial court's decision in the following words:

> The legal standard on which to gauge a jury verdict for remittitur purposes is the "maximum recovery rule." The rule directs the trial judge to determine whether the verdict of the jury exceeds the maximum amount which the jury could reasonably find and if it does, the trial judge may then reduce the verdict to the highest amount that the jury could properly have awarded.
>
> The court's task is to ascertain by scrutinizing all the evidence as to each element of damages, and what amount would be the maximum the jury could have reasonably awarded.

The court went on to analyze in detail each of the five cardinal elements of the claim—past physical and mental pain, future physical and mental pain, future medical expenses, loss of earning capacity, and permanent disability and disfigurement—and to determine the damages appropriate to each. Based on the analysis, the appellate court upheld the jury's award.

In this case, the court based its finding on the potential of the jury verdict. Consideration was given to similar cases as well as to the presentation in the trial court of expert testimony by economists, psychiatrists, and other physicians relating to the extensive future medical care that would be required. Expert testimony is how an attorney demonstrates, with some degree of precision, his or her client's potential estimated future losses, including pain and suffering.

Impairment of earning capacity

In the case of Helen Britton, the loss of future earning capacity was a recoverable loss. Expert testimony was given at the time of trial to demonstrate this segment of the plaintiff's damages. Evidence of the plaintiff's preinjury potential for employment was presented to the jury. In addition, the total

---

[1] 377 F. Supp. 136 (E. D. La. 1974)

estimated years of the patient/plaintiff's inability to work as a result of her injury was presented. Finally, the estimated compensation for such types of employment was given to compute the estimated potential loss of earnings. This total computation is classified as the loss of earning capacity. Loss of past earnings sustained between the date of injury and the time of trial—earnings that are not otherwise readily identifiable—is likewise proved by various forms of evidence.

Where the injured plaintiff is self-employed or possibly works for an employer on a commission basis, the amount of wage loss is generally proved by evidence of past profits, past commissions, or the amount of compensation someone else received for similar work during the period of time in question. For example, a real estate salesperson may be unable to work for a period of time because of an injury caused by someone else's negligent conduct. At the time of trial, the injured plaintiff would need to prove his or her loss of past earnings based on the value of the time loss incurred. The jury would be presented with evidence of the plaintiff's past earnings—for instance, commissions earned on sales during the previous year—and the employer or fellow employees would be called to testify that the injured plaintiff was an energetic salesperson who continually worked on a regular basis before his or her injury. The injured plaintiff would also need to establish, with testimony by similar salespersons or brokers in the general geographic area, the average number of sales and commissions earned on those sales for the period in question. This would tend to demonstrate the money value of the sales and commissions that the injured plaintiff could have earned for the period. If the real estate market became depressed during the period of time in question, the jury would probably discount the plaintiff's claimed loss. And, if the real estate market showed an increase during the period, the jury would take this into account when assessing money damages.

Loss of future earning capacity

Plaintiffs may also recover money damages for the impairment of their earning capacity in the future. As with the loss of past earnings based on potential lost profits or commissions, plaintiffs have to prove with some degree of certainty that they would sustain a loss of earnings in the future because of an inability to work in certain fields or capacities. A fifteen-year-old adolescent who, prior to his or her injury, had a low IQ and poor academic grades would probably have an insurmountable task in proving to a jury that he or she would have become a world-famous brain surgeon with the potential of earning a million dollars per year had it not been for the injury. In contrast, an injured plaintiff could conceivably convince a jury of a significant loss of earning capacity where the evidence demonstrates that the plaintiff has completed most of his or her college education with high academic grades and has been accepted to medical school. However, without some clear evidence of a long-standing desire to become a neurosurgeon, the injured plaintiff may have difficulty proving his or her loss of earning capacity based on the average earnings of a neurosurgeon for the period of time claimed. Thus, the injured plaintiff may be restricted to comparing his or her future earnings to those of a general practitioner in assessing losses attendant to future earning capacity.

In calculating the loss of earning capacity, the jury is presented with the picture of a total loss. More specifically, the injured plaintiff is claiming that he or she has been prevented from using his or her ability in a particular profession or occupation. The period of time used to compute the amount of damages begins when the injured plaintiff would have entered the profession or occupation and started earning money. The projected loss of earnings based on capacity ends with the average work-life expectancy of the plaintiff in the particular profession or occupation. In the case of a diminished life expectancy, this life expectancy of the injured plaintiff is used in place of the work-life expectancy.

Evidence by the injured plaintiff may include actuarial tables and testimony from a statistician or an economist who can present the jury with statistics on the average earnings associated with the particular profession or occupation. The economist or statistician would undoubtedly present the jury with statistics from several different professions or occupations that the injured plaintiff might have entered. The amount of compensation associated with each profession or occupation would likewise be presented. In this way, the injured plaintiff would be given a greater degree of latitude in arguing his or her claimed loss of earning capacity should a particular juror disbelieve the plaintiff's contention that he or she would have gone into a specific or particular occupation or profession had it not been for the injury.

If the loss claimed is based on the plaintiff's inability to work in an occupation or profession in which he or she was previously employed, the claim for the loss of future earning capacity is based on the present value of earnings for the probable period of disability. Just as in the case demonstrating to the jury the value of lost time incurred in the past, the injured plaintiff may also demonstrate that he or she has worked in a particular occupation before the injury and that, because of the injury, he or she will be continually incapacitated from returning to that occupation for a specified period of time in the future. If the disability is permanent, the specified period of time may be his or her work-life expectancy.

Compared to this is the situation in which the plaintiff has been precluded from going into a particular occupation or profession. In this case, an economist could also project the present value of earnings for that particular occupation or profession and the potential increases in income based on the standard rate of inflation.

Future medical care and other expenses

Just as recovery is allowed for the loss of future earnings or earning capacity, the injured plaintiff is allowed recovery for future medical or other expenses necessary to cure or relieve him or her from the effects of the injury. However, these expenses must be relatively certain to be incurred by the plaintiff in the future. To demonstrate this potential loss, the plaintiff would introduce evidence in the form of testimony from doctors or other professionals. The purpose of this testimony would be to demonstrate the potential loss.

In the Helen Britton case, the jury was presented with evidence that a certain number of future surgeries would be necessary, with an estimated loss for each surgery based on the present cost for such surgical procedure. The jury is only allowed to consider the present value of such services, and is not supposed to take into account any potential increase in the cost for a particular procedure at some future time. The same is true for nursing services or other professional care that the injured plaintiff could prove, with a reasonable degree of certainty, would be incurred.

Not only is the jury allowed to consider awarding damages for future medical care or other professional services, but other expenses that may reasonably be anticipated because of the injury may be presented to the jury for consideration. The plaintiff may present evidence to the jury that he or she has always done certain household chores, such as cooking, housecleaning, gardening, and so on. The jury could then consider evidence that, due to the injury, the plaintiff will be required to hire domestic help in the future because the injury prevents him or her from doing those chores. Again, the jury may only consider the present value of the costs for such services. They may not speculate that such costs may increase in the future. In addition, the injured plaintiff can only present evidence concerning the period that these services would be required because of his or her inability to perform them. Evidence of the plaintiffs incapacity to perform such chores would undoubtedly come from the medical opinions of the plaintiff's treating doctors. Evidence of the need for hiring such domestic help to perform such chores may come from the plaintiff, his or her spouse, or other sources that demonstrate that such chores exist.

For example, the patient who resides in an apartment or condominium where he or she is not required to do yard work would be unable to prove to a jury any potential need for hiring a gardener in the future based on testimony that he or she may someday purchase a home with a yard. Such an element of damage is mere speculation and is not allowed by the courts. In contrast, the plaintiff who owns a large home with a yard could present evidence that he or she will be required by his or her incapacity to hire a regular gardener in the future.

Pain and suffering

The elements of general damages that may be recovered by an injured plaintiff include pain and suffering. It has long been established in the law that the injured plaintiff may recover damages for physical pain, suffering, and mental anguish. This includes not only suffering from the date of the injury to the time of trial but also suffering that is reasonably certain to result from the injury in the future. There is no fixed standard of any kind against which damages for pain, suffering, and mental anguish may be measured. This element of damage may mean different things to different people. Ultimately, the responsibility for fixing a reasonable amount as compensation is left to the jury, subject to the control of the court.

The complexity of life in our modern society gives rise to innumerable ways in which a person can become less happy. Accordingly, skillful attorneys have become very articulate in breaking down into elements the forms of happiness claimed as losses due to injury. For example, the jury has been allowed to award general damages for the plaintiff's loss of his or her sense of smell, touch, taste, sight, or hearing. The skillful attorney whose injured client has a life-long hobby of making fine wood carvings may strongly argue that his or her client has sustained, and will in the future sustain, great mental anguish due to his or her inability to ever do wood carvings again because of the injury. Likewise, an injured plaintiff whose hobby is gourmet cooking and who is a connoisseur of fine wines and cheeses would undoubtedly argue that great mental suffering and anguish has been sustained, and will be sustained in the future, because the injury deprived him or her of the ability to taste or smell.

Assume for the moment that the gourmet cook has no interest or dexterity in doing fine wood carving and that the plaintiff whose hobby is fine wood carving eats only foods that are bland in taste and lacking in aroma. In the case of the wood carver, he or she would be hard-pressed to argue having sustained great mental suffering or anguish because of the loss of the ability to smell or taste. In contrast, the gourmet cook might be able to argue successfully to the jury that he or she sustained severe mental anguish or suffering because of an injury that caused numbness or grip-loss to the hands and thereby prevented him or her from holding cooking utensils.

Juries have been burdened with the task of assessing and awarding general damages for physical and mental pain and suffering based on myriad premises—including the mental suffering sustained by a virgin of strict religious faith because her hymen was ruptured by a doctor during a physical examination.[2] Other arguments for the awarding of general damages have included the fear of death, increased stuttering, nervousness, insomnia, inability to drive a car, fear of injury to an unborn child, and, most commonly, scars and other disfigurements.

The question of whether or not a woman should recover more for facial scars than a man has often been raised. Although juries have traditionally been somewhat more sympathetic to a woman, modern trends have demonstrated that juries generally base their assessment of the amount of mental or physical pain on numerous factors. Accordingly, the jury would tend to consider where the scar is located, whether the woman is young or old, married or unmarried, and whether the scar is likely to be a constant embarrassment.

In addition, modern juries have tended to award greater damages if the scar or disfigurement is likely to inhibit the person's ability to work in a particular occupation. For example, a jury would probably award a successful

---

[2]*Templin v. Erkekedis*, 119 Ind. App 171, 84 N.E. 2d 728 (1949).

free-lance fashion model, whether a man or a woman, greater-than-average general damages for pain and suffering due to a conspicuous scar or disfigurement. In assessing the amount of damages, the jury might also consider evidence of the plaintiff's high motivation and ambition within the profession or occupation.

Finally, it should be noted that some jurisdictions have limited the amount of compensation that a jury may award for general damages. For example, the relevant Massachusetts law requires a court to instruct the jury that if they find a medical malpractice defendant liable, they may not award the plaintiff more than five hundred thousand dollars for pain and suffering, loss of companionship, embarrassment and other items of general damages unless they find special circumstances specified by the statute.[3]

DAMAGES FOR EMOTIONAL PAIN AND SUFFERING

Traditionally, and in the majority of jurisdictions today, general damages have not been awarded to a plaintiff for mental pain and suffering that are not associated with some physical injury. However, a California case has allowed for such compensation. This decision reasoned that such an injury is readily discernible because the field of psychiatry has become an exacting science. Therefore, an actual **neurosis** cannot be faked by an injured plaintiff; the manifestations of such neuroses can be readily identified by a trained psychiatrist.

However, the majority of states do not follow the California court's rationale. For example, the plaintiff may not recover damages for mental pain and suffering based on fear alone when a physician or registered nurse specializing in the field of cardiology mistakenly tells the patient/plaintiff that he or she is on the verge of a heart attack. Such compensation is only allowed where such fear manifests itself in some physical form, such as insomnia, hives, nervous twitching, or other physical manifestations that are readily discernible and cannot be faked. Likewise, the majority of states do not allow recovery for the plaintiff whose only claimed injury is mental suffering caused by observing injury to another person.

Case example: *Whetham v. Bismarck Hospital*

In the North Dakota case of *Whetham v. Bismarck Hospital*,[4] mental suffering was the claimed result of observing injury to another person. In this case, Mrs. Whetham gave birth to a daughter named Tami Lynn in Bismarck Hospital. An employee of the hospital, in Mrs. Whetham's presence, dropped Tami Lynn

---

[3]M.G.L. chapter 231, section 60H.

[4]*Whetham v. Bismarck Hospital*, 197 N.W. 2d 678 (N.D. 1972).

onto the tile floor of the hospital. Mrs. Whetham asserted that, as a direct result of the careless and negligent handling of her daughter by the employee, Tami Lynn struck her head on the floor with such force and violence that she suffered a fractured skull. As a direct and proximate result of that negligence, Mrs. Whetham was forced to watch her daughter fall to the floor and to hear the sound of the impact. Because of this, Mrs. Whetham claimed, she suffered severe emotional and mental shock for which she sought money damages. She also sought damages for the additional medical expenses required for Tami Lynn's care and for the prolonged hospitalization she incurred while the child received the care. No claim was being made on behalf of Tami Lynn because the full residual effects of her injuries had not yet been ascertained.

The Supreme Court of North Dakota, in deciding this case, first looked to the two leading cases in the state of California dealing with the issue of whether liability may be predicated on fright or nervous shock induced solely by the plaintiff's observation of negligently caused danger or injury to a third person.

Stopping point to the liability

The first case cited was that of *Amaya v. Home Ice, Fuel & Supply Co.*[5] In the case of *Amaya*, the court pointed out that there must be a stopping point in the liability of a negligent defendant. To the extent that the law intervenes in any area of human activity and declares that for certain consequences of that activity the actor shall be civilly liable for damages, both the individual actor and society as a whole feel the effects of the restraint: a psychological effect in the form of a lessening of incentive and an economic effect in the form of the cost of insurance necessary to enable the activity to continue. The law further recognizes that no activity could survive in an unlimited progression of such effect. Accordingly, when the general social utility of an activity is deemed to outweigh the particular interest with which it may clash, important policy reasons dictate that some limits be set to liability for its consequences.

The law in California and in many other jurisdictions that have ruled on the question provides that an actor who is merely negligent is not liable to a person who claims injury through fright or shock induced by conduct directed not to the person himself or herself but to a third person. Thus, in cases where a defendant's conduct involves negligent driving of a motor vehicle, the courts conclude that to extend liability to spectators who are not themselves in danger would place an unreasonable burden on users of the highways. Because the industrial society in which we live becomes still more complex as the use of streets, highways, and airways increases, a certain percentage of accidents appears to be statistically inevitable. And losses will inevitably accompany those accidents.

The present system of insurance attempts to compensate for such losses and to spread the cost of compensation over those who do not, as well as those

[5]29 Cal. Rptr. 33, 379 P. 2d 513 (1963)

who do, cause such losses. The system of insurance protection would be overtaxed if it attempted to absorb the far-reaching extension of liability that would follow from allowing a person recovery of damages for mental suffering caused by witnessing a trauma to some third person. Further, the courts have noted that many activities of everyday life are either uninsurable or customarily involve persons who are uninsured. Yet, those activities may well give rise to the type of "spectator injury" that involves mental suffering. The courts have concluded that the social utility of such activities outweighs the somewhat speculative interest of individuals who wish to be free of the risk of mental suffering in witnessing trauma to some third person.

In addition, in the case of Mrs. Whetham, the court stated that,

[a]s long as our system of compensation is based on the concept of fault, we must also weigh the moral blame attached to the defendant's conduct. Here is felt the difference between the social importance of conduct that negligently causes harm and conduct that is intended to do so. It is often said that in the latter case that the defendant will be held liable for a broader range of consequences because, as the consequences are intended, they are the more foreseeable. But in many intentional tort cases the defendant has been held liable under the reasoning for consequences far beyond those which he actually intended. It follows that, once more, foreseeability is not the real answer. Rather, the increased liability imposed on an unintentional wrong-doer appears to reflect the psychological fact that solicitude for the interest of the actor weighs less in the balance as his moral guilt increases and the social utility of his conduct diminishes.

Reasonable foreseeable injury

In 1968, only five years after the case of *Amaya*, and after changes in the membership of the court, the California Supreme Court overruled the *Amaya* case in the case of *Dillon v. Legg*.[6] The court, speaking for the majority in *Dillon*, maintained that the difficulties of adjudication should not frustrate the principals from finding a remedy for every substantial wrong while at the same time realizing that potentially infinite liability should be limited. It therefore concluded that the law of torts holds a defendant **amenable** only for injuries to others that were reasonably foreseeable to the defendant. Noting that the court was dealing with a case in which the plaintiff suffered a shock that resulted in physical injuries, and confining its opinion to that case, the court stated:

In determining, in such a case, where the defendant should reasonably foresee the injury to plaintiff, or in other terminology, where the defendant owes plaintiff a duty of due care, the courts will take into account such factors as the following: (i) whether plaintiff was located near the

---

[6] 69 Cal. Rptr. 72, 441 P. 2d 912 (1968)

scene of the accident, as contrasted with one who was a distance away from it; (2) whether the shock resulted from the direct emotional impact on the plaintiff from the sensory and contemporaneous observance of the accident, as contrasted with learning of the accident from others after the occurrence; (3) whether plaintiff and the victim are closely *related*, as contrasted with an absence of any relationship or the presence of only a distant relationship.

After laying down these guidelines, the California Supreme Court concluded that all of the factors listed were present in the Dillon case.

Ruling in the Whetham *case*

In making its judgment, the North Dakota Supreme Court went on to cite the Restatement of Torts, which states

> that if the actor unintentionally causes emotional distress to another, he is subject to liability to the other for resulting illness or bodily harm if the actor should have realized that his conduct involved an unreasonable risk of causing the distress, otherwise than by knowledge of the harm or peril of a third person, and from facts known to him should have realized that the distress, if it were caused, might result in illness or bodily harm; this rule has no application to illness or bodily harm of another which is caused by emotional distress arising solely from harm or peril to a third person, unless the negligence of the actor has otherwise created an unreasonable risk of bodily harm to the other. This applies only where the negligent conduct of the actor threatens the other with emotional distress likely to result in bodily harm because of the other's fright, shock, or other emotional disturbance, arising out of fear for his *own* safety, or the invasion of his *own* interest, and it has no application where the emotional distress arises solely because of the harm or peril to a third person, and the negligence of the actor has not threatened the plaintiff with bodily harm in any other way. Thus, by way of illustration, the restatement points out that where the actor negligently runs down and kills a child in the street, and its mother, in the immediate vicinity, witnesses the event and suffers severe emotional distress resulting in a heart attack or other bodily harm to her, she cannot recover for such bodily harm unless she was herself in the path of the vehicle, or was in some other manner threatened with bodily harm to herself otherwise then through the emotional distress at the peril to her child.

Thus, the Supreme Court of North Dakota upheld the trial court's ruling in dismissing the claim of Mrs. Whetham for damages based on mental shock and suffering.

Case example: *Gleitman v. Cosgrove*

In the case of *Gleitman v. Cosgrove*,[7] the New Jersey Supreme Court dismissed a malpractice suit for money damages to an infant and an infant's parents based on their inability to prove that the claimed injuries were a direct and proximate result of the doctor's malpractice.

The first count of the complaint was brought on behalf of Jeffrey Gleitman, an infant, for his birth defects. The second count was brought by his mother, Sandra Gleitman, for the emotional state caused by her son's condition. The third count was brought by his father, Erwin Gleitman, for the costs incurred in caring for Jeffrey. Defendants Robert Cosgrove, Jr., and Jerome Doland were the physicians engaged together in the practice of obstetrics and gynecology in Jersey City. The facts of the case and the holding of the court may be summarized as follows:

> Sandra Gleitman consulted Drs. Cosgrove and Doland in the year 1959. She was examined by Dr. Cosgrove and found to be two months pregnant. She informed him that around March of 1959 she had had an illness diagnosed as German measles. Mrs. Gleitman testified that Dr. Cosgrove, on receipt of this information and on inquiry by her, told her that the German measles would have no effect at all on her child.
>
> Mrs. Gleitman gave birth to Jeffrey on November 25, 1959. Although at first the baby seemed normal, a few weeks later the substantial defect which Jeffrey has in sight, hearing and speech began to become apparent. He has had several operations which have given him some visual capacity, and he attends a special correctional institute for blind and deaf children. His physical condition, which is seriously impaired, was not in dispute.
>
> The theory of plaintiffs' suit is that defendants negligently failed to inform Mrs. Gleitman, their patient, of the effects that German measles might have upon the infant in gestation. Had the mother been so informed, plaintiffs assert that she might have obtained other medical advice with a view to the obtaining of an abortion. Plaintiffs do not assert that Mrs. Gleitman's life or health was in jeopardy during the term of her pregnancy.
>
> The trial judge dismissed the three counts without submitting any of them to the jury. The claim of infant Jeffrey was dismissed for failure to show that the acts of the defendants were the proximate cause of Jeffrey's condition, and the claims of his mother and father were dismissed because the trial judge believed that the suggested abortion would be criminal in the state of New Jersey under New Jersey law.

---

[7]*Gleitman v. Cosgrove*, 49 N.J.22, 227 A.2d 689 (1967).

The state supreme court, in its ruling upholding the trial court's decision, made the following statement:

> In the present case there is no contention that anything the defendants could have done would have decreased the likelihood that the infant would be born with defects. The conduct of defendants was not the cause of infant plaintiff's [Jeffrey's] condition.
>
> The infant plaintiff is therefore required to say not that he should have been born without defects but that he should have not been born at all. In the language of tort law he says: But for the negligence of defendants, he would not have been born to suffer with an impaired body. In other words, he claims that the conduct of defendants prevented his mother from obtaining an abortion which would have terminated his existence, and that his very life is "wrongful."
>
> The normal measure of damages in tort actions is compensatory. Damages are measured by comparing the condition plaintiff would have been in, had the defendants not been negligent, with plaintiff's impaired condition as a result of the negligence. The infant plaintiff [Jeffrey] would have [the court] measure the difference between his life with defects against the utter void of nonexistence, but it is impossible to make such a determination. This Court cannot weigh the value of life with impairments against the nonexistence of life itself. By asserting that he should not have been born, the infant plaintiff makes it logically impossible for a court to measure his alleged damages because of the impossibility of making the comparison required by compensatory remedies. . . . We hold that the first count of the complaint on behalf of Jeffrey Gleitman is not actionable because the conduct complained of, even if true, does not give rise to damages cognizable at law.
>
> The mother and father stand in a somewhat different position from the infant. They are equally subject to the factual circumstance that no act by the defendants could have decreased the likelihood that the infant would be defective. However, Mrs. Gleitman can say that an abortion would have freed her of the emotional problems caused by the raising of a child with birth defects; and Mr. Gleitman can assert that it would have been less expensive for him to abort rather than raise the child.
>
> A considerable problem is raised by the claim of injury to the parents. In order to determine their compensatory damages, a court would have to evaluate the denial to them of the intangible, unmeasurable, and complex human benefits of motherhood and fatherhood and weigh these against the emotional and money injuries. Such a proposed weighing is similar to that which we have found impossible to perform for the infant plaintiff. When the parents say that their child should not have been born, they make it impossible for a court to measure their damages in being the mother and father of a defective child.
>
> Denial of the claim for damages by adult plaintiffs is also required by a close look at exactly what it is they are here seeking. The thrust of

their complaint is that they were denied the opportunity to terminate the life of their child while he was an embryo. Even under our assumption that an abortion could have been obtained without making its participants liable to criminal sanctions, substantial policy reasons prevent this Court from allowing tort damages for the denial of the opportunity to take an embryonic life.

A dissenting opinion in this case was expressed by one of the Justices and was joined, in part, by a second Justice. Basically, the dissenting Justice stated that Dr. Cosgrove breached his duty of care to Mr. and Mrs. Gleitman by misleading them into a false sense of security—that is, by letting them believe that the German measles would have no effect on the child then in gestation. In reliance on this misrepresentation, Mrs. Gleitman was deprived of the free choice to safely and lawfully abort the pregnancy. Instead, she permitted the pregnancy to proceed and gave birth to a child with severe birth defects. The Justice concluded that, although the law cannot relieve the heartache and undo the harm, it could afford some reasonable measure of compensation toward alleviating the financial burdens of raising the child. In declining to do so, the law is permitting a wrong with serious consequential injury to go wholly unredressed, which is neither just nor compatible with expanding principles of liability in the field of torts.

The dissenting Justice felt very strongly that compensatory damages could be calculated in providing the minor child with necessaries of life such as special schooling, extraordinary medical services, and so on.

The *Gleitman* case is sharply contrasted with similar cases filed against physicians and pharmaceutical houses based on the assertion of "wrongful life," probably because of the delicate subject of abortion dealt with in the *Gleitman* case. In the cases dealing with "wrongful life," the courts have upheld compensatory damages against physicians for the costs of raising a child due to the physician's misdiagnosis of sterility or the failure to inform patients of the potential for pregnancy associated with a particular method of birth control. The fact that the parents were misled to **abstain** from methods of birth control other than the one they were using has formed the basis for recovery of damages. However, such damages have been limited to recovery by the parents only. In a 1990 case, the Supreme Judicial Court of Massachusetts allowed recovery for the negligent performance of a sterilization procedure where the physician had guaranteed that future pregnancies would be prevented by the procedure.[8] The damages in such cases include the cost of the unsuccessful procedure, the costs associated with pregnancy, the wife's lost earning capacity, if any, cost of care for any other children while the mother recovers, the husband's loss of consortium, the wife's pain and suffering relating to the pregnancy and birth, cost of subsequent sterilization procedure, and the emotional distress of both parents. Child-rearing costs may be allowed if there is proof that sterilization was undertaken for financial reasons.

---

[8]*Burke v. Rivo*, 406 Mass. 764, 551 N.E.2d 1 (1990).

The *Gleitman* case should not be confused with cases dealing with compensatory damages recoverable by a child as a result of medical malpractice occurring to the child before he or she is born. Such cases have dealt largely with the physician's prescribing to the mother medication with known **propensities** to cause birth defects. Where the child who is later born does suffer from such birth defects, he or she may maintain an action against the physician for negligently prescribing the medication, and if the child dies of such injuries, an action can be maintained for the child's wrongful death. Likewise, many cases have held the pharmaceutical laboratory liable for failing to warn of the potential of birth defects caused by a woman taking certain medications during pregnancy.

Other cases have dealt with the use of X-ray examinations with a pregnant woman whose unborn child is in the first stages of embryonic development. Actions have been maintained and damages awarded to the parents and the child for birth defects allegedly sustained as a result of such examinations.

LOSS OF CONSORTIUM

Traditionally, the common law recognized that a husband was legally entitled to his wife's various earnings and services. The courts protected the husband's right to these assets against interference by third parties. This action against negligent persons who caused injury to a wife resulting in the husband's loss of her services was and is known as an action for loss of **consortium**. Because the common law did not recognize the wife as having a legal interest in her husband's personal property, she was barred from recovery under the doctrine of loss of consortium.

In modern times, with the advent of equal rights and equal protection under the law, the common law doctrine affording this remedy exclusively to the husband has lost its validity. Today the majority of courts permit both spouses to bring a claim for loss of consortium.

The main emphasis on the damage element in this claim has shifted away from mere economic loss to the loss of companionship, society, and affection. Although the loss of consortium could be viewed as a wholly independent injury of the spouse, most jurisdictions regard it as a **derivative** claim, Thus, the spouse claiming loss of consortium may maintain the action only as long as the injured spouse is able to maintain a claim against the negligent person for causing his or her injury. Further, many states limit a claim for loss of consortium to spouses. Therefore, many jurisdictions disallow any claim asserted by the child of an injured parent where the child's action is based on loss of society, love, and affection. Likewise, claims by parents solely for loss of companionship of their injured child have been barred from recovery, although a 1975 Wisconsin decision did allow such a claim.[9] Other courts considering such claims have not, however, followed the Wisconsin decision.

---

[9]*Shockley v. Prier*, 66 Wis. 2d 394, 225 N.W.2d 495 (1975).

The rationale for shifting recovery to intangible things such as love, companionship, society, and affection in a loss of consortium action arose out of attempts to prevent the plaintiff from receiving a double recovery. Currently, the courts recognize a husband and wife as constituting a "family unit." Thus, to award a wife damages based on proof that she was required to hire a babysitter to pick her child up from day care and then to award her husband damages for loss of consortium in a similar amount for having to hire a babysitter would be, in effect a double recovery. The jury may consider only once the wages paid to the babysitter. However, the jury may also consider the husband's additional loss in being forced to hire a gardener to care for their garden if the evidence established that the wife's hobby was gardening.

In addition a jury may not award loss of earnings and earning capacity to a husband who is injured as a result of professional or other negligent conduct and also award the wife a similar amount for the loss of her husband's financial support. Such an award is not allowed because it would be a duplication of the husband's loss of earnings, both past and future. However, the wife can maintain an action for loss of consortium where the husband's injuries preclude him from doing such household chores as gardening or washing the car. Also, the husband can maintain an action for damages for loss of consortium in having to hire a babysitter as in the previous example. Damages for loss of consortium are allowed as long as the damages sought in either action are not duplicated.

As previously mentioned, the majority of states do not allow recovery for purely emotional or mental suffering as a result of another person's negligent conduct. The loss of consortium action may therefore be maintained by a husband or wife only where there has been a physical injury to the other spouse as a result of such negligent conduct. This is precisely what is meant by a **derivative action** in a lawsuit. The spouse's action is not independent but is *derived* from the other spouse's action.

Finally, courts have repeatedly held that the loss of consortium claim derives from the relationship of marriage and the rights of the parties in a marriage. Accordingly, unmarried cohabitants cannot maintain a loss of consortium claim, nor can married persons when the injury at issue occurred before the marriage.

PUNITIVE DAMAGES

We have thus far been dealing with the compensatory damages that a person may recover due to an injury sustained as a result of the negligent conduct of another person. Where a patient sustains a severe burn from a diathermy, ultrasound, or similar therapeutic instrument because the instrument was improperly set up, used, or maintained, the injured person may receive compensatory damages. We have seen that these damages include additional medical expenses to cure and relieve the effects of the injury; loss of earnings and earning capacity; pain, mental suffering, and anguish; and other damages reasonably or necessarily incurred as a result of the injury.

However, what if the medical assistant, nurse, practitioner, physical therapist, or other qualified professional decides to find out whether, where a little heat does a little good, a lot of heat would do a lot better? To find out, the professional intentionally sets the diathermy machine way above the recommended level of heat output, and the patient sustains severe, disabling burns. Should this patient be limited to receiving only compensatory damages? In this case, the law recognizes the imposition of *punitive damages.*

Punitive damages are damages assessed by a judge or jury for the purpose of punishing the wrongdoer. They are intended to set an example, to let it be known that this type of conduct will not be tolerated. Such damages are designed to make the wrongdoer think twice before he or she acts in the same or similar manner again. However, some jurisdictions, including Massachusetts, do not allow punitive damages unless a specific statute provides for them.

Note that, in the preceding example, the medical assistant, nurse, physical therapist, or other professional increases the dosage to the patient intentionally but without ill will. The machine is set up in an effort to help rather than hurt the patient. However, this distinction is of little consequence when dealing with intentional wrongs and the imposition of punitive damages. The crucial test is whether the act that causes the injury is performed intentionally, rather than accidentally or through mere negligence. Where the act is intentional, punitive damages may be assessed. Where the act is accidental or negligent, punitive damages may not be assessed unless the injured person can clearly demonstrate that such conduct amounts to gross misconduct. Such gross misconduct must constitute a willful and wanton disregard for the patient's welfare.

Consider the following example. Mr. Jones is involved in an automobile accident at approximately 11:00 P.M. one Friday night. He is taken to the local hospital, where the emergency-room physician orders certain X-rays to be taken. Mr. Jones is transferred by stretcher from the emergency room to the X-ray department by emergency-room personnel.

Regular hours for staff of the X-ray department end at 5:00 P.M. on Friday. However, a radiological technologist (X-ray technician) remains on call or is otherwise available by telephone for emergency situations. An emergency-room staff member telephones the technologist at his home and informs him that an emergency patient at the hospital needs to have certain X-rays taken.

The emergency-room staff member is unaware that the radiological technologist has been drinking alcoholic beverages at home and is inebriated. The technologist comes to the hospital after rinsing his mouth with mouthwash to disguise the odor of alcohol on his breath.

During the course of positioning Mr. Jones for various X-ray views, the technologist accidentally hits him with a piece of X-ray equipment, thereby causing him severe injuries. Thereafter, it is discovered that the radiological technologist was drunk while performing the examination on Mr. Jones.

Following a lengthy recovery from the injuries sustained while being X-rayed, Mr. Jones consults Ms. Trudeau, a local attorney. The attorney then files a suit against the hospital, the X-ray department, the radiological technologist, the emergency-room staff member, and the emergency-room doctor for negligence in failing to properly supervise and conduct the X-ray examination. The technologist is also sued for punitive damages based on gross willful and wanton misconduct.

In the argument to the jury, Ms. Trudeau emphasizes the evidence that has been brought out at trial. First the attorney points out that this was not the first time that the technologist was intoxicated while on duty. The hospital had prior knowledge of his previous conduct through other personnel and should have anticipated that such conduct would continue. Knowing this, the hospital was negligent in keeping the technologist on its payroll.

Second, the emergency-room nurse and emergency-room physician were likewise negligent in failing to supervise the X-ray examination, since they also knew of previous incidents in which the radiological technologist conducted examinations on patients while under the influence of alcohol.

Finally, the radiological technologist admitted that he accidentally struck Mr. Jones with a piece of X-ray equipment, thereby causing Mr. Jones injury. However, the technologist's attorney argues that the injury to Mr. Jones was caused by the technologist's negligence, which was not intentional. The attorney argues that the technologist was not sober enough to formulate an intent to do the act that caused the injury. Without such specific intent to do the act, the law cannot impose punitive damages.

In rebuttal to this argument Ms. Trudeau points out to the jury that the act of consuming alcohol by the technologist was a voluntary one. The technician had been intoxicated in the past, and he knew that his ability to perform his duties would be severely impaired by the influence of alcohol. Therefore, he could reasonably foresee that such impairment was likely to cause an injury to a patient while the patient was being positioned on the X-ray table. Knowing all these things, the technologist nevertheless voluntarily consumed alcohol, realizing that at any time he could be summoned to the hospital to perform an X-ray examination. Thus, his conduct in voluntarily consuming alcohol amounted to gross misconduct. The conduct was willful and showed a wanton disregard for the safety of any patient for whom he might be called to do an X-ray examination. The jury concurred with this argument and imposed punitive damages of $50,000 against the radiological technologist, in addition to compensatory damages.

The act of the radiological technologist that allowed the imposition of punitive damages was not the striking of Mr. Jones with a piece of X-ray equipment, but rather the voluntary consumption of alcohol when the technologist was on emergency call. The technologist knew, or reasonably should have known, that his judgment and physical ability to perform the requested

X-ray examination would be severely impaired. Had the technician not been drinking and the same injury occurred, punitive damages would not have been imposed, since the act that caused the injury would undoubtedly have been construed as mere negligence. It was the act of enhancing the potential for causing injury that allowed the jury to impose punitive damages as a form of punishment. The jury's decision was a way of saying to the technologist, "We hope the $50,000 imposed on you personally as a form of punishment makes you think twice before you again consume alcohol while on duty."

In subsequent chapters, we will be dealing with the intentional torts according to which punitive damages may be imposed above the awarding of nominal, compensatory, and general damages. Such intentional torts include assault, battery, defamation of character, invasion of privacy, intentional infliction of emotional distress, malicious prosecution, and abuse of process.

CRIMINAL PENALTIES

Some cases involve the imposition of criminal penalties for conduct that is not only tortious but also tantamount to criminal activity. For example, in the case in the previous section involving the intoxicated radiological technologist, the state could bring a criminal action against him for violating a criminal law or statute, such as being drunk in a public place. This would be in addition to, and separate from, Mr. Jones's legal action and recovery of damages. In addition, had the injury occurred to Mr. Jones while the technologist's license was suspended or revoked because of such prior misconduct, the state could bring its own independent criminal action against the technologist for violation of the law requiring him to hold a valid state license when performing X-ray examinations on patients. Thus, if the state statute or regulation prescribed that any person performing an X-ray examination with a suspended or revoked license could be placed in jail for a period not to exceed six months or fined in an amount not to exceed $1,000, or both, the technician would also be faced with criminal prosecution, in addition to the civil action brought by Mr. Jones.

Finally, even if the technologist's license was not under suspension at the time he injured Mr. Jones, the technologist might be brought before his state licensing agency (as discussed in Chapter 1) to answer for his unprofessional conduct in caring for a patient while drunk.

EXAMPLES / QUESTIONS / PROJECTS

1. Mrs. Gonzalez had an abdominal operation approximately ten years ago. During the course of the operation, a large set of sponge forceps was left in her abdomen. Mrs. Gonzalez made an uneventful recovery from the opera-

tion and for ten years was unaware of what she was carrying around in her body. After a routine chest X-ray, the radiologist noticed the end of the forceps and ordered an X-ray of Mrs. Gonzalez's abdomen, which revealed the sponge forceps. Shortly thereafter, Mrs. Gonzalez had another operation, which cost $3,000, to have the forceps removed, and made an uneventful recovery. She then obtained the services of an attorney, who brought suit against the hospital and staff where the initial operation took place seeking $500,000 in general and special damages and $1,000,000 in punitive damages. Will Mrs. Gonzalez prevail?

Answer: Mrs. Gonzalez will undoubtedly prevail on the issue of liability against the hospital and its staff regarding her first operation based on her successful ability to use the doctrine of *res ipsa loquitur* in establishing negligent conduct. However, Mrs. Gonzalez will be somewhat less than successful obtaining a large award in damages as she requests. First, she will not recover punitive damages against the hospital because, by invoking the doctrine of *res ipas loquitur,* she is implying that someone was negligent in his or her conduct. Punitive damages are only awarded in cases where the conduct of the wrong-doer either is intentional or amounts to gross misconduct. Such gross misconduct must be a willful and wanton disregard of the patient.

Mrs. Gonzalez will undoubtedly recover her out-of-pocket expenses for the second operation. Also, the jury will undoubtedly award her general damages for pain and suffering sustained as a result of the second operation. However, the jury will probably disregard any claim for damages for general pain and suffering sustained during the last ten years because Mrs. Gonzalez was totally unaware of the forceps in her body during that time. There is no indication that the forceps caused her any discomfort or inconvenience or was in any way incapacitating.

The facts clearly indicate that Mrs. Gonzalez made an uneventful and complete recovery following the surgery to remove the forceps. Thus, the jury will undoubtedly disbelieve any claim for future medical care or loss of earning capacity or other similar claims. Mrs. Gonzalez will probably be awarded costs incurred in bringing the lawsuit, such as the fee required by the court to file the lawsuit, the amount of money expended to have the marshal serve a copy of the complaint on the defendants, and so on. However, the costs of the lawsuit do not include reimbursement for the attorney's fees expended in bringing the action.

2. *Martha is in need of orthodontic work to straighten her teeth. She enters into a written contract with Dr. Young, a local orthodontist, in which she pays Dr. Young the sum of $200 as a down payment and agrees to pay $50 per month until the full amount of $2,000 has been paid. Dr. Young, in turn, agrees to take all steps necessary to straighten her teeth with braces. When Martha comes in for her first treatment, she is informed by the assistant that Dr. Young has decided not to do the work. The assistant then*

refunds all the money paid by Martha. Because Dr. Young is the only orthodontist within a fifty-mile radius, Martha brings an action against the doctor to compel him to perform the work under the terms of their contractual agreement. Will she prevail?

> **Answer:** No. The law has long recognized that the doctrine of specific performance may not be used to compel the performance of a personal service contract. In other words, when personal services are involved, specific performance may not be used to enforce the contract. To do so would be a form of slavery or involuntary servitude. More importantly, the court would have no way of knowing whether the services were of the exact quality bargained for.

3. *In example 2, would Martha be able to sue Dr. Young for money damages because of his refusal to perform the contract?*

> **Answer:** Yes, if Martha can show she sustained money damages because of the doctor's breach of the written agreement. Such damages may include travel to and from the nearest available orthodontist to have her teeth straightened and any charges by another orthodontist in excess of those that Dr. Young was to have charged.

4. *Would Dr. Young have a valid defense based on the doctrines of rescission and restitution of the contract?*

> **Answer:** Probably not. There is no indication that Martha did not have the ability to continue making payments on a periodic basis as she contracted to do. This fact would tend to hinder Dr. Young in his attempts to demonstrate the applicability of his argument that he rescinded the contract rather than merely breaching it. There is no question that he made restitution by restoring Martha's down payment to her. However, there was no performance required of Martha other than periodic payment for services rendered under the contract. If Dr. Young could clearly demonstrate that Martha did not have the ability to make such periodic payment, or that she did not intend to pay for some reason, then Dr. Young might prevail in his argument.

5. *In the preceding example, would Martha prevail in an action against Dr. Young for restitution of her down payment if she expressed her intent to rescind their agreement prior to the doctor's undertaking to render the contracted treatment?*

> **Answer:** Probably yes. Martha could prevail against the doctor in this action if she could show that she expressed her intent to rescind their agreement prior to the doctor's taking any affirmative steps toward rendering treatment. Thereafter, the doctor could be paid for his services on a quantum merit basis for the reasonable value of services he had already rendered. Thus, if Dr. Young got special supplies or incurred laboratory costs or expenses in obtaining molds of

Martha's teeth, he could charge Martha for the reasonable value of these services. However, Martha could rescind their contract prior to any steps being undertaken by the doctor. Thereafter, the doctor could maintain an action against Martha for breaching their contractual agreement as long as he could clearly demonstrate he was ready, willing, and able to perform the orthodontic services under their contract.

CHAPTER EIGHT

CONTRIBUTORY NEGLIGENCE, COMPARATIVE FAULT, AND ASSUMPTION OF RISK

Key Terms

deliberation	emancipate	estop
incompetent	actionable	carte blanche

This chapter deals with major defenses to lawsuits based on an injured person's own negligent conduct. There are basically two major defenses with which we need to be concerned. The first is *comparative fault* or *contributory negligence.* The second is *assumption of risk.* Comparative fault deals with a proportionate share of negligence assessed against two or more negligent defendants who cause a person's injury. It is not a true defense that is asserted against the plaintiff's action; it is merely a defense made by one defendant that asserts that he or she should not be held accountable to the full extent of any award or verdict rendered in favor of the plaintiff because another person also contributed to the injury.

Illustrations of informed consent forms will be presented in discussing the defense of assumption of risk by the patient. These illustrations may be used in practice.

CONTRIBUTORY NEGLIGENCE

The common law and some states today recognize contributory negligence by the injured plaintiff as a complete defense to the action or lawsuit. Where the injured plaintiff has contributed in any degree toward his or her own injury, he or she is completely prevented from recovering damages in an action against the defendant for negligent conduct—even if the plaintiff's conduct in contributing to his or her own injury was minor in comparison to the negligent conduct of the defendant.

Consider the following example. Helen Green injures her right ankle as a result of falling off her bicycle and is examined at Dr. Walters's office for the injury. Dr. Walters X-rays the ankle and determines that Helen has sustained a severe fracture. Dr. Walters tells Helen that he does not wish to put a plaster cast on the ankle and leg until the swelling in the ankle has gone down. This is sound medical practice. He tells Helen to return the following day to have the cast applied but gives her no further instructions.

That evening, the swelling in the ankle decreases substantially, and the pain associated with the swelling is not as severe. Consequently, Helen proceeds to walk on the affected foot and ankle. The pain is not severe because she has been taking pain medication and because she does not place much weight on the ankle when walking. Nevertheless, the fracture is further displaced.

The next day, when Helen returns to Dr. Walters to have the plaster cast put on the leg and ankle, Dr. Walters has another X-ray taken that reveals that surgery will be needed to correct the displaced fracture.

Helen Green then files a lawsuit against Dr. Walters for failing to properly advise her not to walk on the ankle. At trial, it is established that the standard of care owing to the patient would have been to properly advise her not to walk on the fractured ankle. Thus, the jury concludes that Dr. Walters is guilty of professional negligence in this regard.

However, Dr. Walters asserts as a defense that Helen was contributorily negligent by failing to use common sense in walking on the affected ankle. He further argues that Helen knew of his intent to immobilize the ankle with a plaster cast the following day when the swelling decreased. He contends that it was not the act of failing to properly advise her, but rather her walking on the affected foot and ankle, that caused the displaced fracture. Thus, he argues, her contributory negligence in aggravating the injury should bar her recovery of damages.

In the states that recognize contributory negligence as a complete defense, Dr. Walters would not be held liable for malpractice, even though his negligent conduct may far exceed any negligent conduct committed by Helen in furthering her own injury.

COMPARATIVE NEGLIGENCE

The majority of states today recognize the doctrine of comparative negligence as a defense to a charge of negligent conduct asserted by the plaintiff. The doctrine of comparative negligence came into being because the courts recognized that the doctrine of contributory negligence was all too commonly unfair to the plaintiff, Many were the cases where the defendant was 99 percent at fault for causing the plaintiff's injury, but, because the jury determined that 1 percent of the plaintiff's injury was caused by the plaintiff himself or herself, the defendant totally escaped liability. Because of this unfair result, the doctrine of comparative negligence came into existence.

The doctrine of comparative negligence is applied in the following manner. The jury is requested to render a verdict in the plaintiff's favor if it is found that the defendant is in any way negligent. The jury is then requested to reduce any award for the plaintiff's injuries by the amount of the plaintiff's own contributory negligence.

Consider the following example. Nathan McGregor breaks his arm and goes to Dr. Rogers, who applies a plaster cast. Nathan's arm is very swollen when the cast is applied. Dr. Rogers tells Nathan to return the following week to have the cast and arm rechecked. Nathan knows that the purpose of the plaster cast is to immobilize his arm so that it will heal properly.

By the following day, the swelling in Nathan's arm has gone down considerably, and he is able to move his arm about freely within the cast. However, he does not return to Dr. Rogers to have the cast and arm rechecked, even though he knows that his arm should be completely immobilized. Throughout the week, Nathan continually uses the hand and arm, causing the fracture to become displaced. Thereafter, surgical intervention becomes necessary to properly set the fractured bones.

Nathan brings a lawsuit against Dr. Rogers for failing to wait until the swelling had gone down before applying the plaster cast to his arm. He further alleges that Dr. Rogers is guilty of malpractice based on the absence of any instruction to return to the doctor's office in the event that the cast became loose.

Dr. Rogers defends Nathan's allegations on the basis of the fact that Nathan knew that, unless his arm was immobilized, further injury would occur. Dr. Rogers further contends that Nathan knew, or should have known, to return to the doctor's office when the cast became loose. His failure to return to have the cast and arm rechecked constituted comparative negligence on his part in causing his own injury.

Before submitting the case, the judge instructs the jury that, should it find Dr. Rogers negligent, it is to assess the overall damages attributable to Nathan's injury based on the assumption that Dr. Rogers was 100 percent negligent. Further, should the jury find that Nathan was comparatively negligent in causing his own injury, it is then to reduce the amount of its award by the percentage of fault attributable to Nathan.

Following its **deliberations,** the jury returns a verdict in favor of Nathan and against Dr. Rogers. The verdict is based on its finding that Dr. Rogers was negligent in applying the cast while the arm was still swollen and failing to properly advise Nathan to return to the office if the cast became loose. The jury finds that, because of Dr. Rogers's negligence, Nathan sustained $20,000 in compensatory damages. However, the jury also finds that Nathan was 50 percent negligent in failing to use common sense and return to Dr. Rogers when the cast became loose. His continued use of the arm with the knowledge that it should be kept completely immobile caused one-half of his overall injury. Thus, the total award is reduced by 50 percent—the extent of Nathan's comparative negligence in causing his own injury. Nathan can then collect only $10,000 from Dr. Rogers.

COMPARATIVE FAULT

The doctrine of comparative fault in assessing liability against multiple parties was mentioned briefly in the example of *Ybarra v. Spangard* presented in Chapter 6. Mr. Ybarra was allowed to assert negligent conduct against all the defendants in that case because he was asleep and unaware of which defendant or defendants caused his injury. Much the same is true in cases dealing with a distribution of liability based on comparative fault among various defendants.

Where more than one person causes the plaintiff's injury, the jury is allowed to assess the percentage of liability of each individual defendant. Should Dr. Smith and Dr. Jones each cause their patient injury, the jury could properly conclude that a percentage of the patient's injury was due to the negligent conduct of Dr. Smith, and the remainder was due to the negligent conduct of Dr. Jones.

Most states, however, recognize the doctrine of *joint and several liability.* This doctrine means that, where the plaintiff is injured by more than one person, the plaintiff may collect the entire jury award from any one of the defendants. The primary importance of the doctrine of comparative fault and the assessment of liability on a percentage basis between multiple defendants is in determining shares of the contribution. The contribution is generally allocated between the defendants themselves rather than with the plaintiff.

Consider the following example. Dr. Freeman and Dr. Henry both negligently cause injury to Hope Ann, their patient. Following a jury trial, Hope Ann receives a verdict in the amount of $50,000. The jury further finds that 50 percent of Hope Ann's injury was due to the negligent conduct of Dr. Freeman, and 50 percent was due to the negligent conduct of Dr. Henry.

Dr. Freeman pays the full $50,000 to Hope Ann. He then obtains a contribution from Dr. Henry of $25,000 for that portion of the jury award associated with the percentage of comparative fault assessed against Dr. Henry in causing Hope Ann's injury.

The doctrine of joint and several liability is most commonly applied in conjunction with the doctrine of comparative fault. The doctrine of joint and several liability was discussed previously in Chapter 4, which deals with concurrent causation and joint and several liability.

ASSUMPTION OF RISK

Informed express consent

Consent by the patient constitutes a complete defense when the patient assumes all the risk or adversity connected with the examination or treatment. The patient must be aware of all the potential risks involved and voluntarily give his or her consent for such treatment.

Before performing surgical procedures (except in the case of emergency, life-saving measures), the physician or hospital generally obtains a signed consent form from the patient. Most commonly, this form outlines all the risks and hazards of the particular surgical procedure, including the risk of anesthesia, which could cause injury or death. This consent or authorization to treat and/or operate is given by patients themselves or someone authorized to act on their behalf. The expressed consent may be either written or oral. However, the consent given by the patient must be founded on an understanding of what is to be done and of all the potential risks involved. The physician or other professional must make the patient aware of all the potential hazards of the procedure or treatment.

Explanation must be given to the patient in nontechnical terms before such consent can be considered valid. Should the patient not fully understand what the procedure entails or is otherwise misled as to the risks involved, the consent is not valid. An invalid consent will not constitute a defense based on the patient's assumption of the risk of the procedure or operation. Thus, not only must the patient be told of all the potential hazards and risks of the procedure, but he or she must understand them as well.

The patient must give consent voluntarily. Any misrepresentation or fraud in obtaining the consent nullifies it. Thus, a false representation to a patient that an operation or treatment is necessary to save the patient's life or to preserve the patient's health is tantamount to fraud. Such a misrepresentation of a material fact regarding a reason for the procedure makes any consent the patient may give null and void.

Implied consent

We have previously studied cases dealing with express and implied contracts. Consent to treat or otherwise perform certain procedures on a patient may likewise be either express or implied. In *express consent*, one party conveys certain information, such as all the risks involved in a procedure, in exchange for the patient's written or verbal expression that he or she understands all the risks and consents to the procedure. Such consent has also been termed *informed consent*.

Implied consent arises much like the implied contract discussed in Chapter 2. In this situation, the patient or consenting party gives no verbal expression or formal written consent for treatment. For example, implied consent arises when the patient who seeks medical attention at an emergency room for a possible fractured arm receives an X-ray examination to determine whether the arm is actually broken. The patient is told only that an X-ray examination will have to be conducted to make this determination. In response, the patient remains silent, and the procedure is conducted. It is common knowledge that diagnostic X-ray procedures are not generally considered to be extremely hazardous. The patient would be hard-pressed to maintain a lawsuit against the doctors, emergency-room personnel, or X-ray facility for failing to inform him or her of all the potential hazards of X-rays.

However, the preceding example should not be confused with some diagnostic X-ray procedures, which are potentially hazardous. Procedures done in the operating room implementing sterile techniques (such as angiograms) are examples of such procedures. In such instances, mere silence by the patient would undoubtedly not be enough to demonstrate that the patient understood all the attendant risks and validly gave his or her consent. Therefore, such procedures would only be performed after the doctor, hospital, or other professional had obtained the patient's express consent.

The law recognizes that a patient impliedly consents to basic, standard treatment in the physician's office. Where the patient remains silent after the doctor, dentist, nurse, medical assistant, or dental assistant has explained the purpose and nature of the treatment involved, implied consent is assumed to have been given. However, one must be cautious, since such explanation to the patient must be made in terms that the patient can understand. Further, the

```
                                                          A.M.
        Date_____  Time_____P.M.

    I have been informed by Dr. _____ of the nature, risks, possible
  alternative methods of treatment, possible consequences and possible complications

  involved in the treatment by means of _____

  _____

  for the relief of _____

  Nevertheless, I authorize Dr. _____to administer such treatment to me.


                                      Signed _____
                                             (Patient or person authorized
                                                to consent for patient)

  Witness_____
```

ILLUSTRATION 8.1 CONSENT TO TREATMENT (REPRINTED WITH PERMISSION OF THE
AMERICAN MEDICAL ASSOCIATION, *MEDICOLEGAL FORMS WITH LEGAL ANALYSIS,*
COPYRIGHT 1991, AMERICAN MEDICAL ASSOCIATION)

type of treatment involved must be such that any ordinary, reasonable person
would be expected to remain silent rather than give an express consent. A jury
who did not believe that an ordinary person would remain silent regarding
consent to such treatment would tend to disbelieve that all risks of this treatment or procedure were explained to the patient by the health professional in
attendance.

When in doubt, the health professional should obtain a valid written
consent from the patient that outlines all the potential risks involved in the
procedure or treatment. Standard consent forms for an operation, anesthesia,
or other medical service are given in Illustrations 8.1 through 8.4. These illustrations have been adopted and approved by the American Medical Association.

Like all forms in this book, the wording in each of the following consent
forms is very general and may need to be specifically tailored for use with a
particular patient or case, or in a specific jurisdiction (for example, the legal
requirements in a particular state may not permit use of one or more of the
following forms or may require use of a specific form or particular wording
prescribed by state law).

The main idea in any consent form, however, is to put into written form
the fact that all risks attendant to the particular procedure or operation have
been explained to the patient. The particular procedure or operation must be
listed on the consent form, which must be signed and dated by the patient. This

1. I authorize the perfomance upon _____
                                        (myself or name of patient)

of the following operation _____
                                        (state name of operation)

2. I understand that the operation is to be performed at _____,
a teaching institute.

3. I undertand that the operation, the medical services rendered in conjunction
with the operation, and the post-operative care are to be performed and rendered
by those individuals selected and deemed qualified by the teaching staff of the

_____.
(name of the institution)

Witness_____   Signed _____
                                          (Patient or person authorized
                                           to consent for patient)

ILLUSTRATION 8.2   CONSENT TO OPERATION, ANESTHETICS, AND OTHER MEDICAL
SERVICES AT TEACHING INSTITUTION (REPRINTED WITH PERMISSION OF THE
AMERICAN MEDICAL ASSOCIATION, *MEDICOLEGAL FORMS WITH LEGAL ANALYSIS,*
COPYRIGHT 1991, AMERICAN MEDICAL ASSOCIATION)

written form is nothing more than evidence of the patient's express consent.
Generally, written consent is not required by law, nor does the law require any
specific form to be used. Having consent in writing does, however, offer some
evidence of the patient's informed consent. General or "blanket" consent forms
which give a doctor or other health care provider unlimited authority and
discretion should be avoided.

Moreover, there are instances in which a patient's written consent is
required. For example, Massachusetts law (Massachusetts General Laws
[M.G.L.] Chapter 111, section 70F) prohibits any health care facility, physician,
or other health care provider from (1) testing any person for the presence of the
HTLV-III antibody or antigen without first obtaining the subject's written
informed consent; (2) disclosing the results of such a test to any person other
than the subject of the test without the subject's written informed consent; or
(3) disclosing the identity of the subject of such tests to any person without the
subject's written informed consent. That statute defines written informed consent as follows: a written consent form for each requested release of the results
of an individual's HTLV-III antibody or antigen test, or for the release of
medical records containing such information. Further, the statute specifies that
such consent form shall state the purpose for which the information is being
requested and shall be distinguished from written consent for the release of

Date_____ Time_____A.M.
P.M.

1. I authorize the perfomance upon _____
                                      (myself or name of patient)

of the following operation _____
                              (state nature and extent of operation)

to be performed by or under the direction of Dr._____.

2. I consent to the performance of operations and procedures in addition to or different from those now contemplated, whether or not arising from presently unforeseen conditions,which the above named doctor or his associates or assistants may consider necessary or advisable in the course of the operation.

3. I consent to the administration of such anesthetics as may be considered necessary or advisable by the physician responsible for this service, with the exception of

_____.
(state "none,"spinal anesthesia,"etc.)

4. The nature and purpose of the operation, possible alternative methods of treatment, the risks involved, the possible consequences, and the possibility of complications have been explained to me by Dr. _____ and by _____.

5. I acknowledge that no guarantee or assurance has been given by anyone as to the results that may be obtained.

6. I consent to the photographing or televising of the operations or procedures to be performed, including appropriate portions of my body, for medical, scientific or educational purposes, provided my identity is not revealed by the pictures or by descriptive texts accompanying them.

7. For the pupose of advancing medical education, I consent to the admittance of observers to the operating room.

8. I consent to the disposal by hospital authorities of any tissues or body parts which may be removed.

9. I am aware that sterility may result from this operation. I know that a sterile person is incapable of becoming a parent.

10. I acknowledge that all blank spaces on this document have been either completed or crossed off prior to my signing.

(Cross out Any Paragraphs Above Which Do Not Apply)

Witness_____   Signed_____
                                   (Patient or person authorized
                                   to consent for patient)

ILLUSTRATION 8.3 CONSENT TO OPERATION, ANESTHETICS, AND OTHER MEDICAL SERVICES (REPRINTED WITH PERMISSION OF THE AMERICAN MEDICAL ASSOCIATION, *MEDICOLEGAL FORMS WITH LEGAL ANALYSIS,* COPYRIGHT 1991, AMERICAN MEDICAL ASSOCIATION)

any other medical information (which means that a general consent for release of medical records is not sufficient for the release of HTLV-III testing information). Finally, the statute states that an HTLV-III test means a licensed screening antibody test for the human T-cell lymphotrophic virus type III.

                                                                        A.M.

Date_____ Time_____ P.M.

1. I authorize the performance upon _____
                                        (myself or name of patient)

of the following operation _____
                                        (state name of operation)

to be performed by or under the direction of Dr. _____.

2. The following have been explained to me by Dr. _____.

   A. the nature of the operation _____.
                                         (describe the operation)
_____

   B. The purpose of the operation _____.
                                         (describe the purpose)
_____

   C. The possible alternative methods of treatment _____.
                                   (describe the alternative methods)
_____

   D. The possible consequences of the operation _____.
                                  (describe the possible consequences)
_____

   E. The risks involved _____.
                                    (describe the risks involved)
_____

   F. The possibility of complications _____
                                 (describe the possible complications)
_____

3. I have been advised of the serious nature of the operation and have been advised that if I desire a further and more detailed explanation of any of the foregoing or further information about the possible risks or complications of the above listed operation it will be given to me.

4. I do not request a further and more detailed listing and explanation of any of the items listed in paragraph 2.

Witness_____   Signed _____
                                        (Patient or person authorized to consent for patient)

ILLUSTRATION 8.4 CONSENT TO OPERATION, ANESTHETICS, AND OTHER MEDICAL SERVICES (ALTERNATE FORM) (REPRINTED WITH PERMISSION OF THE AMERICAN MEDICAL ASSOCIATION, *MEDICOLEGAL FORMS WITH LEGAL ANALYSIS,* COPYRIGHT 1991, AMERICAN MEDICAL ASSOCIATION)

Lack of Informed consent

In the majority of states, the patient/plaintiff in cases dealing with the lack of informed consent may maintain an action based on battery. The types of conduct that may be considered battery are discussed in Chapter 9. The plaintiff may obtain punitive damages against the professional for unauthorized treatment or rendering of a diagnostic procedure even if the operation, treatment, or procedure is performed with the utmost care. The Appellate Court of New York State has held that uninformed consent is tantamount to no consent at all. However, where informed consent has been given, the defense of assumption of risk acts as a complete bar to the plaintiff's case.

Reasonable disclosure

Informing the patient of all potential risks and hazards of the procedure requires the doctor to make reasonable disclosure to his or her patient of the nature, probable consequences, and possible dangers of the suggested or recommended treatment. However, the Kansas Supreme Court has held that such duty does not mean that a doctor is under an obligation to describe in detail all the possible consequences of treatment. The Kansas court reemphasized that a physician has a duty to disclose as much as a reasonable medical practitioner would disclose under similar circumstances. This reemphasizes the principle of standard of care previously discussed in this text.

Courts in other jurisdictions, such as Arizona and California, have made similar rulings. They have held that the duty of a physician to disclose is determined by the normal practice of his or her profession in his or her particular community. In these cases, the courts have reemphasized that all reasonable people must understand that some risk is inherent to surgery and similar procedures.

The courts have long accepted that a physician or other allied health professional need not inform the patient of all the *remote* risks or consequences of a treatment or procedure. Nevertheless, there is a duty to reasonably inform the patient of *recognized* risks or potential adverse reactions to the treatment or procedure being performed. Many courts view this duty as a duty to disclose all material risks and define a material risk as one that a reasonable person in the position of the patient would likely find significant in deciding whether or not to undergo the recommended treatment, procedure, or operation. Where such an objective standard of disclosure is followed, professional standards are not conclusive. Rather, they are one factor to be considered in determining whether or not the disclosure was reasonable. In addition to disclosure of the material risks, some courts also require that a description of alternative courses of action and the patient's prognosis if he or she refuses treatment be given.

Finally, some courts have excused a physician's failure to make an otherwise required disclosure where it reasonably appeared that to disclose would have unreasonably affected the patient's health.

Legal Incompetence

Consent to render treatment is invalid if the patient is legally **incompetent** to give his or her consent. Legal incompetence means that the patient is either not an adult or has been found by the court to be insane or incompetent. Consent for treatment in such cases may be given on behalf of the patient by a natural parent, legal guardian, or the court. Consent for treatment, unless otherwise authorized by statute, may be given only by the natural parent or legal guardian as established by the court for a minor child. A minor child is a person below the age of majority as set by state statute. California recognizes eighteen as the legal age of majority. An **emancipated** minor is considered an adult by the courts. The emancipated minor may validly and legally give his or her consent for medical or dental treatment. Where treatment is rendered on behalf of a minor child without such legally obtained consent, the professional rendering such treatment may be held liable, even if the treatment is successful.

Emergency treatment

There are cases where rendering emergency treatment to save a minor's life is necessary. In such situations, the courts have routinely held that the minor's parent would impliedly consent to the rendering of such emergency first-aid treatment. These cases also turn on the fact that a consent for treatment could not be obtained by a judge in time to save the minor child's life. In addition, the Good Samaritan laws of the majority of states would apply in shielding the person from liability based on battery where such a person renders such emergency treatment at the scene of an accident.

There are cases in which the courts have held that rendering treatment in emergency situations other than at the scene of an accident to save a minor's life was not **actionable** where a judge authorized such treatment after the fact. Most of these cases have dealt with blood transfusions given to the minor to save his or her life without the express or implied consent of the minor's parents. Some of these cases have also shielded the person or institution rendering such emergency life-saving treatment where the parent has withheld consent for treatment of the minor.

Oral consent

Anything other than strictly emergency, life-saving treatment procedures should not be conducted on a minor without the parent's or legal guardian's authorization. This restriction includes situations where the minor child has been taken by someone other than his or her parent or legal guardian to the emergency room of a hospital, clinic, or physician's office for treatment. Such authorization may take the form of an oral consent on behalf of the minor by the parent or legal guardian via a telephone conversation. One word of caution in obtaining such verbal consent: the person receiving the consent should accurately note the conversation and the name of the person with whom they speak. It is also wise to have two office staff members listen and verify by their signature on the child's chart or medical record that consent has been given by the parent or legal guardian. One should also record the date and time of the conversation on the minor child's chart or medical record. This procedure, if followed, provides evidence in any lawsuit that valid consent has been obtained.

This procedure is especially important in cases dealing with parents who are separated or divorced or who have otherwise dissolved their marriage. Often one parent is given exclusive custody of a minor child. In cases where the child receives treatment based on the noncustodial parent's consent for treatment, the custodial parent may be **estopped** or otherwise barred from asserting a lawsuit based on lack of consent against the person rendering treatment.

Blanket consent

Another fairly common situation arises where the parents of a minor child leave the child with a babysitter, grandparent, or other relative for a brief period of time. Most parents in today's society realize that the babysitter, grandparent, or other relative could not validly give consent for treatment of the minor in the parent's absence. Accordingly, parents may give the babysitter or relative a written consent that may be presented to a physician or treating facility. This consent authorizes treatment of the minor when or where necessary. Many states recognize the validity of this blanket consent; others, such as California, restrict such blanket consent for treatment by requiring that certain information must be included in the consent form.

Restrictions on blanket consent

Where blanket consent is restricted, the following information may be required: providing the full name of the minor or incompetent person for whom consent is given; giving definite inclusive dates for which the consent will be valid; and having the consent signed and dated by one or both parents of the minor or by the legal guardian of the minor or incompetent person. Restrictions have further been recognized by outlining the general kinds of treatments that may be administered under such circumstances.

For example, a parent may expressly authorize treatment at any emergency-room facility or doctor's office by a licensed medical doctor. Such treatment may include rendering X-ray examinations, laboratory tests, or other recognized forms of treatment, including emergency surgical operations and blood transfusions to save the minor's life. The parent may expressly state that the consent will be valid only for a specified period of time. The parent then dates and signs the authorization and gives it to the babysitter or relative to hold in the event that treatment of the minor becomes necessary. The parent may also include permission to use a photocopy of the consent instead of an original. This would allow treatment at multiple treating facilities or on separate occasions by different doctors or facilities when treatment became necessary.

The authorization for consent to treat the minor or incompetent could also be restricted to treatment only by a specified physician or treatment facility. In such cases, the parent would give a copy of the consent to the babysitter or relative indicating that treatment of the minor or incompetent may only be done by the specified physician or facility. The parent or legal guardian would give the original consent to the treating physician or facility to be attached to the minor's or incompetent's medical chart or record. An example of a standard parental consent to treatment by a school physician form is given in Illustration 8.5. This form has been adopted and approved by the American Medical Association. It is general in format and language and may be altered in terminology to fit a particular case, a particular allied health profession, or a particular jurisdiction.

Elective procedures

Even when specific authorization or consent for treatment of the minor or incompetent person has been given to the babysitter or relative by the parent or legal guardian, note should be made of whether or not consent is restricted to emergency treatment only. When a relative or close friend to whose care the minor has been entrusted by the parent feels that an elective procedure may be of benefit to the minor, the authorization may be held invalid for that procedure if only emergency treatment has been authorized. In such situations, express consent by the parent must be obtained for the elective treatment or procedure.

Consider as an example the case where the minor has been entrusted to the care of his grandparents while his parents are on vacation. The parents give the grandparents a written consent for emergency treatment of the minor child. During the parent's absence, the grandparents decide that the minor should be given a smallpox vaccination, which is not an emergency procedure. The court could hold in this situation that authorization for this procedure is invalid without the express consent of one of the parents.

Another example is the case where the person to whom the minor has been entrusted has the child X-rayed by a local mobile chest X-ray unit or health department. The chest X-ray is not associated with any authorized treatment. This examination is not an emergency and is not being done for treatment purposes. The court would probably hold that this examination does not fall within the authorization or consent for treatment given by the parents.

I authorize _____, M.D., director of the School Health
Department at _____ or the person acting in his stead in his
(name of college or university)
absence to provide such regular health care including immunization procedures to
my child _____, a student at the college, as is necessary for my
(name)
child's health and best interests as well as the best interests of the student body.

    I authorize the director or his representative to act on my behalf in case my child
is victim of major accident, injury or illness when immediate medical or surgical care
is needed, provided, _____ M.D. or his representative make dili-
gent effort first to notify me of the situation and obtain my preferences. If such efforts to get in touch with me are unsuccessful I authorize _____,
M.D., (or one person designated to act in his stead in his absence) to take such action
and give such consent on my behalf as his judgment dictates.

_____   _____
        (Date)   *(Signature of parent or guardian)*

**ILLUSTRATION 8.5 AUTHORIZATION TO SCHOOL HEALTH PHYSICIAN (REPRINTED
WITH PERMISSION OF THE AMERICAN MEDICAL ASSOCIATION, *MEDICOLEGAL FORMS
WITH LEGAL ANALYSIS,* COPYRIGHT 1991, AMERICAN MEDICAL ASSOCIATION)**

Thus, before the examination could be conducted on the minor, express consent would have to be obtained from a parent or legal guardian of the minor or
incompetent.

    Carte blanche parental consent or authorization may, in many instances,
be held invalid, Discretion by the physician or treatment facility should be
exercised in those situations where the physician or facility has been given an
authorization. Every attempt should be made to obtain the express consent of
the parent or legal guardian of the minor or incompetent before going forward
with any examination or treatment, especially where the examination or elective treatment procedure is felt to fall outside the written authorization.

Stepparents

    Another interesting situation arises where the consent is being given by a
stepparent. Some jurisdictions have held that a stepparent may validly give
consent for the examination or treatment of a stepchild. However, other states
hold that a consent may be given only by the natural parent or legal guardian
of the child. In these states, because the stepparent is not a legal guardian of the
minor, he or she may not give a valid consent for the minor's treatment or
examination.

    To avoid legal problems in such situations, the natural parent may give
the stepparent a valid written consent for the treatment in the same way that

such consent is given to a babysitter, grandparent, or other person to whom temporary custody of the child has been entrusted. Also, stepparents can obtain legal guardian status from the court for the limited purpose of authorizing treatment of the minor. A copy of the court order should be given to the physician or treatment facility to be maintained in the minor's chart.

Responsibility for payment

One final note in obtaining the parent's or legal guardian's consent for treatment of the minor or incompetent is that the parent or legal guardian is responsible for payment of any such treatment or examination. As previously discussed in the chapter on contractual obligations, all states recognize that, if a minor is not legally competent to authorize his or her own medical treatment, he or she is not legally competent to enter into a legally binding contract. Thus, payment for any such treatment or examination can be obtained from the parent or legal guardian.

Remembering that a contract is a promise in exchange for a promise, the parent impliedly agrees to pay for such treatment of the minor by giving a valid consent for treatment. As long as the patient is below the legally recognized age of adulthood or has not been emancipated, the parent or legal guardian is responsible for the child or adolescent's well being—including obtaining and paying for medical examinations and/for treatment when necessary.

Consent by spouses

Before leaving the subject of consent by one person on behalf of another, we need to briefly examine the issues involved in cases of abortion, sterility, artificial insemination, and similar situations. Many states require consent by both husband and wife before sterilization of one of the parties may be obtained. Likewise, cases dealing with artificial insemination require consent by both husband and wife. As to abortion, the United States Supreme Court has held that state laws requiring the consent of the father of the fetus to the mother's plan to abort are unconstitutional. In *Planned Parenthood v. Danforth*,[1] the Supreme Court said that to permit such a requirement would violate a woman's fundamental right to privacy, which was recognized in *Roe v. Wade*,[2] the landmark case concerning abortion.

In sterilization and artificial insemination cases, one party is not giving consent on behalf of the other party; rather, consent is being given by the spouse who is not undergoing the procedure. The rationale for obtaining such consent is that sterilization and artificial insemination procedures have a direct

---

[1]*Planned Parenthood of Missouri v. Danforth*, 428 U.S. 52 (1976).

[2]*Roe v. Wade*, 410 U.S. 113 (1973).

effect on the nonpatient spouse. Accordingly, many doctors and treatment facilities will not sterilize a wife or husband without the other's consent. Such procedures involve the ability of the parties to bear children, which is viewed as an individual right of both the husband and the wife separately. An example of a request for sterilization is given in Illustration 8.6; this standard form is adopted and approved by the American Medical Association. Note that both the husband and wife are requested to sign the authorization. Their signatures must also be witnessed by some noninterested party to the procedure. This noninterested party may be the medical assistant, nurse, or other staff member of the physician doing the procedure.

A.M.

Date_____Time_____P.M.

We the undersigned husband and wife, each being more than twenty-one years

of age and of sound mind, request Dr._____, and assistants of his

choice, to perform upon _____, the following operation:
(name of patient)

_____
(state nature and extent of operation)

It has been explained to us that this operation is intended to result in sterility although this result has not been guaranteed. We understand that a sterile person is NOT capable of becoming a parent.

We voluntarily request the operation and understand that if it proves successful the results will be permanent and it will thereafter be physically impossible for the patient to inseminate, or to conceive or bear children.

Signed _____
(Husband)

Signed _____ [16]
(Wife)

Witness_____

This form is intended to be used where the primary purpose rather than the incidental result is sterilization.

[16]The question of the necessity of the consent of the patient's spouse to a voluntary sterilization has never been litigated. It would appear that such consent is not necessary, although it may be desirable. The statutes in Georgia, North Carolina and Virginia which specifically authorize voluntary sterilization require the written consent of the patient's spouse.

ILLUSTRATION 8.6 REQUEST FOR STERILIZATION (REPRINTED WITH PERMISSION OF THE AMERICAN MEDICAL ASSOCIATION, MEDICOLEGAL FORMS WITH LEGAL ANALYSIS, COPYRIGHT 1991, AMERICAN MEDICAL ASSOCIATION)

Valid consent by a minor

Modern society and the law recognize certain situations in which an uneman-cipated minor may validly give his or her consent for treatment. These situa-tions vary greatly from state to state, but are generally restricted to cases of venereal disease, birth control methods, drug or alcohol dependency and/or abortions. Where permitted, the unemancipated minor may be examined and/or treated by medical personnel without needing to obtain the parents' con-sent. In fact, notification of the parents of the minor seeking treatment or examination may constitute an invasion of the minor's right to privacy. An invasion of the minor's right to privacy could subject the doctor, medical assistant, nurse, or other practitioner to severe civil penalties in an action brought by the minor.

Within this restricted area, the minor may receive information, contra-ceptives, treatment for venereal disease, and/or therapeutic abortion. In these cases, responsibility for payment for the services rendered rests with the minor.

Judicial by-pass hearings for minors

Some states have instituted a judicial by-pass hearing procedure for pregnant minors who are unable to obtain parental consent for an abortion, or who have determined that they are unable to discuss the pregnancy and decision to undergo an abortion with their parents. Under such a procedure the minor may appear before a judge to seek permission to proceed with her plans for an abortion. Though the procedure in such hearings varies, the Massachusetts procedure is illustrative.

In Massachusetts, a pregnant minor who has decided to undergo an abortion and who cannot or chooses not to obtain the consent of her parents may petition a Superior Court judge for a hearing. The minor has the right to an attorney to represent her without charge at all stages of this proceeding. Once a hearing is scheduled, the minor has a confidential hearing with a judge who, through detailed questioning, determines whether the minor is mature enough to give informed consent for an abortion. If the court finds her mature enough, the court is simply saying that she is now free to make her own decision as to whether or not to undergo an abortion. The court is not consenting to the abortion on her behalf; rather, the court is saying that the decision is technically and legally hers. Therefore, the court's order will authorize the physician to proceed with the abortion if the minor elects to undergo the procedure.

If the court decides that she is immature, the court must proceed to the second step of the hearing and determine whether or not an abortion is in the minor's best interest. If the court finds that an abortion is in her best interest, the court will authorize the physician to proceed with it. Note, however, that the minor is still free to change her mind and not undergo an abortion, even if the court has decided that it is in her best interest.

Advance directives

Advance directives are, generally, directions that a person gives concerning his or her medical care in advance of the time when such decisions actually have to be made. That is, an individual may execute (sign) a Living Will, or other similar document, that specifies whether he or she wants certain drugs or treatments that may prolong life to be withheld or withdrawn if he or she is in a terminal condition with no reasonable likelihood of recovery. Typically such a document is executed in the presence of witnesses and, possibly, a Notary Public while a person is mentally alert and in good health. It may be revoked by the patient at any time after making it.

Although not all states have Living Will statutes, other types of advance directives may be recognized. For example, Massachusetts, by statute [M.G.L.] Chapter 201D), allows a competent adult, called the principal, to designate an agent to make health care decisions for the principal if the principal becomes unable to make such decisions for himself or herself. Called a Health Care Proxy, this document (see Illustration 8.7) also allows the principal to appoint an alternate agent in the event that the original health care agent becomes unavailable, unwilling, or incompetent to serve. The powers given to the health care agent are broad, although the principal is allowed to limit them if he or she so desires. To minimize potential conflict of interest problems, the statute also provides that the health care agent or alternate must not be an operator, administrator, or employee of a hospital, clinic, nursing home, rest home, Soldiers Home or other health care facility where the principal is a patient at the time of the making of the health care proxy unless the agent is also related to the principal by blood, marriage, or adoption. The health care proxy must be signed by the principal, or by a person signing at the principal's direction if the principal cannot sign, in the presence of two witnesses. Signing before a Notary Public is not required.

Since federal law now requires that all persons and facilities (including hospitals) receiving payments through Medicare and Medicaid must explain to patients seeking care or treatment from them their rights under the law of the state where they are located, health care providers should familiarize themselves with the options patients have in their states.

Examples of informed consent

Illustration 8.8 through 8.14 are excellent examples of written consent forms developed by the American Medical Association. Note that each form briefly describes the treatment or other procedure and contains an acknowledgment that the patient has been given information about alternatives, risks, and possible outcomes.

MASSACHUSETTS HEALTH CARE PROXY

TO MY FAMILY, DOCTORS, AND ALL THOSE
CONCERNED WITH MY CARE:

1. Appointment

I, _____(the principal), residing at _____ , being a competent adult at least eighteen years of age or older, of sound mind and under no constraint or undue influence, hereby appoint the following person to be my HEALTH CARE AGENT under the terms of this document:

Name: _____

Address: _____

_____

Telephone(s): _____

In so doing, I intend to create a Health Care Proxy according to Chapter 201D of the General Laws of Massachusetts. In making this appointment, I am giving my Health Care Agent the authority to make any and all health care decisions on my behalf, subject to any limitations I state in this document, in the event that I should at some future time become incapable of making health care decisions for myself.

2. Alternate Appointment (Completion of this section is optional but recommended)

I hereby appoint the following person to serve as my Health Care Agent in the event that my original Health Care Agent is not available, willing or competent to serve and is not expected to become available, willing or competent to make a timely decision given my medical circumstances, or in the event that my original Health Care Agent is disqualified from acting on my behalf.

Health Care Agent (alternate):

Name: _____

Address: _____

_____

Telephone(s): _____

3. Powers Given to Health Care Agent

A.   I give my Health Care Agent full authority to make any and all health care decisions for me including decisions about life-sustaining treatment, subject only to the limitations I state below.

ILLUSTRATION 8.7 MASSACHUSETTS HEALTH CARE PROXY

B. My Health Care Agent shall have authority to act on my behalf only if, when and for so long as a determination has been made that I lack the capacity to make or to communicate health care decisions for myself. This determination shall be made in writing by my attending physician according to accepted standards of medical judgment and the requirements of chapter 201D of the General Laws of Massachusetts.

C. The Authority of my Health Care Agent shall cease if my attending physician determines that I have regained capacity. The authority of my Health Care Agent shall recommence if I subsequently lose capacity and consent for treatment is required.

D. I shall be notified of any determination that I lack capacity to make or communicate health care decisions where there is any indication that I am able to comprehend this notice.

E. My Health Care Agent shall make health care decisions for me only after consultation with my health care providers and after full consideration of acceptable medical alternatives regarding diagnosis, prognosis, treatments and their side effects.

F. My Health Care Agent shall make health care decisions for me only in accordance with my Health Care Agent's assessment of my wishes, including my religious and moral beliefs, or, if my wishes are unknown, in accordance with my Health Care Agent's assessment of my best interests.

G. My Health Care Agent shall have the right to receive any and all medical information necessary to make informed decisions regarding my health care, including any and all confidential medical information that I would be entitled to receive.

H. The decisions made by my Health Care Agent on my behalf shall have the same priority as my decisions would have if I were competent over decisions by any other person, including a person acting pursuant to a durable power of attorney, except for any limitation I state below or a specific Court Order overriding this Health Care Proxy.

I. If I object to a health care decision made by my Health Care Agent, my decision shall prevail unless it is determined by Court Order that I lack capacity to make health care decisions.

J. Nothing in this proxy shall preclude any medical procedure deemed necessary by my attending physician to provide comfort care or pain alleviation including but not limited to treatment with sedatives and painkilling drugs, non-artificial oral feeding, suction, and hygienic care.

ILLUSTRATION 8.7 CONTINUED

K.   (Optional) I specifically limit my Health Care Agent's authority as follows:

_____

_____

_____

4.   Revocation

This Health Care Proxy shall be revoked upon any of the following events:

A.   my execution of a subsequent Health Care Proxy,

B.   my divorce or legal separation from my spouse where my spouse is named as my Health Care Agent;

C.   my notification to my Health Care Agent or a health care provider orally or in writing or by any other act evidencing a specific intent to revoke the Health Care Proxy.

5.   Statement of Health Care Agent and Alternate (Optional)

Health Care Agent:

I have been named by the principal as the principal's Health Care Agent in this document.

(Please check one):

___ I am **not** an operator, administrator or employee of a hospital, clinic, nursing home, rest home, Soldiers Home or other facility defined in section 70E of chapter 111 of the General Laws of Massachusetts where the principal is presently a patient or resident or has applied for admission.

___ I am an operator, administrator or employee of a hospital, clinic, nursing home, rest home, Soldiers Home or other facility defined in section 70E of chapter 111 of the General Laws of Massachusetts where the principal is presently a patient or resident or has applied for admission, and I am also related to the principal by blood, marriage, or adoption.

I have read this document carefully and. accept the appointment.

_____

Signature of Health Care Agent

ILLUSTRATION 8.7   CONTINUED

Health Care Agent (alternate):

I have been named by the principal as the principal's Health Care Agent in this document.

(Please check one):

___ I am not an operator, administrator or employee of a hospital, clinic, nursing home, rest home, Soldiers Home or other facility defined in section 70E of chapter 111 of the General Laws of Massachusetts where the principal is presently a patient or resident or has applied for admission.

___ I am an operator, administrator or employee of a hospital, clinic, nursing home, rest home, Soldiers Home or other facility defined in section 70E of chapter 111 of the General Laws of Massachusetts where the principal is presently a patient or resident or has applied for admission, and I am also related to the principal by blood, marriage, or adoption.

I have read this document carefully and accept the appointment.

_____

Signature of Health Care Agent (alternate)

6. Signature of Principal

I hereby sign my name on this date, _____, to this Health Care Proxy in the presence of two witnesses.

Signature: _____

Complete here if the principal is physically incapable of signing:

I hereby sign the name of the principal at the principal's direction and in the presence of the principal and two witnesses.

Name of Principal: _____

Name of Signatory: _____

Date: _____

Address of Signatory: _____

_____

ILLUSTRATION 8.7   CONTINUED

7. Witnesses

Witness 1:

I, the undersigned, have witnessed the signing of this document by the principal or at the direction of the principal and state that the principal appears to be at least eighteen years of age, of sound mind and under no constraint or undue influence. I have not been named as Health Care Agent or alternate Health Care Agent in this document.

Signature: _____

Name (print): _____

Address: _____

_____

Date: _____

Witness 2:

I, the undersigned, have witnessed the signing of this document by the principal or at the direction of the principal and state that the principal appears to be at least eighteen years of age, of sound mind and under no constraint or undue influence. I have not been named as Health Care Agent or alternate Health Care Agent in this document.

Signature: _____

Name (print): _____

Address: _____

_____

Date: _____

ILLUSTRATION 8.7 CONTINUED

Date_____ Time _____ A.M.
P.M.

1. I authorize the performance upon myself of the following operation

_____ performed by or under the direction of Dr._____.

(state the name of operation)

2. It has been explained to me that this operation is intended to result in my sterility, but no such result has been guaranteed.

3. 1 understand that a sterile person is NOT capable of becoming a parent.

4. I understand that if the operation proves successful the results will be permanent and it will thereafter be physically impossible for me to inseminate, or to conceive or bear children.

5. The nature of this operation, the possible alternative methods of treatment, the risks involved, the possible consequences, the possibility that the operation may be unsuccessful, and the possibility of complications have been explained to me by

Dr._____ and by_____.

Signed _____

Witness _____

I have read the above **Request for Sterilization** and do hereby consent to the operation under the terms therein set forth as the spouse of _____.

Signed _____.

Date _____ Time _____.

ILLUSTRATION 8.8   REQUEST FOR STERILIZATION (ALTERNATE FORM) (REPRINTED WITH PERMISSION OF THE AMERICAN MEDICAL ASSOCIATION, MEDICOLEGAL FORMS WITH LEGAL ANALYSIS, COPYRIGHT 1991, AMERICAN MEDICAL ASSOCIATION)

Read this consent form carefully. Make sure you understand all of it before you decide to have a sterilization. Make your decision only after careful thought. The decision is your free choice. You are free to withdraw your consent at any time prior to the sterilization.
For patients receiving health services supported in whole or in part by Federal or State financial assistance, your decision at any time not to be sterilized will not result in a withdrawal or withholding of any benefits provided by programs to projects to which you might otherside be entitled. The sterilization procedure will not be performed until at least 72 hours after the date and time shown on this consent.

1. I _____ hereby request and authorize Dr._____ and/or his associates to perform upon me at the hospital one of the following elective (that is, optional) sterilization procedures. I have been informed that there is the possibility that the above named physician may not be available to perform the sterilization proceduere; in that event, I request and authorize that the sterilization procedure be performed by one of his associates.

ILLUSTRATION 8.9   CONSENT FOR ELECTIVE FEMALE STERILIZATION (REPRINTED WITH PERMISSION OF THE AMERICAN MEDICAL ASSOCIATION / *MEDICOLEGAL FORMS WITH LEGAL ANALYSIS,* COPYRIGHT 1991, AMERICAN MEDICAL ASSOCIATION)

[Cross Out Inapplicable Paragraph]

"Laparoscopic sterilization" is an operation to prevent a woman from ever becoming pregnant by sealing and, in some cases, cutting each of the fallopian tubes. These tubes normally carry the eggs from the ovaries to the uterus or womb. Cutting or severing each tube prevents eggs from reaching the uterus. The patient is placed under general, regional or, in very rare instances, local anesthesia. The abdomen is inflated with gas and an instrument called a "laparoscope" is inserted into a small cut near the navel. The laparoscope is a tube which allows the surgeon to look around the abdomen. Once the fallopian tubes are located, a second small cut may be made in the abdomen a few inches below the laparoscope and another instrument called "cautery forceps" are inserted. In some cases, all the instruments go through the one cut. The cautery forceps are applied to each of the fallopian tubes in turn, and use electricity to seal each tube and, in some cases, divide it. (Some surgeons prefer to use clips or elastic bands to pinch the tube closed instead of severing it). The abdomen is then deflated and the cuts are sewn shut or closed with clips or tape.

A "tubal ligation sterilization" is an operation to prevent a woman from ever becoming pregnant by tying off and removing a section of each of the fallopian tubes. These tubes normally carry the eggs from the ovaries to the uterus or womb. Cutting a section out prevents eggs from reaching the uterus. The patient is placed under either general, regional or, in very rare instances, local anesthesia, depending upon the judgement of her physician and her preference. A cut is made in the lower abdomen or vagina and the fallopian tubes are located. The tubes are held and a portion of each tube is tied off with surgical suture. These portions of tube may then be cut off and removed. Following this, the cut in the abdomen or vagina is sewn shut.

2. **This operation is intended to result in permanent sterility. I fully understand that this operation is intended to be permanent and that if I want to become pregnant or bear children in the future I should not have this operation. I understand that the operation may not make me sterile. I acknowledge that no guarantees have been made to me that I will be sterile as a result of this operation.**

3. I authorize the administration of local anesthesia by the above named physician and/or his associates, or a regional or general anesthetic by or under the supervision of an anesthesiologist. My doctors have explained to me that whenever an operation is done which requires an anesthetic there are some risks to me associated with the anesthetic, and not necessarily with the operation. These risks involve sore throat, mild tongue or mouth damage, severe headaches, pneumonia, or, in extremely rare instances, even death.

4. I have been informed that, as with any surgical procedure, there are risks which may occur, such as infection, bleeding, damage to the organs other than my tubes which may require additional surgical procedures on an emergency basis or, in extremely rare instances, death, I also understand that if there is a complication, I may have to stay in the hospital for a longer period of time.

5. I understand that there may be benefits associated with having sterilization performed. If the sterilization is successful, I will never again have to use a temporary method of birth control (such as the pill or the IUD) and will not have to worry about becoming pregnant again.

6. I recognize that during the operation unexpected conditions may require my doctors to perform additional or different procedures than those described above. Since I may be under anesthiesia or otherwise unable to give my consent to this treatment during the sterilization, I hereby authorize and request that the physician performing this operation and his assistants or designees perform such other procedures

(cont'd)

ILLUSTRATION 8.9 (CONTINUED)

as are, in the exercise of good professional judgment, necessary and desirable, I understand that these procedures may include surgery as well as other forms of treatment. The authority granted in this paragraph shall extend to remedy all conditions found during the operation that require treatment, whether or not known at the time this operation is commenced.

7. I have been told that there are a number of other ways than sterilization that may prevent pregnancy, such a birth control pills, intrauterine device, contraceptive foam, contraceptive diaphragm and condoms (rubbers). These methods, unlike sterilization, are not intended to be permanent. I also know that it is possible for a man have a sterilization procedure.

8. This surgery is being done at my request. I am at least 21 years of age. I understand and it has been explained to me that I may change my mind about having this operation or the type of operation I wish at any time before the operation is done without prejudicing my future care and that no benefits to which I might otherwise be entitled may be withdrawn or withheld from me by reason of a decision not to be sterilized.

9. I understand that government regulations require that this sterilization may not be performed sooner than 72 hours following my signing of this Consent. I understand that I should use this 72 hour period to think over my decision to be sterilized and that if I want to change my mind, I may do so. The above named physician has offered to answer any questions I may have at any time concerning the sterization procedure.

10. I have read and fully understand this "Consent for Elective Female Sterilization" the nature and purpose of this procedure, its advantages and possible risks, discomforts and complications, if any, as well as possible alternative methods of family planning which were explained by the above physician. All blanks have been completed or crossed off prior to my signing

_____   _____
Date   Signature of Patient

                                                                    A.M.
                                      Time_____P.M.

Witness to the Explanation and Signature

_____   _____
Namer of Witness-Please Print   Explainer's signature

_____
Signature of Witness

_____
Signature of Physician

ILLUSTRATION 8.9   (CONTINUED)

We the undersigned, husband and wife, request

Dr. _____ and assistants of his choice to perform upon

_____ the operation know as a vasectomy which is a

(name of husband/patient)

severance of the vas deferens which conducts sperm and to do such things as are deemed necessary to such operation including the administration of any anesthetic of his choice.

It has been explained to both of us that this operation is intended to result in sterility. We understand that a sterile person is not capable of inducing or causing conception or reproduction of a child. We also understand that the operation may not result in sterility and that no guarantee that sterility will be the result of the operation, has been given to either of us.

We give our consent and agreement, individually and jointly, to the performance of the vasectomy operation and understand that, if it proves successful, the results may be permanent and it will be impossible for the patient to beget or induce the conception or reproduction of a child.

We, individually and jointly, assume all risks and consequences to the vasectomy operation, whether or not it is successful in sterilizing the patient for a temporary or permanent period of time and further agree to indemnify and save blameless the aforementioned doctor, his assistants and the Hospital and its employees and agents in the event any action is brought against them or any of them because of a misrepresentation of our marital status, knowingly or otherwise.

We further release said doctor, his assistants and the Hospital and its employees and agents from liability for any and all claims and demands whatsoever we or our heirs, executors, administrators or assigns may have against any of them by reason of any matter relative or incident to such operation.

_____ 19___   _____

Date   Signature of Husband/patient

_____ 19___   _____

Date   Signature of Husband/patient

_____

Witness

_____

Witness

ILLUSTRATION 8.10 CONSENT TO VASECTOMY (HUSBAND AND WIFE) (REPRINTED WITH PERMISSION OF THE AMERICAN MEDICAL ASSOCIATION, *MEDICOLEGAL FORMS WITH LEGAL ANALYSIS,* COPYRIGHT 1991, AMERICAN MEDICAL ASSOCIATION)

I hereby request that Dr._____ and assistants of his choice, perform on me the operation know as a vasectomy which I understand consists of severing of the vas deferens which conducts sperm and to do such things as are deemed necessary to such operation including the administration of any anesthetic of his choice.

I represent and warrant that I am not lawfully married and am over the age of legal consent to such surgical operation under the law of the State of Illinois, and understand that the physician named above, others acting in collaboration with him, his assistants, and the Hospital and its employees and agents are acting in reliance upon my statements.

It has been explained to me that this operation is intended to result in sterility. I understand that a sterile person is not capable of inducing or causing conception or reproduction of a child. I also understand that the operation may not result in sterility and that no guarantee that sterility will be the result of the operation, has been given to me. If the operation is successful in causing sterility such condition may be permanent and irreversible.

I hereby give my consent and agreement to the performance of the vasectomy operation, assume all risks and consequences involved and further agree to indemnify and save blameless the aforementioned doctor, his assistants and the Hospital and its employees and agents in the event any action is brought against them or any of them because of a breach of the representations and warranties made by me herein. I further release said doctor, his assistants and the Hospital and its employees and agents from liability for any and all claims and demands whatsoever I or my heirs, executors, administrators or assigns may have against any of them by reason of any matter relative or incident to such operation.

Date:_____   _____
                                                                            Signature of Consenting Party
                                                            A.M.
Time:_____P.M.

                                                            If Consenting Party
Witnesses: **is other than patient:**

_____   _____
Signature of Witness   Signature of Consenting Party

_____   _____
Signature of Witness   Relationship

ILLUSTRATION 8.11   CONSENT TO VASECTOMY (SINGLE INDIVIDUAL) (REPRINTED WITH PERMISSION OF THE AMERICAN MEDICAL ASSOCIATION, *MEDICOLEGAL FORMS WITH LEGAL ANALYSIS*, COPYRIGHT 1991, AMERICAN MEDICAL ASSOCIATION)

Date_____ Time_____ A.M.
P.M.

1. I authorize and consent to the performance upon _____
                                                    (myself or name of patient)
of a therapeutic abortion to be performed by or under the direction of
Dr._____.

2. I acknowledge that I have been informed by Dr.(s)_____

_____

that in his (their) opinion further progress of _____
                                                     (myself of name of patient)
pregnancy would gravely endanger or imperil the life of _____
                                                     (myself of name of patient)
and that in his (their) opinion, it is medically necessary to perform a therapeutic abortion.

3. I consent to the performance of operations and procedures in addition to or different from those now contemplated, whether or not arising from presently unforeseen conditions, which the abovenamed doctor or his associates or assistants may consider necessary or advisable in the course of the operation.

4. I consent to the administration of such anesthetics as may be considered necessary or advisable by the physician responsibile for this service, with the exception

of _____

_____
                              (state "none", "spinal anesthesia", etc.)

5. The nature and purpose of the operation, possible alternative methods of treatment, the risks involved, the possible consequences, and the possibility of

complications have been explained to me by Dr. _____

and by_____.

6. I acknowledge that no guarantee or assurance has been given by anyone as the results that may be obtained.

7. I acknowledge that all blank spaces on this document have either been completed or crossed off prior to my signing.

[Cross Out Any Paragraphs Above Which Do Not Apply]

Witness_____ Signed_____
                                                    (Patient or person authorized to
                                                     consent for patient)

ILLUSTRATION 8.12 CONSENT TO THERAPEUTIC ABORTION (REPRINTED WITH PERMISSION OF THE AMERICAN MEDICAL ASSOCIATION, *MEDICOLEGAL FORMS WITH LEGAL ANALYSIS,* COPYRIGHT 1991, AMERICAN MEDICAL ASSOCIATION)

Date_____Time_____ A.M.
P.M.

I hereby acknowledge that I have received from_____,

M.D., a booklet containing information on the use, effectiveness, and known hazards

of oral contraceptives, including _____, and that I have been
(insert name of product)

informed by said _____, M.D., of the possible serious side-effects of
such oral contraceptives, including but not limited to phlebitis, thromboembolism,
breakthrough bleeding and hepatic disease and informed of alternative methods of
contraception. I further acknowledge that I understand such information and warn-
ings.

I understand that such oral contraceptives are prescribed for the intended purpose of preventing future pregnancies, but no guarantees or assurances of the results
of the use of such oral contraceptives have been given by anyone. I, nevertheless,

request _____, M.D., to prescribe for me, or for _____
(insert name and relationship)

the oral contraceptive_____.
(insert name of product)

Witness_____ Signed_____
(Patient or person authorized)

**ILLUSTRATION 8.13 REQUEST FOR PRESCRIPTION OF ORAL CONTRACEPTIVES
(REPRINTED WITH PERMISSION OF THE AMERICAN MEDICAL ASSOCIATION,
MEDICOLEGAL FORMS WITH LEGAL ANALYSIS, COPYRIGHT 1991, AMERICAN MEDICAL
ASSOCIATION)**

I acknowledge that _____ M.D., has informed me of the nature and purpose of intrauterine contraceptive devices, including _____.

(insert name of device)

I understand that such device is placed in the uterus of a female patient for the intended purpose of preventing future pregnancies, but that it is not invariably effective in preventing pregnancy. I further acknowledge that no guarantee or assurance has been given by anyone as to the results to be obtained from the placement and use of such device within the uterus.

I have been informed by _____, M.D., of alternative methods of contraception and of the risks and possible complications which may arise from the placement and use of such intrauterine contraceptive device, including but not limited to perforation of the uterus by the device, expulsion of the device, infection, pain and cramps.

I nevertheless, request and consent to the placement of such intrauterine contraceptive device within my uterus or the uterus of _____

(insert name and relationship)

by _____, M.D.

Witness_____   Signed_____

(Patient or person authorized to
consent for the patient)

ILLUSTRATION 8.14 REQUEST AND CONSENT FOR PLACEMENT OF INTRAUTERINE CONTRACEPTIVE DEVICE (REPRINTED WITH PERMISSION OF THE AMERICAN MEDICAL ASSOCIATION, *MEDICOLEGAL FORMS WITH LEGAL ANALYSIS,* COPYRIGHT 1991, AMERICAN MEDICAL ASSOCIATION.

Date_____ Time_____

A.M.
P.M.

We, _____and _____, being husband and wife and both of legal age, authorize Dr. _____and such assistants as he may designate, to inseminate the wife artificially, and to use the semen of (the husband) (the husband and a donor or donors) (a donor or donors) for this purpose. We authorize him to employ such assistants he may desire to assist him.

We understand that even though the insemination may be repeated as often as recommended by Dr. _____, there is no guarantee on his part or assurance that pregnancy or full term pregnancy will result.

We agree to rely upon the sole discretion of Dr._____ in the selection of qualified donors and never to seek to discover the identity of any donor. We agree that following the insemination, Dr. _____ may destroy all records and information concerning the identityof the donor or donors.

We, and each of us, acknowledge our obligation to care for and support and otherwise treat any child born as the result of such artificial insemination in all respects as though it were our natural born child.

We understand that if pregnancy shall result, there is the possibility of complications of childbirth or delivery, or the birth of an abnormal infant or infants, or undesirable hereditary tendencies of such issue, or other adverse consequences.

(CROSS OUT ANY WORDS ABOVE WHICH DO NOT APPLY)

Signed _____
(Husband)

Signed _____
(Wife)

ILLUSTRATION 8.15 CONSENT TO ARTIFICIAL INSEMINATION (REPRINTED WITH PERMISSION OF THE AMERICAN MEDICAL ASSOCIATION, *MEDICOLEGAL FORMS WITH LEGAL ANALYSIS,* COPYRIGHT 1991, AMERICAN MEDICAL ASSOCIATION)

Consent forms should be amended periodically as procedures and techniques change. If your facility provides patients with written materials concerning procedures, the consent form should also contain blanks that the patient should fill in with information found only in the brochure describing the particular procedure. This would be further evidence that the patient read the brochure and understood all the risks regarding the procedure. As long as the recognized procedure is followed as outlined, the patient would be hard pressed to maintain an action for negligence or battery because the doctor would have an affirmative defense based on the patient's assumption of the risk of the procedure or treatment.

EXAMPLES/QUESTIONS/PROJECTS

1. *Draft a consent to treatment form for your child authorizing your own family physician, hospital, or similar institution to provide medical care to your child while you are on vacation, using the necessary criteria for a valid consent contained in this chapter. If you do not have a minor child, pretend that you do for the purposes of this project.*

2. *Prepare a standardized consent form for treatment of any particular procedure routinely used in your office or hospital that you feel would satisfy the requirements of an informed consent using the necessary criteria as set forth in this chapter.*

3. *Elizabeth is sixteen years old. She has been examined and prescribed birth control pills by Dr. Stern without her parent's consent. More importantly, the parents do not know that she has been to see Dr. Stern at all. One day, she comes to Dr. Stern complaining of an ingrown toenail. Is Dr. Stern liable for prescribing her birth control medication? May Dr. Stern treat her for the ingrown toenail without her parent's consent?*

   Answer. Under most states' laws, Dr. Stern may examine and/or treat minors for birth control, abortion, or other obstetrical matters. Not only may such procedures be performed without parental consent, but the doctor would violate a minor patient's right to privacy if he or she were to notify the parents of the treatment. However, the doctor may not treat the minor patient for anything else without parental consent, even though he or she has been treating the minor for birth control. Thus, Dr. Stern could not treat the ingrown toenail without consent to such treatment by the minor's parents.

4. *Mr. Hall is prescribed medication by Dr. Stern. This medication causes drowsiness, and Dr. Stern warns the patient of this adverse affect. More importantly, Dr. Stern discusses the hazards of driving an automobile after taking this medication. Mr. Hall follows the doctor's advice and refrains from driving an automobile. However, Mr. Hall sustains a severe injury to his hand while using a power saw after taking the medication. Would Dr. Stern be liable to Mr. Hall for failing to warn him to also refrain from using dangerous power tools.*

   Answer: Probably not. If Mr. Hall was warned by the doctor of the medication's adverse affects in causing drowsiness to the extent that he should refrain from driving an automobile, common sense would dictate that he should also refrain from any other hazardous activities. In this situation, Dr. Stern would probably escape liability based on Mr. Hall's comparative negligence and/or the assumption of risk in taking the medication and performing a potentially hazardous activity. Mr. Hall was specifically warned that the medication would cause drowsiness. It is just as foreseeable that he would become drowsy while using a power tool as that he would become drowsy while driving an automobile.

5. *Draft a form that could be used in a medical office for a patient about to undergo testing for the HIV (HTLV-III) virus, making sure your draft complies with the provisions of the Massachusetts statute (law) as set forth earlier in this chapter.*

Chapter Nine

ASSAULT AND BATTERY

Key Terms

apprehension	unprivileged	aggressor
punitive damages	malice	battery
	assault	

Not only are assault and battery tortious acts giving rise to civil liability, but they may also be considered criminal activity. An **assault** is an unlawful attempt or threat to commit battery, coupled with the present ability to inflict injury on another person. A **battery** is any unprivileged, willful, unlawful, and intentional touching of another person. Harmful or offensive touching or contact with another person is the essence of battery. It is distinct from a mere assault, which is the causing of an **apprehension** or fear, of such contact.

ASSAULT

Mere words, however threatening, will not normally amount to an assault in the absence of the ability to carry out the harmful or offensive touching of the other person. The terms *assault* and *battery* are commonly misused, particularly in pleadings and judicial opinions. Assault rarely occurs in the allied health professions; battery is the wrong most commonly committed.

However, an assault may be committed when, for example, a nurse tells a patient that he will place the patient in leather restraints if she does not stop summoning him or other aides to her room merely to change the channel on the television she is watching. It is immaterial whether or not the nurse has, or believes he has, the ability to place the patient in leather restraints. An assault has been committed if he intends to put the patient in apprehension of being placed in leather restraints and if the patient believes that he has the ability to carry out the threat. This does not mean that the patient may recover $1,000,000 from the nurse as **punitive damages.** The patient would have to show that some injury, such as a legitimate apprehension or fear, has been inflicted on her by the nurse's threat. The nurse may also be held accountable to the patient on other grounds. His threatening words may lead to liability being imposed for an intentional infliction of emotional distress, which is another intentional tort, even though mere words, however, offensive or threatening, will not generally amount to an assault in the technical sense. Finally, the nurse could possibly assert a number of defenses to bar the patient's recovery of damages.

For a *criminal assault* to take place, one person must have present ability to injure the other person; it is immaterial whether or not the other person is placed in apprehension of injury. This is the main difference between a criminal assault and a civil assault, where the other person need only *believe* that the wrongdoer has the ability to injure.

BATTERY AND ITS DEFENSES

A battery in the civil context is the **unprivileged** touching of one person by another. The tort carries the elements of duty, breach of duty, causation, and damages, just as in negligence actions. In addition, an unprivileged touching must accompany the other four basic elements.

The key words that form the basis of this tort are *unprivileged touching.* Thus, consent by the patient to the touching is a complete defense to allegations of this type of misconduct. However, as will be discussed throughout this chapter, the consent must be actual and freely given, with full knowledge of all surrounding facts and circumstances. For example, a surgical operation performed without consent is a battery. A battery is also committed when the doctor is authorized to perform one operation and goes beyond the scope of the consent given by the patient to the specific procedure—as when the doctor performs an additional surgical procedure not associated with the originally intended procedure.

Any unnecessary mishandling of the patient may amount to a battery where a particular treatment is done following the patient's consent to such treatment. For example, a patient may consent to having a low-back X-ray examination. The patient implies his or her consent for the radiologic technologist to move him or her for positioning. However, this implied consent does not go so far as to allow the technologist to twist and contort the patient's body to the point of inflicting pain or injury.

Another example is the case in which the patient consents to be given an injection by a medical assistant. If the medical assistant intentionally twists the needle around during the injection procedure for the purpose of inflicting pain, such mishandling of the patient would amount to battery. Also, battery has been held against a dentist who pulled three of a patient's teeth when the patient consented to the extraction of only one tooth.

It makes no difference that the doctor does not charge the patient for the additional procedure. Further, the asserted conduct cannot be defended on the grounds that the patient would have given his or consent if he or she had been asked in advance.

Breach of Duty

All persons have an inherent duty to refrain from hitting, kicking, stabbing, poking, injecting, or even kissing another person without that person's freely given consent. The doing of such acts without another person's freely given consent constitutes a breach of the duty to refrain from such conduct. As discussed in negligence actions, where such offensive touching is done as a matter of mere accident, the elements of battery have been established when the touching is intentional and when it is done without the other person's freely given consent or is otherwise unprivileged. To constitute battery, the touching need not be done with the intent to harm the other person. It is the act of touching voluntarily undertaken with specific intent by the wrongdoer that elevates this conduct from wrongful, negligent conduct to the status of battery.

Case example

Consider the following example. One day, while playing, Bobby Carson steps on a rusty nail, breaking the skin. The wound is open and fairly deep. Mrs. Carson takes Bobby to the doctor for an examination and treatment.

On their arrival at the office, the wound is cleaned while Mrs. Carson is present. Thereafter, Dr. Baxter looks at the wound and notes that it does not require any stitches. He then requests his medical assistant to apply anti-bacterial ointment to the wound and bandage the foot accordingly. While the medical assistant is out of the room, Dr. Baxter indicates to Mrs. Carson that Bobby should have a tetanus shot. Mrs. Carson explains to the doctor that Bobby recently had a tetanus shot, which, she feels, makes this particular treatment unnecessary. Dr. Baxter makes no further comment about the injection.

Thereafter, Dr. Baxter's medical assistant enters the room with the intention of giving Bobby a tetanus shot. When she sees the syringe and needle, Mrs. Carson again explains her position that the injection is unnecessary. The medical assistant then states that this is a matter of office policy in such cases and proceeds to give the injection.

Bobby, being a typical seven-year-old boy, kicks and screams when he is given the injection. In addition, he has a minor reaction to the tetanus injection. Bobby also becomes fearful and apprehensive toward doctors in general because of the experience. Finally, Mrs. Carson is charged for the tetanus shot that Bobby received.

As previously discussed under the topic of informed consent, Mrs. Carson is the only authorized person present who can give consent to Dr. Baxter, and his staff for Bobby's treatment. In the majority of cases, patients merely follow the doctor's recommendations concerning treatment. However, Mrs. Carson told Dr. Baxter that she did not feel that the injection was necessary in this particular case. The position was reemphasized to the medical assistant. A battery was committed by the office medical assistant when she gave Bobby the injection. Bobby was given the shot intentionally and without the mother's consent (or Bobby's). Also, the giving of the injection was not privileged; a privileged touching would be completely defensible under the law.

Intentional conduct of battery

Even though only minor harm has been done in this case, a lawsuit based on the intentional conduct of battery could nevertheless be maintained against the medical assistant for giving the shot. Also, a lawsuit could probably be maintained against Dr. Baxter under the doctrine of respondeat superior for his negligence in not telling the assistant not to give the injection. A suit for battery could also be maintained against Dr. Baxter as well as the medical assistant if Mrs. Carson could demonstrate that Dr. Baxter told the assistant to give the injection after the mother expressed her disapproval. In this situation, the medical assistant would be viewed as an extension of Dr. Baxter in doing the offensive touching.

The medical assistant's motive in giving Bobby the injection was not to cause him harm, but rather to prevent further harm. However, the elements of battery itself do not turn on the existence or nonexistence of ill will in the person committing the act. Rather, it is the intent to do an act that is not otherwise privileged that forms the foundation of battery. Thus, the conduct is intentional when a nurse or medical assistant gives a patient more medication than has been ordered because of his or her feeling that the patient would benefit more from the increased dosage. A suit could be maintained with an award of punitive as well as compensatory damages should harm result to the patient as a result of such conduct. Where the patient/plaintiff in a lawsuit can further demonstrate that the intentional act was done with ill will or **malice** toward the patient—a jury would undoubtedly impose a larger amount of punitive damages against the wrongdoer.

Finally, as the foregoing discussion of criminal penalties suggests, the more aggravating the injury inflicted with ill will or malice toward the patient, the greater the likelihood that such conduct will be considered criminal and will entail criminal penalties, such as imprisonment.

Direct Force Not Required

To constitute battery, the wrongdoer need not use direct force against the victim or ever directly touch the victim. It is enough that the wrongdoer simply sets in motion a force that ultimately causes physical harm.

Case example

The principle of transferred intent is illustrated by the following example. Mr. Clark is a chronic alcoholic whose bloodstream continuously contains some concentration of alcohol. He is also a regular patient of Dr. Smead, receiving oral medication in the form of pills from Dr. Smead for an illness unrelated to his alcoholism. Mr. Clark is routinely drunk and somewhat discourteous to the office personnel of Dr. Smead when he is at the doctor's office.

One day, Jonathan Carlisle, Dr. Smead's medical assistant, decides to teach Mr. Clark a lesson. Instead of giving Mr. Clark his routine supply of pills, he substitutes Antabuse® for some of the medication. This drug, which converts ethyl alcohol into a highly virulent poison, causes violent reactions in persons who ingest alcohol while on the medication. The medical assistant's motives are not entirely malicious. He merely feels that the reaction might alert Mr. Clark to the physically harmful effects of his chronic alcoholism.

Defense and response

Thereafter, Mr. Clark takes some of the Antabuse®, becomes violently ill, and needs to be hospitalized. He then brings a lawsuit against the medical assistant for battery. Mr. Carlisle defends his actions on two grounds. The first is that his motive in giving Mr. Clark the Antabuse® was to help him see the error of his ways, not to cause him harm. The court quickly dispenses with this argument on the grounds that the act of giving Mr. Clark the specific medication was done intentionally, not accidentally.

The second argument asserted by the medical assistant in his defense is that a battery was not committed in the technical sense. Mr. Carlisle asserts that it was not he but the medication that caused the reaction. Therefore, if battery is indeed the unprivileged touching by another, Mr. Clark's action for battery could not be maintained. The court, however, sides with Mr. Clark's attorney's use of the following analogy to establish the contention of battery.

The technical definition of battery would be met if the medical assistant intentionally injected Mr. Clark with Antabuse®. If he held syringe and needle and injected the harmful solution into Mr. Clark, he would be committing a "harmful touching," since Mr. Clark did not consent to such an injection.

Likewise, Mr. Clark, knowing that a violent reaction would result, would not consent to allowing the medical assistant to place a pill of Antabuse® in his mouth. Therefore, the technical term of unprivileged touching would be met if the medical assistant placed the pill of Antabuses® into Mr. Clark's mouth under such circumstances. The question then arises, What is the difference in tricking Mr. Clark into placing the pill into his own mouth? Of course, the answer is that there is no difference.

As in the cases dealing with proximate cause discussed in Chapter 4, the courts have relied on the unbroken chain of events in their analysis of such cases to establish the tort of battery. In the preceding example, the handing of the Antabuse® pills to Mr. Clark constitutes the battery. This battery is the proximate cause of Mr. Clark's taking the medication and having the violent reaction.

Injury of a third person

Transferred intent is one area of the law of battery in which the courts have viewed the factual situations somewhat consistently. These are cases where the wrongdoer intends to commit a harmful, unprivileged act on another and, while attempting to commit the act, actually injures a third person. In the preceding example, if another patient, Mr. Jones, had suffered a violent reaction because he had mistakenly received the Antabuse® that the medical assistant intended to give to Mr. Clark, the medical assistant could not escape liability by asserting as a defense that his intent was to cause Mr. Clark to experience the reaction and not Mr. Jones. The courts have long established that such intent by the medical assistant would be transferred from Mr. Clark to Mr. Jones.

Self-defense

The law has long recognized that anyone is privileged to use reasonable force in defending himself or herself against a battery or threatened battery (assault). The privilege is one of defense against the assault or battery and not one of retaliation. The privilege terminates when the initial **aggressor** has withdrawn and the battery is no longer threatened. The privilege exists when the defendant (the person using the force) reasonably believes that it is necessary to protect himself or herself against the offensive touching (battery), even though there may in fact be no necessity to use any force at all. In other words, a reasonable mistake on the part of the person who defends him- or herself will protect him or her from civil liability.

However, the privilege is limited to the use of force that is, or reasonably appears to be, necessary for protection against the threatened battery. Thus, differences in age, size, and relative strength are proper considerations for a jury to examine relating to a defense based on self-defense. Insults, verbal threats, or other kinds of abusive language in and of themselves, without the present ability to carry out such threats, do not give a person the right to respond with physical force. In this regard, the following example is illustrative.

Case example

Mr. Curtis brings his fifteen-year-old son Randy into the emergency room of a local clinic because Randy has cut his foot. Although the wound is minor, the emergency room doctor tells Mr. Curtis that Randy should have a tetanus shot. Mr. Curtis agrees with the doctor.

Shortly thereafter, a nurse comes into the emergency room with a hypodermic needle and syringe. Mr. Curtis knows that his son does not like shots and that Randy has acted violently in the past toward people who have given him shots. Nevertheless, Mr. Curtis makes no comment to the nurse that Randy has a history of kicking, screaming, and crying when receiving an injection.

Randy starts to back off a little when the nurse approaches him, but she has no reason to believe that he will retaliate with physical force. She considers him, at fifteen years of age, to be a "big boy." In fact, he is 5 feet 11 inches tall and weighs 185 pounds.

As the nurse approaches him Randy punches her in the face and breaks her nose. Subsequently, the nurse brings a lawsuit against Randy's father for her injuries on the grounds that Randy's conduct amounted to battery and that Mr. Curtis was negligent in not informing her of Randy's previous violence. Mr. Curtis responds to the allegations in the lawsuit on the grounds that a parent cannot be held liable for tortious conduct committed by a minor child; that such conduct should have been anticipated by the nurse; and, that Randy acted in self-defense, a charge that would completely bar the nurse from recovering damages.

Defense and response

As for the first defense asserted by Mr. Curtis, that a parent may not be held liable for the tortious conduct of a minor child, the outcome frequently is decided according to the provisions of a state statute. However, the nurse would probably prevail on the grounds that Mr. Curtis knew of his son's prior misconduct regarding injections from other doctors and nurses. He had no reason to believe that his son would not act again as he had in the past. Therefore, the jury would probably assess liability against Mr. Curtis for failing to warn the nurse that Randy might physically retaliate. The court would probably find that Mr. Curtis at the very least had a duty to warn the nurse of the prior instances of retaliation. This finding would also keep Mr. Curtis from asserting a defense based on the grounds that Randy's conduct should have been anticipated by the nurse.

Punitive damages against the parent

Many jurisdictions hold that, where a parent has knowledge of a child's potential for dangerous conduct and fails to take action against such conduct, punitive damages may be assessed against the parent for the minor's wrongful acts. The courts seem to be split on assessing punitive damages against the parent on the basis of two different theories. The first is the theory that the parent's failure to warn or take affirmative action is in and of itself tantamount to willful and wanton misconduct. Such willful and wanton misconduct would justify the awarding of punitive damages to the plaintiff. Another theory on which to base liability for the imposition of punitive damages is that the child is an extension of the parent. This latter theory is not frequently asserted and constitutes the view taken by a minority of states.

The principal factors in assessing punitive damages against parents for the wrongful misconduct of a child seem to be the nature of the act, the age of the child or his or her mental capacity, and the child's ability to distinguish right from wrong. Thus, where dangerous propensities exist in a fifteen-year-old who is 5 feet 11 inches tall and weighs 185 pounds, the courts will generally allow the awarding of punitive damages against the parent. The parent's willful and wanton failure to warn of the child's dangerous propensities when the parent knows of such propensities forms the basis for the awarding of punitive damages and elevates this conduct out of the arena of mere negligence. (In contrast, where the child is of "tender years," that is eight or nine years of age, punitive damages are generally not allowed in the majority of jurisdictions without some definite evidence that the parent knew the child could do physical harm.) In the present example, punitive damages would undoubtedly be based on the fact that Mr. Curtis's failure to warn the nurse or otherwise take affirmative action relating to Randy's potential misconduct was tantamount to willful and wanton misconduct. This willful and wanton failure to warn ultimately resulted in the nurse's broken nose.

Aggression or self-defense?

The jury would probably also find in the nurse's favor in the third defense asserted by Mr.Curtis. The jury would almost certainly not be swayed by the argument that Randy acted in self-defense when he received the tetanus shot. The analysis of the court or jury in assessing liability and awarding damages would probably be based on the fact that the nurse was not committing either an assault or a battery when she approached Randy and started to give him the injection. Because Randy's father had given his consent to the treatment, the nurse was not committing a battery when she gave Randy the tetanus shot. Rather, her conduct in giving the injection was privileged.

When Randy hit the nurse in the nose, he became an aggressor. More important, such an act of aggression or retaliation could undoubtedly be demonstrated to be intentional rather than merely reactive. Thus, the technical element of battery could be established by the nurse against Randy, and she could undoubtedly collect for her injury from Randy's parents for all medical expenses incurred, loss of earnings and/or earning capacity, future medical care, and so on, as previously discussed.

However, the nurse may or may not be able to receive an award of punitive damages against Randy for his intentional act in striking her nose. Many jurisdictions would allow her to maintain an action against Randy for punitive damages because of his age and physical stature, even though he was a minor at the time he broke her nose. But many jurisdictions do not allow punitive damages to be assessed against minor children for their intentional acts. Such jurisdictions rationalize the position taken on the basis of the fact that a minor does not understand the total nature and extent of his or her conduct. Without such an understanding, the minor's conduct could not be considered intentional and could not be subject to punitive damages.

Suffice it to say that, under any theory, the nurse would undoubtedly prevail in being awarded compensatory damages for the injuries she sustained as a result of Randy's conduct. In fact, she would prevail even if she had not given Randy the injection but had merely been approaching him with the syringe and needle at the time he struck her or had merely made a comment to Randy or his father that she intended to give Randy the injection a few minutes later.

As this example makes clear, the nurse did not express or imply her consent to Randy to punch her in the nose. Thus, the technical element of battery was met when Randy hit her.

Consent

On the basis of previous examples, it should be evident that consent is the key factor in determining whether or not a battery has been committed. Consent is also the key factor in determining whether the conduct of the medical assistant, nurse, technician, doctor, or other professional is defensible. In the allied health field, examination or treatment usually involves touching the patient. The key question is whether or not such touching is privileged or otherwise consented to by the patient.

Consent must be either expressly or impliedly given by the patient before such examination or treatment may be rendered. We have seen that an exception to this rule is where such treatment is undertaken in an emergency, lifesaving situation. The law presupposes that the patient would give his or her consent to such life-saving treatment rather than die.

Most cases dealing with consent, whether express or implied, involve surgical operations. However, all examinations or treatments conducted by a physician, dentist, optometrist, nurse, medical assistant, physical therapist, radiological technologist, or other allied health professional must be consented to by the patient before they can be rendered. It would be impossible to cover in this text every possible situation involving the issue of consent in specific types of examinations or treatments. The reader could certainly think of many uncited examples in which liability could be assessed against a professional on the basis of the lack of the patient's consent. To aid in this interpretation and application to each person's specific profession, the basic ground rules of informed consent are set forth in the section of Chapter 8 dealing with implied consent and the assumption of risk. In a lawsuit based on the tort of battery, the defense of express or implied consent, in which the patient has assumed the risk in the examination or treatment being conducted, is a complete defense that bars the patient from recovering damages.

EXAMPLES / QUESTIONS /PROJECTS

1. *Kevin Ky has just been involved in a severe accident at home and has gone to Dr. Yoshimura's office with a deep laceration to his forearm. On his arrival at the office, the medical assistant immediately rushes Kevin into the minor surgery room and summons Dr. Yoshimura. Seeing Kevin in intense pain, Dr. Yoshimura gives Kevin an injection of a narcotic drug to ease the pain. The medical assistant then cleans the wound and controls the bleeding.*

Knowing further treatment will involve surgery, the medical assistant then requests Kevin to sign a consent for treatment, which Kevin does, and the surgery is performed. Is the consent for treatment valid?

> **Answer:** Probably not. Informed consent means just that: the patient must be informed of all the consequences inherent to the procedure. In this situation, the patient has been given a narcotic drug that may and probably does alter his senses and ability to comprehend exactly what he is being informed about. Thus, since he gives his consent under the influence of a drug, the consent is not valid informed consent.

2. *Jane is a medical assistant who works in Dr. Smith's office. Her duties include giving physical therapy to patients. Dr. Smith tells Jane to put Bill Johnson in traction for neck injuries he sustained in an automobile accident. Dr. Smith instructs Jane to increase the amount of tension to the point where Bill begins complaining of pain.*

Jane hooks Bill up to the traction machine and begins increasing the amount of tension to his neck. She continues to increase the amount of traction until Bill indicates he feels a slight pain in his neck. However, Jane tells Bill that the amount of tension is very slight and that he could probably stand a little more. She then increases the amount of tension to his neck, which greatly increases the amount of pain in Bill's neck. Is Jane liable for any ensuing injury under any theory or theories of law previously studied?

> **Answer:** Yes. Jane could be held accountable for any injury sustained if her action of increasing the amount of tension amounts to negligent conduct. Jane was given instructions to use her discretion in adjusting the traction machine. However, the doctor told Jane to adjust the tension only to the point at which Bill first experienced pain. The tension added after that point could be considered mishandling of the patient amounting to battery. Bill consented to the treatment by implication. However, this implied consent would probably be viewed by a jury as given only to the point of first experiencing pain. Thereafter, Bill would not have consented to the treatment as given by Jane.

CHAPTER TEN

DEFAMATION OF CHARACTER

Key Terms

publication	republication	disseminate
per se	loathsome	indemnify
per quod	moral turpitude	indemnification
recitation	prima facie	garnish
	malicious	

Defamation of character is injury to a person's character, fame, or reputation by false and **malicious** statements. In other words, the statement or statements must be intentionally false and malicious. For example, the statement "John is a thief" intentionally carries with it the connotation that John steals. The court would have little difficulty determining that the person making the statement intends for anyone hearing it to think that John steals. And John would have little difficulty demonstrating that this statement is defamatory if he can prove that it is false. Finally, inherent in the definition is the fact that the statement or statements must be publicized.

Publication means that the statement is transmitted to a third person other than the patient or party to whom the statement refers. Publication of the statement may be demonstrated where the statement is made to the person to whom the statement refers and is overheard and understood by some third person. The third person need not believe that the statement is intended to be defamatory for the statement to constitute the tort of defamation of character. The tort of defamation of character is an intentional tort and thus, carries the potential for punitive damages as well as compensatory damages to be awarded by a jury on behalf of the defamed.

Defamation of character actually consists of two torts: slander, which is oral, and libel, which is written. Slander and libel have some common elements. Both libel and slander require the plaintiff to prove that the defendant defamed the plaintiff. That is, the plaintiff must prove that the defendant used oral or written language that would tend to hold the plaintiff up to scorn, hatred, ridicule, or contempt in the minds of any considerable and respectable class in the community.[1] In addition, slander and libel are subdivided into statements that are defamatory **per se** and statements or words that are defamatory *per quod.*

SLANDER

The term *slander* refers to statements that are spoken by the defaming party. For example, a medical assistant tells a patient in the physician's office that another patient, Chuck Brown, is a dead beat who notoriously refuses to pay his bills. If the statement about Chuck Brown is untrue, and the person to whom the statement is being directed understands the term *dead beat*, a cause of action (lawsuit) can be maintained by Chuck Brown against the medical assistant for slandering his name and reputation. In this example, the term *dead beat* is characterized by the medical assistant as a person who notoriously refuses to pay his bills. If the term were used without further explanation of its meaning, it would have to be understood as defamatory by the person whom it was intended to describe.

---

[1]*Ingalls v. Hastings & Son Publishing Co.*, 304 Mass. 31, 22 N.E.2d 657 (1939).

As previously mentioned, publication means that the statement is understood by a third person. For example, if the medical assistant made the statement to a person who only speaks and understands Spanish, Chuck Brown would be hard-pressed to demonstrate that the Spanish-speaking person understood what the medical assistant was saying about him. Thus, the publication element for the maintenance of this wrongdoing would undoubtedly fail to be upheld.

The courts in most states have required that the person about whom the slanderous statement is being made must demonstrate actual damages before he or she may maintain an action for punitive damages. People routinely call one another names. When someone calls another person a jackass in front of a third person, the person about whom the statement is being made must demonstrate actual compensatory suffering before he or she may receive punitive damages against the person making the statement. Obviously, the courts would be flooded with defamatory cases involving slanderous statements if it were not necessary to show actual compensatory damages. Every time someone called another person a bum, a jerk, a dingbat, or some other name in the presence of other persons, the person about whom the statement was made could file a lawsuit against the person or persons who made the statement. In any case, the majority of these cases would undoubtedly fall by the wayside, ending in verdicts in favor of the defense, because of the absence of evidence that the statement was made maliciously, with ill will or with intent to cause injury.

Maliciousness

A slanderous statement must be intended to be malicious. In other words, the person making the statement must intend the statement to be injurious to the fame, character, or reputation of the person about whom the statement is made. Many defendants have properly asserted that the statement was made in jest and that all persons hearing the statement understood that to be the case. Such asserted defenses have been successful in proving that the statement could not be considered malicious.

It should be noted, however, that the plaintiff (the party to whom the statement refers) need only show that the defendant (the party making the statement) had no reasonable grounds to believe the statement to be true when the statement was made to constitute maliciousness. Therefore, maliciousness should not be confused with a purposeful intent to damage a person's reputation, character, or fame. Actual ill will toward the person to whom the statement refers is not technically an element of the wrong, The mere **recitation** or **republication** of a defamatory statement previously made by another person where there is no reasonable grounds to believe such statement to be true is enough to demonstrate liability against the republishing party. However, where the defamed person can demonstrate malice or ill will, the jury will be more likely to impose a larger amount of punitive damages against the person who made the statement.

SLANDER BY ALLIED HEALTH PROFESSIONALS

In the authors' experience, allied health professionals are somewhat lax in making statements about patients or others without reasonable grounds for believing that such statements are true. Health care professionals frequently discuss patients in elevators, cafeterias, and other public areas of health care facilities with little or no thought about who might be within earshot of the conversation. This may simply be thoughtless or it may be due to a lack of understanding of the potential seriousness of this type of conduct or of the patient's potential for recovering punitive damages against the person making the statement. Some typical situations involving slanderous statements may be seen in the following examples.

Case example 1

Nurse Ross and Nurse Rivera both work in a hospital. One night, while both are on duty, Nurse Ross is reviewing the chart of a patient whose attending physician is Dr. Tanaka.

While reviewing the patient's chart, Nurse Ross makes the following comment to Nurse Rivera about Dr. Tanaka's chart entries, prescription orders, and generalized chart notations: "This is a typical example of Dr. Tanaka's practice. That guy is nothing but a quack; it's a wonder the licensing board hasn't revoked his license to practice medicine."

Nurse Rivera, who knows that Dr. Tanaka is sometimes behind in chart recording, thereafter tells the hospital administrator of the incident and of Nurse Ross's comment. In response, the hospital administrator calls Dr. Tanaka before the hospital review board and confronts him with the accusation of Nurse Ross. Because Dr. Tanaka has not completed one particular patient chart, his hospital privileges are suspended until the patient's chart is completed. There is no other evidence that Dr. Tanaka is a "quack" or that he has made an improper diagnosis or conducted improper medical treatment on any of his patients.

The statement that a doctor is a quack calls into question the doctor's practice of medicine or ethics. Accordingly, such a term in and of itself *(per se)* has been repeatedly found by juries to be intended to injure a doctor's reputation, not only in the medical community but also among the general public. Such terms are slanderous *per se*. Thus, Dr. Tanaka could maintain a lawsuit based on slander against Nurse Ross for calling him a quack.

Nurse Ross further clarifies what she means by the term *quack* in her statement: she indicated that the doctor's license should be revoked, thus taking away any defense she might have that the statement was made in jest. Nurse Rivera shows that she has been led to believe that the statement is true when she goes to the hospital administrator.

Since the general statement is false, Dr. Tanaka could successfully maintain an action against Nurse Ross for defaming his reputation in the medical community—particularly if he could demonstrate that the other doctors were more behind in charting than he was. Also, he could undoubtedly demonstrate that he suffered monetary loss in having his hospital privileges suspended on the basis of the false statement.

Further, there is a strong indication that Dr. Tanaka could maintain an action against Nurse Ross for the imposition of punitive damages. A demonstration by Dr. Tanaka that Nurse Ross made the statement as a gesture of ill will toward him would formulate the basis for the awarding of punitive damages. For example, Dr. Tanaka may demonstrate to a jury that the primary reason Nurse Ross made the statement was because he had personally reprimanded her for something she failed to do for one of his patients as ordered on that patient's chart.

Case example 2

In the following example, the statement is overheard by a third person. Steve Rosenberg, a nurse, and Betty Pastore, a ward clerk, work in the local hospital. One night, during visiting hours, while Al Tarcher's wife is seated in the waiting room adjacent to the nurses station, Steve makes a statement to Betty about Dr. Gregory, Al Tarcher's attending physician. Steve comments, "It's a wonder Dr. Gregory's patients put up with her. She's never on time during hospital rounds. Her patients must sense her lax attitude toward their care. She's always behind in charting, even though she's a very conscientious doctor, and she rarely explains to her patients their condition or the treatment they are receiving."

Overhearing the conversation, Mrs. Tarcher discusses the comments of Steve Rosenberg with her husband. Neither Mrs. Tarcher nor her husband know the specific times that physicians are expected to make hospital rounds. However, they believe that the doctor should have been present during visiting hours to explain Al's condition and progress to them. Mr. Tarcher therefore discharges Dr. Gregory because of the statement of Nurse Rosenberg plus the fact that the doctor was not present during visiting hours.

In this example, the discharge of Dr. Gregory is based solely on Nurse Rosenberg's comments, even though he qualifies his comments by saying that Dr. Gregory is a very good doctor. The comment about her lax attitude, her not making rounds at appropriate times, and her being behind in patient charting influence Al Tarcher to discharge Dr. Gregory.

A clear demonstration by Dr. Gregory that the majority of doctors make hospital rounds at various, unspecified times would tend to demonstrate that the statement by Nurse Rosenberg was untrue and defamatory. The doctor could further demonstrate the untruthfulness of the statement by showing that all her patient charts were current. Evidence that she routinely made hospital rounds at a time when Nurse Rosenberg was not on duty but that she was otherwise punctual would also demonstrate the lack of truth of the statement and the lack of reasonableness on the part of Nurse Rosenberg in believing his own comments to be true.

Dr. Gregory would probably prevail in her defamation of character action against Nurse Rosenberg for compensatory damages. She could demonstrate having suffered actual money damages in her discharge from the care of Al Tarcher. The more she could demonstrate that Nurse Rosenberg lacked reasonable belief in the truth of his own comments, the greater the likelihood that she could also maintain her action against Nurse Rosenberg for punitive damages.

Nurse Rosenberg's comment that Dr. Gregory is always late in doing hospital rounds may not have been intended or otherwise construed as being defamatory in and of itself. After all, who cares? Al Tarcher is in a hospital where he receives care primarily from nurses and other hospital personnel. However, Mrs. Tarcher understands the statement to connote that Dr. Gregory does not care about her patients. This connotation—that she is tardy and behind in her charting—renders the defamatory sting, not the mere words themselves.

Case example 3

Dr. McCormick is a sole practitioner. Doris Miller, one of Dr. McCormick's medical assistants, handles patient billing and account collections for Dr. McCormick. Among her various office duties, based on Dr. McCormick's office policy, is the responsibility for telephoning individual patients when their bills become ninety days past due. The purpose of telephoning patients is to warn them that the bill will be turned over to a collection agency unless payment is made immediately. Doris's desk and telephone are located in the front-office area adjacent to the patient waiting room.

One day, Doris Miller telephones Kim Santa to admonish him for being late in paying his bill. Because another medical assistant has not properly credited Kim Santa's account, Doris is unaware that Mr. Santa paid his account in full the week before.

Pursuant to office policy, Doris states that Mr. Santa must pay his bill immediately or be subject to having the bill turned over to a collection agency for further legal proceedings. Doris does not believe Mr. Santa's explanation that he has already paid his bill in full. At this point, she calls him a deadbeat and states that the matter will be turned over to a collection agency if he does not come into the office immediately with proof of payment. The patients seated in the waiting room overhear the one-sided conversation in which Doris calls Mr. Santa by name. One of the patients who overhears the conversation is a banker from whom Mr. Santa is trying to obtain a business loan. Based on Doris's statement, the banker turns down the loan.

Kim Santa, with proper counseling from an attorney, could probably maintain an action for slander against both Doris Miller and Dr. McCormick for defaming Mr. Santa's character and his reputation within the community. Kim Santa could demonstrate that he suffered actual compensatory money damages when the banker refused to give him a loan based on the comment that he was a deadbeat. This comment carried with it the connotation that Kim does not pay his bills on time.

Kim could maintain an action against Dr. McCormick because Doris was acting in her authorized capacity as the doctor's medical assistant. Her routine telephoning of patients regarding their past-due bills was standard operating procedure in Dr. McCormick's practice. Not only did she have the apparent authority to act in the manner she did, she was also given actual authority by Dr. McCormick to contact patients for the specific purpose of threatening them with collection unless they paid their bill immediately. Dr. McCormick could argue that Doris Miller was not authorized to call people deadbeats. However, the average jury would likely find that the purpose of the telephone call, as established by office procedure, carried with it the authority to call a person a disparaging name. Thus, after adequately demonstrating that he suffered compensatory money damages, Kim Santa could maintain an action against both Doris Miller and Dr. McCormick for punitive damages.

The action for slander could not have been maintained without the banker's overhearing the one-sided conversation of Doris Miller. Liability arose from the publication of the statement. Better office policy, which would prevent liability, would be to make such telephone calls in private, in an area away from waiting patients. Remember, it is not defamation of character to make a statement directly to the person to whom the statement refers. Defamation only arises when publication of the statement is made to some third person. Therefore, be it a physician's office, physical therapy office, laboratory, X-ray department, or other practice catering to the general public, discussions with the patient about his or her bill should be conducted outside the earshot of other patients. If followed, this procedure would be successful in circumventing the potential hazards of retaliation by a disgruntled patient in a court of law based on a suit for defamation of character.

Case example 4

The circumstances in the following example demonstrate the potential hazards of voicing one's personal opinion regarding a patient's treatment for an illness. Richard Carter and Amy Stein are medical assistants who work for Dr. Winston in a local clinic. Dr. Winston's clinic has a waiting room adjacent to a back-office alcove where medication is kept and minor laboratory work is done by the assistants. Patients awaiting the results of laboratory work are routinely found in the waiting area.

One day, Mrs. Davis overhears a conversation between Richard Carter and Amy Stein about her husband, Michael Davis, who was examined by Dr. Winston the previous day. Mrs. Davis is completely unaware that her husband had been examined by the doctor. Richard states to Amy that he does not care what Dr. Winston has written on Mr. Davis's chart, it is his belief that Michael Davis has venereal disease. In support of his belief, Richard notes that Mr. Davis is a traveling salesman and that Dr. Winston gave him a large dose of penicillin for what was claimed to be an upper respiratory infection.

Mrs. Davis, a jealous woman, accuses her husband of infidelity based on the conversation she has overheard. She persists in harassing him to get him to confess, even though he explains that he was treated for what he believes to be a cold. Finally, in desperation, Michael Davis takes his wife to Dr. Winston to have the doctor explain to her that Michael has in fact been treated for an upper respiratory infection and not for venereal disease.

Dr. Winston confirms Michael Davis's claim and finds out, in questioning Mrs. Davis, that she has based her accusation on a conversation between two of his medical assistants. Dr. Winston confronts Amy Stein, who confirms the substance of the conversation and the statements made by Richard Carter. Dr. Winston then promptly fires Richard Carter from his employment.

Analysis of this example should indicate that the least that can happen to Richard Carter is that he is fired from the employment of Dr. Winston. Mr. Davis would have much difficulty asserting an action for slander against Richard, since no actual compensatory damages can be demonstrated. After all, only Michael's wife and Amy Stein, the other assistant, are recipients of the statement. Mrs. Davis does not dissolve her marriage from her husband as a result of the statement, and the only real harm that Michael can demonstrate is the harassment he has received from his wife.

However, Michael might be able to maintain an action against Richard Carter for negligent infliction of emotional distress, which is recognized as another type of tortious conduct in some jurisdictions. This lawsuit would be based on Richard Carter's knowledge that patients do routinely sit outside the alcove and can overhear such conversations. The mental anguish suffered by Michael as a result of the statements made by Richard could be sufficient to demonstrate Michael's damages.

More important, an action for defamation of character could be maintained by Michael against Richard Carter in those jurisdictions that recognize that a statement that a person has a **loathsome** disease constitutes slander *per se*. In those states, Michael could maintain an action for punitive damages against Richard after demonstrating that his actual damages are at least nominal. Nominal damages could include the cost of gas used in going to the doctor's office for the purpose of clarifying the nature of Michael's illness.

PER SE DEFAMATORY WORDS

The common law recognizes that words that by themselves render a defamatory sting are considered defamatory *per se*. Statements that accuse a woman of unchastity, accuse a person of having a loathsome disease, disparage a person's profession, or accuse a person of committing a crime are considered defamatory without any further explanation. However, there is no uniform agreement about the kind of crime the accusation addresses that is actionable. Some states say the crime must be a felony such as arson, rape, murder, mayhem, burglary, or other major offense. Others say the crime must be one that involves **moral turpitude**. Thus, accusing someone of a misdemeanor such as driving a vehicle while under the influence of alcohol or running a stop sign would not constitute slander or defamation *per se*.

Words that disparage a person's profession are in many states considered defamatory on their face. For example, calling a doctor a quack or a butcher or calling an attorney a shyster has been held to constitute defamation *per se*.

Words that accuse a woman of being a hooker, a streetwalker, or a "lady of the evening" or that in some other way indicate her unchastity have likewise been held to be defamatory *per se*. And statements that depict a person as suffering from a loathsome disease such as leprosy, syphilis, or some similar venereal disease have also been held to be defamatory *per se*.

The person to whom the statements refer need not *demonstrate* that such statements rendered a defamatory sting. Further, jurisdictions recognizing such statements to be defamatory *per se* often do not require the plaintiff to demonstrate that he or she suffered actual compensatory damages. Such states enable the plaintiff to seek a claim for punitive damages against the person who made the statement even though the plaintiff suffered no compensatory loss. In other words, the statement itself demonstrates that it was made with the intention of ridiculing the person to whom it was directed. Such ridicule is tantamount to malice or ill will.

In the example cited in the preceding section, Michael Davis could maintain an action for defamation of character against Richard Carter in many jurisdictions. His success in such an action would be predicated on showing that the words that accused him of having a venereal disease were tantamount to defamation *per se*. Accordingly, Mr. Davis would not need to demonstrate that he actually suffered public ridicule or other actual money damages in order to maintain his action against Richard Carter for punitive damages. The words accusing him of having a loathsome disease would in and of themselves be enough to demonstrate that the statement was made by Richard with malicious intent to injure his reputation or subject him to ridicule. Such ridicule could easily be demonstrated by Michael Davis based on his wife's continued harassment.

PER QUOD DEFAMATORY WORDS

Words that by themselves are not necessarily defamatory but are understood by another person to carry a defamatory sting are classified as defamatory *per quod*. Calling a person a deadbeat may not in and of itself render a defamatory sting. However, where Doris Miller's statement calling Kim Santa a deadbeat is overheard by the banker, it is the banker's interpretation of the term *deadbeat*, coupled with a telephone call regarding Kim's bill, that renders the defamatory sting and makes the statement slanderous.

Where the words are not defamatory *per se* actual compensatory damages must be established by the plaintiff before he or she may maintain an action for punitive damages against the person who made the statement. In the case of Kim Santa, (assuming he could show that he would have gotten the loan if the banker hadn't heard Davis Miller's statement), he could demonstrate that he suffered actual monetary loss when the banker turned down the loan. Meeting this prerequisite, he could thereafter maintain an action against Doris Miller and possibly Dr. McCormick for punitive damages. The purpose of this form of punishment would be to teach them to think twice before making, or allowing to be made, such statements about other people in the future.

RUMORS AND REPUBLICATION

Undoubtedly, every reader of this text has at some point been guilty of conveying rumors or gossip. Gossip about other people, whether true or untrue, is as commonplace in modern American society as apple pie and the American flag. No discussion of slander would be complete without an analysis of the potential legal hazards of gossip and rumors. We have already seen that the person making a slanderous or otherwise defamatory statement about another person may be held liable to that person for damages. These include not only compensatory or actual money damages but also punitive damages for making the untrue statement. The key phrase here is "the person making the slanderous statement." Caution should be exercised by third persons who hear and repeat defamatory statements.

As previously discussed, a person may be held liable for making an untrue statement about another person without reasonable grounds for believing such a statement to be true. The statement must subject the person to whom it refers to public ridicule or must injure his or her character, fame, or reputation. As we have seen, the tort (wrong) is complete by the mere intent to make the statement. No ill will is necessary to demonstrate malicious intent in making the statement.

Doctrine of republication

The *doctrine of republication* means that all persons who convey or reconvey to another person a false and malicious statement that injures a third person's character, fame, or reputation may be held just as liable as the person who made the original statement. Thus, where Richard Carter made the false statement to Amy Stein about Michael Davis having venereal disease, Richard may be held liable for a lawsuit base on such slanderous statements. However, Amy Stein may likewise be held liable in a suit for damages based on defamation of Michael's character if she then reconveys the original statement to some other person. The suit would be based on the premise that Amy republished the statement. Republication of the statement by Amy must include the implication that the defamatory statement is true. When it is understood by some other person to render a defamatory sting to Michael's fame, character, or reputation, Amy can be held accountable for slander.

Republication of a statement that then gives rise to a suit for defamation of character has included cases where the persons republishing the statement did not necessarily believe the truth of the allegation. However, the person to whom the statement was republished did believe the statement to be true and damaging to the defamed person's character, fame, or reputation. Amy Stein might not have believed the statement made by Richard Carter. Had she nevertheless conveyed the statement to some other person who did believe it to be true, she could be held accountable in a lawsuit based on republication of a slanderous statement.

Amy could not use as a defense the fact that she attributed the statement to Richard Carter. Mere republication of the false defamatory statement would be sufficient for Michael Davis to maintain his action for slander against Amy as well as against Richard.

Preventing republication

However, it is a defense to an action for defamation of character to report that the statement was made about a person for the purpose of stopping any further republication—that is, any further spreading of the rumor. Cases on the subject have largely dealt with the presentation of evidence that such republication of the statement was done to save a person's character rather than to expand the rumor.

Remember the example of Nurse Ross, Nurse Rivera, and Dr. Tanaka in which Nurse Rivera reported the slanderous statement to the hospital administrator. Nurse Rivera would escape liability in any lawsuit brought by Dr. Tanaka against her for republication of the statement because she reported it to the hospital administrator. Of course, she would have to demonstrate, through testimony of the hospital administrator and others, that she was merely reporting that a defamatory statement had been made by Nurse Ross about Dr. Tanaka, as opposed to carrying a tale or rumor about the doctor. In the cited example, Nurse Rivera's true intent in reporting the statement to the hospital administrator is unclear. However, in the absence of any facts or justification for the reporting, the ultimate damage suffered by Dr. Tanaka was restriction in his ability to practice within the confines of the hospital. He could undoubtedly maintain at least a **prima facie** case against Nurse Rivera for defamation of character in republishing a slanderous statement to the hospital administrator. Nurse Rivera would then have the obligation to make a rebuttal.

A way of restating or reporting a slanderous statement that would not amount to republication may be seen in the example of Richard Carter and Amy Stein. Amy reported to Dr. Winston the comment made by Richard because she felt it was unjustified and possibly defamatory. Such reporting would not amount to republication regarding Michael Davis's alleged venereal disease. In this regard, Amy would be reporting the comment to the doctor in an attempt to short-circuit or otherwise prevent further republication or direct publication of the untrue statement about Mr. Davis. For this reason, Amy would have a complete defense in any lawsuit brought by Mr. Davis for republication of the slanderous statement to Dr. Winston.

Using caution In republishing statements

From the analysis of the two cited examples, it should be clear that it is one thing to report one's belief that a defamatory statement about a person has been made to some third person and another thing to convey a rumor regarding a person's character, reputation, fame, or professional conduct. Be cautious in clarifying your position and intent when conveying any statement that you have no reason to believe is true, especially for the strict purpose of reporting that the statement was made by another person. Indicate to the person to whom you are conveying the statement that you are merely reciting the statement for the purpose of reporting your feeling that the statement may be defamatory. Merely reporting that a statement was made, without any expression of belief or disbelief of its truth, may still subject the reporting person to liability based on republication.

LIBEL

Traditionally, libel is a written defamatory statement, in contrast to slander, which is a spoken defamatory statement. However, libel has been expanded in modern society to include defamatory statements conveyed through the medium of radio and television. The main distinction between libel and slander is that defamatory statements that are libelous are generally more permanently affixed or reach a greater number of people. The law has made this distinction between libelous and slanderous defamatory statements because memory tends to fade over time. A defamatory statement printed in a newspaper, magazine, or other periodical publication is likely to be encountered and understood by a greater number of persons than a statement spoken by an individual. Also, the chances of the publication's being reread in the future by someone who may not have initially heard or understood the defamatory statement are greater than the chances of a defamatory statement's being repeated by word of mouth. Thus, the potential for the continuous injury of a person's character, fame, or reputation in the community sometime in the future is vastly enhanced.

The law has met this enhancement by allowing the defamed person the potential for recovering punitive damages without demonstrating any actual compensatory loss at the time the initial statement is published. The potential of future compensatory damage arising from the statement makes it unnecessary for the plaintiff to demonstrate actual damages at the time of trial. This distinguishes this element of the lawsuit based on libel from the corresponding element of the lawsuit based on slander.

Extent and forms of libel

To constitute libel, a statement need not be published in a circular, magazine, newspaper, or other publication of general circulation to the public at large. It is enough that the statement is written and may be viewed by persons at sometime in the future. Thus, where a defamatory statement has been made about a patient on his or her medical chart, such statement is considered libelous because the chart, including any defamatory statement, may be reviewed by numerous people in the future, including treating physicians, institutions, therapists, attorneys, and the courts. Such defamatory statements are considered libelous because the patient could potentially suffer criticism, ridicule, or diminishment of his character, fame, or reputation at sometime in the future.

Just as with cases dealing with slander, libel has been divided by many courts into *libel per se* and *libel per quod*. Statements that deal with the chastity of a woman, accuse another of a crime, disparage a person's profession, or accuse another of having a loathsome disease are considered libelous per se. Statements that do not render a defamatory sting without further clarification of the terms or of the character of the person about whom the statement is made are considered libelous *per quod*.

False and unprivileged publication constituting libel is not confined to mere statements in written form. Libel may also take the form of a picture, a three-dimensional effigy, or some other image or object that some third person might identify and associate with the defamed person. Such an image or object that exposes the person to hatred, ridicule, or contempt, that causes the defamed to be shunned or avoided or that injures his or her reputation is considered libelous.

Case example

A libelous statement relating to medical chart entries may be seen in the following example. Mr. and Mrs. Nelson, both patients of Dr. Lawrence, are periodically seen in his office for various ailments, Mr. Nelson is a pleasant individual, soft-spoken and somewhat reserved. He gets along well with Dr. Lawrence and all of Dr. Lawrence's office personnel.

In contrast, Mrs. Nelson is an obstinate, demanding, boisterous person who is generally not liked by the office personnel. Likewise, she is not Dr. Lawrence's favorite patient because of her demanding demeanor and attitude and her tendency to be overbearing.

Mr. Nelson goes in to Dr. Lawrence's office one day with the chief complaint that he is upset and nervous. This nervousness causes his stomach to be "tied up in knots," and he has been experiencing nausea and vomiting that he attributes to his nervousness. The symptoms are quite real, even though Mr. Nelson cannot give a reason or a cause for his nervousness. Dr. Lawrence decides that the best approach to take in treatment of the condition is to hospitalize Mr. Nelson for further examinations.

Dr. Lawrence dictates an admitting history and physical examination of Mr. Nelson, which is transcribed by hospital personnel. Dr. Lawrence makes the statement in the history and physical examination that the nervousness causing Mr. Nelson's symptoms are undoubtedly due to his "constantly nagging wife. A wife like Mrs. Nelson would certainly drive anyone crazy and give them an ulcer."

Mr. Nelson remains in the hospital for four days. His stomach disorder is ultimately diagnosed as a severe case of influenza, and his nervousness attributed to extreme fatigue caused by his job, though this information is not recorded in his medical record.

Subsequently, Mr. and Mrs. Nelson move from the area and request to have their medical records transferred to Dr. Smith, their new family doctor. On their receipt, Dr. Smith reviews all the prior medical records, including the admission summary prepared by Dr. Lawrence regarding the hospitalization of Mr. Nelson. When Mr. Nelson later goes to Dr. Smith with the chief complaint of nausea and vomiting, Dr. Smith indicates to Mr. Nelson that his nausea and vomiting may possibly be due to his "constantly nagging wife," as outlined in the previous medical records. This comment is made even though Dr. Smith has never even seen or met Mrs. Nelson. Thereupon, Mrs. Nelson brings an action against Dr. Lawrence for defaming her character and reputation.

Just as in the cases dealing with slander, calling Mrs. Nelson a "constantly nagging wife" may not in and of itself constitute a defamatory sting. However, coupled with the statement is Mr. Nelson's hospitalization and treatment for nausea and vomiting. Absent from the prior hospital admission record is the fact that Mr. Nelson's nervous condition was due to his job. Thus, anyone reading the statement in the hospital records—for example, a subsequent physician or his office personnel—would tend to shun or avoid Mrs. Nelson. A jury would probably find that the statement as written in the medical records constitutes libel.

Libel of persons receiving public assistance

Another example of a written statement constituting libel by rendering a defamatory sting has emerged in cases where people are receiving public assistance. Commonplace throughout the United States are indigent persons who, among other public assistance benefits, may receive medicare, medicaid, medical, or some similar medical subsistence allowance provided by the federal or local government. It is common knowledge that the government agency rarely pays 100 percent of the charges incurred for professional services rendered. In addition, peer review committees established by the administrating agency on behalf of the federal or local government have heavily scrutinized medical charges and have, in some cases, taken the position that some medical charges are excessive. This, in turn, has caused much hard feeling among doctors, hospitals, and other health care professionals and institutions that treat patients on such programs.

Instances of "welfare fraud" committed by the professional rendering treatment and by individuals on the program have been widely publicized. Also, stories have been written and songs have been recorded about welfare recipients driving expensive cars and living in expensive homes at the taxpayer's expense. Through public accusations in the media, popular recordings, and personal contacts with persons on the welfare rolls, a popular stereotype has emerged of the "typical welfare recipient"—a person of questionable integrity and cleanliness. Little material has been written, spoken, or otherwise **disseminated** describing a welfare recipient as a person of impeccable character or reputation.

Problems can easily arise in defaming a welfare recipient's character, fame, or reputation in the community by using the stereotyped phrase "typical welfare recipient." Interestingly enough, defamation can arise from a mere assertion of the patient's status as a welfare recipient without some clarification of the meaning of the statement.

For example, where a nurse or medical assistant discloses to a fellow nurse, assistant, or other professional that a patient is a "typical welfare recipient," the use of the term *typical* may be sufficient to constitute an action for damages based on defamation of the patient's character. Such an action would be especially well supported when the patient receives less than adequate care from the professional or institution to which he or she is referred. Just as in the case of Mrs. Nelson, the "constantly nagging wife" in the previous example, the patient may be able to maintain an action for punitive damages where he or she has been shunned or avoided by subsequent treatment personnel because of being classified as a "typical welfare recipient." The description of the patient as "typical" coupled with the popular connotation of the term *welfare recipient* renders the defamatory sting. For this reason, the patient may have little difficulty demonstrating adequately to a judge or jury that such a statement was made with the motive of ill will toward the patient.

Libel in other forms

As previously stated, defamation in a nonwritten form may nevertheless be viewed as libel. Remember that a statement is libelous when more permanency of the defamatory sting becomes permanently associated with the person or, when the statement is disseminated in a form in which many persons may hear and understand it. Originally, the strictness of the law in this interpretation of libel disallowed recovery for statements broadcast over radio and television. Such defamatory statements were considered slander because they were verbal. The courts today, however, have recognized that most radio and television programs are recorded on tape. The program may be rebroadcast, just as the written statement may be reprinted. For this reason, the courts now take the position that, when defamatory statements are made about a person on a radio or television broadcast, such statements are considered libel. The rationale has been put forward that such statements, when made over these media, reach a far greater number of people. The defamed person's reputation and chances for suffering actual compensatory damages are greater because of the potential for rebroadcasting the program in the future.

The courts have likewise held that photographs, cartoons, and even dolls depicting a person in a light that subject that person to public ridicule, scorn, hatred, or ill will or otherwise cause the person to be shunned or avoided may constitute libel in defaming that person's character, fame, or reputation in the community. Why, then, do we not see libel suits filed daily by the president of the United States, members of Congress, and movie and television actors and actresses stemming from political and theatrical cartoons published in newspapers or magazines?

One defense to defamation of character based on libel has been recognized by the courts in cases where the person being depicted in a cartoon or statement has notoriety or is otherwise a public figure, and the subject of the cartoon or statement published is newsworthy. The courts have recognized this defense to the action of libel by the person disseminating the material or information. However, this defense only applies to *newsworthy* situations about public figures or to persons who are currently newsworthy. It does not apply to the average patient or to the person who may live next door to you.

DEFAMATION OF UNIDENTIFIED PERSONS

One last area of caution should be explored before leaving the topic of defamation of character: situations in which the defamatory statement is made about an unidentified person. These situations arise where the person making the defamatory statement does not specifically name the person to whom the comment refers but in other words identifies that person. It makes no difference whether the statement is slanderous or libelous, defamation *per se* or defamation *per quod*—the previously cited rules regarding defamation apply in these situations as well.

Consider the following example. Nurse Kent works at the local hospital. During a conversation with three or four other hospital staff members, she states that one of the nurses who works at the hospital must be a "streetwalker" because she looks like one. Everyone participating in the conversation understands Nurse Kent's comment as implying that the nurse is a prostitute. However, Nurse Kent does not tell the other nurses to whom the statement refers.

If only one nurse at the hospital wears flashy street clothing, short uniforms on duty, gaudy jewelry; and heavy makeup—often considered the signs of a prostitute—that nurse would undoubtedly have a cause of action against Nurse Kent for defamation of character. Although this is an extreme example, many similar situations arise in offices and hospitals, where rumors, gossip, and other small talk are commonplace.

Where untrue statements are made about the condition, attitude, or other characteristics of a patient whose name remains anonymous but who is identified by other means, the patient may be able to maintain an action for defamation of character against the person or persons making or republishing the statement. For example, where the defamatory statement is made about a male patient in a ward with only one male patient, that patient would have little difficulty demonstrating that the defamatory statement was about him. Likewise, where a defamatory statement is made about the only red-haired physical therapist, the only Hispanic radiological technologist, or the only nurse on a particular shift whose demeanor resembles an army sergeant's, the defamed would not be hard-pressed to demonstrate that the statement concerned him or her.

We cannot overstress the importance of refraining from gossip and the spreading of rumors, even though several defenses against liability are available in defamation of character cases. Caution should likewise always be exercised when discussing a patient's history, diagnosis, prognosis, or bill or when expressing other personal opinions about a patient or fellow professional. Nothing is to be gained by disseminating a false or malicious statement, whether originally or by republication. At the very least, a person may receive a reprimand for spreading false rumors; more probably, one will incur loss of employment or a lawsuit.

One final note on dealing with intentional torts in general and with defamation of character cases in particular: Doctors and many professional personnel carry malpractice insurance for the purpose of defending and **indemnifying** themselves against lawsuits for tortious conduct. However, it is against public policy, and in many states, governed by statute, that the insurance company cannot insure a person for **indemnification** of his or her intentional acts amounting to tortious conduct. That is, the insurance company may be obligated to defend an action brought by a patient against a professional for defamation of character or some other intentional tort. However, the insurance company would not be obligated to pay the injured person any award for punitive damages made against the wrongdoer. Thus, any award for punitive damages against a wrongdoer is assessed against that person only. The successful plaintiff may attach the wrongdoer's house and force a sheriff's sale, **garnish** his or her wages, or use any other legal means to secure payment on the judgment.

DEFENSES TO DEFAMATION OF CHARACTER

One defense to defamation of character that has already been mentioned is the case where the person making the statement is merely republishing it for the purpose of reporting that the statement was made. This reporting contrasts with republication of the statement as a matter of unfounded gossip.

But truth is the main defense to actions based on defamation of character. If the allegedly defamatory statement, taken as a whole, is true, there is no basis for an action of defamation to be asserted. Truth is a complete defense to the plaintiff's right to recovery.

However, the more abstract the statement that forms the basis of the defamatory action, the less likely it is that the defense of truth can be maintained. When the statement is abstract, the person whose reputation has been injured may be able to demonstrate to the judge or jury that the statement can have many connotations. Only one or two of these connotations could be asserted as being true, leaving the balance of the others untrue. Remember that it is the connotation understood by the person hearing or reading the statement or publication that forms the basis for the injured party's right to recovery. Thus, truth may not be asserted as a complete defense to the statement, even though the statement was not meant to be defamatory. For example, a medical assistant or nurse may be depicted by a fellow professional as a "blue-eyed sex goddess." Even though the medical assistant or nurse is an attractive, blue-eyed woman, truth may not be asserted as a complete defense to the statement. It makes little difference that the person making the statement actually meant it as a compliment. If the medical assistant or nurse could demonstrate that some of the persons who heard the statement viewed it as implication of unchastity, the defense of truth would fail.

EXAMPLES / QUESTIONS / PROJECTS

1. Ken Stuart is angry at Dr. Horton and his office staff, particularly with Barbara, the front-office assistant, who turned his account over to a collection agency for nonpayment of his bills. One day, Ken sees Barbara standing three patrons back from him at the checkout counter in the supermarket. At this time, he comments to another patron and to the clerk at the store "There's Barbara, the butcher's assistant." Everyone who hears Ken's statement knows that Barbara works for Dr. Horton. Could Dr. Horton and Barbara maintain an action against Ken for defamation of character?

Answer: Both Dr. Horton and Barbara could undoubtedly maintain an action against Ken based on defamation of character. Dr. Horton could maintain the action because the term "butcher" disparages his profession and is thus defamatory *per se*. In most states, Dr. Horton would not have to show that he actually suffered compensatory damages to maintain his action for punitive damages against Ken because of the *per se* connotation of the statement.

Likewise, Barbara could maintain a similar action against Ken for defaming her character. Although the phrase "butcher's assistant" constitutes defamatory words against the doctor, the phrase carries the connotation that Barbara, as the doctor's assistant, stands in the same light. Such defamatory words disparage her profession as well as the doctor's and are thus defamatory *per se*. In most states, Barbara would not need to demonstrate actual compensatory damages to maintain her action against Ken for punitive damages.

2. *Another example is when the medical assistant telephones Amy Lou Smith and states in jest that "Your pregnancy test is positive." If Amy Lou is subsequently turned down for a job by a prospective employer who is a patient seated in the office waiting room and who hears the statement, could she maintain an action against the medical assistant based on defamation of her character?*

Answer: Yes. The medical assistant would be somewhat hard-pressed to argue as a defense that the statement was made merely as a practical joke. The connotation understood by the prospective employer is the key to Amy's ability to maintain her action based on defamation of her character. She could show she suffered compensable damages by the fact that she was subsequently turned down for a job because the prospective employer would not hire her due to pregnancy. Once compensable damages are established, Amy would be able to seek the imposition of punitive damages against the medical assistant to make that person think twice before making "practical-joke" statements about people in the future.

3. *Kate Blake routinely pays her bills in cash. Recently she paid General Hospital for services rendered when she was treated in the emergency room. However, the bookkeeping department of General Hospital failed to make the proper notation that payment had been made and the hospital turned her account over to a collection agency to obtain payment. The collection agency thereafter, without contacting Kate or investigating any further, reported General Hospital's action and the alleged outstanding balance to a credit-*

reporting agency. Kate did not discover all this activity until she was rejected for a home mortgage loan and was told that the reason for the rejection was the outstanding account with General Hospital. Could Kate maintain an action for defamation of her character?

Answer: Yes. She could maintain a libel action against the hospital because it wrongfully turned her account over to the collection agency. Additionally, she could maintain an action against the collection agency for libel in republishing the original false accusation regarding her account. In an action based on libel, she need not show she suffered actual compensatory damages before seeking punitive damages against these defendants.

CHAPTER ELEVEN

INVASION OF PRIVACY AND FALSE IMPRISONMENT

Key Terms

invasion of privacy
malice
intentional infliction of
emotional distress

emancipate
derisive

false imprisonment
duress
arrest

In defamation of character cases, as noted in the previous chapter, truth is a complete defense. However, this defense should not be taken to mean that patients or other persons cannot maintain an action against a medical assistant, nurse, or other professional for making or republishing true statements about them—especially when the true statements injured their character, fame, or reputation.

INVASION OF PRIVACY

The recognized tort of **invasion of privacy** is of relatively modern origin. The action may provide a remedy to a person for damages sustained when an action based on defamation of character would fail because the statement is true.

Premises for damages

The main premise in establishing and awarding damages in an invasion of privacy case is that a direct wrong has been suffered by a person because of a statement published without any regard to the effect that the publication might have on the property, business, financial interests or community standing of the individual. The damages awarded are essentially the same as those associated with defamation of character. However, the damages are not awarded because of an injury to the character or reputation of the injured party but because of a violation of the individual's right to privacy and peace of mind. This right includes the right to be left alone to live an ordinary, private life without being subjected to unwarranted or undesired publicity. In defamation of character cases, in contrast, the damages arise from the dissemination of false and misleading statements that primarily concern one's reputation.

Malice is not an element of the tort of invasion of privacy, and, without the element of malice, punitive damages may not be obtained by the injured plaintiff. However, the tort of **intentional infliction of emotional distress** has often been associated and claimed as an additional cause of action by an injured plaintiff in his or her suit based on invasion of privacy. The injured plaintiff in many jurisdictions may maintain an action for punitive damages where he or she can demonstrate that the information was disseminated or the statements were made by the wrongdoer with the motive of causing the person actual injury.

Remember that the motive of ill will is tantamount to malice. The successful plaintiff, in demonstrating that the information was released by the wrongdoer with the intent to cause emotional distress, would be entitled to receive punitive damages in addition to compensatory damages.

Privacy of minor women

It is now generally recognized that a female patient who has not reached the age of majority or is otherwise **emancipated,** such as being married or in the military, may seek medical attention in certain situations without the express authorization of her parent or legal guardian. Examinations or treatment for the limited purpose of detecting venereal disease or pregnancy or prescribing legally recognized methods of birth control do not require the parent's consent in many states. In these situations, the minor is treated as an adult for all intents and purposes. Accordingly, any statements about such examinations or treatment may not be made to third parties without the express consent of the patient. To disseminate materials such as the patient's chart or to make statements regarding the girl's treatment to some third person would subject the person making the statement to the risk of a lawsuit based on the invasion of the patient's privacy.

For example, if a minor, unmarried girl has been examined by a doctor for possible pregnancy, she could maintain an action against a medical assistant or nurse based on her right to privacy if the medical assistant or nurse telephones the girl's home and reports the laboratory finding to the mother, father, stepmother, stepfather, brother, sister, or anyone other than the patient herself. In addition, an action could possibly also be maintained against the doctor or treatment facility based on the doctrine of *respondeat superior* (see Chapter 5).

Inadvertence as an inadequate defense

A similar situation often arises when the medical assistant or hospital or office staff person telephones the patient regarding payment of his or her bill. We have seen that the patient may maintain an action for defamation of character should untrue statements be made and heard by someone other than the patient. However, where the statement is true, the patient may still maintain an action for invasion of privacy if the statement is overheard by some third person, such as the patient's banker. Neither inadvertence nor mistake is a defense to the cause of action by the injured person based on the violation of his or her right to privacy. Thus, mere inadvertence in not knowing that the patient's banker was seated in the waiting room and overheard the conversation would not be a defense to the action brought by the patient based on the invasion of privacy. Likewise, the medical assistant or nurse reporting the results of the pregnancy examination in the previous example could not maintain a complete defense where she gave the results of the pregnancy test to the minor's mother inadvertently, thinking that she was talking to the minor girl.

INVASION OF PRIVACY IN THE HEALTH CARE SETTING

The unwarranted disclosure of a person's private affairs, the unauthorized, noncommercial use of a photograph of a person, or the commercial exploitation of a picture or a person's name has traditionally given rise to an action for invasion of privacy. However, the tort has been expanded to include other areas that might give rise to a violation of a person's right to privacy.

In the realm of the examination and treatment of patients, the truth is that most professionals are merely trying to get their job done. Routinely, medical assistants, nurses, aides, and other allied health professions punch a time clock. They are subjected to constant pressure to get the job done throughout their working day. Hence, many professionals attempt to take shortcuts in handling or transporting patients while carrying out their routine duties.

Patients are commonly requested to disrobe for examinations or treatments. Unless express consent has been given by the patient, persons other than those rendering the examination or treatment are not allowed to be present. This includes all nonessential personnel, both medical and nonmedical.

Nevertheless, how many times has a patient wearing only a thin, open-backed patient gown been lying on the X-ray table when someone from the housekeeping department of the hospital has come in to clean a sink? How many times has a nurse, aide, or other medical assistant transported a patient down a hospital hallway wearing only a thin patient gown? How many times has a patient wearing such a gown been requested to walk in front of other patients en route to the office laboratory? How many times have disrobed patients been exposed to students, medical assistants, nurses, aides, technicians, or other nonessential students or personnel? In all these situations the patient's right to privacy has been severely violated. In fact, insensitivity to privacy issues, among other things, has led some states to pass legislation concerning patients' rights. For example, a Massachusetts statute (M.G.L. chapter 111, section 70E) provides that every patient of a medical facility, as defined in the statute, shall have the right, among others, to privacy during medical treatment or other rendering of care.

Where the medical assistant, nurse, technician, or other essential medical personnel allow this invasion of privacy to occur, they may be held liable to the patient. Remember that mere inadvertence or mistake is not a defense to the invasion of a patient's privacy. The only defense that can properly be asserted is based on the patient's expressly given, informed consent.

The defense of implied consent can also be raised in cases dealing with life-threatening situations. However, this defense might not be successful in cases dealing with the patient's right to privacy, since it is the presence of nonessential personnel that gives rise to the cause of action by the patient. Accordingly, the patient may properly assert that consent was not given to the presence of nonessential medical or nonmedical personnel when the life-saving procedure was undertaken by essential personnel.

It has also been held that photographs depicting a patient's ailment, affliction, or injury may not be taken without the patient's express authorization. To do so is to violate the patient's right to privacy. The rationale of the courts has been that the photographs are not in and of themselves necessary in rendering a diagnostic impression and could easily be viewed by persons that the patient may not wish to see them. This rationale would hold true even where the photographs are taken for the purpose of educational illustration.

However, photographs depicting a child's bruised body, apparent broken bones, or other injuries in cases dealing with suspected child abuse may be permitted by a law-enforcement agency to demonstrate that the minor child has been abused by his or her parent or others. Such permission may constitute a complete defense or bar to recovery of damages for violation of the minor's right to privacy. The court-appointed guardian representing the child in the child abuse case could authorize the taking of such photographs on behalf of the child's well-being, even though such authorization is given after the fact.

Similarly, a state may have a law such as that in Massachusetts under which certain health care professionals including doctors, emergency medical technicians, dentists, nurses, chiropractors, and many others are required to report evidence of child abuse. That law (M.G.L. chapter 119, section 51A) provides, among other things, that any hospital personnel preparing a report of suspected serious physical injury resulting from abuse inflicted upon a child, is permitted to take photographs of the areas of trauma visible on such a child.

NEWSWORTHY OR PUBLIC FIGURES

We have seen that there is no defense to invasion of privacy actions where a statement is made about a person whose life is not a matter of public interest. In addition, there is no defense where the statement or material disseminated is untrue and the person to whom the statement or material refers is otherwise newsworthy or a public figure. In lawsuits filed by actors and actresses against persons who make untrue statements publicized in television and movie magazines or newspapers, the dissemination of false and misleading information about the actor's or actress's private life has been held defamatory by the courts and juries, even though such persons are constantly in the public eye. Such statements or materials are held to be defamatory because they are untrue.

However, a defense does exist to making statements or disseminating material about persons who voluntarily undertake to expose themselves to publicity, such as candidates for public office, actors and actresses, and others who submit themselves to being viewed with notoriety by the general public. This defense is a complete bar to any suit brought by such a person against another based on a violation of his or her right to privacy. Of course, the statement or material that forms the basis of the lawsuit must be true and not otherwise defamatory. In addition, it must be newsworthy if it is to be properly and affirmatively asserted as a complete defense.

The California Appellate Court, in the case of *Cohen v. Marx*, held that "a person by his accomplishments, fame, or mode of life, or by adopting a profession or calling which gives the public a legitimate interest in his doings, affairs, or character, is said to become a public personage, and thereby relinquishes a part of his right to privacy."[1]

This case involved a prize fighter who had been retired from the ring for approximately ten years. The court denied the fighter recovery based on a **derisive** comment made by a radio comedian.

Newsworthiness

Political cartoons depicting the president, members of his cabinet, members of Congress, judges, and others are commonly found in newspapers and magazines. These public figures are subject to the constant ridicule of writers and cartoonists. However, the next time you read an article or glance at a cartoon, notice that such depiction is generally founded on a current event in the news. Because of the newsworthiness of the article or caricature, liability cannot be asserted. Also, the defense is based on the federal guarantees of the First Amendment of the U.S. Constitution dealing with a person's right to freedom of speech and freedom of the press. The cartoonist or publishing agency's right to freedom of the press, expression, or speech outweighs the public figure's right to privacy.

The term *newsworthiness* has traditionally been associated with actors, actresses, and other public figures. It has also been associated with professionals and others who are involved in newsworthy events. The subject matter of the publication has generally been disseminated to the public at large, making the subject matter newsworthy.

Right to privacy of health professionals

The issue of newsworthiness brings up the interesting situation where a hospital, doctor's office, or other institution causes to be posted a statement or other material about one of its employees. Although the specific depiction or statement may be true, is that person's right to privacy being violated when the subject matter is used as a reprimand or as an educational tool for other hospital personnel?

Consider the following example. Registered nurse Bill Patel has done something unorthodox in his treatment of one of his assigned patients. The hospital administration publishes a description of Bill's conduct in printed

---

[1]*Cohen v. Marx*, 94 Cal. App. 2d 704, 211 P. 2d 320 (1950).

form on the hospital bulletin board to set an example for other nurses to refrain from such conduct. Bill is then shunned by his fellow employees.

Does the publication on the hospital bulletin board constitute defamation of Bill's character? The answer is probably yes. However, the hospital administration would have a complete defense because the statement is true.

Does the publication by the hospital administration on the hospital bulletin board constitute an invasion of Bill's privacy? Probably not, since the information placed on the bulletin board is certainly "newsworthy" at the hospital in relation to the proper care of patients. The statement is placed in a particular area of the hospital where it will be viewed only by medical personnel and not by members of the general public. Further, the judge or jury hearing the case would be told that the subject matter of the statement set forth Bill's conduct in a professional capacity relating to the care and treatment of hospital patients.

What about a case in which the hospital administration publishes on the hospital bulletin board the fact that Bill was arrested and forfeited bail for being drunk in a public place while on vacation the previous summer? Bill could probably maintain an action against the hospital administration for invasion of his privacy. Since this arrest and conviction did not relate to hospital business and was not otherwise connected with Bill's professional conduct as a nurse, publication of this information would undoubtedly constitute a violation of his right to privacy. The petty offense would not be newsworthy at the time the information was placed on the hospital's bulletin board. This would likewise be the case in situations where "truthful" rumors or gossip was spread by doctors, nurses, or other allied health professionals regarding the social activities of their fellow employees or constituents.

Grounds for legal action

There are instances, however, in which public figures may maintain an action for invasion of their right to privacy. How many times have you seen a photograph of the president of the United States looking over his shoulder? Probably often. In contrast, how many times have you seen a photograph depicting the president from behind wearing nothing but an open-backed patient gown? The existence of such a photograph, let alone its publication, without his express authority would constitute a violation of his right to privacy. The same standards apply to other public figures, including, but not limited to, professional entertainers, politicians, and persons charged with criminal offenses. In other words, the taking or disseminating of the photograph or the disseminating of other truthful information regarding that person without some justification of its newsworthiness may constitute a violation of that person's right to privacy. It is not enough to maintain as a defense that the public would like to see a photograph of this nature or know the information published.

The courts have also held that a person may be held liable for invasion of another person's privacy where that person is not a public figure or person of notoriety but where the information may be newsworthy. The cases are split on this issue. Some cases have held that, where the information is given by the doctor, medical assistant, nurse, or other professional, the patient has a cause of action against the professional for disseminating such information if it is not found to be newsworthy. Similarly, other cases have held that the newsworthiness of the information disseminated may be a bar to recovery by the plaintiff. This may be true even though the information was initially given or formulated under the terms of confidentiality between the patient and the physician, medical assistant, or nurse. However, some courts have held that publication of confidential communications, including the results of examinations or treatments, constitute a violation of the patient's right to privacy, even though the information is newsworthy. Such information excludes matters that demonstrate a patient's criminal activity. In this regard, the courts have held that the patient's right to privacy outweighs the potential newsworthiness of a story. When the confidential communication to the physician, medical assistant, nurse, or other health professional makes the patient newsworthy, the defense that the story and the person are newsworthy would not be available. An example of this might be seen in the cases dealing with what have been termed "test tube babies." The procedure of fertilization outside the mother's womb, conducted in a confidential manner, may be newsworthy, However, to broadcast the mother's name to the world, without her consent over television and radio in connection with describing the procedure would violate her right to privacy.

Necessary communication of Information

Situations constantly arise within the allied health professions where the patient's condition or suspected illness must be reported to a public health agency—for example, in cases dealing with hepatitis or other highly contagious diseases. Venereal diseases, child abuse, and knife and gunshot wounds are other examples of such situations. The dissemination of this information to the public agency is required by code or statute. This requirement is a complete defense to any action brought by a patient on the basis of either defamation of character or invasion of the patient's privacy. However, caution should be exercised that the information be given only to the proper public health agency and in the manner prescribed by the code or statute.

We have also seen cases dealing with office or hospital policy in turning over a patient's bill to a collection agency or reporting nonpayment to a credit agency. Again, caution should be exercised that the information be given only to the proper agency. At no time should such information be conveyed by telephone or other means where some third party, such as another patient, might overhear. Further, nonauthorized medical personnel associated with the doctor's or hospital's practice should not have access to information regarding the patient's condition or the status of his or her bill. The patient may also be able to maintain an action against the person transmitting the information where such information is confidential and not intended to be publicly available.

QUALIFIED PRIVILEGE

As just described, the privilege of disclosure is a defense to a claim based on defamation of character or violation of a person's right to privacy where the disclosure has been made to the public health department as required by law. This defense applies even in cases where a report of an alleged child abuse by the parents of a minor child is made to the health department or other law-enforcement agency and is later found to be untrue. The previously discussed Massachusetts law on mandated reporting of suspected child abuse provides, for example, that, "[n]o person so required to report shall be liable in any civil or criminal action by reason of such report." It further provides that, "[n]o other person making such report shall be liable in any civil or criminal action by reason of such report if it was made in good faith;" (and as long as the person making the report is not the abuser). Likewise, reporting to a credit bureau the bad reputation of a patient for paying his or her bill is generally recognize as a qualified privilege that is asserted in the interest of protecting others.

Thus, it is possible that in some jurisdictions, a doctor, medical assistant, nurse, and other professional could advise some third person, such as a next-door neighbor, to refrain from face-to-face contact with a patient because the patient has a highly contagious disease. The fact that the patient has a highly contagious disease may properly be asserted as a defense to any action brought by the patient for violation of his or her right to privacy. This defense may also be properly asserted, and may formulate a complete bar to recovery by the patient, where the statement is made to the third party as a warning to refrain from personal contact with a patient until such time as confirmation can be made about whether the patient has in fact contracted a highly contagious disease.

It should be noted that this "qualified" statement is not made with ill will toward the patient. Rather, it is made to the interested third person for his or her protection. More important, the statement has been qualified, and the person to whom the statement is directed knows that further testing will be necessary to establish the fact that the patient has the disease. Based on this qualification, the statement on its face is not defamatory *per se*.

Finally, a qualified privilege exists in disseminating material or comments relating to a patient's condition where such dissemination is made in court or is otherwise connected with a legal or administrative proceeding. Where the patient has brought a lawsuit against someone for personal injury or has filed a worker's compensation claim, the patient has placed his or her physical and/or mental condition in issue within the lawsuit or administrative proceeding. Providing the patient's attorney or insurance company with a copy of the medical chart, photographs of the patient, or a narrative report would not be an invasion of the patient's right to privacy.

However, an original, signed authorization by the patient requesting the facility or professional to release medical or hospital information should be obtained before any such information is released. (For examples of authorization forms, see Illustrations 11.1 through 11.5.) Such forms safeguard the person releasing the information from any action asserted on the basis of a patient's right to privacy. An exception to this requirement is seen in cases where the medical information is being sought via a valid court order. In these cases, the court order completely bars any action brought by the patient against the hospital, treatment facility, or professional disseminating the requested material.

However, only material requested in the subpoena or explicitly authorized by the patient may be given to the person requesting such information. Should the hospital, treatment facility, or professional disseminate more than the information specifically requested or authorized, the patient may have a valid action for violation of his or her right to privacy against the person or institution releasing the unauthorized information. Thus, where the subpoena requests the medical or dental office to release the patient's billing records, an invasion of privacy action could be maintained if the medical or dental assistant were to release any other information, such as the medical or dental chart, regarding the patient's treatment.

FALSE IMPRISONMENT

Like invasion of privacy, **false imprisonment** is the unlawful violation of a person's right—in this case, the right to personal liberty. Although this tortious conduct has rarely been asserted as a basis for a lawsuit against doctors,

---

1. I authorize Dr._____ to disclose complete information to _____ concerning his medical findings and treatment of the undersigned from on or about _____, 19___ until date of the conclusion of such treatment.

2. Further, I authorize him to testify, without limitation, as to all of his medical findings and the treatment administered to the undersigned, in any legal action, suit, or proceedings to which I am, or may become, a party; and I waive on behalf of myself and any persons who may have an interest in the matter, all provisions of law relating to the disclosure of confidential medical information.

Witness_____   Signed _____

                                            Place_____

                                            Date_____

ILLUSTRATION 11.1 AUTHORIZATION FOR DISCLOSURE OF INFORMATION BY PATIENT'S PHYSICIAN (REPRINTED WITH PERMISSION OF THE AMERICAN MEDICAL ASSOCIATION, *MEDICOLEGAL FORMS WITH LEGAL ANALYSIS*, COPYRIGHT 1991, AMERICAN MEDICAL ASSOCIATION)

Date_____ Time_____ A.M.
P.M.

I authorize and request the _____ Hospital, and the physicians who attended me while I was a patient in said hospital during the approximate period from _____, 19___ to _____, 19___, to furnish to _____ all information concerning my case history and the treatment, examinations or hospitalization which I received, including copies of hospital and medical records.

Witness_____   Signed_____

ILLUSTRATION 11.2 AUTHORIZATION TO FURNISH INFORMATION (REPRINTED WITH PERMISSION OF THE AMERICAN MEDICAL ASSOCIATION,, *MEDICOLEGAL FORMS WITH LEGAL ANALYSIS*, COPYRIGHT 1991, AMERICAN MEDICAL ASSOCIATION)

I authorize Dr._____ to disclose complete information to _____ concerning the results of a physical examination of the undersigned made or to be made on _____, 19_____, and to testify, without limitation, as to all findings of said physical examination, in any legal action or judicial proceedings to which I am, or may become, a party; and I waive on behalf of myself and any persons who may have an interest in the matter, all provisions of law relating to the disclosure of information acquired through said examination.

Witness _____   Signed _____

                                 Place _____

                                 Date _____

ILLUSTRATION 11.3 AUTHORIZATION FOR DISCLOSURE OF INFORMATION BY EXAMINING PHYSICIAN (REPRINTED WITH PERMISSION OF THE AMERICAN MEDICAL ASSOCIATION, *MEDICOLEGAL FORMS WITH LEGAL ANALYSIS*, COPYRIGHT 1991, AMERICAN MEDICAL ASSOCIATION)

nurses, medical assistants, and other health professionals, situations have arisen that could give rise to the claim.

For example, following a course of treatment, a hospitalized person is requested by the hospital to pay the bill. His or her discharge from the facility is made contingent on fulfillment of this request. Such a threat coupled with further confinement may be viewed as a restriction of that patient's personal liberty and freedom. This restriction could give rise to the charge of false imprisonment against the facility.

Physical force or coercion is not the only criterion for the wrongful conduct of false imprisonment. The claim may also arise when a person is being restrained by threats of force or **duress**. The tort of false imprisonment

To Dr._____:
I authorize you to furnish a copy of the medical records of _____,

(state name of patient or "myself")

covering the period from _____, 19_____ to _____, 19_____ or to allow those

records to be inspected or copied by_____. I release you from all legal
responsibility or liability that may arise from this authorization.

Witness_____   Signed _____

                                                          Date _____

ILLUSTRATION 11.4 AUTHORIZATION FOR EXAMINATION OF PHYSICIAN'S RECORDS (REPRINTED WITH PERMISSION OF THE AMERICAN MEDICAL ASSOCIATION, *MEDICOLEGAL FORMS WITH LEGAL ANALYSIS,* COPYRIGHT 1991, AMERICAN MEDICAL ASSOCIATION)

AUTHORIZATION FOR RELEASE OF MEDICAL INFORMATION

TO: _____

          _____

          _____

          _____

I,_____, authorize you, upon receipt of this Authorization For Release of Medical Information or a photocopy hereof, to release to my attorney, Melinda Drew, all medical information concerning me in your possession, custody, or control. You are further authorized to provide my attorney with copies of any and all documents concerning me, including history, findings, x-ray and laboratory findings, treatment recommendations, diagnosis and prognosis.

Please note that you are prohibited from releasing any medical information concerning to me to any other person or entity without my specific written consent.

Cross out if inapplicable:

This Authorization includes permission to release any psychiatric or psychological information you have concerning me.

This Authorization includes permission to release any drug or alcohol dependency information you have concerning me.

                                                          _____

                                                          Signature of patient

                                                          _____

                                                          Date of Birth

Dated:

ILLUSTRATION 11.5 AUTHORIZATION FOR THE RELEASE OF MEDICAL INFORMATION

may thus be asserted when such comments come from hospital personnel and the patient is not discharged because payment of the bill has not been made. The tort of false imprisonment, like the tort of battery, is an intentional wrong. Accordingly, in some jurisdictions, punitive damages may be maintained if the patient can successfully prove he or she was falsely restrained by the hospital or treatment facility. The patient need not have been **arrested** for the tort of false imprisonment to apply.

The tort of false imprisonment could also properly be maintained in situations where a person is confined to a mental institution on the recommendation of some third person other than a court of law. Such confinement may be based on the statement by one spouse that the other spouse is "crazy." Thereafter, the person is confined in the institution for observation for what is supposed to be a brief period of time. The tort of false imprisonment could be maintained by the patient if further justification were not given by the treatment facility, doctors, psychiatric technicians, or other personnel that continued confinement was necessary to keep the patient from harming himself or herself or others.

EXAMPLES / QUESTIONS / PROJECTS

1. *Could a doctor or his office personnel be held liable for violation of a patient's right to privacy because office policy has patients sign in with other patients on a log or sheet when visiting the doctor or clinic?*

   Answer: Many offices and clinics routinely use patient sign-in sheets. As patients enter the office, they are requested to sign their name so that their chart can be pulled from the file cabinet. Hence, with the possible exception of the first patient all patients who enter the office are able to read the names of other patients who have been seen that day. A possible defense to any asserted claim by a patient for violation for his or her right to privacy may be maintained on the basis of the patient's implied informed consent. Each patient that signs the log obviously knows from looking at the other names on the log that other patients will see his or her name as well. Thus, if the patient wants to conceal his or her identity, he or she can refuse to sign the log. In any case, the patient will certainly be seen by the other patients in the office waiting room.

   However, one must remember that patients often blindly follow what office policy dictates. Thus, it might be considered a violation of a minor female's right to privacy if she is being examined or treated for an unwanted pregnancy without her parents' consent and her mother sees her daughter's name on the patient log.

2. *Mr. Hough is a patient of Dr. Clausen, Mr. Hough is being treated for injuries sustained as a result of an automobile accident. At the same time, a lawsuit is pending in which Mr. Hough is suing the other driver for causing him injuries. Sam Johnson, a famous plaintiff's attorney specializing in automobile accidents, telephones your office. Mr. Johnson requests you as a medical assistant to provide him with a copy of Mr. Hough's medical or dental chart and a copy of all charges incurred for treatment as a result of the accident in question. Mr. Johnson indicates that the matter is proceeding to trial the next day, and he will send a messenger over to pick up the copies in about an hour.*

What would you do in this situation?

> **Answer:** Remember that the release of any medical or dental information about a patient may be held to be a violation of that patient's right to privacy, without a valid court order or express authorization written, signed, and dated by the patient. This holds true even though you know that Mr. Johnson is, in fact, representing Mr. Hough regarding the automobile accident.

3. *How many other examples of common office or hospital policy procedures can you think of that may be held to constitute a violation of a patient's right to privacy?*

4. *Would a medical or dental assistant be liable for violation of a patient's right to privacy where the assistant files a lawsuit in a small claims court for collection of a bill and the patient's banker hears about the pending lawsuit from the medical or dental assistant himself or herself?*

> **Answer:** No. The filing of a lawsuit is a matter of public record. Even where the banker telephones the office to check on the patient's credit and finds out about the lawsuit, there is a complete defense to any action brought by the patient based on invasion of privacy. However, where the medical or dental assistant telephones all other known creditors of the patient, including the patient's banker, to notify them of the pending lawsuit for collection of the debt, the patient could possibly prevail in a lawsuit against the medical or dental assistant based on invasion of privacy. The patient could argue that other creditors would not have known of the pending lawsuit had it not been that the medical or dental assistant intentionally informed the creditors of the pending litigation. It could be argued that such an intentional act was performed with ill will or malice toward the patient.

5. *In the preceding example, would it make any difference that the patient was a judge of a local court? Is a judge a public figure? (Class discussion.)*

Chapter Twelve

MALICIOUS PROSECUTION AND ABUSE OF PROCESS

MALICIOUS
PROSECUTION

ABUSE OF PROCESS

DEFENSES TO MALICIOUS
PROSECUTION

EXAMPLES/QUESTIONS/
PROJECTS

Key Terms

meritorious
frivolous

judgment debtor

extort
demean

Malicious prosecution is tortious conduct that may entitle the defendant in an action to redress. The term implies that the plaintiff has sued the defendant with malice and without justifiable cause. The unjustifiable litigation has caused damage to the defendant's reputation as well as the expense of defending the proceedings.

Abuse of process is similar to the tortious conduct of malicious prosecution. The main distinction is that malicious prosecution is the initiation of a lawsuit, whereas abuse of process is the use of a rightful legal process for improper means.

MALICIOUS PROSECUTION

Malicious prosecution, often referred to as wrongful civil proceedings when brought in the civil rather than the criminal context, is a separate and distinct lawsuit from the main action brought by the patient/plaintiff. It starts with the patient/plaintiff's inability to demonstrate that the named defendant in the original, or underlying, action has anything to do with the patient/plaintiff's injury. In fact, the patient/plaintiff's only purpose in bringing the underlying action against this particular defendant has been harassment or personal gain. The underlying action has no **meritorious** grounds for recovery.

An example of malicious prosecution is to be found in cases where a patient brings an unfounded action against a medical assistant for causing that patient's injury. Even though the medical assistant had no connection whatsoever with the patient's examination and/or treatment, the patient sues the medical assistant unjustly for an injury that was caused by others. In this situation, the medical assistant has a cause of action against the patient/plaintiff in a subsequent lawsuit for malicious prosecution.

Most commonly, underlying case situations involve lawsuits brought by patients against doctors, medical assistants, nurses, and other professionals for professional negligence. When the lawsuit is based on malpractice, rarely can a malicious prosecution action by the defendant be maintained at a later time. This is because of the reasonable belief on the part of the plaintiff, by and through his or her attorney, that the action has validity and merit. Thus the underlying lawsuit is not being prosecuted against the doctor, medical assistant, nurse, dental assistant, or other professional solely on the basis of malice. The lawsuit is based on the plaintiff's firm belief that his or her injury was caused by someone's professional negligence as the facts are applied to the law on malpractice, which is a legal interpretation by the attorney.

The main reason for discussing the tortious conduct of malicious prosecution is its relevance to cases dealing with collection of payment. As noted in examples cited in previous chapters, lawsuits may be maintained by patients who have been defamed because of one-sided conversations about their bill. Should the medical assistant or hospital collection manager choose to bring a lawsuit against such a patient for collection of his or her bill, caution should be exercised that the bill has not previously been paid or that other credit arrangements have not been made. A lawsuit against the patient for nonpayment of a bill where the bill has already been paid can lead to retaliation by the patient in a suit for malicious prosecution. The wrongful conduct in bringing the lawsuit is considered intentional; mere mistake or inadvertence is no defense to an action based on malicious prosecution.

Consider the following example. Joan, Dr. Lee's medical assistant, is in charge of collecting on past-due bills. The account of Mr. Mallia, a patient of Dr. Lee, indicates that he owes a balance of $100. Mr. Mallia has paid this balance in full, but the ledger card was not properly credited.

The medical assistant contacts Mr. Mallia for payment of his bill, but Mr. Mallia explains to the assistant that the bill has been paid in full. Not believing him, the assistant files a lawsuit in small claims court for collection of the debt. Mr. Mallia successfully defends the lawsuit by showing the judge a receipt and cancelled checks for payment of the bill. The judge rules in Mr. Mallia's favor, finding that the debt has been paid.

Mr. Mallia thereafter brings an action against Dr. Lee and the medical assistant for malicious prosecution. The basis of his action is that the medical assistant **demeaned** his reputation within the community by filing the **frivolous** lawsuit. Does he win the case?

The answer is yes. Mr. Mallia not only collects for compensatory damages for out-of-pocket expenses in defending the prior lawsuit dealing with collection of his account, but he may also be entitled to punitive damages against Dr. Lee and the medical assistant for the sake of example. Malicious prosecution is intentional tortious conduct. The intentional conduct of the medical assistant acting on behalf of Dr. Lee may lead to an award of punitive damages.

ABUSE OF PROCESS

Abuse of process is rarely found in medical malpractice situations but is often found in collection matters. Consider the following example. Mr. Kim, a patient of Dr. Black, owes Dr. Black $500 for dental services rendered. The bill has been outstanding for some time, and Dr. Black's dental assistant brings an action against Mr. Kim in small claims court for payment of the bill. The dental assistant appears on behalf of her employer against Mr. Kim. The court finds against Mr. Kim and orders that payment be made.

Thereafter, the dental assistant files a request to have Mr. Kim appear before the court on a **judgment debtor** proceeding. The purpose of this proceeding, as explained in subsequent chapters dealing with collections matters, is to force Mr. Kim to provide certain credit information, including bank balances, the name and address of his employer, and a list of his various assets. Mr. Kim provides this information under oath.

The dental assistant, acting on behalf of the dentist, does not seek to levy against Mr. Kim's assets or to garnish his wages for payment of the judgment. She does, however, drag Mr. Kim back into court every two weeks for another judgment debtor hearing. This is abuse of a civil process.

The dental assistant is entitled to obtain debtor information by means of judgment debtor hearings. However, in the preceding example, the legally available civil process is being abused by the dental assistant on behalf of Dr. Black. The only reason the assistant is compelling the attendance of the debtor is to harass him. She makes no attempt to collect the bill other than to repeatedly drag the patient/debtor back into court. Therefore, the patient could file an action against the dentist and his assistant for abuse of a civil process, and he could obtain compensatory and, possibly, punitive damages against them if he could demonstrate that he was being taken to court merely for the sake of harassment.

DEFENSES TO MALICIOUS PROSECUTION

Reliance on the advice of an attorney may be good defense against malicious prosecution, provided that there is a full disclosure of the facts to the attorney and a resulting honest belief based on the law relating to the specific type of conduct of the defendant in the underlying case. However, the defendant in the malicious prosecution action must have disclosed all pertinent and material facts within his or her knowledge to the attorney to successfully invoke this defense. Thus, a defense based on the attorney's recommendation of a valid legal cause of action in the underlying suit must be based on *all* the facts of the case. The attorney's interpretation of the law relating to such facts and advice to the client regarding a legal basis for a lawsuit prevents the defendant in the underlying case from asserting that the underlying case is based solely on malice.

Consider the following example. Susan claims that she sustained an injury because of medical malpractice. She discusses the case with her attorney, explaining that Dr. Richards, the doctor's medical assistant, radiological technologist (X-ray technician), laboratory technician, and front-office personnel failed to properly set her broken arm. The attorney then files an action against all the personnel for failure to render proper treatment.

Susan's attorney actively serves all the named parties to the lawsuit. Each individually named defendant is forced to hire an independent attorney to represent his or her individual interests in the lawsuit. Later, it is discovered that only the doctor was responsible for setting the fractured arm. The radiological technologist, laboratory technician, front-office personnel, and medical assistant had nothing to do with the examination and/or treatment of Susan. Nevertheless, the attorney continues prosecuting all named defendants to the lawsuit, even after the radiological technologist and the laboratory technician requested to be dismissed from the case. The jury returns a verdict in favor of Susan against the doctor only.

The other health professionals named in the case could thereafter maintain an action against the attorney and the patient for malicious prosecution. It was clearly demonstrated in the underlying suit that none of these named defendants had anything to do with Susan's injury. Nonetheless, the attorney and/or Susan chose to prosecute them in an attempt to **extort** money in possibly settling the case.

EXAMPLES / QUESTIONS / PROJECTS

1. *Illustration 12.1 on the following pages lists questions that may be gone into regarding a judgment debtor's assets and other liabilities at a judgment debtor hearing. Where the judgment was obtained against a former patient, such questions may be asked by the medical assistant, dental assistant, collection manager, or other authorized representative of the doctor or hospital to whom the money is owed.*

2. *Sam Smith, Dr. John's patient, files an action on his own behalf, without the advice of an attorney, for dental malpractice. His complaint alleges that Dr. John was negligent in performing dental work involving a root canal. However, the real reason for the lawsuit is that Dr. John charged Mr. Smith what he thought to be an overinflated amount for the services. May Dr. John initiate and win a lawsuit against Mr. Smith based on malicious prosecution?*

   Answer: Dr. John could possibly be successful in an action based on malicious prosecution against Mr. Smith. However, Dr. John would have to demonstrate that the underlying suit lacked merit and was brought solely for the purpose of escaping payment for the bill. To do this, Dr. John must first win the underlying action to demonstrate its lack of merit regarding alleged dental malpractice. Thereafter, Dr. John could maintain an action against Mr. Smith based on malicious prosecution.

   However should a jury find in favor of Mr. Smith for any reason in the underlying case and award even nominal damages, a malicious prosecution action by Dr. John could not be maintained against Mr. Smith, because a jury determined the underlying case to be meritorious.

3. *Emily Dickstein is treated by Dr. Samules for abdominal pain. Dr. Samules's diagnosis of her condition is ulcer. He treats her with oral medication for this condition. He charges Emily $300 for two examinations and a prescription. Emily does not have the prescription filled, but the abdominal pain nevertheless goes away.*

   Thereafter Emily consults an attorney, conveys all the facts relating to her examinations, and states that she thinks that the bill is exorbitant. The attorney expresses his feeling that the doctor may have misdiagnosed Emily's condition, thereby touching on what may be considered to be malpractice. An action based on malpractice is then filed by the attorney on behalf of Emily. Following a trial on the underlying case, the jury returns a verdict in favor of the doctor. May the doctor thereafter maintain an action against Emily and/or the attorney for malicious prosecution?

Answer: Probably not. To prevail on an action for malicious prosecution it must be demonstrated that the underlying case was based solely on malice. The doctor could not demonstrate that Emily filed the action based on malice, because she relied on the advice of her attorney in prosecuting the suit. Likewise, an action against the attorney by the doctor for malicious prosecution would undoubtedly fail because the attorney formulated an honest belief that the doctor may have misdiagnosed Emily's condition.

```
MUNICIPAL COURT
NORTH ORANGE COUNTY JUDICIAL DISTRICT          DATE_____

CASE NO. _____ VS. _____

NAME _____ SPOUSE_____

ADDRESS_____ PHONE_____

FAMILY AND DEPENDENTS_____

OCCUPATION_____.EMPLOYER_____

ADDRESS_____ HOW PAID?_____

INTEREST IN ANY BUSINESS_____

OTHER INCOME_____

OWN HOME_____ VALUE $_____ MORTGAGE $_____ EQUITY $ _____

HOMESTEADED_____

IF YOU RENT, AMOUNT OF RENT PAID $_____ (MONTHLY) (WEEKLY)

LANDLORD'S NAME & ADDRESS_____

INTEREST IN OTHER REAL ESTATE $_____ ENCUMBERED $_____

DESCRIPTION_____

BANK_____ IN WHOSE NAME?_____

LAST BANK ACCOUNT _____ CLOSED_____

SAFE DEPOSIT BOX_____ WHERE?_____
```

ILLUSTRATION 12.1

CASH ON PERSON $_____ CASH ELSEWHERE $_____

STOCKS, BONDS, SECURITIES_____

INSURANCE_____ KIND_____ PREMIUM $_____

JEWELERY_____ INTEREST IN ESTATE_____

AUTO OR INTEREST THEREIN_____

REGISTERED OWNER_____ LEGAL OWNER_____

VALUE $_____ AMOUNT DUE $_____

OTHER VEHICLES_____ VALUE $_____

PROPERTY PLEDGED OR PAWNED_____

DEBTS OWED TO DEBTOR_____

DEBTS OWED BY DEBTOR _____

_____

ANYONE HOLDING ANY PROPERTY OR INTEREST THEREIN FOR YOU_____

_____

ANY OTHER PERSONAL PROPERTY OTHER THAN WEARING APPAREL OR HOUSEHOLD_____

_____

HAVE YOU DISPOSED OF ANY PROPERTY SINCE SERVICE OF ORDER?_____

PROMISE TO PAY_____

REMARKS_____

_____

_____

_____

ILLUSTRATION 12.1 (CONTINUED)

Chapter Thirteen

WORKERS' COMPENSATION

COMPENSATION FOR
LOST EARNINGS

PERMANENT DISABILITY

REHABILITATION AND
TREATMENT BENEFITS

COMPENSATION FOR PER-
MANENT LOSSES

EXAMPLES/QUESTIONS/
PROJECTS

Key Terms

compensable   permanent disability   temporary disability

Virtually all state governments and the federal government have laws that allow certain benefits or compensation to a worker who sustains injuries as a result of his or her employment. Many states restrict a **compensable** injury to one that occurs as a result of a specific incident or accident. Others, such as California, recognize that the overall effects that constitute the injury may occur as the result of a continuous exposure or trauma in the course of employment, without any specific incident.

For example, this type of injury occurs in cases where an employee is continually exposed to asbestos in his or her job and later develops asbestosis as a result of such exposure. Continuous trauma cases involving injury have included exposure to toxic fumes, the use of hazardous materials, work in a stressful environment, or continuous heavy lifting, bending, or stooping. Injuries have included cardiovascular or heart disorders, injury to internal organs, psychological depression or anxiety, and bone and joint disorders, including spinal injury.

To be compensable, the injury must occur or arise within the course and scope of individual's employment. Many benefits are obtainable by the injured employee where the injury is incurred in this way. These benefits arise as matter of law and are paid either by the employer or by an insurance company from which the employer has purchased coverage for such claims.

Where a workers' compensation act covers an injured employee, the compensation permitted by the statute is the employee's sole recourse against the employer. However, depending on the circumstances of the injury, the employee may be able to bring a lawsuit against another party. If, for example, an employee is injured while working on a machine and the machine is found to be defectively designed, the employee may be able to bring a lawsuit against the manufacturer of the machine even where the employee's sole remedy against his employer is workers' compensation.

COMPENSATION FOR LOST EARNINGS

An injured employee has the right to be compensated for lost earnings he or she may incur as a result of the injury. California, like most other states, limits the amount of compensation that an injured employee may receive. Generally, wage-loss compensation is a percentage of the employee's gross weekly salary, with some maximum amount allowed by a labor code provision or similar statute. In many states, the percentage and total wages allowed is reviewed and changed on a periodic basis, such as yearly. This compensation is termed **temporary disability.**

In certain situations, the injured employee may be entitled to greater compensation than allowed under the labor code. For example, teachers in the state of California who sustain a work-related injury are entitled to compensation for lost income pursuant to the California Education Code. Generally this compensation for temporary disability is greater than that allowed under the California Labor Code.

Employment compensation for lost wages is provided to the employee while his or her condition is in the process of healing and he or she is otherwise unable to do any type of work. The employee is entitled to this temporary disability compensation throughout the healing stage of his or her injury.

In certain situations, the injured employee may be able to continue light work while his or her injury is in the process of healing. The workers' compensation appeals board or similar agency, in describing the patient's condition when the patient is working, often uses such terms as *partial permanent disability* or *partial temporary disability*. In these cases, the injured employee may only receive temporary disability compensation that has been adjusted relative to any actual salary he or she may receive as a result of working. For example, an injured employee would normally work eight hours per day but is precluded from working any more than four hours per day as a result of the injury. The employee would receive his or her normal salary for the four hours worked plus additional compensation for the four hours not worked. However, most jurisdictions that follow this principle limit the compensation to the maximum allowed by law under the compensation acts.

PERMANENT DISABILITY

Another benefit that an injured employee is entitled to receive deals with any **permanent disability** or work restriction caused by the injury. The injured employee commonly receives money compensation for his or her permanent inability to compete in the open labor market for a job. Again, the amount of compensation that the employee may receive is governed by statute and is dependent on the degree or severity of the permanent disability and the type of work that the employee was doing at the time of the injury.

For example, a carpenter who injures her back and sustains a permanent disability that precludes her from work activities requiring repeated bending, stooping, or lifting would receive greater compensation for this injury and work restriction than an attorney who sustains a similar injury. The reason is that the carpenter is required by the nature of her job to do continued lifting, bending and stooping. In contrast, the general work of an attorney does not require such repeated activities. Thus, the carpenter would receive a higher percentage of permanent disability compensation than the attorney. California and most other states do not recognize the pain and suffering associated with the employee's injury as being compensable. However, the inability to work may be based on the employee's subjective complaints of pain. It is the inability to compete with someone else for a job in the open labor market for which the injured employee is being compensated.

REHABILITATION AND TREATMENT BENEFITS

Most states recognize and allow rehabilitation benefits in cases where an injured employee is unable to return to his or her former occupation or profession because of an injury. The employer or insurance company is obligated to send the employee to school to be retrained for another occupation or profession. The type of rehabilitation plan will depend on the injured employee's work restrictions, skills, basic intelligence, ability to comprehend the principles of certain types of job and interest in pursuing a particular occupation or profession.

COMPENSATION FOR PERMANENT LOSSES

In addition to compensation for lost earnings and for permanent disability, many states also allow compensation for disfigurement and/or the permanent loss of a bodily function. For example, in Massachusetts, persons who have sustained permanent losses of sight, hearing, arms, legs, or other bodily functions, or who have a permanent disfigurement, are entitled to receive an additional benefit called specific compensation, whether or not this loss is causing the person total or partial disability.

The injured employee is also entitled to be examined and/or treated for the injury by doctors, institutions, psychiatrists, or psychologists, chiropractors, physical therapists, dentists, or any other similar practitioners or technicians. All such examinations or treatments—including treatment that is initially received following the injury as well as all injury-related treatment that is necessarily rendered throughout the patient's life—are at the employer's or the insurance company's expense. Also, some states recognize that an injured employee is entitled to be examined by a physician, chiropractor, psychiatrist or psychologist, or any other health practitioner for the sole purpose of proving a contested claim of injury. This examination is termed a medical/legal examination. The need to prove a contested claim of injury arises only in cases where the injured employee has filed an application for workers' compensation benefits before the workers' compensation appeals board or a similar agency. Again, these examinations are authorized by statute and are required to be paid by the employer or insurance company on behalf of the patient (employee).

Persons employed by a state or private employer are most commonly covered by workers' compensation benefits as defined by the statute or code of the state in which they work or are injured. Federal employees (such as postal workers), maritime employees working on ships, and railroad employees are covered for workers compensation benefits by federal statutes. In either case, the benefits and compensation that the employee may receive are similar. It is primarily the procedure that the employee, his or her attorney, or the medical assistant follows in obtaining such benefits that distinguishes the two systems.

EXAMPLES / QUESTIONS / PROJECTS

1. *Is John's injury work related if it occurs in his employer's parking lot when he has already walked out and is on his way home?*

    Answer: Yes. With very few exceptions, an injury to the patient/employee that occurs in the employer's parking lot may be considered work related. Had it not been for the patient's employment, he or she would not have parked his or her car in the employer's parking lot. Thus, in these situations, the accident causing injury is generally considered incidental to the patient's employment.

2. *Would a patient's injury be work related if the injury is the result of an automobile collision occurring two blocks away from her employment when she is on her way home?*

    Answer: Most commonly, no. When the patient/employee leaves the premises of her employer, she is free to travel in any direction chosen. Unless the employee is on an errand for her employer at the time, injuries resulting from an accident would fall outside the course and scope of employment.

3. *How many work-related injuries can you name. Include continuing trauma, where the patient's overall condition is caused by continuous exposure or by the types of job duties he or she is performing. (Class discussion.)*

CHAPTER FOURTEEN

LITIGATION PROCEEDINGS

Key Terms

accusation	incarceration	consort
information	manslaughter	statute of limitations
indictment	murder	toll
grand jury	heir	ultimate facts
informant	complaint	discovery
	tribunal	

As discussed in previous chapters, there are three basic types of litigation: criminal, civil, and administrative. In criminal litigation, the people of a state or of the United States, by and through the city attorney, district attorney, or U.S. attorney, bring an action against an individual or institution on the basis of the violation of some statute or ordinance. The initiation of this type of lawsuit stems from the filing of an **accusation,** an **information,** or an **indictment.** The accusation, information, or indictment is the formal charge asserted on behalf of the people of the state or of the United States alleging that certain criminal conduct has been committed by the person named in the charges. The main difference between the filing of an information or accusation and the filing of an indictment is that an information or accusation is generally filed as a result of a criminal offense committed in the presence of a police officer. The officer in his or her official capacity makes a formal charge against the person, and the charge is merely passed on for formal prosecution to the district attorney or other counsel acting on behalf of the government.

An indictment is similar to an accusation or information in that it is a formal charge asserted on behalf of the people against an individual or institution relating to the individual's or institution's criminal activities. The indictment, however, is issued by a **grand jury** and is followed by a grand jury investigation of alleged criminal activities by the individual or institution. The U.S. attorney, district attorney, city attorney, or other counsel acting on behalf of the government or state presents the grand jury with evidence that has been collected or received by law-enforcement agencies. Following presentation of this material, the grand jury decides whether the evidence is sufficient to establish criminal conduct on the part of the person or institution.

Should the grand jury believe that the evidence is sufficient, an indictment is issued charging that person or institution informally. Thereafter, the person or institution is formally charged, and a warrant is issued for the person's arrest. In the case of criminal misconduct of an institution, the prosecuting attorney may request the court to issue other warrants involving seizure of materials. In addition, the prosecuting attorney may request closure of the institution and the issue of warrants for the arrest of certain individuals within the institution.

Pretrial hearings are generally held, whether prosecution of the case is based on an information or an indictment. For example, hearings will be held at the defendant's request to ask the court to suppress certain items in evidence that may have been illegally seized or obtained. This is especially true in serious offenses, such as felonies. In addition, there may be a defense request for the prosecution to provide defense counsel with the names of certain **informants.**

Preliminary hearings are also held in which a judge listens to the testimony of prosecuting witnesses to determine whether or not the government has a prima facie case demonstrating criminal conduct on the part of the defendant. The defendant's attorney is given the opportunity to cross-examine these witnesses to demonstrate their lack of credibility or otherwise attack the prosecution's case. The charges against the defendant are dismissed should the court find that there is insufficient evidence to warrant proceeding with the case. The matter proceeds to a jury trial should the court find that the prosecution has made a prima facie case against the defendant.

The defendant in all criminal cases has a constitutional right to have his or her case tried before a jury of his or her peers. This right may be waived by the defendant, whereupon the case would be tried before a judge only. The process of trying a case to a judge sitting without a jury is referred to as a bench trial. The prosecuting attorney may not elect to have the case tried before a judge without the express consent of the defendant being charged.

CRIMINAL CONDUCT

Criminal conduct is generally divided into three categories. Minor infractions are those, such as traffic citations, for which the penalty for disobeying the law is generally the imposition of a fine. Misdemeanors are generally associated with criminal conduct for which the penalty may be a fine and/or **incarceration** for a period not to exceed one year. Felonies are major crimes for which the penalty is generally incarceration in a state or federal penitentiary for a period exceeding one year. In addition to incarceration, fines may also be imposed against the defendant by the court.

There are very few instances in which a person can be charged with an infraction within the confines of the allied health professions. Most commonly, criminal conduct amounts to either a misdemeanor or a felony. Depending on the state or jurisdiction, common misdemeanors include the unauthorized possession of a hypodermic syringe or certain classes of drugs. In addition, the alteration of medical records for the purpose of deception is commonly classified as a misdemeanor.

Injury or death of a patient

Depending on the circumstances and the amount of aggravation, battery may take the form of a misdemeanor or a felony. The conduct would probably be termed a misdemeanor assault and battery where the touching is only minor and causes very little injury to the patient. However, the unlawful touching may be escalated to felonious assault and/or battery if the unlawful touching amounts to disfigurement of the patient. The crime of mayhem may also be asserted and prosecuted where the unlawful touching amounts to severe disfigurement.

Where a patient dies as a result of intentional or negligent conduct, such conduct may amount to felonious criminal activity. Such activities include negligent homicide, **manslaughter,** and second- or first-degree **murder.**

There has been much litigation in the United States over the issue of removing patients from life-support systems. Since the issue is a controversial one, suffice it to say that, absent a valid court order, a nurse, medical assistant, or anyone other than an attending physician should refrain from participating in any activity dealing with the cessation of treatment in the use of life-support systems. When a patient dies because treatment is stopped or a life-support system is removed without a valid court order, authorization by the lawful **heirs** of the patient, or clear demonstration that the clinical death of the patient has occurred, inquiry and prosecution are almost certain to ensue.

Possession of medication or syringes

Another common situation that occurs all too frequently and is tantamount to criminal conduct is the unlawful possession of hypodermic syringes, needles, or medication. Persons who use a hypodermic syringe and/or needle at home for some hobby or craft are generally not prosecuted for unauthorized possession. But the risk of criminal prosecution is vastly enhanced when a syringe or needle is obtained for the purpose of injecting medication into oneself or a member of one's family. When one obtains nonprescribed medication for oneself or others, one also runs the risk of criminal prosecution for such conduct, whether or not the medication is a narcotic. If the medication is a narcotic, such conduct may be felonious.

For example, consider the case in which a nurse, medical assistant, or technician obtains a syringe, needle, and some antibiotic without any specific authorization from a doctor for the purpose of treating members of his or her family for upper respiratory infections, influenza, and so on. The nurse or technician's conduct in giving the medication to other members of the household without a physician's prescription is tantamount to practicing medicine without a license—even though the antibiotic may have originally been given to the nurse or technician by a doctor for his or her personal use. Such conduct constitutes a felony for which the technician or nurse may be prosecuted. Where injury occurs as a result of a reaction to the medication, criminal prosecution may very well follow.

First aid or medical practice?

One of the most common legal questions asked by allied health professionals relates to the distinction between first aid and the practice of medicine. Medical assistants, nurses, technicians, and other nonphysicians practicing in rural areas are generally confronted with complex situations. These situations skirt the edge or boundary that separates the practice of medicine from authorized conduct amounting to first aid or otherwise falling within that person's legal mandate to practice. Obviously, a nurse, medical assistant, or other nonphysician performing open heart surgery on a person would be practicing medicine without a license and would be subject to criminal prosecution, whether or not the surgery was totally successful and saved the patient's life. It is the act itself that constitutes the criminal conduct.

But what about the situation where a patient comes into the doctor's office and asks the medical assistant or nurse what he or she would suggest for a headache? The medical assistant or nurse who tells the patient to take two aspirins and go to bed might technically be considered to be practicing medicine without a license. If the patient taking the aspirins has a perforated ulcer or is on anticoagulant therapy, he or she could very possibly die. A strong argument that the medical assistant or nurse was practicing medicine could be made in both the criminal context and the civil context if the patient were to take the aspirins on the recommendation of the medical assistant or nurse because of his or her apparent expertise in the field of medicine.

Similarly, pharmacists are continually requested by patrons to give their expert advice about the types of medication that work best for certain types of symptom. The pharmacist who makes such recommendations does so at his or her peril. Such a recommendation, if mistaken, could subject the pharmacist to civil liability. More important, some jurisdictions recognize this conduct to be a criminal activity in the form of practicing medicine without a license. The likelihood of prosecution depends on the specific recommendation made by the pharmacist to the patron, the type of medication involved, and similar related circumstances. The pharmacist can tell the patron the chemical makeup of over-the-counter medications, but any further recommendation of specific medications for certain symptoms may amount to criminal conduct.

Fortunately, guidelines have been established by the American Red Cross and the American Medical Association identifying the types of conduct that do not constitute the practice of medicine. Within these guidelines are definitions of conduct that may be performed by nonphysicians in emergency situations.

For example, *first aid* has been defined as immediate and temporary care given to a victim until the services of a physician can be obtained. Many authorized first aid practices and techniques for various types of injuries, bites, poisonings, and so on are found in the American Red Cross first aid handbook. In addition, hospitals and similar institutions have prescribed certain guidelines for emergency-room nurses and other emergency personnel, such as registered nurses working in intensive care or cardiac care units. These guidelines encompass the "standing orders," which are procedures the nurses may follow in the physician's absence. These guidelines often allow the nurse or technician to administer certain drugs, including intravenous injections for cardiac arrest. However, the importance of staying within the boundaries of first aid or of the standing orders cannot be overemphasized. Nurses or technicians performing procedures or techniques or administering any medications other than those authorized in the guidelines may subject themselves to criminal prosecution for the practice of medicine. In addition, civil liability may also be imposed by the patient against the nurse, assistant, or technician where an injury is caused by treatment that falls outside the guidelines.

Multiple allegations

The district attorney, U.S. attorney, city attorney, or other counsel for the state or federal government is not limited to charging a defendant with only one allegation of criminal conduct. Remember the situation where the nurse, medical assistant, or technician gave members of his or her household antibiotics without the medication being prescribed by physician? The prosecution attorney acting on behalf of the state or federal government could bring charges against the professional for practicing medicine without a license. Criminal charges could also be maintained for the nonauthorized possession of a hypodermic syringe, a needle, and medication. Finally, criminal charges could also be maintained against the professional for negligent homicide, manslaughter, or murder in the event that a family member died as a result of an allergic reaction to the antibiotic. Criminal charges could include a combination of any of these, with the exception of duplicate charges dealing with the death itself.

Situations dealing with injectable medication are emphasized only because of the speed of the potential reaction generally associated with such medication. The giving of oral medication, with the possible exception of over-the-counter medications such as aspirin, would likewise subject the nonphysician to the same criminal charges.

CIVIL LITIGATION

Myriad laws deal with the relationships between persons in institutions, corporations, and the like. Laws dealing with the transferring of real property, with contracts, and with personal injury were touched on at the beginning of this text. Lawsuits dealing with personal injury actions have likewise been divided into categories—such as battery, assault, negligent infliction of physical injury and emotional distress, and abandonment of patient—and have been discussed in some detail. All these types of lawsuit involve one person suing another person or an institution. The patient/plaintiff in these situations is either seeking money damages for his or her injuries, requesting the court to impose some type of restriction, or compelling performance of some obligation.

Civil litigation is initiated by a person called the *plaintiff*, who files a complaint with the clerk of the court against the other person or entity, called the *defendant*. The amount of damages sought by the plaintiff or the type of relief the plaintiff requests will determine where the complaint is filed. In cases dealing with a request for damages not exceeding a minimal amount of money, the complaint is filed in a municipal court, a district court, or a justice court, depending on the state. In Massachusetts, a case involving an amount in controversy equal to or less than $25,000 is filed in the district court. The case is filed in the superior court if the plaintiff's damages for which he or she seeks compensation exceeds $25,000. If one party lives in one state and the other party lives in another state and the amount of money in controversy exceeds $50,000, the case may be filed in the federal court on the basis of a "diversity of citizenship" between the plaintiff and the defendant.

With few exceptions, all civil cases follow the same procedural steps from beginning to end. The exceptions to this general rule are found in some court systems in states that limit certain procedural steps in the litigation process. For example, the courts in some areas of California have limited certain procedural discovery tools (depositions, interrogatories, requests for admission, and so on; see Chapter 15) available to the parties for the purpose of expediting litigation and increasing the possibility of settlement between the parties themselves. Also, small claims actions in Massachusetts and in many other states generally do not allow procedural discovery, such as depositions and interrogatories, between the parties. And small claims actions may not allow either of the parties to be represented by an attorney, except in appeals made from a small claims judgment by a defendant. In California, such an appeal is heard in the Superior Court and is basically nothing more than a retrial of the case, with the exception that the parties may be represented by an attorney. In Massachusetts, such appeals are heard by a six person jury in the district court.

All procedural steps to a civil lawsuit are discussed in the following sections and in subsequent chapters.

Notification of the defendant

Some states, such as California, require notification of the potential defendant in any medical malpractice case of the intent to file a lawsuit based on medical malpractice. Cases asserted against the health care provider require the patient/plaintiff to outline the conduct on the part of the defendant that is alleged to have constituted professional negligence and to have caused an injury to the patient/plaintiff. California requires that this notice be given to the doctor or other health care provider ninety days prior to the filing of any lawsuit based on medical malpractice. The purpose of this notice is to give the doctor or other health care provider adequate notification of the patient's grievance and an opportunity to respond to the allegations in an attempt to circumvent the necessity of a formal lawsuit. The California statute states the following:

> No action based upon the health care provider's professional negligence may be commenced unless the defendant has been given at least ninety days prior notice of the intention to commence the action.
> No particular form of notice is required but it shall notify the defendant of the legal basis of the claim and the type of loss sustained, including with specificity the nature of the injuries suffered.

If the notice is served within ninety days of expiration of the applicable Statute of Limitations, the time for the commencement of the action shall be extended ninety days from the service of the notice.

"Health care provider" means any person licensed or certified . . . pursuant to the Osteopathic Initiative Act or the Chiropractic Initiative Act or licensed pursuant to [the] . . . Health and Safety Code.[1]

Professionals to whom such notice must be given include dentists, physicians, and hospitals. Medical assistants, nurses, radiological technologists, laboratory technicians, registered physical therapists, and similar medical professionals are excluded from the notice requirement. Any attorney who files litigation without first giving the ninety-day notice as required is subject to professional discipline by the state bar association. However, failure to give the ninety-day notice does not otherwise invalidate the filing of the lawsuit.

No prescribed form of the notice has been established by the statute. The form most commonly used is a simple letter directed to the physician, dentist, chiropractor, or hospital (see Illustration 14.1).

As previously mentioned, the rationale for the ninety-day notice requirement is to enable the doctor to respond to the charges without the necessity of litigation. The notice in Illustration 14.1 would enable the doctor to respond without incurring legal expenses in defending his position. For example, he might explain that he did not repair the hernia and was in no way connected with the trauma to the elbow, or he might present some other valid defense to the allegation. The doctor would also want to turn the matter over to his malpractice insurance carrier immediately for its investigation and response to the allegation in the letter.

If the matter is not resolved within the ninety-day period required in California or those jurisdictions requiring similar notice, plaintiff's counsel would undoubtedly file a complaint alleging medical malpractice against the doctor or institution. The attorney would then request that a summons be issued on the complaint. The summons demands that the alleged defendant or, in the case of an institution, an authorized representative of the facility answer the allegations formally before the court.

Other states, such as Massachusetts, do not have a notice requirement. However, there may be other specific procedures required in medical malpractice lawsuits. For example, Massachusetts law (M.G.L. chapter 231, section 60B) requires that every action for malpractice brought against a provider of health care be heard by a **tribunal** consisting of a single judge of the superior court, a physician licensed to practice medicine in Massachusetts, and an attorney authorized to practice law in Massachusetts. If the defendant health care provider is not a physician, a representative of the field of health care from which the claim arose takes the place of the physician on the tribunal. At the hearing the plaintiff must present an offer of proof (usually an opinion of an expert in the same medical field as the defendant), after which the tribunal

---

[1]California Code of Civil Procedure, sections 364:365.

```
                    M.L. COWDREY, ATTORNEY
                       111 E. First Street
                        Anytown, CA
```

November 13, 1982

RE: JACK COLTRAINE

The undersigned has been retained by Mr. Jack Coltraine to represent him in a
claim arising from your professional treatment rendered him in July 1977.

As I understand it, my client was treated for repair of a left inguinal hernia,
which he incurred as a direct result of his employment. At that time, you
undertook to treat his complaint. Apparently, during the course of treatment
by you, Mr. Coltraine suffered trauma to his elbow that was unknown to him at
the time and subsequently diagnosed as right ulnar neuropathy, probable
pressure palsy.

Often there is more than one version of what occurred during a situation such
as this. Therefore, before proceeding, I am extending you this opportunity
to provide me with your account of the incident.

Please consider this official notice as required by Section 364 of the California Code of Civil Procedure.

In the event that you are covered by insurance for such loss, please place a
copy of this letter in the hands of your insurance carrier. In the event that
you do not carry insurance against such loss, or desire to proceed with settlement negotiations directly, please contact the undersigned within 15 days of
the date of this letter.

Thank you for your anticipated courtesy and cooperation in resolving this
matter in an expeditious and amicable manner.

Very truly yours

Michael L. Cowdrey

ILLUSTRATION 14.1   NOTIFICATION OF INTENT TO FILE LAWSUIT

must determine if the evidence presented by the plaintiff, if it were properly
substantiated, "is sufficient to raise a legitimate question of liability appropriate for judicial inquiry, or whether the plaintiff's case is merely an unfortunate
medical result."

The statute further defines health care provider as, among others, physicians, hospitals, clinical or nursing homes, dentist, nurses, optometrist, podia-
trists, chiropractors, physical therapists, psychologists, or acupuncturists.

If the tribunal decides that the plaintiff's offer of proof would not, if substantiated, raise a question of liability appropriate for a court to look into, and the plaintiff wants to pursue the lawsuit, the tribunal will order the plaintiff to post a bond with the court in the amount of $6,000, payable to the defendant for costs assessed in the case. Thus, if the plaintiff ultimately loses the case, the bond is forfeited to the defendant for the purpose of defraying his or her costs of the litigation. If the plaintiff does not file the bond within the time specified, the case is dismissed.

The complaint and its component parts

The **complaint** is the civil counterpart to a criminal accusation, information, or indictment. The main difference lies in the fact that the complaint is filed by or on behalf of an individual person or entity, whereas the criminal accusation, information, or indictment is filed on behalf of the people of a state or of the United States. As previously discussed, the person bringing the lawsuit is the plaintiff, who charges certain misconduct against the defendant.

A sample of a general complaint for medical malpractice is given in Illustration 14.2. This complaint charges a hospital and certain doctors with professional malpractice in failing to properly diagnose and treat a patient/plaintiff for an alleged back injury. In addition, the wife of the patient has also joined in the lawsuit as a party plaintiff alleging a loss of consortium sustained by her as a result of the injuries her husband sustained because of the alleged malpractice. Although this complaint is not asserting any alleged conduct for battery, the plaintiff's attorney could insert a general allegation charging assault and/or battery as a third cause of action if the facts so indicated.

The complaint may be broken down into its component parts. The first paragraph indicates that possibly more than the named defendants were responsible in some way for the plaintiff's alleged injury. The plaintiff is allowed to allege these unknown parties as *DOE defendants* I through some specified number because these potential defendants were not known to the plaintiff at the time the lawsuit was filed.

The second paragraph identifies the hospital where the alleged misconduct causing the plaintiff's injuries occurred. The plaintiff also alleges additional DOE defendants in paragraph 2. The purpose of this allegation is to allow the plaintiff to amend the complaint, if necessary, to set forth the true names of the institution and the true names of any other institutions that may have been involved in the alleged malpractice.

Paragraph 3 identifies the specific doctors involved in the alleged malpractice. Like paragraph 2, paragraph 3 contains an additional allegation that DOE defendants were involved. The plaintiff could amend the complaint to insert their true names and capacities should he later discover that these persons were in some way responsible for his injuries.

(continued on page 200)

```
 1   MICHAEL L. COWDREY
     3345 Wilshire Boulevard
 2   Los Angeles, California

 3

 4

 5   Attorney for Plaintiff

 6

 7

 8            SUPERIOR COURT OF THE STATE OF CALIFORNIA

 9                 FOR THE COUNTY OF ORANGE

10

11   CHARLES L. DAVIN and LILA R. )    CASE NO.
     DAVIN,                       )
12                               )
                  Plaintiffs,    )    COMPLAINT FOR MEDICAL
13                               )    MALPRACTICE
         vs.                     )
14                               )
     JOHN SMITH, M.D.;           )
15   HENRY DEAL, M.D.;           )
     HERBERT C. JUNG, M.D.;      )
16   GENERAL HOSPITAL; and DOES  )
     I through XX, inclusive,    )
17                               )
                  Defendants.    )
18   _____)

19                    FIRST CAUSE OF ACTION

20         Plaintiff, Charles L. Davin, alleges:

21         1.   Plaintiff does not know the true names of the defendants

22   referred herein as DOE I through DOE XX.

23         2.   Plaintiff is informed and believes and upon such infor-

24   mation and belief alleges that defendant, GENERAL HOSPITAL and

25   DOES I and II, inclusive, and each of them, are authorized and

26   licensed to conduct and did conduct a hospital business or

27   business in the State of California, County of Orange, to which

28   hospital or hospitals members of the public were invited, includ-
```

-1-

ILLUSTRATION 14.2 COMPLAINT FOR MEDICAL MALPRACTICE

1 | ing the plaintiff, CHARLES L. DAVIN; that the exact form of

2 | business organization of the defendants, GENERAL HOSPITAL and

3 | DOES I and II, inclusive, and each of them, are unknown to

4 | plaintiff at the time of the filing of this complaint and

5 | plaintiff will ask leave of Court to amend this complaint if

6 | required when the same shall be ascertained.

7 | 3. At all times herein mentioned, JOHN SMITH, M.D., HENRY

8 | DEAL, M.D., HERBERT C. JUNG, M.D., and DOES III through X,

9 | inclusive, and each of them, were and now are physicians and

10 | surgerons duly licensed to practice their professions as provided

11 | by the laws of the State of California and were and now are

12 | engaged in the practice of their profession in the County of

13 | Orange, State of California.

14 | 4. That at all times herein mentioned, defendants, DOES

15 | XI through XX, inclusive, and each of them, were nurses, atten-

16 | dants, employees, assistants, consultants, and the like, of defen-

17 | dants, GENERAL HOSPITAL and DOES I and II, inclusive.

18 | 5. That at all times herein mentioned, defendants, JOHN

19 | SMITH, M.D., HENRY DEAL, M.D., HERBERT C. JUNG, M.D., GENERAL

20 | HOSPITAL, and DOES I through XX, inclusive, and each of them,

21 | were the agents, servants and employees, assistants and con-

22 | sultants of their co-defendants and were, as such, acting within

23 | the course, scope and authority of said agency and employment,

24 | and that each and every defendant, as aforesaid, when acting as

25 | a principal, was negligent in the selection, hiring and super-

26 | visions of each and every other defendant as an agent, servant,

27 | employee, assistant and consultant.

28 | //

-2-

ILLUSTRATION 14.2 (CONTINUED)

1 6.   On or about January 10, 1979, plaintiff injured his low

2 back. Thereafter, up to and including March, 1980, plaintiff

3 consulted and engaged for compensation, the services of the

4 defendants, and each of them, to examine, diagnose, treat and

5 care for his injury. On and after the date aforesaid, the defen-

6 dants, and each of them, undertook to examine, diagnose, treat,

7 and perform surgery upon plaintiff, and agreed to care for and

8 treat plaintiff and do all things necessary and proper in

9 connection therewith.

10 7.   That in the aforesaid examination, diagnosis, treat-

11 ment, surgery, care and control of the plaintiff, defendants,

12 and each of them, negligently failed to possess and to exercise

13 that degree of knowledge and skill ordinarily possessed and

14 exercised by other physicians and surgeons, hospitals, nurses,

15 attendants and the like, engaged in said profession in the same

16 or similar locality as said defendants, and each of them.

17 8.   As a direct and proximate result of said negligence

18 of the defendants, and each of them, plaintiff was hurt and

19 injured in his health, strength and activity, sustaining injury

20 to his body and shock and injury to his nervious system and

21 person, all of which injuries have caused and continue to cause

22 plaintiff mental, physical and nervous pain and suffering.

23 Plaintiff is informed and believes, and thereon alleges, that

24 said injuries will result in permanent disability to plaintiff.

25 9.   As a proximate result of plaintiff's reliance on

26 statements and representations made to him by the defendants,

27 and as a proximate result of the confidence and trust reposed

28 by plaintiff in the defendants, plaintiff failed to seek any

-3-

ILLUSTRATION 14.2 (CONTINUED)

1 medical treatment or advice to ascertain the true cause of his

2 condition until on or about April, 1980. Plaintiff's failure

3 to ascertain or discover the true condition from which he was

4 suffering, and the cause therefore, was not due to any lack of

5 diligence on his part.

6   10. As a proximate result of said negligence of defendants,

7 and each of them, plaintiff was required to and did and will in

8 the future employ physicians and surgeons to examine, treat and

9 care for him, and did and will in the future incur medical and

10 incidental expenses.

11   11. As a further proximate result of the conduct of the

12 defendants, and each of them, plaintiff was prevented from

13 attending his usual occupation and has thereby suffered a loss of

14 income; plaintiff is informed and believes, and thereon alleges,

15 that by reason of said injuries herein alleged, plaintiff has

16 suffered, and will continue in the future to suffer, a loss of

17 earning capacity.

18   SECOND CAUSE OF ACTION

19   Plaintiff, LILA R. DAVIN, alleges:

20   12. Plaintiff, LILA R. DAVIN, refers to each and every

21 paragraph of the First Cause of Action and incorporates them

22 herein by this reference.

23   13. At all times material herein, plaintiff, LILA R. DAVIN,

24 was and still is married to and is the lawful wife of plaintiff,

25 CHARLES L. DAVIN.

26   14. As a direct and proximate result of the conduct of the

27 defendants as described herein and the injuries and damages

28 resulting therefrom sustained by plaintiff, CHARLES L. DAVIN,

-4-

ILLUSTRATION 14.2 (CONTINUED)

1 | plaintiff, LILA R. DAVIN, has suffered a loss and impairment of

 2 | consortium including extreme mental suffering and a loss and

 3 | impairment of part or all of the benefits incidental to said

 4 | marriage relationship, all to her damage.

 5 | WHEREFORE, plaintiffs pray damage against the defendants,

 6 | and each of them, as follows:

 7 | Plaintiff, CHARLES L. DAVIN:

 8 | 1.   General damages;

 9 | 2.   Medical and incidental expenses;

10 | 3.   Loss of earnings and earning capacity;

11 | 4.   Cost of suit incurred herein; and,

12 | 5.   Such other and further relief as the Court may deem

13 | proper.

14 | Plaintiff, LILA R. DAVIN:

15 | 6.   Loss of consortium;

16 | 7.   Cost of suit incurred herein; and,

17 | 8.   Such other and further relief as the Court may deem

18 | proper.

19 | DATED: October 6, 1980

20 |

21 | By _____

22 | Michael L. Cowdrey
        Attorneys for Plaintiffs

23 |

24 |

25 |

26 |

27 |

28 |

-5-

ILLUSTRATION 14.2 (CONTINUED)

Paragraph 4 of the complaint basically identifies nurses, attendants, employees, assistants, and consultants of the defendant hospital. It also identifies doctors who may have participated in or contributed to causing the plaintiff's alleged injuries. The plaintiff is allowed to insert these unknown persons as DOE defendants because he is unaware of their true names or capacities. Thereafter, should he discover the true names or capacities, he could then amend the complaint to include them.

Paragraph 5 of the complaint merely states that all defendants were acting in **consort** in causing the plaintiff's injuries. The plaintiff is unaware of the actual capacity of the defendants or the relationship between them. However, he is allowed to allege that they all were agents, servants, employees, assistants, and consultants of each of their respective codefendants and are thus responsible under the principle of agency, or the doctrine of respondeat superior, for each other.

Further, the plaintiff has indicated that each was acting in the course, scope, and authority of any such agency or employment relationship. In the event that one of the doctors involved in the lawsuit asserts as a valid defense that he or she did not actively participate in causing the plaintiff's injuries, the plaintiff has already alleged that the doctor was negligent in the selection, hiring, and supervision of his or her agent, servant, or employee, assistant, or consultant should some agency relationship be established by the plaintiff during the course of the lawsuit. The negligent selection or supervision of an employee or agent allows a plaintiff recovery for injuries sustained when the agent is acting on behalf of his or her principal or employer (according to the doctrine of respondeat superior).

Paragraph 6 of the complaint is one of the main charging allegations of the document. It describes the general circumstances and acts that constituted professional negligence, includes the date they occurred, and describes what the plaintiff was being treated for. It also notes that the plaintiff engaged the defendants for compensation, which established a contractual obligation on the part of the defendants to properly treat him. He specifically describes that he retained the defendants for the purpose of examining, diagnosing, and treating him for his underlying injury (condition). He describes that the defendants thereafter undertook to examine, diagnose, and treat him, including performing surgery. They agreed to do everything necessary and proper in connection with the surgery and other treatment. Their agreement established a duty to care for the plaintiff properly.

Paragraph 7 is the other charging allegation. The plaintiff contends that the defendants individually and/or collectively negligently failed to exercise that degree of knowledge and skill ordinarily possessed and exercised by other physicians, surgeons, hospitals, nurses, and other professionals practicing in the same or similar geographic locale. This allegation, in its basic form, means that each of the defendants breached his or her duty of care owed to the plaintiff in treating him for his condition.

Paragraph 8, 9, 10, and 11 are allegations separately describing the injuries and damages sustained by the plaintiff as a result of the negligent conduct of the defendants. Paragraph 8 describes that the plaintiff sustained general damages to his health, strength, and activity and sustained physical and nervous pain and suffering as a *direct* and *proximate result* of the defendants' negligence. Thus, the defendants' negligent conduct was the proximate cause of the injuries and damages the plaintiff sustained.

Paragraph 9 sets forth that the plaintiff was unaware of the alleged malpractice and his resulting injuries until April 1980. This allegation is asserted to stop the **statute of limitations** from barring the plaintiff's ability to bring a lawsuit against the defendants. The plaintiff does not contend that the defendants perpetrated any intentional misrepresentation or fraud to conceal the alleged malpractice. Rather, his failure to ascertain or discover his true condition was due to the confidence and trust he had in his treating doctors. Because of this confidence and trust, he did not seek further medical treatment or ascertain the true cause of his condition until April, 1980. The nondiscovery of his true condition based on the trust and confidence he placed in his doctor stops the "running" of any statute of limitations that would limit the time in which he must file a lawsuit. Note that the statute of limitations may vary from one jurisdiction to another and a lawsuit may not be brought after the statute of limitations has run out. Thus, in Massachusetts, for example, the statute of limitations for an act of medical malpractice committed on an adult is three years. Under the traditional rule, that means that if, for instance, a foreign object such as a clamp is left in a patient's body during surgery, a lawsuit over harm resulting from leaving that clamp must be brought within three years from the time the clamp was left; that is, three years from the time the wrongful conduct occurred. However, it is possible that the abandoned foreign object may not cause problems for many years. Concerned with the injustice of barring a lawsuit by a plaintiff who had no way to discover his or her injury for a period of time, many jurisdictions, including Massachusetts, have adopted a discovery rule. Under such a rule, the statute of limitations is **tolled** (temporarily suspended or stopped) until a person discovers he or she has suffered injury or by exercising reasonable diligence *should* have discovered it.

Paragraph 10 describes the damages sustained by the plaintiff in the form of medical care for curing and relieving him of the effects of his injury sustained as a result of the alleged malpractice. Paragraph 11 further describes the plaintiff's damages as consisting of his loss of earnings and earning capacity. Both types of damages are commonly referred to as compensatory damages, which are compensation paid to the plaintiff for actual out-of-pocket expenses.

As previously mentioned, the second cause of action deals with the complaint alleged by the patient's wife for loss of consortium. The spouse of an injured party may join a lawsuit on the basis of the loss of consortium or conjugal society of his or her spouse as a result of the injury caused by the negligence of the defendants. This subject is discussed in some detail in

Chapter 7. This loss is generally pleaded as the spouse's damages apart from the physically injured plaintiff's damages. Such loss may include the necessity of obtaining the services of a gardener to do yard work, the services of a maintenance person to do minor repairs on the family residence, and so on. However, such damages may not be duplicated or charged twice against the defendant. Thus the husband and wife cannot both allege loss of the husband's earnings.

Attorney's certificate of merit

The attorney representing the plaintiff in some jurisdictions must file a *certificate of merit* indicating that he or she has reviewed the facts of the case (see Illustration 14.3). The certificate of merit must also include the fact that the attorney has consulted at least one physician or surgeon licensed to practice in the state of the alleged malpractice. The certificate must also include the attorney's reasonable belief, based on the physician's review and consultation, that malpractice has been committed. If the attorney has consulted at least three physicians who have refused to express an opinion or to review the facts, he or she is allowed to file the attorney's certificate of merit indicating that he or she has consulted three physicians who have refused to express an opinion or review the case.

The attorney and his or her client may be subject to the filing of a malicious prosecution action by the defendant/doctor or hospital unless an attorney's certificate of merit is filed. The malicious prosecution action could only be filed where the doctor or hospital successfully defended the plaintiff's action by demonstrating that no malpractice was committed.

The answer

Following the filing of the complaint by the plaintiff's counsel and the issuance of a summons on the complaint by the court clerk, a copy of the summons and complaint is generally served on the defendants named in the lawsuit. Thereafter, each party served with the summons and complaint is given a certain amount of time in which to answer or otherwise plead (respond) to the complaint. California allows thirty days for this response to be filed with the court clerk. Massachusetts allows twenty days. This response, or *answer,* may be required to take the form of a general or specific denial of each individual paragraph of the plaintiff's complaint. In many jurisdictions, however, the defendant is allowed to file a *general denial* to the complaint. A general denial basically asserts that the defendant generally and specifically denies each and every paragraph in the complaint. However, a general denial is not allowed in certain situations and in some jurisdictions. In such cases, the defendant must admit to factual contentions that he or she knows to be true and may generally and specifically deny those matters that are not true or are not known by the defendant to be true. The denial may be based on a lack of

```
1    MICHAEL L. COWDREY
     3345 Wilshire Boulevard
2    Los Angeles, California

3

4

5    Attorneys for Plaintiff

6

7

8              SUPERIOR COURT OF THE STATE OF CALIFORNIA

9                    FOR THE COUNTY OF ORANGE

10

11   CHARLES L. DAVIN and LILA      )    CASE NO.
     R. DAVIN,                      )
12                                  )
                  Plaintiffs,       )    ATTORNEY'S CERTIFICATE
13                                  )
         vs.                        )
14                                  )
     JOHN SMITH, M.D., et al.,      )
15                                  )
                  Defendants.       )
16   _____)

17          I, MICHAEL L. COWDREY, declare:

18          I have reviewed the facts in this case, and I have

19   consulted with at least one physician and surgeon who is licensed

20   to practice in this State, and whom I reasonably believe to be

21   knowledgeable in the relevant issues in this case.  I have con-

22   cluded that on the basis of such review and consultation, there

23   is a reasonable and meritorious cause for commencing this action.

24          DATED:  October 6, 1980.

25

26                              _____
                                Michael L. Cowdrey
27

28
```

ILLUSTRATION 14.3   CERTIFICATE OF MERIT

sufficient information and belief regarding those matters asserted in the complaint.

The defendant may also assert certain affirmative defenses in response to the plaintiff's allegation, in addition to a denial of the allegations contained in the complaint. Such affirmative defenses may include the allegation that the plaintiff caused or contributed to his or her own injury by failing to follow the treatment recommended by the defendant. Another affirmative defense, commonly asserted in cases dealing with surgery, is the patient's assumption of a known risk attendant to the procedure. If the risk was actually known and assumed by the patient/plaintiff, he or she is barred from recovery. Another affirmative defense is that the complaint was filed after the lapse of the statute of limitations for an action based on the alleged professional misconduct.

An affirmative defense may be asserted that any recovery by the plaintiff should be reduced by the percentage of comparative fault of the codefendant to the lawsuit, where the injury sustained by the plaintiff/patient was occasioned by the misconduct of a codefendant. The answer is filed with the clerk of the court where the complaint was filed. Illustration 14.4 is an example of an answer alleging a general denial and presenting the affirmative defenses outlined in this section.

Summary

As indicated by the complaint and answer examples given, specific descriptions of the alleged malpractice are absent from the pleadings themselves. All that is required in the complaint is to inform the defendant of the general allegation of negligence. Likewise, a general denial and the setting up of affirmative defenses are all that is required in the answer. Specification of the issues in contention follows during the discovery phase of the litigation or trial before a judge or jury.

The negligent conduct (malpractice) of the defendants described in the complaint (Illustration 14.2) are essentially the same as in the case of *Ybarra v. Spandard* presented in Chapter 5. In this actual case tried in a California Superior Court, the plaintiff was admitted to the defendant's hospital for low-back surgery. When he awoke from anesthesia, he felt severe neck pain. He complained to his treating physician, Dr. Smith, about the neck pain, but Dr. Smith told him that it was probably nothing to worry about. One year later, the plaintiff underwent neck surgery for a herniated disc. The plaintiff had nothing wrong with his neck before the low-back surgery. Apparently, the plaintiff's neck was injured during surgery to his low back.

Note that the complaint only sets forth the general allegations of malpractice and not the **ultimate facts.**[2] The following chapter, dealing with the subject of discovery, explains the methods by which the parties to the lawsuit would ascertain the ultimate facts of the plaintiff's allegations.

---

[2]Both the sample complaint and the answer to complaint—Illustrations 14.2 and 14.4—are taken from an actual case tried in California (The names have been changed).

```
 1  JONES, JONES & ANDERSON
    315 West Third Street
 2  San Jose, California

 3

 4

 5  Attorneys for Defendant
    Herbert C. Jung, M.D.
 6

 7

 8              SUPERIOR COURT OF THE STATE OF CALIFORNIA

 9                     FOR THE COUNTY OF ORANGE

10

11  CHARLES L. DAVIN and LILA    )    CASE NO.   34 30 62
    R. DAVIN,                    )
12                               )
                    Plaintiffs,  )    ANSWER TO COMPLAINT
13                               )
                                 )
         vs.                     )
14                               )
    JOHN SMITH, M.D., et al.,    )
15                               )
                    Defendants.  )
16  _____)

17          COMES NOW the defendant, HERBERT C. JUNG, M.D., and

18  for answer to plaintiff's unverified Complaint on file herein,

19  admits, denies and alleges as follows:

20          1.   Under the provisions of Section 431.30(d) of the

21  California Code of Civil Procedure, this answering defendant

22  denies generally and specifically each and every allegation con-

23  tained in the Complaint, and the whole thereof, and each and

24  every alleged cause of action thereof, and denies that plaintiffs

25  suffered damages in the sum or sums alleged, or in any other sum

26  or sums, or at all, by reason of any act, breach or omission on

27  the part of this answering defendant, or on the part of any agent,

28  servant or
```

                                -1-

ILLUSTRATION 14.4 ANSWER TO A COMPLAINT

1 employee of this answering defendant.

2   2.   This answering defendant denies that he was guilty

3 of any of the conduct as alleged in said Complaint, or otherwise,

4 or at all, and further denies that plaintiffs were injured or

5 damaged, or will be injured or damaged, as a result of any conduct

6 on the part of this answering defendant, either as alleged in

7 said Complaint, or otherwise, or at all.

8   3.   Denies that by reason of any acts or acts, or by

9 virtue of any of the allegations contained in plaintiff's Complaint

10 or otherwise, that plaintiffs are, were or will be entitled to any

11 of the relief sought in their Complaint, or otherwise, or at all.

12

13   FIRST AFFIRMATIVE DEFENSE

14   4.   That the causes of action, and each of them, as

15 stated in plaintiffs' Complaint fail to state facts sufficient to

16 constitute causes of action as against this answering defendant in

17 that said plaintiffs have failed to comply with the provisions of

18 California Code of Civil procedure, Section 364, and give timely

19 notice of plaintiffs' intent to sue.

20

21   SECOND AFFIRMATIVE DEFENSE

22   5.   That the causes of action, and each of them, as

23 stated in plaintiffs' Complaint fail to state facts sufficient to

24 constitute causes of action as against this answering defendant in

25 that said plaintiffs have failed to comply with the provisions of

26 Code of Civil Procedure, Section 411.30, and file a declaration in

27 accordance with said provisions of that Code section at the time

28 //

-2-

ILLUSTRATION 14.4 (CONTINUED)

1 | this lawsuit was filed with the Clerk of the Court.

 2

 3 | THIRD AFFIRMATIVE DEFENSE

 4 | 6.   In the event this answering defendant is found to

 5 | be negligent (which supposition is denied and merely stated for

 6 | the purpose of this affirmative defense), this defendant may elect

 7 | to introduce evidence of any amounts paid or payable, if any, as

 8 | a benefit to plaintiffs, pursuant to Civil Code, Section 3333.1.

 9

10 | FOURTH AFFIRMATIVE DEFENSE

11 | 7.   In the event this answering defendant is found to

12 | be negligent (which supposition is denied and merely stated for

13 | the purpose of this affirmative defense), the damages for non-

14 | economic losses shall not exceed the amount specified in Civil

15 | Code, Section 3333.2.

16

17 | FIFTH AFFIRMATIVE DEFENSE

18 | 8.   In the event this answering defendant is found to

19 | be negligent (which supposition is denied and merely stated for

20 | the purpose of this affirmative defense), this defendant may elect

21 | to have future damages, if in excess of the amount specified in

22 | Code of Civil Procedure, Section 667.7, paid in whole or in part,

23 | as specified in Code of Civil Procedure, Section 667.7.

24

25 | SIXTH AFFIRMATIVE DEFENSE

26 | 9.   If plaintiffs in fact sustained or will sustain any

27 | injuries or damages as a result of any act or omission on the

28 | part of this answering defendant (which supposition is not admitted

-3-

ILLUSTRATION 14.4 (CONTINUED)

1 by this answering defendant, but is merely stated for the purpose
2 of this affirmative defense), then plaintiffs at the time and place
3 alleged in said Complaint were themselves guilty of negligence in
4 failing to exercise that degree of care for the safety and pro-
5 tection of CHARLES L. DAVIN that ordinarily prudent persons would
6 exercise under the premises, and said negligence contributed as a
7 proximate cause in some degree to the injuries and damages being
8 claimed by plaintiffs herein, thereby barring and/or reducing
9 plaintiff's recovery.
10
11   SEVENTH AFFIRMATIVE DEFENSE
12   10.   That the causes of action, and each of them, as
13 stated in plaintiffs' Complaint are barred by the provisions of
14 California Code of Civil Procedure, Section 340.5.
15
16   EIGHTH AFFIRMATIVE DEFENSE
17   11.   This answering defendant contends that there is
18 no basis for liability of said defendant to plaintiffs. However,
19 without withdrawing that position, this defendant alleges in the
20 alternative that should this defendant be found liable to plaintiffs
21 on the Complaint herein, this defendant should, in whole or in part,
22 be indemnified by the other defendants, by those responsible
23 persons and/or entities who would be liable to plaintiffs if joined
24 herein, according to the degree of involvement or responsibility
25 for causing loss to the plaintiffs, and by the plaintiffs to the
26 degree and extent of their contributory negligence or to the
27 extent plaintiffs are found to have assumed the position of any
28 other responsible person and/or entity with whom plaintiffs have

-4-

ILLUSTRATION 14.4 (CONTINUED)

```
1    settled their claims separately or in any other manner have
2    attempted to exonerate.
3         WHEREFORE, this answering defendant prays that the
4    plaintiffs take nothing by their Complaint; that this answering
5    defendant recover his costs expended herein; and for such other
6    and further relief as to the Court may deem proper and just in
7    the premises.
8                              JONES, JONES & ANDERSON
9
10                      By  David Jones
                            David Jones
11                          Attorneys for Plaintiff
                            Herbert C. Jung, M.D.
12
13
14
15
16
17
18
19
20
21
22
23
24
25
26
27
28
                              5.
```

ILLUSTRATION 14.4 (CONTINUED)

EXAMPLES / QUESTIONS / PROJECTS

1. *Would a medical assistant who gives a patient an injection of medication on the express authorization of a doctor be subject to criminal charges if the doctor is not present at the treating facility?*

     Answer: In California and the majority of states, the answer would be yes.

2. *What is a complaint?*

3. *What is a summons?*

4. *What is an indictment?*

5. *Find out what general class of persons is asked to serve on a grand jury in your local community and how they are chosen.*

6. *Use your local law library to research the additional types of response—other than an answer—that may be made to a civil complaint. Define each legal reason for filing each response. (For assistance, check a text on civil procedure.)*

7. *What is a demurrer? What is a motion to strike? How do they differ, and when and by whom are they filed?*

CHAPTER FIFTEEN

DISCOVERY

REQUEST FOR ADMISSIONS

INTERROGATORIES

REQUEST FOR DOCUMENTS
AND OTHER TANGIBLE ITEMS

ORDER COMPELLING A
PLAINTIFF TO UNDERGO A
MEDICAL EXAMINATION

DEPOSITIONS

SUBPOENAS

OBTAINING COPIES OF
PATIENT RECORDS
WITHOUT A SUBPOENA

EXAMPLES/QUESTIONS/
PROJECTS

Key Terms

propound
sanctions
penalty of perjury

notary public
credibility

percipient witness
expert witness
carte blanche

Once the complaint and answer have been filed with the court, a phase of civil litigation termed *discovery* begins. Discovery encompasses information-gathering processes in various forms. Formal procedural devices for obtaining factual information are available to all parties to the lawsuit until the time of trial, or shortly before. Through various procedural steps, the plaintiff obviously wants to demonstrate as specifically as possible that he or she has a valid complaint. Likewise, the defendant to the malpractice or other action wants to gather facts to demonstrate that he or she is not guilty of misconduct as alleged in the plaintiff's complaint. Formal court-sanctioned discovery takes many forms, each of which will be discussed in this chapter.

REQUEST FOR ADMISSIONS

Each party to a lawsuit may request that another party to that lawsuit admit or deny under oath certain factual contentions (see Illustration 15.1). The party **propounding** the request for admissions will make certain factual statements or allegations. The party to whom the request is directed must answer in the form of an unqualified admission or denial of the factual matters asserted. The purpose of this form of discovery is to narrow issues relating to the alleged negligence of the defendant or to establish an ultimate fact about the case. A defendant will attempt to establish an ultimate factual basis to bar the plaintiff's recovery. The plaintiff will attempt to establish an ultimate factual basis to demonstrate the validity of his or her action.

In certain jurisdictions, such as California and Massachusetts, the party to whom the request is directed must answer the request within a specified period of time. All admissions requested will be deemed to have been admitted factually by that party in the event that the response is not made within the time allotted by statute (see Illustration 15.2). In addition, failure to properly provide a factual basis for a qualified denial of a request for admission may be held as an admission on the part of the party to whom the request is directed. In both such cases, the outcome of the litigation may be drastically affected to the detriment of the party to whom the request has been made, since the format of the request is generally drafted to favor the person *making* the request.

Thus, where the plaintiff requests the medical assistant or nurse to admit or deny that he or she was negligent in causing the plaintiff's injuries, a failure to respond on time or to properly qualify a denial would be tantamount to the nurse's or medical assistant's admission that he or she was negligent in causing the injury. Likewise, where a defendant requests that the plaintiff admit or deny that he or she assumed all the risk inherent in the procedure or treatment, the plaintiff's failure to respond on time or otherwise properly qualify a denial would be tantamount to barring the plaintiff's ability to recover damages. This bar would be based on the total defense of the patient's assumption of risk.

Requests for admissions are generally allowed to be propounded only between plaintiffs and defendants. Thus, requests for admissions may not be

```
 1   MICHAEL L. COWDREY
     3345 Wilshire Boulevard
 2   Los Angeles, California

 3

 4

 5   Attorneys for Plaintiff

 6

 7

 8          SUPERIOR COURT OF THE STATE OF CALIFORNIA

 9              FOR THE COUNTY OF SAN DIEGO

10

11   WORKMEN'S AUTO INSURANCE    )    CASE NO. 457099
     COMPANY,                    )
12                               )
                   Plaintiff,    )    REQUEST FOR ADMISSIONS
13                               )
          vs.                    )
14                               )
     MANUEL T. LOPEZ; ARTHUR     )
15   TOVAR LOPEZ; JAVIER MENDOZA )
     JIMENEZ; SOLEDAD TOVAR LOPEZ;)
16   and DOES I through V,       )
     inclusive,                  )
17                               )
                   Defendants.   )
18   _____)

19   TO DEFENDANT, MANUEL T. LOPEZ, AND HIS ATTORNEY OF RECORD:

20          Within thirty (30) days after service of these Request

21   for Admissions, it is requested that you admit the truth of the

22   following in writing under oath pursuant to Code of Civil

23   Procedure, Section 2033:

24       1.   That on December 17, 1979, you purchased an Automobile

25   Insurance Policy Number A 214013 from plaintiff.

26       2.   That on December 17, 1979, said Policy Number A 214013

27   provided coverage for a 1974 Chevrolet Malibu owned by MANUEL T.

28   LOPEZ and ARTHUR TOVAR LOPEZ....
                            -1-
```

ILLUSTRATION 15.1 REQUEST FOR ADMISSIONS (NONMEDICAL)

1 | JIMENEZ pursuant to that action.

2 | 16.   That pursuant to the provisions and exclusions of

3 | Insurance Policy Number A 214013, plaintiff herein is not obligated

4 | to defend defendants MANUEL T. LOPEZ, ARTHUR TOVAR LOPEZ, and/or

5 | SOLEDAD TOVAR LOPEZ in the lawsuit entitled Javier Mendoz Jimenez,

6 | Plaintiff, v. Manuel Tovar Lopez et al., filed in the Superior

7 | Court of the State of California for the County of San Diego, Case

8 | Number 452367 (Complaint for Personal Injuries).

9 | If you fail to comply with the provisions of Section

10 | 2033 of the Code of Civil Procedure with respect to this Request

11 | for Admissions each of the matters of which an admission is

12 | requested will deemed admitted.

13 | DATED: May 21, 1981

14 |

15 | By _____
16 | Michael L. Cowdrey, Esq.
   | Attorneys for Plaintiff
17 | Workmen's Auto Insurance Company

-4-

ILLUSTRATION 15.1 (CONTINUED)

```
 1   MICHAEL L. COWDREY
     3345 Wilshire Boulevard
 2   Los Angeles, California

 3

 4

 5   Attorneys for Plaintiff

 6

 7

 8            SUPERIOR COURT OF THE STATE OF CALIFORNIA

 9                 FOR THE COUNTY OF SAN DIEGO

10

11   WORKMEN'S AUTO INSURANCE        )    CASE NO.  457099
     COMPANY,                        )
12                                   )
                    Plaintiff,       )    NOTICE THAT REQUESTS FOR
13                                   )    ADMISSIONS ARE DEEMED
        vs.                          )    ADMITTED
14                                   )
     MANUEL T. LOPEZ, ARTHUR         )
15   TOVAR LOPEZ , JAVIER MENDOZA    )
     JIMENEZ, SOLEDAD TOVAR LOPEZ,   )
16   and DOES I through V,           )
     inclusive,                      )
17                                   )
                    Defendants.      )
18   _____)

19   TO DEFENDANT, MANUEL T. LOPEZ, AND HIS ATTORNEY OF RECORD:

20            Responses to the Request for Admissions propounded

21   defendant on May 26, 1981, having not been received within the

22   time prescribed by Section 2033 of the Code of Civil Procedure;

23            PLEASE TAKE NOTICE that all Requests for Admissions

24   propounded to defendant on May 21, 1981 are now deemed admitted

25   pursuant to Section 2033 of the Code of Civil Procedure.

26            DATED:  December 2, 1981

27

28                         By _____
                              Michael L. Cowdrey
                              Attorneys for Plaintiff

                              -1-
```

ILLUSTRATION 15.2 NOTICE THAT REQUESTS ARE DEEMED ADMITTED (THIS FORM MUST BE CERTIFIED WHEN MAILED TO BE VALID AND BINDING)

used to seek an admission or denial from a potential witness, expert witness, or other person who is not a named party to the lawsuit.

INTERROGATORIES

Like requests for admissions, *interrogatories* may only be propounded between named parties to the lawsuit. Interrogatories are questions propounded by one party of the lawsuit to another party requesting certain information. Like requests for admissions, the person to whom the questions are directed must provide the requesting party with an answer within a specified period of time.

In addition, the number of interrogatories that may be propounded by one party to another may be limited. For example, the Massachusetts Rules of Civil Procedure permit only thirty interrogatories to be propounded by one party to another. A party wishing to have more than thirty interrogatories answered by another party must obtain the court's permission.

However, if answers to the interrogatories are not provided within the time allotted, no admission of any factual contention is deemed to have been made. The party propounding the questions may request the court to compel the answers from the other party. Further, the court may impose **sanctions** by compelling the defaulting party to pay an amount of money to the party propounding the interrogatories. Sanctions are awarded by the court to compensate the party propounding the interrogatories for the necessity of bringing a motion before the court.

An example of a simple set of interrogatories is found in Illustration 15.3. Questions are usually drafted in a formal form to obtain as much information as possible within the framework of the question. Interrogatory questions propounded by defendants to a lawsuit most commonly request the plaintiff to describe in detail all alleged injuries and damages sustained as a result of the alleged negligence of the defendants. In addition, the plaintiff may be asked to list the names, addresses, and telephone numbers of all physicians, surgeons, nurses, and other professionals who treated the plaintiff for his or her alleged injury. The defendant may also request the plaintiff to compile a list of all specific dates of treatment, the type of treatment, and an itemization of the charges incurred as a result of the treatment. The defendant may request the plaintiff to describe in detail all events and occurrences related to the alleged acts of negligence giving rise to the lawsuit.

Parties may be asked not only for information they already possess but also for information they have the ability to obtain. Thus, even if the plaintiff may not recall all specific dates of treatment and the charges that accompanied that treatment, he or she may nevertheless be required to make a reasonable effort to secure and provide such information.

Like requests for admissions, interrogatories must be answered under oath. This means that the information supplied must be true and correct to the best of the informant's knowledge and ability to know. Exhibits, such as bills or records, may be supplied in lieu of a narrative answer to a question. Further,

```
 1   MICHAEL L. COWDREY
     3345 Wilshire Boulevard
 2   Los Angeles, California

 3

 4

 5   Attorneys for Plaintiff

 6

 7

 8              SUPERIOR COURT OF THE STATE OF CALIFORNIA

 9                    FOR THE COUNTY OF ORANGE

10

11   CHARLES L. DAVIN, et al.,      )     CASE NO.  34-30-62
                                    )
12              Plaintiffs,         )
                                    )     INTERROGATORIES PROPOUNDED
13        vs.                       )     TO GENERAL HOSPITAL, BY
                                    )     PLAINTIFFS
14   JOHN SMITH, M.D., et al.,      )         (Second Set)
                                    )
15              Defendants.         )
                                    )
16   ──────────────────────────────

17   TO DEFENDANT, GENERAL HOSPITAL, AND THEIR ATTORNEYS OF RECORD,

18   ANDREWS & DAVIS:

19        Plaintiffs request that defendant answer under oath,

20   within thirty (30) days, pursuant to Section 2030 C.C.P., the

21   following interrogatories:

22        1.   Was plaintiff operated upon at GENERAL HOSPITAL on

23   February 2, 1979?

24        2.   If your response to the foregoing interrogatory is

25   affirmative, please state:

26        (a)  The name, address and job capacity of each person

27   employed by the hospital who was present in the operating room

28   during the operation (other than the doctors involved);
```

-1-

ILLUSTRATION 15.3 INTERROGATORIES

1   (b)   The name, address and job classification of each

2 employee of yours who attended plaintiff in the recovery room;

3   (c)   The name, address and job classification of each

4 person who attended plaintiff during the twenty-four hours follow-

5 ing plaintiff's release from the recovery room on February 2, 1979.

6   3.   Did you have reported to you any incident involving

7 the plaintiff, at any time during the day of February 2, 1979?

8   4.   If your answer to the previous interrogatory is affirma-

9 tive, state:

10   (a)   The name, address and job classification of all

11 persons who reported any such incident;

12   (b)   A general description of the incident; and,

13   (c)   The present custodian of any such incident report.

14 DATED: March 27, 1981.

16 By _____
      Michael L. Cowdrey
17   Attorneys for Plaintiff

-2-

ILLUSTRATION 15.3 (CONTINUED)

parties to whom questions are directed must provide, if necessary, reasonable explanation for their inability to answer particular questions. Where they have the ability to provide some, but not all, of the information requested, they must provide whatever information they possess. They must also explain their inability to secure the balance of the requested information.

Needless to say, parties to litigation do not like being compelled to answer interrogatories, and, at certain times, interrogatories may in fact be overly broad or overly burdensome. For example, a question requesting a party to supply the names, addresses, and telephone numbers of employers, specific dates worked, and actual wages earned for employment over the past forty years would be overly burdensome where the alleged injury and the loss of earnings and earning capacity are fairly recent. The party to whom questions are directed may object to answering on grounds that the interrogatory is overly broad or overly burdensome.

Thereafter, the party propounding the interrogatory could bring a motion before the court to compel the other party to provide a response should the first party consider the objection invalid. Such a motion would undoubtedly be accompanied by a request for the court to impose sanctions against the other party for failing to provide a proper response to the question.

One way of preventing the courts from awarding sanctions for failure to properly respond to an interrogatory is to request the court to issue a *protective order*. This protective order would prevent the party propounding the interrogatory from obtaining the information. The protective order must be based on some valid showing that the party need not answer as a matter of law or fairness. Protective orders are often sought by parties where the interrogatories contain hundreds of detailed questions, many of which seek the same information. In such cases, the court would probably issue a protective order in favor of the responding party whereby that party need not answer all the questions.

The court may also issue a protective order in favor of the responding party where the information sought is not relevant to the lawsuit. Information protected by some trade, copyright, or patent law may also be protected by a protective order.

In addition, the court may issue a protective order where requested information is not otherwise privileged or protected from discovery. For example, in cases where the information requested would take a great deal of time to compile, the court may give the answering party additional time to provide the requested information.

The court may also impose on the party requesting such information to pay for the expenses of photocopying documents that are being sought directly by questioning. The protection given by the court would also encompass the inability to secure sanctions by the propounding party in the event compliance to the interrogatories is not made within the time allotted by the statute. The protection given by the court may also include precluding the propounding party from obtaining information at the responding party's expense.

REQUEST FOR DOCUMENTS AND OTHER TANGIBLE ITEMS

Another discovery tool that is only allowed between the parties of a lawsuit is one party's request that the other party provide certain documents or other tangible items to be used as evidence at trial. A response to the request, as with other forms of formal discovery, must be made within a certain period of time most commonly governed by code or statute. Generally, the time is very short—that is, twenty or thirty days from the request date.

The propounding party may request the court to compel the production of documents in the event that the party to whom the request is directed fails to respond within the time allotted. The propounding party may also request the court to impose sanctions against the noncooperating party in the form of payment of attorney's fees and costs for bringing the motion before the court.

The party to whom the request is being made may ask the court to issue a protective order where the documents requested are voluminous. A protective order may also be sought where the requested documents would take longer to provide than the time allotted by the code or statute. The party to whom the request is directed may also seek a protective order compelling the requesting party to pay for the copies requested. In addition, the court may also issue a protective order making a response unnecessary where the documents to be provided are protected by some legal privilege—for example, documents containing trade secrets or information qualifying under some other privilege, such as the confidentiality between attorney and client or physician and patient. Illustration 15.4 is an example of a request for production of documents and other tangible items. Illustration 15.5 shows that a document has been served.

ORDER COMPELLING A PLAINTIFF TO UNDERGO A MEDICAL EXAMINATION

Most jurisdictions recognize the defendant's right to have the plaintiff examined by a physician of the defendant's choice, and at the defendant's expense, in cases dealing with personal injury litigation. The purpose of the examination is to enable the defendant to prepare a proper defense to the plaintiff's assertion of permanent residual physical or mental injury. Most commonly, a defendant is given the statutory right to have the patient examined once. Where additional examinations of the patient/plaintiff are requested by one or all of the defendants to the action, the defendant must request the court to issue an order compelling the patient/plaintiff to attend the examinations.

However, some states do not adhere to the absolute right of a defendant to compel the plaintiff to undergo a physical or mental examination. In these jurisdictions, the defendant must seek court approval in the form of a court order to compel the plaintiff to undergo an examination. The examination may

1   (b)   The name, address and job classification of each

2 employee of yours who attended plaintiff in the recovery room;

3   (c)   The name, address and job classification of each

4 person who attended plaintiff during the twenty-four hours follow-

5 ing plaintiff's release from the recovery room on February 2, 1979.

6   3.   Did you have reported to you any incident involving

7 the plaintiff, at any time during the day of February 2, 1979?

8   4.   If your answer to the previous interrogatory is affirma-

9 tive, state:

10   (a)   The name, address and job classification of all

11 persons who reported any such incident;

12   (b)   A general description of the incident; and,

13   (c)   The present custodian of any such incident report.

14 DATED: March 27, 1981.

15

16 By _____

17 Michael L. Cowdrey
   Attorneys for Plaintiff

18

19

20

21

22

23

24

25

26

27

28   -2-

ILLUSTRATION 15.3 (CONTINUED)

```
 1  MICHAEL L. COWDREY
    3345 Wilshire Boulevard
 2  Los Angeles, California

 3

 4

 5  Attorneys for Plaintiff

 6

 7

 8         SUPERIOR COURT OF THE STATE OF CALIFORNIA

 9              FOR THE COUNTY OF ORANGE

10

11  CHARLES L. DAVIN, et al.,      )    CASE NO. 34-30-62
                                   )
12              Plaintiffs,        )
                                   )    INTERROGATORIES PROPOUNDED
13      vs.                        )    TO GENERAL HOSPITAL, BY
                                   )    PLAINTIFFS
14  JOHN SMITH, M.D., et al.,      )    _____
                                   )         (Second Set)
15              Defendants.        )
                                   )
16  _____

17  TO DEFENDANT, GENERAL HOSPITAL, AND THEIR ATTORNEYS OF RECORD,

18  ANDREWS & DAVIS:

19          Plaintiffs request that defendant answer under oath,

20  within thirty (30) days, pursuant to Section 2030 C.C.P., the

21  following interrogatories:

22      1.  Was plaintiff operated upon at GENERAL HOSPITAL on

23  February 2, 1979?

24      2.  If your response to the foregoing interrogatory is

25  affirmative, please state:

26          (a)  The name, address and job capacity of each person

27  employed by the hospital who was present in the operating room

28  during the operation (other than the doctors involved);
```

-1-

ILLUSTRATION 15.3 INTERROGATORIES

```
 1   MICHAEL L. COWDREY
     3345 Wilshire Boulevard
 2   Los Angeles, California

 3

 4

 5   Attorneys for Plaintiff

 6

 7

 8          SUPERIOR COURT OF THE STATE OF CALIFORNIA

 9              FOR THE COUNTY OF SAN BERNARDINO

10

11   CONNIE CALDERON,            )   CASE NO.  OCV 23974
                                 )
12              Plaintiff,       )
                                 )   NOTICE TO PRODUCE DOCUMENTS
13      vs.                      )   PURSUANT TO C.C.P. SECTION
                                 )   2031
14   PRUDENTIAL OVERALL SUPPLY,  )   _____
     et al.,                     )
15                               )
                Defendants.      )
16   _____)

17   TO ONTARIO AUTO TRUCE PLAZA AND ITS ATTORNEYS OF RECORD, MERCER

18   AND GALLGHER:

19          NOTICE IS HEREBY GIVEN that pursuant to C.C.P. Section

20   2031, ONTARIO AUTO TRUCK PLAZA is requested to produce the follow-

21   ing described documents at 3345 Wilshire Boulevard, Los Angeles,

22   California, on April 20, 1983, at 10:00 A.M.:

23      1.   True and correct copies of all medical statements,

24   itemizations, reports, billings, statements and receipts, reflect-

25   ing payments made to or on behalf of Connie Calderon for injuries

26   she received on September 13, 1980, which is the subject of this

27   lawsuit.

28   //
```

-1-

ILLUSTRATION 15.4 REQUEST FOR DOCUMENTS AND OTHER TANGIBLE ITEMS

```
 1        DATED:   March 18, 1983.

 2

 3                          By _____
                              Michael L. Cowdrey
 4                            Attorneys for Plaintiff

 5

 6

 7

 8

 9

10

11

12

13

14

15

16

17

18

19

20

21

22

23

24

25

26

27

28                              -2-
```

ILLUSTRATION 15.4 (CONTINUED)

VERIFICATION

STATE OF CALIFORNIA, COUNTY OF _____

I have read the foregoing _____
_____ and know its contents.

☒ CHECK APPLICABLE PARAGRAPH

☐ I am a party to this action. The matters stated in it are true of my own knowledge except as to those matters which are stated on information and belief, and as to those matters I believe them to be true.

☐ I am ☐ an Officer ☐ a partner _____ ☐ a _____ of _____
_____

a party to this action, and am authorized to make this verification for and on its behalf, and I make this verification for that reason. I have read the foregoing document and know its contents. The matters stated in it are true of my own knowledge except as to those matters which are stated on information and belief, and as to those matters I believe them to be true.

☐ I am one of the attorneys for _____

a party to this action. Such party is absent from the county of aforesaid where such attorneys have their offices, and I make this verification for and on behalf of that party for that reason. I have read the foregoing document and know its contents. I am informed and believe and on that ground allege that the matters stated in it are true.

Executed on _____, 19___, at _____ California.

I declare under penalty of perjury under the laws of the State of California that the foregoing is true and correct.

_____
Signature

ACKNOWLEDGMENT OF RECEIPT OF DOCUMENT
(other than summons and complaint)

Received copy of document described as _____
_____

on _____ 19___.

_____
Signature

PROOF OF SERVICE

STATE OF CALIFORNIA, COUNTY OF LOS ANGELES

I am employed in the county of Los Angeles _____, State of California.

I am over the age of 18 and not a party to the within action; my business address is: _____
3345 Wilshire Boulevard, Los Angeles, CA.

On March 18 _____ 19 83 I served the foregoing document described as _____
NOTICE TO PRODUCE PURSUANT TO C.C.P. SECTION 2031
_____

on interested parties

in this action by placing a true copy thereof enclosed in a sealed envelope with postage thereon fully prepaid in the United States mail at: Los Angeles, California
_____

addressed as follows:

TORRES & TORRES, 3843 Repton Street, Los Angeles, CA

ARVIZU & ARVIZU, 6868 Malibu Street, Los Angeles, CA

☒ (BY MAIL) I caused such envelope with postage thereon fully prepaid to be placed in the United States mail.
Executed on March 18 _____, 19 83, at Los Angeles _____, California.

☐ (BY PERSONAL SERVICE) I caused such envelope to be delivered by hand to the offices of the addressee.
Executed on _____, 19___, at _____, California.

☒ (State) I declare under penalty of perjury under the laws of the State of California that the above is true and correct.

☐ (Federal) I declare that I am employed in the office of a member of the bar of this court at whose direction the service was made.

_____
Signature

ILLUSTRATION 15.5 PROOF THAT A DOCUMENT HAS BEEN SERVED

be limited to the plaintiff's alleged injuries and to determining whether such injuries are permanent.

This physical or mental examination may be used to assert that the plaintiff's claimed injuries either were caused by something other than the alleged negligence of the defendant or are not severe or permanent, as alleged by the plaintiff. The plaintiff may only be required to submit to examinations that are determined to be reasonable, since the examination is being done for the strict purpose of preparing a proper defense. Examinations that are dangerous or carry a risk of further injury to the patient would not be sanctioned by the court. Thus, the court would not compel a plaintiff to undergo a myelogram to establish that he or she does not have a herniated disc—even if the plaintiff underwent a previous myelogram—since the procedure itself carries an inherent risk.

DEPOSITIONS

Unlike the forms of formal discovery previously discussed, *depositions* are not limited only to parties named in the lawsuit. A deposition is oral testimony taken from a party or witness to the litigation. It consists of questions asked of a person called the *deponent* by the attorney(s) to the lawsuit and is quite similar to testimony given in open court. The main difference is that a deposition is generally taken at the attorney's office or some other convenient location. The deponent is nevertheless placed under oath by a certified shorthand reporter, often called a court reporter even though the deposition is taken in an informal atmosphere. The oath that the deponent takes is to tell the truth under the **penalty of perjury** in responding to questions. This is the same oath the deponent would take if he or she were testifying in a court of law or before some administrative judge or tribunal.

All questions and answers are recorded by the certified shorthand reporter, transcribed, and then put together into a booklet called the *deposition transcript.* The original deposition transcript is sent to the deponent for his or her review. The deponent is given the opportunity to make any changes or corrections in his or her testimony by making such changes on the original deposition booklet. The deponent is then asked to sign the original deposition, either under the penalty of perjury or before a **notary public,** after the booklet has been reviewed and any corrections made. The attorneys involved in the lawsuit often stipulate that a copy of the deposition may be used in the event that the original deposition is not signed by the time of trial or corrections or additions to the testimony have not been received within a certain period of time. This copy may be used as though no corrections have been made or as though the deposition transcript has been signed.

The deponent is generally told at the beginning of the deposition the formalities of the deposition procedure. The deponent is also admonished that he or she is testifying under oath and that this testimony carries the same obligation to tell the truth as testimony given in a court of law. In addition, any changes or corrections of major significance made on the deposition transcript regarding the deponent's testimony may be commented on by any attorney should the case proceed to trial. Any significant changes, corrections, or deletions could tend to prove the lack of **credibility** of the party or witness to whom the questions were directed. This reduction in credibility could affect the outcome of the lawsuit.

Many jurisdictions adhere to the position that each party to the lawsuit has a statutory right to obtain the deposition of an adversary party. This statutory right is generally confined to one deposition. Any further requests to obtain the deposition of a previously deposed party may not be obtained without a request and approval by the court. There is no such "once only" restriction on obtaining the deposition of a potential witness who would testify on behalf of one of the parties to the lawsuit. Nevertheless, the parties do not have a **"carte blanche"** right to harrass a potential witness by redeposing that witness again and again.

Compensation may be obtained by a deponent for his or her time spent responding to the deposition, except where the deponent is a party to the litigation. Where a **percipient witness** to the litigation is deposed, most states recognize payment to the witness of a nominal sum by the person requesting his or her testimony. This nominal sum represents compensation for the time incurred by the witness to attend his or her deposition and is designed to compensate him or her for lost wages, travel expenses, and other similar expenses. A percipient witness to the lawsuit may include the physician, dentist, nurse, medical assistant, or other professional who has been treating the patient/plaintiff for his or her alleged injuries. However, questioning may only be directed to the percipient witness regarding facts relating to the plaintiff's treatment and may not include questions that call for the professional to give his or her expert opinion.

The courts and statutes have placed restrictions, including a time limitation, on the requirement that a party or witness attend the deposition. For example, the deposition may not be obtained on a Saturday, Sunday, or holiday without the stipulation of all concerned. In addition, the courts do not require a person to attend a deposition if the deposition is held more than a certain distance from where the lawsuit is filed or the deponent resides.

A deposition may be obtained from a party to a lawsuit merely by giving the party's attorney notice of the intent to take the deposition. However, where the deposition testimony is that of a witness other than a party to the lawsuit, the witness must be subpoenaed for his or her deposition by the attorney requesting the deposition. Where a subpoena is not valid or is not validly served, or where the deposition is restricted because of time or distance, the witness whose testimony is sought need not attend, and the party requesting the deposition cannot tell the court to issue an order of contempt for noncompliance.

Caution should be exercised where the deposition is being sought by service of a subpoena. Most jurisdictions recognize that the personal delivery of a subpoena is not required. Substitute service of the subpoena by leaving it at the deponent's residence or place of business may be sufficient for notifying the deponent. However, the party requesting the deposition must demonstrate to the court that the subpoena was properly served. If proper service can be demonstrated, the person whose deposition testimony is being sought under the subpoena may be held in contempt of court for noncompliance. This charge may include the imposition of a fine and/or incarceration. Further, the court would undoubtedly order the witness to testify at some particular time and place at his or her own expense.

An **expert witness** is a person requested by a party to the lawsuit to give an expert opinion regarding some element of the case. The expert may request and receive compensation in the form of expert witness fees by the party requesting his or her deposition. The expert is not necessarily a percipient witness, who is called to testify about records, specific facts of treatment, or personal knowledge relevant to the particular case in litigation.

For example, the expert may be called as a witness to give his or her opinion of whether or not the defendant committed any acts of malpractice. The expert opinion may also extend to the nature and extent of the plaintiff's injuries and damages. Expert witnesses are routinely used by both plaintiffs and defendants in all litigation dealing with alleged professional negligence. Any witness called to testify, either in court or at a deposition, to give an expert opinion for either side may be compensated for his or her expert opinion. However, compensation is generally based on the amount of money that the professional could have made during the time required for his or her testimony—whether the testimony is obtained in court at trial or by the expert's deposition.

Illustration 15.6 is an example of a form giving notice of the intent of one party's attorney to take the deposition of another party to the lawsuit. Illustration 15.7 is a subpoena that would be served on a witness other than a party to the lawsuit compelling the witness to present himself or herself for deposition at the time and place specified.

SUBPOENAS

A *subpoena* is a document issued by the court and directed to a person, requiring his or her attendance at a particular time and place to testify as a witness to the lawsuit.

A *subpoena duces tecum* is a subpoena used not only to compel witnesses to attend in court but also to require them to provide books, documents, or other tangible items in their possession that may tend to elucidate the subject matter of the trial (see Illustrations 15.7 and 15.8). Compliance with this subpoena generally requires that the witness produce only the documents requested and

```
 1                    LAW OFFICES                (SPACE BELOW FOR FILING STAMP ONLY)
                  Michael L. Cowdrey
 2            SANTA ANA, CALIFORNIA 92701
                    (714) 835-1048
 3

 4

 5    Attorneys for_____

 6

 7

 8

 9

10                                          )   No._____
11                                          )
                                            )
12                                          )
                                            )   NOTICE OF TAKING
13                                          )
                                            )   DEPOSITION
14                                          )
                                            )
15                                          )
      _____)
16    TO:   EACH PARTY HEREIN AND TO THEIR ATTORNEYS OF RECORD:
17          PLEASE TAKE NOTICE that defendant _____
18    will take the deposition of _____
19    on the _____ day of _____, at _____M.
20    at the offices of _____located
21

22    before any Notary Public authorized to administer oaths in the
23    State of California.  Said deposition will continue from day
24    to day until completed, holidays and Sundays excepted.
25    DATED:_____
26

27
                          By_____
28                           Michael L. Cowdrey
```

ILLUSTRATION 15.6 NOTICE OF INTENT TO TAKE DEPOSITION

ATTORNEY OR PARTY WITHOUT ATTORNEY (NAME AND ADDRESS):	TELEPHONE:	FOR COURT USE ONLY
James Smith, M.D.	*(714) 555-5544*	
333 First St.		
Anytown, CA 90000 *In Pro Per*		
ATTORNEY FOR (NAME): *Plaintiff,* ATTORNEY BAR #		

SUPERIOR COURT OF CALIFORNIA, COUNTY OF ORANGE

700 Civic Center Drive West
Post Office Box 838
Santa Ana, CA 92702

PLAINTIFF:
James Smith, M.D.

DEFENDANT:
Donald Johnson

CIVIL SUBPOENA ☐COURT ☒DEPOSITION ☒DUCES TECUM ☐OTHER *(specify)*:	CASE NUMBER: *SC 55 44 55*

THE PEOPLE OF THE STATE OF CALIFORNIA, TO (NAME):

HOPE COWDREY

1. **YOU ARE ORDERED TO APPEAR AS A WITNESS in this action as follows unless you make a special agreement with the person named in item 3:**

    a. Date: *March 6, 1984*   Time: *10:00 a.m.* ☐Dept.: ☐Div.: ☐Room:

    b. Address: *333 First St., Anytown, CA 90000*

2. and you are

    a. ☐ ordered to appear in person.

    b. ☐ not required to appear in person if you produce the records described in the accompanying affidavit in compliance with Evidence Code sections 1560 and 1561.

    c. ☒ ordered to appear in person and to produce the records described in the accompanying affidavit. The personal attendance of the custodian or other qualified witness and the production of the original records is required by this subpoena. The procedure authorized pursuant to subdivision (b) of section 1560, and sections 1561 and 1562, of the Evidence Code will not be deemed sufficient compliance with this subpena.

    d. ☐ ordered to designate one or more persons to testify on your behalf as to the matters described in the accompanying statement. (Code of Civil Procedure section 2019(a)(6).)

3. **IF YOU HAVE ANY QUESTIONS ABOUT WITNESS FEES OR THE TIME OR DATE FOR YOU TO APPEAR, OR IF YOU WANT TO BE CERTAIN THAT YOUR PRESENCE IS REQUIRED, CONTACT THE ATTORNEY REQUESTING THIS SUBPOENA, NAMED ABOVE, OR THE FOLLOWING PERSON, BEFORE THE DATE ON WHICH YOU ARE TO APPEAR:**

    a. Name: *James Smith, M.D.*   b. Telephone number: *(714) 555-5544*

4. **WITNESS FEES:** You are entitled to receive witness fees and mileage actually traveled, as provided by law, if you request them **BEFORE** your scheduled appearance. **Request them from the person named in item 3.**

    If this subpoena requires your attendance at proceedings out of court and you refuse to answer questions or sign as required by law, you must attend a court hearing at a time to be fixed by the person conducting such proceedings.

6. You are ordered to appear in this civil matter in your capacity as a peace officer or other person described in Government Code section 68097.1.

    Date: Clerk of the Court, by _____ , Deputy

> DISOBEDIENCE OF THIS SUBPOENA MAY BE PUNISHED AS CONTEMPT BY THIS COURT. YOU WILL ALSO BE LIABLE FOR THE SUM OF FIVE HUNDRED DOLLARS AND ALL DAMAGES RESULTING FROM YOUR FAILURE TO OBEY.

For Court Use Only

Dated: *Feb. 5, 1984*

Lee A Branch
LEE A. BRANCH, Clerk
County Clerk and Clerk of the Superior Court of the
State of California, in and for the County of Orange

(See reverse for proof of service)

F0182-503.4 (R2/82)

Form Adopted by Rule 982
Judicial Council of California
Revised Effective January 1, 1982

CIVIL SUBPOENA

ILLUSTRATION 15.7 SUBPOENA FOR DEPOSITION AND PROOF OF SERVICE

PROOF OF SERVICE OF CIVIL SUBPEONA

1. I served this ☐subpeona ☒ subpeona duces tecum and supporting affidavit by delivering a copy personally to the person served as follows:

    a. **Person served** (name): *Hope Cowdrey*

    b. **Address where served:** *8382 Montana Rd.*
       Anytown, CA 90000

    c. **Date of delivery:** *Feb. 9, 1984*

    d. **Time of delivery:** *3:55 p.m.*

    e. **Witness fees** *(check one)*
       (1) ☒ were offered or demanded
           and paid. Amount. . . . $ *35.00*
       (2) ☐ were not demanded or paid.

    f. **Fees for service** . . . . $ *25.00*

2. I received this subpeona for service on (date): *Feb. 8, 1984*

3. **Person serving**
    a. ☐ Not a registered California process server.
    b. ☐ Registered California process server.
    c. ☒ Employee or independent contractor of a registered California process server.
    d. ☐ Exempt from registration under Bus. & Prof. Code section 22350(b).
    e. ☐ California sheriff, marshal, or constable.
    f. Name, address and telephone number and if applicable, county of registration and number:

I declare under penalty of perjury under the laws of the State of California that the foregoing is true and correct and that this declaration is executed on (date): *Feb. 9, 1984* . . . .

Wm Henry Jefferson
___(Signature)___

Wm. Henry Jefferson

(For California sheriff, marshal, or constable use only) I certify that the foregoing is true and correct and that this certificate is executed on (date): . . . . at (place): . . . . , California.

_____
(Signature)

ILLUSTRATION 15.7 (CONTINUED)

ATTORNEY OR PARTY WITHOUT ATTORNEY (NAME AND ADDRESS):	TELEPHONE	FOR COURT USE ONLY
James Smith, M.D. *333 First St.* *Anytown, CA 90000* ATTORNEY FOR (NAME): *Plaintiff, In Pro Per*	*(714) 555-5544*	

Insert name of court, judicial district or branch court, if any, and post office and street address:
In the Municipal Court of
CENTRAL ORANGE COUNTY JUDICIAL DISTRICT
700 Civic Center Drive West, Santa Ana
County of Orange, State of California 92701

PLAINTIFF:

James Smith, M.D.

DEFENDANT:

Donald Johnson, et al.

CIVIL SUBPOENA [X] COURT [ ] DEPOSITION [X] **DUCES TECUM** [ ] OTHER *(specify)*:	CASE NUMBER: *C 55 44 55*

THE PEOPLE OF THE STATE OF CALIFORNIA, TO (NAME):

HOPE COWDREY

1. **YOU ARE ORDERED TO APPEAR AS A WITNESS** in this action as follows unless you make a special agreement with the person named in item 3:

> a. Date: *May 5, 1984* Time: *9:00 a.m.* [ ] Dept.: [X] Div.: *4* [ ] Room:
> b. Address: *700 Civic Center Drive West, Santa Ana, CA 92701*

2. and you are

> a. [ ] ordered to appear in person.
> b. [X] not required to appear in person if you produce the records described in the accompanying affidavit in compliance with Evidence Code sections 1560 and 1561.
> c. [ ] ordered to appear in person and to produce the records described in the accompanying affidavit. The personal attendance of the custodian or other qualified witness and the production of the original records is required by this subpena. The procedure authorized pursuant to subdivision (b) of section 1560, and sections 1561 and 1562, of the Evidence Code will not be deemed sufficient compliance with this subpoena
> d. [ ] ordered to designate one or more persons to testify on your behalf as to the matters described in the accompanying statement. (Code of Civil Procedure section 2019(a)(6).)

3. **IF YOU HAVE ANY QUESTIONS ABOUT WITNESS FEES OR THE TIME OR DATE FOR YOU TO APPEAR, OR IF YOU WANT TO BE CERTAIN THAT YOUR PRESENCE IS REQUIRED, CONTACT THE ATTORNEY REQUESTING THIS SUBPEONA, NAMED ABOVE, OR THE FOLLOWING PERSON, BEFORE THE DATE ON WHICH YOU ARE TO APPEAR:**

> a. Name: *James Smith, M.D.* b. Telephone number: *(714) 555-5544*

4. **WITNESS FEES:** You are entitled to receive witness fees and mileage actually traveled, as provided by law, if you request them **BEFORE** your scheduled appearance. **Request them from the person named in item 3.**

5. If this subpeona requires your attendance at proceedings out of court and you refuse to answer questions or sign as required by law, you must attend a court hearing at a time to be fixed by the person conducting such proceedings.

6. You are ordered to appear in this civil matter in your capacity as a peace officer or other person described in Government Code section 68097.1.

> ROBERT B. KUHEL
> Date: Clerk of the Court, by _____, Deputy

> **DISOBEDIENCE OF THIS SUBPOENA MAY BE PUNISHED AS CONTEMPT BY THIS COURT. YOU WILL ALSO BE LIABLE FOR THE SUM OF FIVE HUNDRED DOLLARS AND ALL DAMAGES RESULTING FROM YOUR FAILURE TO OBEY.**

For Court Use Only	Dated: *March 3, 1984*
	James Smith, M.D. (Signature of person issuing subpena) *James Smith, M.D.* (Type or print name) *Plaintiff, In Pro Per* (Title)

(See reverse for proof of service)

F0363-2424 5 (R10/82)

Form Adopted by Rule 982
Judicial Council of California
Revised Effective January 1, 1982

CIVIL SUBPOENA

ILLUSTRATION 15.8 SUBPOENA DUCES TECUM AND PROOF OF SERVICE

PROOF OF SERVICE OF CIVIL SUBPEONA

1. I served this ☐ subpeona ☒ subpeona duces tecum and supporting affidavit by delivering a copy personally to the person served as follows:

   a. **Person served** (name): *Hope Cowdrey*

   b. **Address where served:** *4576 W. Washington Anytown, CA 90000*

   c. **Date of delivery:** *March 7, 1984*

   d. **Time of delivery:** *4:15 p.m.*

   e. **Witness fees** (check one)
      (1) ☒ were offered or demanded and paid. Amount. . . . $ *35.00*
      (2) ☐ were not demanded or paid.

   f. **Fees for service** . . . . $ _____

2. I received this subpeona for service on (date):

3. **Person serving**
   a. ☒ Not a registered California process server.
   b. ☐ Registered California process server.
   c. ☐ Employee or independent contractor of a registered California process server.
   d. ☐ Exempt from registration under Bus. & Prof. Code section 22350(b).

   e. ☐ California sheriff, marshal, or constable.
   f. Name, address and telephone number and if applicable, county of registration and number:

I declare under penalty of perjury under the laws of the State of California that the foregoing is true and correct and that this declaration is executed on (date): *March 7, 1984* . . . .

_____
(Signature)

(For California sheriff, marshal, or constable use only) I certify that the foregoing is true and correct and that this certificate is executed on (date): . . . . at (place): *Anytown,* . . . . , California.

Marsha Middleton
(Signature)

Marsha Middleton

ILLUSTRATION 15.8 (CONTINUED)

ATTORNEY OR PARTY WITHOUT ATTORNEY (NAME AND ADDRESS)	TELEPHONE NO	FOR COURT USE ONLY
James Smith, M.D. 333 First St. Anytown, CA 90000	*(714) 555-5544* ATTORNEY BAR #	
ATTORNEY FOR (Name) Plaintiff, In Pro Per		
Insert name of court judicial district or branch court if any and post office and street address Superior Court of California, County of Orange 700 Civic Center Drive West Santa Ana, CA 92702		

PLAINTIFF	CASE NUMBER
James Smith, M.D.	SC 55 44 55
DEFENDANT Donald Johnson	

DECLARATION FOR SUBPOENA DUCES TECUM

STATE OF CALIFORNIA, COUNTY OF ORANGE

The undersigned states: That he is attorney of record for Plaintiff/~~Defendant~~ in the above entitled action, that said cause was duly set down for trial _May_ _5_ _1984_ at _9:00 a.m._

in Department _One_ of the above entitled Court.

That _Hope Cowdrey_

has in his possession or under his control the following documents:

(Designate and name the exact things to be produced.)

Bank Account records of Donald Johnson

That said books, papers, and documents or other things are material to the proper presentation of his case, and good cause exists for their production by reason of the following facts:

The records are necessary to demonstrate defendant did not pay on his account with a check.

Executed _March 6,_ , 19 _84_ , at _Anytown_ , California.

I declare under penalty of perjury that the foregoing is true and correct.

James Smith, M.D.
(Signature of Declarant)

CRS F0182-517.3 (R2/80)

ILLUSTRATION 15.8 (CONTINUED)

a declaration that all documents requested are being provided. The witness is bound by law to produce such requested documents unless the witness obtains a protective order from the court invalidating this requirement.

A *subpoena duces tecum re: deposition* requires not only that the documents be produced but also that the custodian of records of these documents testify under oath that the requested documents are genuine and complete. The custodian of records to whom the subpoena duces tecum re: deposition is directed may also be required to testify concerning the way that documents are routinely kept, the procedures for making entries in the documents, or other matters relating to the documents themselves.

As a matter of routine, photocopies of the documents may be given to the party requesting them in lieu of the original. The party to whom the subpoena is directed may request a fee for time expended in compiling all the requested documents and for photocopying charges. Where the fee is not governed by statute or the statute provides for a "reasonable fee," a problem generally arises. Many photocopying services used by attorneys provide a flat fee per quarter hour to the custodian of records and other parties to whom the subpoena is directed. This sum represents compensation for administrative costs and time incurred by the custodian of records in compiling the requested documents. However, the medical facility or other person to whom the subpoena is directed may charge a fee for each page copied in addition to the administrative costs of compiling the documents where the person or facility is requested to provide photocopying services.

The custodian of the business records may also be compensated for his or her time and mileage when the subpoena is a subpoena duces tecum re: deposition. This compensation is generally the same as may be charged when the custodian of records is required to testify in court. All such fees are governed by statute in many states.

The request for the deposition fee, administrative fee, or fee for photocopying the documents must be demanded at the time the subpoena is served. If not, such fees and costs are waived by the person or institution to whom the subpoena is directed and may not thereafter be requested. Noncompliance by the custodian of records in providing the documents or attending the deposition may be justified where payment of the *requested* fee was not made when demanded at the time the subpoena was served. However, any person or institution to whom a subpoena is directed should exercise caution when choosing not to comply with the subpoena. Failure to comply or to make alternative arrangements with the attorney requesting the records may result in the attorney obtaining a court order which, if violated, may subject a person to being held in contempt of court.

The following procedure should be followed when accepting subpoenas for requested documents. This procedure will protect one from the wrath of some irate judge over noncompliance. (1) The person to whom the subpoena is served should demand a fee for administrative costs and/or photocopying at the time the subpoena is served. (2) The person accepting the subpoena should

```
┌─────────────────────────────────────────────────────────────────┐
│            AUTHORIZATION FOR RELEASE OF MEDICAL INFORMATION        │
│  TO:                                                              │
│              _____                      │
│                                                                  │
│              _____                      │
│                                                                  │
│              _____                      │
│                                                                  │
│              _____                      │
│                                                                  │
│                                                                  │
│         I,_____, authorize you, upon receipt of   │
│  this Authoriza-                                                 │
│  tion For Release of Medical Information or a photocopy hereof,  │
│  to release to my attor-                                         │
│  ney, Melinda Drew, all medical information concerning me in     │
│  your possession, cus-                                          │
│  tody, or control. You are further authorized to provide my      │
│  attorney with copies of                                        │
│  any and all documents concerning me, including history,         │
│  findings, x-ray and labora-                                    │
│  tory findings, treatment recommendations, diagnosis and        │
│  prognosis.                                                      │
│         Please note that you are prohibited from releasing any   │
│  medical information                                            │
│  concerning to me to any other person or entity without my      │
│  specific written consent.                                      │
│         Cross out if inapplicable:                              │
│         This Authorization includes permission to release any   │
│  psychiatric or psychologi-                                     │
│  cal information you have concerning me.                         │
│         This Authorization includes permission to release any   │
│  drug or alcohol depen-                                         │
│  dency information you have concerning me.                       │
│                                                                  │
│                              _____              │
│                              Signature of patient                │
│                                                                  │
│                              _____              │
│                              Date of Birth                       │
│  Dated:                                                          │
└─────────────────────────────────────────────────────────────────┘
```

ILLUSTRATION 15.9 AUTHORIZATION FOR THE RELEASE OF MEDICAL INFORMATION

immediately telephone the attorney requesting the records to arrange for payment of costs in the event that costs are not paid by the person serving the subpoena. This is especially true in cases where the person or institution is requested to provide photocopies. An agreement on the amount of photocopying costs should be reached between the attorney requesting the documents and the person or institution to whom the subpoena is directed. The requested fee should be paid prior to releasing the records to circumvent any problems in not receiving the requested fee after providing the attorney with the records. These procedural steps are also recommended where documents are being sought pursuant to a release for medical information signed by the patient (see Illustration 15.9).

OBTAINING COPIES OF PATIENT RECORDS WITHOUT A SUBPOENA

California, Massachusetts, and certain other states now have laws that allow a patient to obtain a copy of his or her medical records without the authorization of an attorney. Before the enactment of this California statute, for example, the only way a patient could obtain copies of his or her medical records was either by subpoena or through an attorney who would provide the health care provider with an executed authorization for the release of such records.

The California Health and Safety Code requires that a health care provider supply copies of such records to a patient, former patient, or patient's representative within fifteen days after receiving a written request. A copying fee not to exceed $0.25 per page and reasonable clerical costs may be charged to the patient by the health care provider. X-rays and tracings derived from electrocardiography, electroencephalography, and electromyography could be transmitted to another health care provider within fifteen days after receipt of the written request. This would be in lieu of transmitting such original X-rays and tracings to the patient, former patient, or representative. The statute also guarantees that patients and former patients of health care providers, along with certain representatives of patients and former patients, have the right to inspect health records within five days after presenting a written request and a payment of reasonable clerical costs to the health care provider.

Massachusetts law also requires health care providers, including physicians, surgeons, chiropractors, dentists and nurses to provide at reasonable cost, a copy of a patient's record to the patient or his or her authorized representative.[1] The Massachusetts Board of Registration in Medicine has stated, by regulation, that a charge in excess of 25¢ per page or a clerical fee in excess of $20.00 per hour is an excessive charge for provision of medical records.[2]

However, in many states, a health care provider can refuse inspection or copying of specific mental health records if the provider determines that disclosure would adversely affect the patient or former patient. The patient or former patient could, however, designate a physician or psychologist to inspect or copy such records. In addition, a health care provider can refuse to make a minor patient's records available to the minor's parents or guardian where (1) the provider determines it would have a detrimental effect on the provider's professional relationship with the minor or (2) general laws empower the minor to consent to the care that is the subject of the records.

A "health care provider," as referred to in the California statute, is any health facility, such as a hospital, licensed physical therapist, clinic, home health agency, physician, surgeon, podiatrist, dentist, optometrist, or chiropractor. "Patient records" are records in any form or medium maintained by or in the custody or control of a health care provider relating to the health history,

---

[1]M.G.L. chapter 112, Section 12CC.

[2]243 Code of Massachusetts Regulations, Section 2.07(13).

diagnosis or condition of the patient or relating to treatment provided or proposed to be provided to the patient.

"Patient records" include only records pertaining to the patient in question. They do not include information given in confidence to a health care provider by a person other than another health care provider or the patient. Such material may be removed from any records prior to inspection or copying.

A "patient's representative" is the parent or guardian of a minor or the guardian or conservator of an adult patient. Nothing in the statute may be construed to preclude a health care provider from requiring reasonable verification of identity prior to permitting inspection or copying of patient records, provided such requirements are not used oppressively or discriminatorily to frustrate or delay compliance in providing the records.

As previously indicated, the health care provider may charge a fee of $0.25 per page for copying the records. In addition, he or she may charge $0.50 per page for records copied from microfilm. Any other reasonable clerical costs incurred in making the records available may also be charged to the patient. The health care provider may prepare a summary of the record according to the requirements of the statute in cases where the records are voluminous or the health care provider determines that some entries may be detrimental to the patient if made known to him or her. In such cases, the health care provider should make a summary of the record available to the patient within ten working days from the date of the patient's request. The health care provider can notify the patient that more time is needed because the record is of extraordinary length or because the patient was discharged from a licensed health care facility within the previous ten days. However, thirty days is the maximum time allowed between the request by the patient and the delivery of the summary.

If the health care provider chooses to provide a summary in lieu of the records themselves, the summary shall contain, for each injury, illness, or episode, any information included in the records concerning the following:

1. Chief complaint or complaints, including pertinent history
2. Findings from consultations and referrals to other health care providers
3. Diagnosis, where determined
4. Treatment plan and regime, including medications prescribed
5. Progress of the treatment
6. Prognosis, including significant continuing problems or conditions
7. Pertinent reports of diagnostic procedures and tests and all discharge summaries
8. Objective findings from the most recent physical examination, such as blood pressure, weight, and actual values from routine laboratory tests

9. A list of all current medication prescribed, including dosage and any sensitivities or allergies to medications recorded by the provider

The health care provider may charge no more than a reasonable fee based on actual time and costs for the preparation of the summary. The costs shall be based on a computation of actual time spent preparing the summary for availability to the patient or the patient's representative.

When a health care provider determines that there is a substantial risk of significant adverse or detrimental consequences to a patient in seeking or receiving a copy of mental health records requested, the provider may decline to permit inspection or to provide copies of such records to the patient. However, the provider must make a written record, to be included with the mental health records, noting the date of the request and explaining the health care provider's reasons for refusing to permit inspection or provide copies to the patient. Also included must be a description of the specific adverse or detrimental consequences to the patient that the provider anticipates would occur if inspection or copying were permitted. The health care provider must, however, permit a licensed physician or surgeon, a licensed psychologist, or a licensed clinical social worker designated by the patient to inspect or obtain copies of the mental health records. The health care provider shall inform the patient of the provider's refusal to permit him or her to inspect or obtain copies of the requested records. The provider shall inform the patient of his or her right to require the provider to permit inspection by, or provide copies to, a licensed physician and surgeon, licensed psychologist or licensed clinical social worker designated by written authorization of the patient.

EXAMPLES/QUESTIONS/PROJECTS

1. *Can you think of any reason why the doctor of your office should not be considered the custodian of his or her own records? What about expert witness fees being paid to a doctor acting as the custodian of records and responding to a subpoena duces tecum?*

    Answer: No expert witness fees would be paid.

2. *Assume that you are acting as your own attorney in defending an action brought by a patient against you for malpractice. What questions would you consider relevant and important to your defense in a set of requests for admissions or interrogatories propounded to the patient/plaintiff? (Class discussion and/or individual assignments.)*

Chapter Sixteen

TRIAL

PROCEDURAL STEPS
EXPERT TESTIMONY

CROSS-EXAMINATION
EXAMPLES/QUESTIONS/
PROJECTS

Key Terms

economist

adversary
expert witness

credibility

A criminal defendant has the right to have his or her case tried before a jury of his or her peers. In most, though not all, civil cases, there is also a right to trial by jury. A criminal defendant may waive his or her right to a jury trial and have the case tried before a judge or, in some jurisdictions, before a **tribunal**. In civil litigation, where trial by jury is permitted, the plaintiff has the right to demand a jury trial, even if the defendant doesn't want one. The demand for jury trial is usually made by the plaintiff in his or her complaint.

Most commonly, a jury consists of twelve adult men and women selected from the local community, although some state and federal courts have rules permitting the jury to consist of less than twelve persons.

The court schedules a case to be tried once the plaintiff has filed appropriate papers with the court indicating that the case is ready for trial. The plaintiff indicates that all pretrial discovery has or will be completed within a reasonable time. Generally, the court requires the parties to the action to meet and confer before the court, administrative officer, or designated arbitrator for the purpose of attempting to negotiate a settlement of the case by all concerned. Often termed a *mandatory settlement conference*, this meeting is held just before the scheduled trial date. The matter then proceeds to trial if the parties cannot settle the case out of court.

PROCEDURAL STEPS

The basic procedural steps in a trial include jury selection and an opening statement by the plaintiff's counsel, followed by the presentation of evidence for his or her client's contentions in the form of documents and the testimony of witnesses. This presentation is followed by the opening statement of the defendant's attorney if he or she has not already presented it following the plaintiff's counsel's opening statement. The defendant's counsel presents evidence for his or her client's contentions in the form of documents and the testimony of witnesses to demonstrate that the defendant is not liable to the plaintiff and that the plaintiff did not sustain injury or damages as alleged.

Following the presentation of the defendant's case, both attorneys are allowed to present oral arguments showing how the evidence presented favors their particular contentions. The judge then instructs the jury concerning the law that is applicable to the subject of the litigation. The matter is then submitted to the jury for deliberation and return of their verdict.

Discussion of every possible strategy and procedural step—such as the admissibility of evidence, pretrial motions, posttrial motions, and so on—is beyond the scope of this text. However, expert testimony, a feature of virtually every malpractice case, will be dealt with in the following section.

EXPERT TESTIMONY

Malpractice cases are rarely tried without the testimony of **expert witnesses.** The plaintiff virtually always calls physicians, surgeons, nurses, psychologists, psychiatrists, or other experts to give their expert opinion regarding the standard of care owed to the patient by the defendant at the time of the alleged malpractice. The expert could also testify that the specific conduct—whether an affirmative act or an omission to act where there was a duty to do so— constituted malpractice.

In addition, experts may be called to testify concerning the nature and extent of the patient/plaintiff's injuries, including an estimation of the need for future medical care and the costs for such care. The plaintiff may call an **economist** to give his or her expert opinion about the patient/plaintiff's loss of income caused by the injuries he or she sustained as a result of the alleged malpractice. The economist may also give expert opinion about other reasonable costs that may be anticipated in the future by the patient/plaintiff because of his or her disabling injury. Such costs would include loss of potential future income or earning capacity based on the standard rate of monetary inflation, and future medical costs that may reasonably be anticipated.

The defendant in a malpractice case would present expert testimony by physicians, surgeons, chiropractors, nurses, dentists, or other similarly qualified experts to give their expert opinion of how well the care rendered to the patient/plaintiff measures up to the standard of care owed to him or her by the professional/defendant. The defendant may call additional doctors, dentists, nurses, and other professionals who have examined the plaintiff to give their expert opinion either that the plaintiff has not sustained any injury or that such injury is not a result of any act of malpractice on the part of the defendant. Additional medical experts may be called to testify that the alleged injuries sustained by the plaintiff are not permanently disabling.

In cases where you, as the professional, are being called to testify and give your expert opinion, you are entitled to reasonable compensation for your testimony. Expert witness fees are often allowed by a state code or statute. The expert witness fee is based on the time spent by the expert in reviewing the facts of the case and possibly examining the plaintiff, the actual time spent in court to testify, and the qualifications of the expert in his or her field.

Unless the expert has some direct relationship with the case itself, such as being the plaintiff's treating physician, attorneys are not permitted to go throughout the land issuing subpoenas compelling the attendance and expert testimony of doctors, nurses, technicians, medical assistants, or other allied health professionals. To obtain such expert testimony, the attorney would need to contact the potential witness requesting his or her assistance in providing expert testimony at trial. At this time, the expert should indicate the amount he or she will charge for such testimony, including any fees for the review of records and other facts of the case. Such requested fees should be paid *before* the expert enters the case. This procedure would prevent any further litigation between the attorney and the expert witness based on the attorney's breach of the contractual obligation owed to the expert in providing this service.

Situations arise in lawsuits where a physician, technician, nurse, or other allied health professional is called by a defense attorney to a lawsuit to give his or her professional opinion regarding some examination or treatment of the plaintiff of which the expert has personal knowledge. Because the expert is merely a witness and not a party to the litigation, the only way that the attorney can compel the professional's testimony is by serving him or her with a subpoena to attend and testify at trial. If the subpoenaed professional witness does not attend, the court could issue a contempt citation and a warrant for his or her arrest.

The professional expert called to testify regarding the patient or other matters in the case within his or her own personal knowledge may be deemed to be a percipient witness. Compensation for a percipient witness in such situations is governed by statute, as with any other nonexpert witness. However, testimony may only be directed to the professional's personal knowledge of the patient or case. Unless he or she is given expert witness fees, the professional need not testify regarding his or her expert opinion of the matter in contention. The professional need only tell the judge that an expert opinion is being requested and that the attorney who issued the subpoena compelling the professional's attendance has not paid the professional expert witness fees. Most commonly, the judge will either command the attorney to provide the witness with expert witness fees or will not compel the witness to give his or her expert opinion. Note, however, that this should rarely occur since most attorneys are well aware that expert witnesses are entitled to be compensated for their time.

For those members of the allied health profession who are not routinely called to testify in court or to give their deposition as an expert witness, a few suggestions are in order on the giving of testimony. First, and undoubtedly most important, is to stay within your particular field of expertise. Often attorneys attempt to obtain from a professional witness an expert opinion that is outside their field of expertise—especially when the attorney represents the **adversary** party. Thus, listen to the question carefully. Make sure you understand it before giving your answer. Where the question is requesting information that you feel may be outside your field of expertise, merely respond by stating an opinion that falls within your field of expertise. Decline to express any further opinion that may fall outside your field of expertise. Nothing is more embarrassing to a nurse or medical assistant than to assert for a jury a diagnostic impression or proper treatment procedure that clearly should be given only by a physician, surgeon, dentist, or other person licensed to make such a judgment. Likewise, a technician expressing an opinion regarding the effects of a drug or alcohol on a patient may be drifting far afield from his or her expertise in the field of laboratory technology, even though he or she knows complex biochemical equations and reactions. Such testimony may diminish the credibility of the expert witness and therefore prove embarrassing to that witness.

Second, do not volunteer information that is not being asked unless it clarifies in lay terms something you have already testified to in technical language. To volunteer information only gives an adversary attorney ammunition to attack your **credibility** and also increases the possibility that you may be led into areas outside your particular field of expertise.

Finally, as a professional, your appearance and response to questioning should be professional. You should dress conservatively and respond to questions in a matter-of-fact manner.

CROSS-EXAMINATION

Testimony given by a witness either at his or her deposition or at trial is given under oath. The sworn oath obligates the witness to tell the truth to the best of his or her ability and knowledge. The penalty for intentional lying under sworn oath to tell the truth is that of perjury, a criminal offense that is punishable by incarceration. Assuming that all sworn witnesses would not intentionally give false testimony, important functional aspects regarding the professional's response to questioning as a witness are in order. Cross-examination by an adversary attorney is often upsetting for the person appearing as a witness.

Telling the truth should be interpreted to include not guessing at any answer. If the witness does not know the answer to a specific question he or she should merely state "I don't know" or "I don't recall." Witnesses should not guess only because they feel the question needs to be answered. Also, the witness should be sure that he or she understands each and every question asked before responding. If necessary, the witness should tell the person directing the question that he or she doesn't understand it. The person directing the question must reword or rephrase the question. This is especially true where the question is leading or suggestive of an answer—such as "Isn't it true that you failed to make the chart entry?" Such questions suggest a "yes" answer, when the true answer may be "no." Adversary attorneys often attempt to confuse or badger a witness, especially when the witness's testimony is not expected to be helpful to their case. Witnesses should not become intimidated by the adversary attorney or his or her questions.

EXAMPLES / QUESTIONS / PROJECTS

1. Can a medical, dental, or other professional assistant demand expert witness fees for testifying at trial?

> **Answer:** Yes, if the assistant is being asked questions related to his or her area of expertise.

2. *Should expert witness fees be demanded at the time the attorney requests expert testimony?*

> **Answer:** Yes, if the initial request to testify at a deposition or trial is made by the attorney.

3. *Can the professional refuse to testify at a deposition or trial if subpoenaed as a witness?*

> **Answer:** The expert must present himself or herself at the deposition or trial as required by the subpoena unless the professional has obtained a protective order from the court. However, the professional, whether a physician, medical assistant, or technician, is not required to give expert testimony unless expert witness fees have been demanded and paid by the attorney subpoenaing the expert. When the expert is being asked to give a professional opinion, he or she need only tell the judge that expert witness fees have been demanded and not paid. The attorney subpoenaing the witness may question the expert regarding areas of his or her own personal knowledge about the case or patient; expert witness fees only come into play when the professional is being requested to give an expert opinion.

CHAPTER SEVENTEEN

ACTIONS AGAINST PATIENTS FOR PAYMENT OF THEIR BILLS

MUNICIPAL, DISTRICT,
OR SUPERIOR COURT
ACTIONS

SMALL CLAIMS ACTIONS

WRITS

EXAMPLES/QUESTIONS/
PROJECTS

Key Terms

judgment debtor   judgment creditor   conformed copy

Using the procedural elements of a civil lawsuit discussed in the preceding chapter, this chapter deals with obtaining payment of a patient's bill by litigation. Completed court forms are used as illustrations throughout this chapter to assist the reader in understanding the steps involved from initiation of the lawsuit through case presentation at trial.

MUNICIPAL, DISTRICT, OR SUPERIOR COURT ACTIONS

Cases dealing with claimed damages in excess of a minimal amount may be filed either with the municipal, district, or justice court or with the superior court. Cases where the conflict is based on the breach of a contractual promise or obligation and the amount exceeds some minimal amount, such as $1,500 but less than $15,000, are filed in the appropriate municipal, district, or justice court. Cases where the conflict is based on the breach of a contractual promise or obligation and the amount exceeds some higher minimal amount, such as $15,000 or $25,000 are filed in the appropriate superior court. In addition, the parties to the lawsuit can be represented by an attorney throughout the proceedings, and all forms of formal discovery outlined in Chapter 15 are available to them throughout the litigation.

Most commonly, cases dealing with the breach of a contractual obligation arise in the allied health professions when a patient fails to pay his or her bill for professional services rendered. The physician, dentist, therapist, or institution could retain the services of an attorney and sue in the appropriate court for payment of the patient's bill. The cause of action would be based upon the patient's breach of a contractual obligation owing to the doctor, dentist, therapist, or institution.

The doctor, dentist, therapist, or other individual rendering the professional services may bring the action and act as his or her own attorney in the case. In fact, anyone may act as his or her own attorney in any type of lawsuit. However, the individual dentist, physician, therapist, or other professional may not be represented by one of his or her medical or dental assistants unless the assistant is a licensed attorney.

The preprinted court forms given in Illustrations 17.1 and 17.2 are the pleadings that the individual professional may file with the municipal court in California against the patient for nonpayment of the patient's bill. The preprinted forms given in Illustration 17.3 through 17.5 are forms that may be completed and filed when the patient/defendant fails to answer the charges in the complaint within thirty days after it has been served. The court or clerk in this situation would enter a judgment in favor of the individual professional/plaintiff to the case.

The preprinted court form given in Illustration 17.6 is completed and filed by the individual professional/plaintiff to indicate that all matters of discovery have been completed and that the case is ready for trial on the merits

(continued on page 257)

NAME AND ADDRESS OF ATTORNEY:		FOR COURT USE ONLY:

NAME AND ADDRESS OF ATTORNEY:
James Smith, M.D.
333 First St.
Anytown, CA 90000

TELEPHONE NO:
(714) 555-5544

ATTORNEY FOR (Name): Plaintiff, In Pro Per

FOR COURT USE ONLY:

Insert name of court, judicial district or branch court, if any, and Post Office and Street Address:
**MUNICIPAL COURT OF CALIFORNIA COUNTY OF ORANGE
ORANGE COUNTY JUDICIAL DISTRICT**

ADDRESS:

PLAINTIFF: James Smith, M.D.

DEFENDANT: Donald Johnson

SUMMONS

CASE NUMBER
SC 55 44 55

NOTICE! You have been sued. The court may decide against you without your being heard unless you respond within 30 days. Read the information below.

If you wish to seek the advice of an attorney in this matter, you should do so promptly so that your written response, if any, may be filed on time.

¡AVISO! Usted ha sido demandado. El tribunal puede decidir contra Ud. sin audiencia a menos que Ud. responda dentro de 30 días. Lea la información que sigue.

Si Usted desea solicitar el consejo de un abogado en este asunto, debería hacerlo inmediatamente, de esta manera, su respuesta escrita, si hay alguna, puede ser registrada a tiempo.

1. TO THE DEFENDANT: A civil complaint has been filed by the plaintiff against you. If you wish to defend this lawsuit, you must, within **30** days after this summons is served on you, file with this court a written response to the complaint. Unless you do so, your default will be entered on application of the plaintiff, and this court may enter a judgment against you for the relief demanded in the complaint, which could result in garnishment of wages, taking of money or property or other relief requested in the complaint.

DATED: . . . ., Clerk, By _____ , Deputy

2. NOTICE TO THE PERSON SERVED: You are served
   a. [X] As an individual defendant.
   b. [ ] As the person sued under the fictitious name of: . . . .
   c. [ ] On behalf of: . . . .
      Under: [ ] CCP 416.10 (Corporation)   [ ] CCP 416.60 (Minor)
             [ ] CCP 416.20 (Defunct Corporation)   [ ] CCP 416.70 (Incompetent)
             [ ] CCP 416.40 (Association or Partnership)   [X] CCP 416.90 (Individual)
             [ ] Other:
   d. [X] By personal delivery on (Date): April 28, 1983

A written response must be in the form prescribed by the California Rules of Court. It must be filed in this court with the proper filing fee and proof of service of a copy on each plaintiff's attorney and on each plaintiff not represented by an attorney. The time when a summons is deemed served on a party may vary depending on the method of service. For example, see CCP 413.10 through 415.50. The word "complaint" includes cross-complaint, "plaintiff" includes cross-complainant, "defendant" includes cross-defendant, the singular includes the plural.

(See reverse for Proof of Service)

Form Adopted by Rule 982
Judicial Council of California
Revised Effective January 1, 1979

SUMMONS

CCP 412 20, 412 30, 415 10

F850-2402.8 (R7/82)

ILLUSTRATION 17.1 SUMMONS

PROOF OF SERVICE

(Use separate proof of service for each person served)

1. I served the

   a. ☒ summons ☒ complaint ☐ amended summons ☐ amended complaint

   b. On defendant (Name):   *Donald Johnson*

   c. By serving (1) ☐ Defendant (2) ☒ Other (Name and title or relationship to person served): *Helen Johnson, defendant's wife*

   d. ☒ By delivery at ☒ home ☐ business (1) Date of: *April 28, 1983*
      (2) Time of: *8:45 p.m.* (3) Address: *41563 N. Adams St. Anytown, CA 90000*

   e. ☐ By mailing (1) Date of: (2) Place of:

2. Manner of service: (Check proper box)

   a. ☐ **Personal service.** By personally delivering copies. (CCP 415.10)

   b. ☐ **Substituted service on corporation, unincorporated association (including partnership), or public entity.** By leaving, during usual office hours, copies in the office of the person served with the person who apparently was in charge and thereafter mailing (by first-class mail, postage prepaid) copies to the person served at the place where the copies were left. (CCP 415.20(a))

   c. ☒ **Substituted service on natural person, minor, incompetent, or candidate.** By leaving copies at the dwelling house, usual place of abode, or usual place of business of the person served in the presence of a competent member of the household or a person apparently in charge of the office or place of business, at least 18 years of age, who was informed of the general nature of the papers, and thereafter mailing (by first-class mail, postage prepaid) copies to the person served at the place where the copies were left. (CCP 415.20(b)) **(Attach separate declaration or affidavit stating acts relied on to establish reasonable diligence in first attempting personal service.)**

   d. ☐ **Mail and acknowledgment service.** By mailing (by first-class mail or airmail) copies to the person served, together with two copies of the form of notice and acknowledgment and a return envelope, postage prepaid, addressed to the sender. (CCP 415.30) **(Attach completed acknowledgment of receipt.)**

   e. ☐ **Certified or registered mail service.** By mailing to address outside California (by registered or certified airmail with return receipt requested) copies to the person served. (CCP 415.40) **(Attach signed return receipt or other evidence of actual delivery to the person served.)**

   f. ☐ Other (Specify code section):
      ☐ Additional page is attached.

3. The notice to the person served (Item 2 on the copy of the summons served) was completed as follows (CCP 412.30, 415.10, and 474):

   a. ☒ As an individual defendant.

   b. ☐ As the person sued under the fictitious name of:

   c. ☐ On behalf of:
      Under: ☐ CCP 416.10 (Corporation)   ☐ CCP 416.60 (Minor)   ☐ Other:
      　　　 ☐ CCP 416.20 (Defunct corporation) ☐ CCP 416.70 (Incompetent)
      　　　 ☐ CCP 416.40 (Association or partnership) ☒ CCP 416.90 (Individual)

   d. ☒ By personal delivery on (Date): *April 28, 1983*

4. At the time of service I was at least 18 years of age and not a party to this action.

5. Fee for service: $ *10.50*

6. Person serving

   a. ☒ Not a registered California process server.
   b. ☐ Registered California process server.
   c. ☐ Employee or independent contractor of a registered California process server.
   d. ☐ Exempt from registration under Bus. & Prof. Code 22350(b)

   e. ☐ California sheriff, marshal, or constable.
   f. Name, address and telephone number and if applicable, county of registration and number:

I declare under penalty of perjury that the foregoing is true and correct and that this declaration is executed on (Date): *April 28, 1983* at (Place): *Anytown,* , California.

Ani Egglester
　　　　(Signature)

(For California sheriff, marshal or constable use only)
I certify that the foregoing is true and correct and that this certificate is executed on (Date): at (Place): , California.

　　　　(Signature)

A declaration under penalty of perjury must be signed in California or in a state that authorizes use of a declaration in place of an affidavit; otherwise an affidavit is required.

ILLUSTRATION 17.1 (CONTINUED)

ATTORNEY OR PARTY WITHOUT ATTORNEY (NAME AND ADDRESS)	TELEPHONE	FOR COURT USE ONLY

James Smith, M.D.
333 E. First St.
Anytown, CA 90000

TELEPHONE: *(714) 555-5544*

ATTORNEY FOR (NAME): *Plaintiff, In Pro Per*   ATTORNEY BAR #

SUPERIOR COURT OF CALIFORNIA, COUNTY OF ORANGE
700 Civic Center Drive West
Post Office Box 838
Santa Ana, CA 92702-0838

PLAINTIFF: *JAMES SMITH, M.D.*

DEFENDANT: *DONALD JOHNSON*

[X] DOES 1 TO *10, Inclusive.*

CONTRACT
[X] **COMPLAINT**   ☐ **CROSS-COMPLAINT**

CASE NUMBER

1. This pleading, including attachments and exhibits, consists of the following number of pages: *4 (attach copy of Mr. Johnson's Billing Ledger)*

2. a. Each plaintiff named above is a competent adult
      ☐ **Except** plaintiff *(name):*
        ☐ a corporation qualified to do business in California
        ☐ an unincorporated entity *(describe):*
        ☐ other *(specify):*

   b. [X] Plaintiff *(name):* *James Smith, M.D.*
        ☐ has complied with the fictitious business name laws and is doing business under the fictitious name of *(specify):*
        [X] has complied with all licensing requirements as a licensed *(specify):* *Medical Practitioner*

   c. ☐ Information about additional plaintiffs who are not competent adults is shown in Complaint—Attachment 2c.

3. a. Each defendant named above is a natural person
      ☐ **Except** defendant *(name):*   ☐ **Except** defendant *(name):*
        ☐ a business organization, form unknown   ☐ a business organization, form unknown
        ☐ a corporation   ☐ a corporation
        ☐ an unincorporated entity *(describe):*   ☐ an unincorporated entity *(describe):*
        ☐ a public entity *(describe):*   ☐ a public entity *(describe):*
        ☐ other *(specify):*   ☐ other *(specify):*

   b. The true names and capacities of defendants sued as Does are unknown to plaintiff.

   c. ☐ Information about additional defendants who are not natural persons is contained in Complaint—Attachment 3c.

   d. ☐ Defendants who are joined pursuant to Code of Civil Procedure section 382 are *(names):*

(Continued)

If this form is used as a cross-complaint, plaintiff means cross-complainant and defendant means cross-defendant.
Form Approved by the
Judicial Council of California
Effective January 1, 1982
Rule 982.1(20)

COMPLAINT—Contract

CCP 425.12

F0182-592 (12/81)

ILLUSTRATION 17.2 COMPLAINT-CONTRACT

SHORT TITLE:
James Smith, M.D. vs. Donald Johnson, et al.

CASE NUMBER

COMPLAINT—Contract

Page two

4. [X] Plaintiff is required to comply with a claims statute, **and**
    a. [X] plaintiff has complied with applicable claims statutes, **or**
    b. [ ] plaintiff is excused from complying because *(specify)*:

5. [ ] This action is subject to [X] Civil Code section 1812.10 [ ] Civil Code section 2984.4.

6. This action is filed in this [ ] county [X] judicial district because
    a. [X] a defendant entered into the contract here.
    b. [X] a defendant lived here when the contract was entered into.
    c. [X] a defendant lives here now.
    d. [X] the contract was to be performed here.
    e. [ ] a defendant is a corporation or unincorporated association and its principal place of business is here.
    f. [ ] real property that is the subject of this action is located here.
    g. [ ] other *(specify)*:

7. [ ] The following paragraphs of this pleading are alleged on information and belief *(specify paragraph numbers)*:

8. [ ] Other:

9. The following causes of action are attached and the statements above apply to each: *(Each complaint must have one or more causes of action attached.)*
    [ ] Breach of Contract   [X] Common Counts
    [ ] Other *(specify)*:

10. PLAINTIFF PRAYS
    For judgment for costs of suit; for such relief as is fair, just, and equitable; and for
    [X] damages of $ *2,000.00*
    [X] interest on the damages [ ] according to proof [X] at the rate of ___*7%*___ percent per year
    from *(date)*: *4/5/83*
    [ ] attorney fees [ ] of $ _____ [ ] according to proof.
    [X] other *(specify)*: *Costs of Suit.*

James, Smith, M.D.

. . . .
(Type or print name)

James Smith, M.D.
(Signature of plaintiff or attorney)

(If you wish to verify this pleading, affix a verification.)

Page two

ILLUSTRATION 17.2 (CONTINUED)

SHORT TITLE:	CASE NUMBER:
James Smith -vs- Donald Johnson	

___FIRST___ **CAUSE OF ACTION—Common Counts**   Page __3__
(number)

ATTACHMENT TO ☒ Complaint ☐ Cross-Complaint

(Use a separate cause of action form for each cause of action.)

CC-1. Plaintiff *(name):*   James Smith, M.D.

alleges that defendant *(name):*   Donald Johnson

became indebted to ☒ plaintiff ☐ other *(name):*

a. ☒ within the last four years
    (1) ☒ on an open book account for money due.
    (2) ☐ because an account was stated in writing by and between plaintiff and defendant in which it was agreed that defendant was indebted to plaintiff.

b. ☒ within the last ☒ two years ☐ four years
    (1) ☐ for money had and received by defendant for the use and benefit of plaintiff.
    (2) ☒ for work, labor, services and materials rendered at the special instance and request of defendant and for which defendant promised to pay plaintiff
        ☒ the sum of $ *2,000.00*
        ☐ the reasonable value.
    (3) ☐ for goods, wares, and merchandise sold and delivered to defendant and for which defendant promised to pay plaintiff
        ☐ the sum of $
        ☐ the reasonable value.
    (4) ☐ for money lent by plaintiff to defendant at defendant's request.
    (5) ☐ for money paid, laid out, and expended to or for defendant at defendant's special instance and request.
    (6) ☐ other *(specify):*

CC-2. $ *2,000.00* , which is the reasonable value, is due and unpaid despite plaintiff's demand, plus prejudgment interest ☐ according to proof ☒ at the rate of __7%__ percent per year from *(date):* 4/5/83

CC-3. ☐ Plaintiff is entitled to attorney fees by an agreement or a statute
    ☐ of $
    ☐ according to proof.

CC.4. ☒ Other: *Costs of suit.*

62 Form Approved by the
Judicial Council of California
Effective January 1, 1982
Rule 982.1(22)   **CAUSE OF ACTION—Common Counts**   76C815 12-82
RC112   CCP 425.12

ILLUSTRATION 17.2 (CONTINUED)

ATTORNEY OR PARTY WITHOUT ATTORNEY *(Name and Address)*	TELEPHONE NO.:	*FOR COURT USE ONLY*
James Smith, M.D. *333 First St.* *Anytown, CA 90000* ATTORNEY FOR *(Name)*: *Plaintiff, In Pro Per*	*(714) 555-5544*	

In The Municipal Court of
CENTRAL ORANGE COUNTY JUDICIAL DISTRICT
700 Civic Center Drive West, Santa Ana
County of Orange, State of California 92701

PLAINTIFF: *James Smith, M.D.*	
DEFENDANT: *Donald Johnson*	

REQUEST TO ENTER DEFAULT	CASE NUMBER: *SC 55 44 55*

1. **TO THE CLERK** Enter the default on the complaint or cross-complaint of defendant *(names)*:

Donald Johnson

2. Check applicable items and apply credits below

  a. ☐ Enter default only

  b. ☐ Enter clerk's judgment for restitution of the premises only and issue a writ of execution on the judgment (CCP 1169)

  c. ☒ Enter clerk's judgment under CCP 585(a) *(Complete declaration under CCP 585.5, below)*

  d. ☐ I request a court judgment under CCP 585(b), (c), 989, etc. *(Testimony required. Apply to clerk for hearing date, unless court will enter judgment on affidavit under CCP 585(d).)*

e. Judgment to be entered	Amount	Credits Acknowledged	Balance
(1) Demand of complaint	$ *2,000.00*	$ *∅*	$ *2,000.00*
(2) Attorney fees	$	$	$
(3) Interest *7%*	$ *5.00*	$ *∅*	$ *5.00*
(4) Costs *(see reverse)*	$ *45.00*	$ *∅*	$ *45.00*
(5) **TOTAL**	$ *2,050.00*	$ *∅*	$ *2,050.00*

Date: *May 8, 1983*

James Smith, M.D.
.... *(TYPE OR PRINT NAME)*

▶ _____
(SIGNATURE OF PLAINTIFF OR ATTORNEY FOR PLAINTIFF)

DECLARATION UNDER CCP 585.5

3. This action

  a. ☐ is ☒ is not on a contract or installment sale for goods or services subject to CC 1801, etc. (Unruh Act).

  b. ☐ is ☒ is not on a conditional sales contract subject to CC 2981, etc. (Rees-Levering Motor Vehicle Sales and Finance Act).

  c. ☒ is ☐ is not on an obligation for goods, services, loans, or extensions of credit subject to CCP 395(b).

I declare under penalty of perjury under the laws of the State of California that the foregoing is true and correct.

Date: *May 8, 1983*

James Smith, M.D.
.... *(TYPE OR PRINT NAME OF DECLARANT)*

▶ *James Smith M.D.*
.... *(SIGNATURE OF DECLARANT)*

(Continued on reverse)

FOR COURT USE ONLY	Default entered as requested on *(date)*: By	☐ Default NOT entered as requested. *(State reason on reverse)*

F 0363-2416.6 (R6/83)

Form Adopted by the
Judicial Council of California
982(a)(6) [Rev. July 1, 1983]

REQUEST TO ENTER DEFAULT
Declaration under CCP 585.5, Declaration of Mailing,
Memorandum of Costs, and Declaration of Nonmilitary Status

CCP 585

ILLUSTRATION 17.3 REQUEST TO ENTER DEFAULT

SHORT TITLE:	CASE NUMBER:
James Smith, M.D. -vs- Donald Johnson	SC 55 44 55

DECLARATION OF MAILING (CCP 587)

4. a. [X] On *(date)*: May 8, 1983 , a copy of this Request to Enter Default was mailed first-class, postage prepaid, in a sealed envelope to each defendant's attorney of record, or if none, to each defendant at defendant's last known address, as follows *(addresses)*:

Donald Johnson
41563 N. Adams St.
Anytown, CA 90000

b. [ ] The addresses of the following defendants and of their attorneys of record are unknown to plaintiff and his attorney *(names)*:

I declare under penalty of perjury under the laws of the State of California that the foregoing is true and correct.

Date: May 8, 1983

Julia Eggleston
(TYPE OR PRINT NAME)
▶ Julia Eggleston
(SIGNATURE OF DECLARANT)

MEMORANDUM OF COSTS

5. Costs and disbursements are as follows (CCP 1033½):

a. Clerk's filing fees . . . . $ 35.00
b. Process server's fees . . . . . $ 10.00
c. CCP 1039 supplemental costs $
d. Other *(specify)*: . . . . $
e. $
f. **TOTAL** . . . . $ 45.00
g. [ ] Costs and disbursements are waived.

I am the attorney, agent or party who claims these costs. To the best of my knowledge and belief the foregoing items of cost are correct and have been necessarily incurred in this cause.

I declare under penalty of perjury under the laws of the State of California that the foregoing is true and correct.

Date: May 8, 1983

Julia Eggleston
(TYPE OR PRINT NAME)
▶ Julia Eggleston
(SIGNATURE OF DECLARANT)

DECLARATION OF NONMILITARY STATUS

6. No defendant named above in item 1 is in the military service so as to be entitled to the benefits of the Soldiers' and Sailors' Civil Relief Act of 1940 except
[X] none [ ] the following *(names)*:

I declare under penalty of perjury under the laws of the State of California that the foregoing is true and correct.

Date: May 8, 1983

Julia Eggleston
(TYPE OR PRINT NAME)
▶ Julia Eggleston
(SIGNATURE OF DECLARANT)

982(a)(6) [Rev. July 1, 1983] **REQUEST TO ENTER DEFAULT** Page two

ILLUSTRATION 17.3 (CONTINUED)

James Smith, M.D.
333 First St.
Anytown, CA 90000
(714) 555-5544

Attorney(s) for Plaintiff, In Pro Per

MUNICIPAL COURT OF CALIFORNIA, COUNTY OF ORANGE
CENTRAL ORANGE COUNTY JUDICIAL DISTRICT
700 Civic Center Drive West, Santa Ana

James Smith, M.D.

Plaintiff(s)

vs.

Donald Johnson

(ABBREVIATED TITLE)   Defendant(s)

CASE NUMBER

SC 55 44 55

**JUDGMENT BY DEFAULT
BY CLERK**

In this action   Donald Johnson

sued herein only on a contract for recovery of money or damages, having been regularly served with

summons and copy of complaint, having failed to appear and answer plaintiff's complaint within the

time allowed by law, and the default of said defendant...... having been duly entered, upon application

of plaintiff to the Clerk for Judgment:

It is adjudged that plaintiff........ have and recover from said defendant........ the sum of

Principal $ 2,000.00

Attorney fee $

Interest $ 5.00

Costs $ 45.00

Total $ 2,050.00

I hereby certify this to be a true copy of the Judgment in the above case.

Entered in Judgment Book

ROBERT B. KUHEL
Clerk of the above-entitled Court

on...   By ...., Deputy

F0363-2428.2 (R10/82)

JUDGMENT BY DEFAULT BY CLERK

ILLUSTRATION 17.4   JUDGMENT BY DEFAULT BY CLERK

James Smith, M.D.
333 First St.
Anytown, CA 90000
(714) 555-5544

Default of Defendant entered

by ....
Deputy Clerk

Attorney(s) for *Plaintiff, In Pro Per*

IN THE MUNICIPAL COURT, CENTRAL ORANGE COUNTY JUDICIAL DISTRICT
700 Civic Center Drive West, Santa Ana, California 92701
COUNTY OF ORANGE, STATE OF CALIFORNIA

James Smith, M.D.
Plaintiff(s)

No. *SC 55 44 55*

VS.

JUDGMENT BY DEFAULT
BY COURT

Donald Johnson
Defendant(s)
(ABBREVIATED TITLE)

Date.. , Hon. .... Judge.

In this action the Defendant(s), *Donald Johnson*

having been regularly served with summons and copy of complaint, having failed to appear and answer the complaint of Plaintiff(s) within the time allowed by law, and the default of said Defendant(s) having been duly entered, upon application of Plaintiff(s) to the Court, and

( ) after having heard the testimony and considered the evidence,

( ) a declaration under C.C.P. 585.4, in lieu of testimony, having been considered, the Court ordered the following judgment:

WHEREFORE, IT IS ORDERED AND ADJUDGED that

plaintiff........ have and recover from said defendant........ the sum of

Principal Sum $ *2,000.00*

Attorney Fee $ ....

Interest $ *5.00*

Costs $ *45.00*

Total $ *2,050.00*

Done in open Court this date: *May 5, 1983* .

I hereby certify this to be a true copy of the Judgment in the above case.

Entered in Minute Book No. ....

Page...........................

on ....

ROBERT B. KUHEL,
Clerk of the above-entitled Court

By .... , Deputy

F0363-2429.1 (R10/82)

JUDGMENT BY DEFAULT BY COURT

ILLUSTRATION 17.5 JUDGMENT BY DEFAULT BY COURT

Name, Address and Telephone No. of Attorney requesting setting:

James Smith, M.D.
333 First St.
Anytown, CA 90000
(714) 555-5544

Attorney(s) for Plaintiff, In Pro Per

Space Below for Use of Court Clerk Only

| MEMORANDUM TO SET CASE FOR TRIAL | IN THE MUNICIPAL COURT OF CENTRAL ORANGE COUNTY JUDICIAL DISTRICT COUNTY OF ORANGE, STATE OF CALIFORNIA 700 CIVIC CENTER DRIVE WEST, SANTA ANA | Case Number C 55 44 55 |

James Smith, M.D. _____ vs. Donald Johnson _____
Plaintiff(s)   Defendant(s)

I hereby represent to the court that this case is at issue, and request that it be set for trial.

Nature of the case ___Breach of Contract___

Jury trial ___Is Not___ demanded. Time necessary for trial: ___One-half Day___
          (IS OR IS NOT)   (ESTIMATE CAREFULLY)

This case ___Is Not___ entitled to legal preference in setting. _____
          (IS OR IS NOT)   (IF SO, STATE REASONS)

The following dates are NOT acceptable to me: _August 8, 1983 to August 24, 1983_

Names, addresses and telephone numbers of attorneys for other parties, or of parties appearing in person:

Donald Johnson
41563 N. Adams St.
Anytown, CA 90000

Dated _April 11, 1983_   _James Smith M.D._
                              (NOTE: MUST BE SIGNED BY ATTORNEY OR PARTY REQUESTING SETTING)
                              James Smith, M.D.

This space for use of court clerk only

The above-entitled case has been set for trial in MASTER CALENDAR Division	Card notice of trial mailed _____
	Entered on calendar by _____
on at M.	Entered in register by _____

Rules for the Municipal Courts, Rule 507-519
See also local court rule.
C.C.P. Sec. 591,592,594

F0363-2418.1 (10/78)

MEMORANDUM TO SET CASE FOR TRIAL

ILLUSTRATION 17.6   MEMORANDUM TO SET CASE FOR TRIAL

DECLARATION OF SERVICE BY MAIL

My _Business_ address is _333 First St., Anytown, CA 90000_
(BUSINESS/RESIDENT)

I am, and was at the time herein mentioned mailing took place, a citizen of the United States, _Employed_
(EMPLOYED/RESIDENT)

in the County where said mailing occurred, over the age of eighteen years and not a party to the above entitled cause.

On _April 11, 1983_ I served the foregoing document by depositing a copy thereof, enclosed in separate,

sealed envelope, with the postage thereon fully prepaid, in the United States mail at _Anytown_
(CITY OR POSTAL AREA)

_____, County of _Orange_ _____. California, each of which

envelopes was addressed respectively as follows:

Donald Johnson
41563 N. Adams St.
Anytown, CA 90000

Executed on _April 11, 1983_, at _Anytown,_ _____. California.

I declare under penalty of perjury that the foregoing is true and correct.

Julia Eggleston
(SIGNATURE OF DECLARANT)
Julia Eggleston

ILLUSTRATION 17.6 (CONTINUED)

of the discovery. This form is filed in cases where the patient/defendant has filed a formal answer to the plaintiff's complaint.

The preprinted form given in Illustration 17.7 is completed and presented to the court after a judgment is entered against the defendant/debtor. The court clerk then has the order signed by a judge of the court and sets a specific date and time for the appearance of the **judgment debtor.** The form is then returned to the **judgment creditor** (plaintiff in the case cited). A photocopy of this declaration and order is then personally served on the judgment debtor compelling his or her attendance at court at the specified date and time.

The judgment debtor (defendant in the case cited) is placed under oath to tell the truth under the penalty of perjury at the time of his or her appearance in court. The judgment creditor is then allowed to ask the judgment debtor any questions regarding the judgment debtor's assets, bank accounts, or employment status, or any other questions that would aid the judgment creditor in obtaining payment on the judgment.

The court would issue a warrant for the judgment debtor's arrest in the event that he or she failed to appear at the scheduled time of the hearing. In addition, the court may find the judgment debtor in contempt of court for failing to respond truthfully to the judgment creditor's questions. Contemptuous conduct of this nature may subject the judgment debtor to immediate incar-

Name, Address and Telephone No. of Attorney	Space below for use of Court Clerk only

James Smith, M.D.
333 First St.
Anytown, CA 90000
(714) 555-5544

Attorney(s) for *Plaintiff, In Pro Per*

WARNING

FAILURE TO APPEAR IN COURT IS PUNISHABLE BY IMPRISONMENT IN THE COUNTY JAIL AND/OR FINE.

DECLARATION AND ORDER FOR APPEARANCE OF JUDGMENT DEBTOR	In The **MUNICIPAL COURT** of CENTRAL ORANGE COUNTY JUDICIAL DISTRICT 700 Civic Center Drive West, Santa Ana COUNTY OF ORANGE, STATE OF CALIFORNIA	CASE NUMBER *SC 55 44 55*

James Smith, M.D. .... vs. .... *Donald Johnson* ....

Plaintiff(s)   Defendant(s)

DECLARATION

For the purpose of securing an order requiring..... *DONALD JOHNSON* ....

...., judgment debtor in the above-entitled action, to appear and answer concerning his property, applicant represents and states: that/he is the

Authorized agent for the ....judgment creditor in the above-entitled action; ^she

that judgment was entered in the above-entitled action on....... *May 11, 1983* ....

against the above-named debtor; that said judgment has not been satisfied; that said debtor's residence or place of business is either in the County of Orange or within 150 miles of the place of trial;
(applicable items checked)

[X]   that execution may properly be issued at this time upon said judgment;

[X]   that execution has been issued and has not been returned;

[X]   that the above-named debtor has not been examined;

[ ]   that the above-named debtor was last examined on..;*

[ ]   that affidavit or declaration in support of application for order under section 715 Code of Civil Procedure is filed herewith.

I declare under penalty of perjury that the foregoing is true and correct.

Julia Eggleston   Julia Eggleston
(Signature of Declarant)

COURT ORDER FOR APPEARANCE OF JUDGMENT DEBTOR

To.......... *Donald Johnson* ....

It is ordered that you, the above-named debtor......... appear personally on..
(day of week)

the.....................day of...19........, at the hour of..................o'clock........M., at 700 Civic Center Drive West, in the City of Santa Ana, County of Orange, State of California, before the Judge of the said Court or a referee appointed by him, then and there to answer concerning your property.. is hereby appointed to serve a copy of this order. Div. ....

Dated this...........................day of ...., 19........

(SEAL)

....
Judge of the Above-entitled Court

FAILURE TO APPEAR SUBJECTS THE PARTY SERVED TO ARREST AND PUNISHMENT FOR CONTEMPT OF COURT. Proof of Service must be filed three days before the date of hearing.

*"A judgment debtor may not . . . be required to appear and answer more frequently than every four months." (Sec. 714 C.C.P.)

CRS F0363-2456.4 (R11/82)

DECLARATION AND ORDER FOR APPEARANCE OF JUDGMENT DEBTOR

C.C.P. 714,
715, 2015.5
1209, 1218

ILLUSTRATION 17.7 DECLARATION AND ORDER FOR APPEARANCE OF JUDGMENT DEBTOR

DECLARATION OF SERVICE (By Person Other Than Sheriff, Constable or Marshal)

I was, at the time of the service of the papers herein referred to, over the age of eighteen years and not a party to the within-entitled action: I served the within order by delivering to and leaving with the person or persons personally, hereinafter named, a copy thereof, at the address and on the date set forth opposite each name of said person or persons, in the County of Orange

_____ State of California, to wit:

Name of Person Served*	Street Address and City Where Served	Date of Service
Donald Johnson	41563 N. Adams St. Anytown, CA 90000	August 4, 1983

Fee for Service $___3.00___ , Mileage $___4.50___ , Total $___7.50___ .

I declare under penalty of perjury that the foregoing is true and correct.

Executed on ___August 4, 1983___ , at ___Anytown___ , California

___Art Eggleston___ Art Eggleston
Signature of Declarant

C.C.P. 2015.5

*If service is upon a corporation, partnership, or association, state its name and the official title of person to whom copy of within is delivered.
Any person who willfully makes an improper service of an order directed to a judgment debtor to appear and answer concerning his property which subsequently results in his arrest is guilty of a misdemeanor.

CERTIFICATE OF SERVICE (By Sheriff, Constable or Marshal)

I hereby certify that I served the within order by delivering to and leaving with the person or persons personally, hereinafter named, a copy thereof, at the address and on the date set forth

opposite each name of said persons in the County of Orange _____ ,
State of California, to wit:

Name of Person Served	Street Address and City Where Served	Date of Service

Fee for Service $_____ , Mileage$_____ , Total $_____ .

Dated_____   _____
                                                                    Marshal

At_____ , California

                    By_____
                                            Deputy Marshal

C.C.P. 410, 474

_____

ILLUSTRATION 17.7 (CONTINUED)

_____

ceration and might also subject the judgement debtor to criminal proceedings on the basis of his or her perjured testimony.

The preprinted form examples have been completed using typewriter *italic* entries for illustration purposes only. Some courts will accept only typewritten completed forms using a specific size type. Some courts will never accept forms completed by hand, although others will. A telephone call to the clerk of the court will usually resolve any questions about a particular court's requirements.

SMALL CLAIMS ACTIONS

Medical and dental assistants are usually conscientious in not allowing a patient's bill to become excessive. Accordingly, most situations regarding collection of the patient's bill deal with cases where the amount in question is less than the minimal amount necessary to file a lawsuit in a municipal, district, justice or superior court. In such cases, the physician, dentist, physical therapist, or institution could file an action against the patient in the small claims court for payment of the bill and could be represented by an authorized agent or employee other than an attorney. Thus, the medical or dental assistant may present the case on behalf of his or her employer in small claims actions. Except for an action by an attorney on his or her own behalf, an attorney is usually not allowed to present a case on behalf of a client in a small claims action. However, an attorney may represent *either* party in the action where the unsuccessful defendant appeals the case to the superior court.

The plaintiff or party bringing the action in small claims court generally files a preprinted form with the court clerk alleging certain facts that have given rise to his or her grievance. A summons is issued on the complaint, commanding the appearance of the defendant before the judge or tribunal. A **conformed copy** of the complaint and the original summons is then given to the party bringing the action. Thereafter, the plaintiff gives the original summons and conformed copy of the complaint to a sheriff, marshal, constable, or some other approved adult person to serve on the defendant. The plaintiff may not himself serve the defendant with these papers. However, in Massachusetts, as in some other states, the clerk's office mails the plaintiff's small claims complaint to the defendant via Certified Mail, Return Receipt Requested and mails an additional copy of the complaint to the defendant via regular first-class mail. It is only if the defendant does not pick up the Certified Mail copy *and* the first-class mail copy is returned undelivered that the plaintiff would have the Complaint served by a sheriff, constable, or the like.

Once the defendant has received a copy of the summons and complaint, he or she may file a cross-complaint against the plaintiff for any possible grievance the defendant may have. No formal answer is generally required, in contrast to those cases where the matter is filed in the municipal, district, justice, or superior court. Both parties have the right to subpoena witnesses to testify on their behalf at trial. However, no formal discovery, such as requests for admissions or interrogatories, is associated with a small claims action. Also, neither party has a right to have the case tried before a jury. All cases are initially tried before a judge or tribunal, even where the matter has been appealed to the superior court by the defendant. However, some jurisdictions, including Massachusetts, allow a jury trial when the defendant appeals after losing in the Small Claims Court.

At trial, the party bringing the action or an authorized representative presents the factual contentions of the obligation that forms the basis of the party's lawsuit. The defendant thereafter is given the opportunity to respond to the charges or allegations asserted by the plaintiff. Then the matter is submitted for a decision by the judge or tribunal. If judgment is entered in favor of the defendant, the plaintiff has no right to appeal the decision, and the case is considered ended. However, should a judgment be rendered in favor of the plaintiff and against the defendant, the defendant has the right to appeal the decision to a court of higher, jurisdiction. In the state of California, this higher court is the superior court. In Massachusetts, as previously mentioned, the defendant may appeal for a jury trial which is held in the district court. The case is retried before the higher court tribunal, at which stage the parties may be represented by an attorney. Once presented to the judge of the higher court, the case is submitted for his or her decision, and the decision of the judge is final and binding on the parties to the action.

Illustrations 17.8 through 17.10 present preprinted forms that may be obtained from the court clerk's office. Any questions or assistance needed in completing these small claims court forms will be given by the clerk. This is in direct contrast to lawsuits in higher courts where the court clerk may not aid or assist any parties in completing forms attendant to the litigation.

The successful plaintiff to the small claims action may obtain an order for the appearance of the judgment debtor in the same manner as discussed in the preceding section on municipal court actions. The form given in Illustration 17.7 is also used for this purpose in small claims actions.

WRITS

As many readers of this text have undoubtedly figured out, it is one thing to obtain a judgment against a patient/defendant and another to collect the money. Collecting money on the judgment is often difficult, if not impossible. Rarely do defendants voluntarily pay the plaintiff; usually the plaintiff has to take some affirmative action to execute or otherwise collect money on the judgment. Several affirmative actions may be undertaken.

One of the methods commonly used is to garnish the wages of the employed judgment debtor by obtaining a writ of garnishment or similar wage-reduction order from the court that rendered the judgment on behalf of the plaintiff. The writ of garnishment is then given to a sheriff, marshal or constable to serve on the employer of the judgment debtor. Once the employer

INFORMATION FOR PLAINTIFF

1. You may file your claim here if:

   a. You are at least 18 years of age; if you are under 18, you must obtain special forms and information from the clerk.

   b. You have made an oral or written demand on the defendant for payment of the claim and the claim has not been paid.

   c. (1) At least one **defendant now resides** or a **corporate defendant does business** in this judicial district;

      (2) **Injury** to person or **damage** to personal property **occurred** in this judicial district;

      (3) **Defendant entered into or signed a contract** in this judicial district.

      (4) The **obligation was to be performed** in this judicial district

      (5) **Defendant resided** or a **corporate defendant did business** in this judicial district **at the time the contract was entered into**

2. You may file your claim for any amount up to and including $1,500. If your claim is for more than $1,500, you may file in small claims court if you reduce your claim to $1,500 and give up your right to recover the excess.

3. You must be the original owner of a claim. You cannot sue on an assigned claim, unless you are a trustee in bankruptcy or a holder of a conditional sales contract purchased for your portfolio of investments and not as an assignee for collection.

4. If your claim is against a corporation, you must furnish the sheriff or other server with the name and address of an officer or authorized agent of the corporation. If you do not know this information, you may obtain it from either the corporation itself, the County Clerk, or the Secretary of State (Capitol Building, Sacramento, 95814, 916/445-2900).

5. If you are suing a governmental agency, you must first have completed any required claim procedure. The law may require you promptly to file a claim against the agency.

6. The defendant must be served with a copy of the claim and order at least **five** days before the trial date if defendant resides within this county, and **fifteen** days before the hearing date if defendant resides outside this county. You may not serve the claim and order yourself.

   a. The clerk may attempt to serve the claim and order by mail providing for a return receipt for a fee of $3.00 for each defendant to be served.

   b. If the defendant is not served by mail, you must arrange to have defendant served by the sheriff, marshal or constable or any other person over the age of 18 who is not a party to the action. The person serving the papers should promptly sign and complete a declaration of service which must be delivered to the clerk before the trial date.

7. Have your witnesses appear personally to testify at the trial. At your request the clerk will issue subpenas for the witnesses you need. Also bring to the trial everything necessary to establish your claim: books, papers, repair bills, or other exhibits.

8. You have no right to appeal on your claim. The defendant, however, may appeal. If defendant files a claim against you, you may appeal any judgment against you on defendant's claim.

9. If the court allows your claim

   a. First ask the losing party to pay the amount of the judgment.

   b. If the losing party does not pay, the court does not collect for you.

      (1) The clerk at your request and for a fee will issue papers necessary to levy on defendant's assets such as bank account, wages or other income or property.

      (2) For an additional fee, the sheriff, marshal or constable will levy on the defendant's assets if you can furnish him with a description and location of the assets.

   c. When you are paid in full, you must sign and file a satisfaction of judgment.

10. If the case is settled before the date of hearing, date, sign and file dismissal with the clerk.

11. If you claim auto damages, you must bring a repair bill or two or more estimates.

OVER

F0363-2501.8 (1/82)

INFORMATION FOR PLAINTIFF
(SMALL CLAIMS)

CCP 116

ILLUSTRATION 17.8   INFORMATION FOR PLAINTIFF (SMALL CLAIMS)

---

12. If the Defendant fails to appear at the trial, you cannot obtain a judgment unless you complete and file with the clerk the Declaration of Non-Military Service, certifying that the defendant is not in the military service of the United States.

13. The fee for filing in small claims court is $6.00 if you have not filed more than 12 claims in this court in the past 12 months. The fee is $12.00 if you have filed 12 or more claims in this court in the past 12 months.

14. If you cannot afford the fee for filing a small claims case or the cost of serving the claim on the other party, you should tell the Clerk. You will be given a form that you can fill out and sign to request that the court permit you to file your case without paying these fees.

15. A small claims advisor is available to give assistance without any charge. This service is available to both plaintiffs and defendants in small claims cases. Neither the county nor the advisors may be held liable for any losses as a result of advice given to either party. If you want advisor assistance, call 714/834-2502.

ILLUSTRATION 17.8 (CONTINUED)

of the judgment debtor has been served with the writ of garnishment, the employer is then legally obligated to surrender a certain percentage of the judgment debtor's salary to the marshal. The marshal then turns the money over to the judgment creditor.

Another method commonly employed is a judgment debtor hearing, which was discussed earlier in this chapter in the section on municipal court actions. With the information obtained at the judgment debtor hearing, the judgment creditor can obtain a writ of execution or other appropriate writ for the attachment of the judgment debtor's property (see Illustration 17.11).

To obtain a writ may require payment of a small fee to the court clerk. In addition, the judgment creditor is generally required to pay the marshal or constable to carry out the requirements of the writ. These fees, which are paid by the judgment creditor, are added to the amount of the judgment. The judgment creditor may be reimbursed. The fee paid to the marshal is generally minimal in cases dealing with merely serving a writ of execution for garnishment of the judgment debtor's wages. However, the cost for the sheriff, marshal, or constable to act may be very expensive. The judgment creditor may be required to pay the sheriff, marshal, or constable's office the amount of the sheriff's, marshal's, or constable's salary where the judgment creditor seeks a writ for the sheriff, constable, or marshal to act as a "keeper in the judgment debtor's business." It is not uncommon for the sheriff, marshal, or constable's office to charge up to $200 per day to sit at the business establishment of the judgment debtor for the purpose of collecting any money that is received by the debtor during the day.

In addition, the judgment creditor is obligated to pay storage fees where personal property of the judgment debtor is attached by the sheriff, marshal, or constable. Storage fees must be paid until either the property is sold at public sale or the judgment (debt) is paid by the judgment debtor. As previously mentioned, these additional costs are added to the underlying judgment and are collectable in the same manner as the judgment.

IN THE MUNICIPAL COURT CENTRAL ORANGE COUNTY JUDICIAL DISTRICT
SMALL CLAIMS DIVISION, COUNTY OF ORANGE, STATE OF CALIFORNIA

700 Civic Center Drive West, Santa Ana, Ca. 92701

Plaintiff

James Smith, M.D.

CASE NUMBER

S.C.

55 44 55

Defendant

Donald Johnson

CLAIM OF PLAINTIFF

I, the undersigned, declare that the defendant(s) is indebted to the Plaintiff in the sum of $ _____ *450.00* _____ , not including court costs for: *Medical bill for medical services rendered to defendant*

between December 16, 1982 and May 1, 1983.

and that plaintiff has demanded payment of this sum and it has not been paid.

A. ☒ that the obligation sued on was entered into or was to be performed in this judicial district;

B. ☐ that the injury to persons or to personal property occurred in this judicial district;

C. ☒ that defendant resides in this judicial district or resided in this judicial district when the contract was entered into.

I understand that although I may consult an attorney, I cannot be represented by an attorney at the trial in the small claims division and I have no right to appeal from a judgment on my claim.

Plaintiff has filed in the past 12 months (check one box) ☒ 0 - 11 ☐ 12 or more small claims cases in this court.

I declare under penalty of perjury that the foregoing is true and correct.

Executed on _____ *June 6, 1983* _____ at Santa Ana, California.

_____
Signature of declarant

COSTS ADVANCED BY PLAINTIFF

COURT NOTATIONS

Fee for filing	$ *10.00*	
Certified Mail	$ ____	
Personal Service	$ *7.00*	
Total	$ *17.00*	

REGISTER OF ACTIONS

_____ CLAIM OF PLAINTIFF FILED. ORDER ISSUED FOR DEFENDANT(S)

_____ TO APPEAR FOR TRIAL ON _____ AT _____

_____ ORDER with copy of Claim of Plaintiff

Mailed to Defendant by certified mail ( )

Delivered to Plaintiff for personal service ( )

_____ Return filed, showing service was made on defendant(s)

F0363-2503.12 (R 1/82)

(over)

ILLUSTRATION 17.9   CLAIM OF PLAINTIFF

IN THE MUNICIPAL COURT CENTRAL ORANGE COUNTY JUDICIAL DISTRICT
SMALL CLAIMS DIVISION, COUNTY OF ORANGE, STATE OF CALIFORNIA

Plaintiff

700 Civic Center Drive West, Santa Ana, Ca. 92701

CASE NUMBER

S.C.

Defendant

CLAIM OF PLAINTIFF
(COPY)

I, the undersigned, declare that the defendant(s) is indebted to the Plaintiff in the sum of $_____ , not including court costs for:

_____

_____

and that plaintiff has demanded payment of this sum and it has not been paid.

A. ☐ that the obligation sued on was entered into or was to be performed in this judicial district;

B. ☐ that the injury to persons or to personal property occurred in this judicial district;

C. ☐ that defendant resides in this judicial district or resided in this judicial district when the contract was entered into.

I understand that although I may consult an attorney, I cannot be represented by an attorney at the trial in the small claims division and I have no right to appeal from a judgment on my claim.

Plaintiff has filed in the past 12 months (check one box)   ☐ 0 - 11   ☐ 12 or more small claims cases in this court.

I declare under penalty of perjury that the foregoing is true and correct.

Executed on_____ at Santa Ana, California.

_____
Signature of declarant

YOU MUST PROVIDE YOUR OWN INTERPRETER IF ONE IS NEEDED IN COURT.
USTED TIENE QUE PROVEER SU PROPIO INTERPRETE SI ES NECESARIO EN SU CAUSA.

ORDER

The People of the State of California, to the within-named defendant(s): YOU are hereby directed to APPEAR and answer the foregoing claim in the above-entitled Court at 700 Civic Center Drive West, City of Santa Ana, County of Orange, State of California;

TRIAL ON_____ AT _____

			TRIAL DATE
Reset for	, at	m. in Div.	
Reset for	, at	m. in Div.	
Reset for	, at	m. in Div.	

AND HAVE WITH YOU THEN AND THERE ALL BOOKS, PAPERS and WITNESSES —

needed by you to establish your defense to said claim; and you are further notified that in case you do not so appear, Judgment will be given against you for the amount found by the COURT to be due upon said claim, but not more than stated in the plaintiff's declaration and, in addition costs of the action, including costs of service of the order.

DATED_____19_____

Robert B. Kuhel
Clerk of the Municipal Court
Central Orange County Judicial District
County of Orange, State of California

_____
Deputy

F0363-2503.12 (R 1/82)

(SEE INFORMATION FOR DEFENDANTS — OVER)

ILLUSTRATION 17.9 (CONTINUED)

INFORMATION FOR DEFENDANT IN SMALL CLAIMS ACTIONS

1. When you have been served with plaintiff's claim in an action filed against you in the Small Claims Division you may:

    a. Make an out-of-court settlement with the plaintiff before the date set for trial, and file the plaintiff's dismissal with the clerk of the court (Plaintiff has this form of dismissal), or,

    b. Make no appearance at the trial, in which case the plaintiff may be given a judgment by default for the amount claimed, plus costs, or

    c. Appear on the date set for trial with all BOOKS, LEASES, PAPERS AND WITNESSES needed to establish your defense. At your request, the clerk will issue subpoenas for attendance of any witnesses you may need.

2. If you have a claim against the plaintiff, you may file in the Small Claims Division a "Claim of Defendant" against him for not more than $1500. Forms for this purpose may be obtained from the clerk.

3. If you reside within this county and are served with plaintiff's claim less than 5 days before trial, or if you reside outside this county and are served less than 15 days before trial, you may, if you choose, personally appear and request the court to postpone the trial.

4. If you are not at least 18 years of age, you should inform the clerk in order to obtain an appointment by the court of a guardian ad litem to protect your interest.

5. See the clerk for forms and procedure on appeal.

6. A small claims advisor is available to give assistance without any charge. This service is available to both plaintiffs and defendants in small claims cases. Neither the county nor the advisors may be held liable for any losses as a result of advice given to either party. If you want advisor assistance, call 714/834-2502.

ILLUSTRATION 17.9 (CONTINUED)

The most popular way of obtaining collection on the judgment in cases dealing with small claims actions is to force the judgment debtor to attend a judgment debtor hearing or to garnish the judgment debtor's wages. The costs to the judgment creditor are minimal, and generally the debt is successfully collected.

The following preprinted examples (Illustrations 17.12–17.14) entitled application for earnings withholding order, instructions to levy on the bank account of the judgment debtor, and marshal instructions may be obtained from the court clerk or the marshal's office. The italic typewritten portions of these forms represent the parts that must be completed individually. As with all court documents, these forms must be typewritten, unless your state courts allow otherwise.

SMALL CLAIMS DIVISION OF THE CENTRAL ORANGE COUNTY MUNICIPAL COURT
PLAINTIFF'S STATEMENT

_SC 55 44 55_

SMALL CLAIMS NO.

1. Please read carefully the instructions appearing below before filling out this form:

   a. If you are suing one or more individuals, give full name of each.
   b. If you are suing a business owned by an individual, give the name of the owner and the name of the business he owns.
   c. If you are suing a partnership, give the names of the partners and the name of the partnership.
   d. If you are suing a corporation, give its full name.
   e. If your claim arises out of a vehicle accident, the driver of the other vehicle must be named, and the registered owner of the other vehicle should also be named.

2. State your name and residence address, and the name and address of any other person joining you in this action. If this claim arises from a business transaction, give the name and address of your business.

   a. Name _James Smith, M.D._

   Address _333 First St., Anytown, CA 90000_   Phone No. _(714) 555-5544_

   b. Name _____

   Address _____ Phone No. _____

3. State the full name and address of each person or business you are suing:

   a. Name _Donald Johnson_

   Address _41563 N. Adams St., Anytown, CA 90000_

   b. Name _____

   Address _____

   c. Name _____

   Address _____

4. State the amount you are claiming. $ _450.00_

   Plaintiff has filed _(check one box)_
   ☒ 0-11   ☐ 12 or more
   small claims cases in this Court in the past 12 months.

5. Describe briefly the nature of your claim:

Medical bill for medical services rendered to defendant
between December 16, 1982 and May 1, 1983

6. If your claim IS NOT a vehicle accident, give address where debt was entered, or was to be performed, or where damage was incurred.

333 First St. ,   Anytown,   CA 90000

(Number)   (Street)   (City)

7. Fill out this section if your claim arises out of a vehicle accident:

   a. Date on which accident occurred: _____ , 19____ .
   b. Street or intersection and city or locality where accident occurred:

   c. If you are claiming damages to a vehicle, were you the registered owner of that vehicle on the date of the accident?
   ☐ Yes   ☐ No

8. I have received and read the form entitled "Information to Plaintiff." I declare under penalty of perjury that the foregoing is true and correct.

Date _November 8, 1983_

James Smith M.D. James Smith, M.D.

Signature

Ⓡ F0363-2502.1 (R9/82)

ILLUSTRATION 17.10 PLAINTIFF'S STATEMENT

NAME AND ADDRESS OF JUDGMENT CREDITOR:	TELEPHONE	FOR COURT USE ONLY

NAME AND ADDRESS OF JUDGMENT CREDITOR:

James Smith, M.D.
333 First St.
Anytown, CA 90000

TELEPHONE
(714) 555-5544

ATTORNEY FOR (Name) *Plaintiff, In Pro Per*

FOR COURT USE ONLY

Insert name of court, judicial district or branch court, if any, and post office and street address:
MUNICIPAL COURT OF CALIFORNIA, COUNTY OF ORANGE, SMALL CLAIMS
CENTRAL ORANGE COUNTY JUDICIAL DISTRICT
Address: 700 Civic Center Dr. West, Santa Ana, CA

PLAINTIFF

James Smith, M.D.

CASE NUMBER:
S.C. *55 44 55*

DEFENDANT

Donald Johnson

FOR RECORDER'S USE ONLY

WRIT OF EXECUTION	[X] **MONEY JUDGMENT** [ ] **JOINT DEBTOR**	[ ] **POSSESSION OF** [ ] **REAL** [ ] **PERSONAL PROPERTY**

1. To the Sheriff or any Marshal or Constable of the County of:
   You are directed to satisfy the judgment described below, with interest and costs and your costs and disbursements, as provided by law. This writ may not be used for a levying officer's sale of a dwelling house as defined in CCP 690.31.

2. To any registered process server: You are authorized to serve this writ only, in accord with CCP 687.

3. Judgment creditor (Name):

   James Smith, M.D.

4. Judgment debtor (Name and address):
   [ ] Additional name and address on reverse.

   Donald Johnson
   41563 N. Adams St.
   Anytown, CA 90000

5. Judgment entered on (Date):

   May 8, 1984

6. Notice of sale under this writ [X] has not been requested
   [ ] has been requested as set forth on the reverse.

7. [ ] Joint debtor information set forth on the reverse.

8. [X] Real or personal property described on the reverse.

(SEAL)

9. Total judgment as entered
   a. Principal: _ _ _ _ _ _ _ _ _ _ _ _ _ $ *2,000.00*
   b. Attorney fees: _ _ _ _ _ _ _ _ _ _ _ $
   c. Interest: _ _ _ _ _ _ _ _ _ _ _ _ _ _ $ *5.00*
   d. Costs: _ _ _ _ _ _ _ _ _ _ _ _ _ _ _ $ *45.00*
   e. Total (Add 9a,b,c,d): _ _ _ _ _ _ _ $ *2,050.00*
10. Total judgment and accruals
    a. Interest (On item 9e) as adjusted for payments and partial satisfactions (Per filed affidavit CCP 682.2): _ _ _ _ _ _ _ _ _ _ _ _ _ _ _ $
    b. Costs (Per filed memo of costs after judgment): _ _ _ _ _ _ $ *14.00*
    c. Total (Add 9e,10a,b): _ _ _ _ _ _ $ *2,064.00*
11. Net balance due on judgment
    a. Payments and partial satisfactions: _ _ _ _ _ _ _ _ _ _ _ _ $
    b. Net balance due before issuance of writ (Subtract 11a from 10c): $ *2,064.00*
    c. Fee for issuance of writ: _ _ _ _ _ $ *11.00*
    d. Net balance due on date of writ (Add 11b,c): _ _ _ _ _ _ _ _ _ _ $ *2,075.00*
12. Levying officer: Add the following daily interest from date of writ to date of levy (legal rate per year on 9e or 11b, whichever is less): _ _ _ _ _ _ _ $ *0.38*

Dated:

Robert B. Kuhel Clerk, By _____ Deputy

NOTICE TO JUDGMENT DEBTOR: SEE REVERSE FOR IMPORTANT INFORMATION

(Continued on reverse)

Do NOT use this form for levy and sale of a dwelling house as defined in CCP 690.31. The singular includes the plural

Form Approved by the
Judicial Council of California
Revised Effective January 1, 1979

WRIT OF EXECUTION

15 USC §1673, CCP 681 et seq.
690.1 et seq, 690.50, 692a,
989-994, 1032.6, 1033 et seq

F0363-2509.1 (R 11/82)

ILLUSTRATION 17.11   WRIT OF EXECUTION

Continued Items

4. ☐ Additional judgment debtor (Name and address):

⌐   ⌐¬⌐   ¬

L   L ⌐ JL   ⌐

6. ☐ Notice of sale has been requested by (Name and address):

⌐   ⌐¬⌐   ¬

L   L ⌐ JL   ⌐

⌐   ⌐¬⌐   ¬

L   L ⌐ JL   ⌐

7. ☐ Joint debtor was declared bound by the judgment (CCP 989-994)

    a. On (Date):   a. On (Date):
    b. Name and address of joint debtor: b. Name and address of joint debtor:

⌐   ⌐¬⌐   ¬

L   L ⌐ JL   ⌐

    c. ☐ Additional costs against certain joint debtors (Itemize):

8. ☒ Judgment was entered for possession of the following
    a. ☐ Real property.
    b. ☒ Personal property ☐ if delivery cannot be had, then for the value (Itemize in 8c) specified in that judgment or supplemental order.
    c. Description: *All funds in Bank Account Number 019-90402-5 of Donald Johnson held at First National Bank, 4556 W. Center, Anytown, CA, to the amount to satisfy judgment.*

NOTICES TO JUDGMENT DEBTOR

YOU MAY BE ENTITLED TO FILE A CLAIM EXEMPTING YOUR PROPERTY FROM EXECUTION. IF SO, YOU MUST DO SO WITHIN 10 DAYS FROM THE DATE YOUR PROPERTY WAS LEVIED UPON BY DELIVERING TO THE LEVYING OFFICER AN AFFIDAVIT OF EXEMPTION, TOGETHER WITH A COPY THEREOF, AS PROVIDED IN SECTION 690.50 OF THE CODE OF CIVIL PROCEDURE. IF YOU WISH TO SEEK THE ADVICE OF AN ATTORNEY IN THIS MATTER, YOU SHOULD DO SO PROMPTLY SO THAT AN AFFIDAVIT, IF ANY, MAY BE FILED ON TIME.

PERSONAL PROPERTY REMAINING ON THE PREMISES DESCRIBED IN ITEM 8a AT THE TIME OF ITS RESTITUTION TO THE LANDLORD WILL BE SOLD OR OTHERWISE DISPOSED OF IN ACCORDANCE WITH SECTION 1174 OF THE CODE OF CIVIL PROCEDURE UNLESS THE TENANT OR THE OWNER PAYS THE LANDLORD THE REASONABLE COSTS OF STORAGE AND TAKES POSSESSION OF THE PERSONAL PROPERTY NOT LATER THAN 15 DAYS AFTER THE TIME THE PREMISES ARE RESTORED TO THE LANDLORD.

ILLUSTRATION 17.11 (CONTINUED)

ATTORNEY OR PARTY WITHOUT ATTORNEY *(Name and Address)*:	TELEPHONE NO.:	LEVYING OFFICER *(Name and Address)*:

ATTORNEY OR PARTY WITHOUT ATTORNEY *(Name and Address)*: TELEPHONE NO.: (714) 555-5544

James Smith, M.D.
333 First St.
Anytown, CA 90000

ATTORNEY FOR *(Name)*: Plaintiff, In Pro Per

LEVYING OFFICER *(Name and Address)*:

NAME OF COURT, JUDICIAL DISTRICT OR BRANCH COURT, IF ANY:
Orange County Municipal Court
700 Civic Center Drive West, Santa Ana, CA 90000

PLAINTIFF:
James Smith, M.D.

DEFENDANT: Donald Johnson

APPLICATION FOR EARNINGS WITHHOLDING ORDER (Wage Garnishment)	LEVYING OFFICER FILE NO.	COURT CASE NO.: SC 55 44 55

TO THE SHERIFF OR ANY MARSHAL OR CONSTABLE OF THE COUNTY OF Orange

1. The judgment creditor *(name)*: James Smith, M.D.

   requests issuance of an Earnings Withholding Order directing the employer to withhold the earnings of the judgment debtor (employee).

Name and address of employer	Name and address of employee
Associated Container Corp. 16859 Wilson Ave. Anytown, CA 90000	Donald Johnson 41563 N. Adams St. Anytown, CA 90000

Social Security Number *(if known)*: 211-00-5555

2. The amounts withheld are to be paid to
   a. [X] The attorney (or party without an attorney) named at the top of this page.
   b. [ ] Other *(name, address, and telephone)*:

3. a. Judgment was entered on *(date)*: May 1, 1983
   b. Collect the amount directed by the Writ of Execution unless a lesser amount is specified here:
      $ 2,075.00

4. [ ] The Writ of Execution was issued to collect delinquent amounts payable for the **support** of a child, former spouse, or spouse of the employee.

5. [ ] Special instructions *(specify)*:

6. *(Check a or b)*
   a. [X] I have not previously obtained an order directing this employer to withhold the earnings of this employee.
      —OR—
   b. [ ] I have previously obtained such an order, but that order *(check one)*:
      [ ] expired at least 10 days ago.
      [ ] was terminated by a court order, but I am entitled to apply for another Earnings Withholding Order under the provisions of Code of Civil Procedure section 706.105(h).
      [ ] was ineffective.

James Smith, M.D.
. . . .
(TYPE OR PRINT NAME)

▶ James Smith, M.D.
(SIGNATURE OF ATTORNEY OR PARTY WITHOUT ATTORNEY)

I declare under penalty of perjury under the laws of the State of California that the foregoing is true and correct.

Date: May 7, 1983
James Smith, M.D.
. . . .
(TYPE OR PRINT NAME)

▶ James Smith, M.D.
(SIGNATURE OF DECLARANT)

F 0328-158.1 (R6/83)

Form Adopted by the
Judicial Council of California
982.5(1) (Rev. July 1, 1983)

APPLICATION FOR EARNINGS WITHHOLDING ORDER
(Wage Garnishment)

CCP 706.121

ILLUSTRATION 17.12 APPLICATION FOR EARNINGS WITHHOLDING ORDER (WAGE GARNISHMENT)

J.C. BYHAM
Marshal, Orange Co.

Case No. _SC 55 44 55_

You are hereby instructed to levy on the bank account of the following named:

Donald Johnson
_____
Defendant

First National Bank
_____
Name of Bank

4556 W. Center St.
_____
Address of Bank

Anytown, CA 90000
_____
City

Account number, if known: _019-90402-5_ _____

Accept $ _2,075.00_ _____, plus cost of the levy to satisfy this case

James Smith, M.D. _James Smith, M.D._
_____
Signature of Atty. or Litigant

_(714) 555-5544_
_____
Telephone No.

Note: All communications, refunds due and collections received will be directed to the name and address listed below:

James Smith, M.D.
_____
Name

333 First St.
_____
Address

Anytown, CA   90000
_____
City   State   Zip Code

SPECIAL NOTICE: This bank levy will be served within the next few days. The bank has 10 days in which to answer the levy and a copy of the bank's answer will be mailed to you. Please allow one month to receive any collections. Absolutely no status checks will be given by phone; you must submit a written request for such information.

Central Division
700 Civic Center Dr West
Room K-100
Santa Ana, CA 92701

ILLUSTRATION 17.13 INSTRUCTIONS TO LEVY ON THE BANK ACCOUNT OF THE JUDGMENT DEBTOR

Marshal, Orange County

$ _34.00_____ _____4_____
  ADVANCE   DIVISION

Case Number _SC 55 44 55_

Orange County
Municipal Court
              COURT

James Smith, M.D.   _Donald Johnson_
     PLAINTIFF   VS   DEFENDANT

YOU ARE HEREBY INSTRUCTED TO:

LEVY DATES: _5/7–5/12/83_

F/ATTEMPT: _____

Serve Earnings Withholding Order on:

Associated Container Corp.
16859 Wilson Ave.
Anytown, CA 90000

Re: Donald Johnson, employee

ACCEPT _$ 2,075.00_____ PLUS COST OF THE LEVY TO SATISFY THIS CASE.

XX _James Smith M.D_   _May 7, 1983_
   SIGNATURE OF ATTY. OR LITIGANT   DATE

TELEPHONE _(714) 555-5544_

NOTE: ALL COMMUNICATIONS, REFUNDS DUE AND COLLECTIONS RECEIVED WILL BE DIRECTED TO THE NAME AND ADDRESS LISTED BELOW:

TYPE OR
PRINT NAME _James Smith, M.D._

ADDRESS _333 First St._

CITY_Anytown, CA_____ ZIP CODE _90000_

F0328-101.6 (R 3/78)   ORIGINAL

MAP GRID: _____ FEES: $ _____

SERVED _____

TITLE _____

LEFT WITH _____

TITLE _____

PERSONAL SERVICE ☐   M.A. YES ☐ NO ☐
SUBSTITUTE SERVICE ☐
HOME ADDRESS ☐   BUSINESS ADDRESS ☐
BOXES CHECKED ON SUMMONS
  ☐ YOU ARE SERVED AS AN IND. DEFT.
  ☐ FICTITIOUS NAME
  ☐ YOU ARE SERVED ON BEHALF OF
UNDER: ☐ CCP416.10 ☐ CCP416.60 ☐ OTHER
       ☐ CCP416.20 ☐ CCP416.70
       ☐ CCP416.40 ☐ CCP416.90
☐ SERVED   ☐ POSTED   ☐ NOT FOUND
☐ NO SERVICE ☐ COPY MAILED ☐ CANCELLED

#1 AGE _____HAIR _____HT _____WT _____
☐ FEMALE
☐ MALE   DATE _____ TIME _____ A.M.
                                            P.M.

DEPUTY'S NAME   I.D. NO.

#2 AGE _____HAIR _____HT _____WT _____
☐ FEMALE
☐ MALE   DATE _____ TIME _____ A.M.
                                            P.M.

DEPUTY'S NAME   I.D. NO.

DOCKET NO.

ILLUSTRATION 17.14 MARSHAL INSTRUCTIONS

EXAMPLES / QUESTIONS / PROJECTS

1. *Obtain from a local court or court clerk all forms necessary to bring a small claims court action against Brian Thompson, a patient who owes the doctor $300. Complete all forms necessary to file the action. You may use your doctor's name and address or a fictitious name and address for all persons in this example. The following forms should be included: a summons and complaint; a judgment; and a declaration and order for appearance of judgment debtor.*

2. *Prepare a list of questions that you intend to ask the judgment debtor at the hearing. (Refer to Illustration 12.1 as an example.)*

3. *Obtain from the court, court clerk, or marshal's office all forms necessary to garnish a judgment debtor's salary. Complete these forms using the parties in example 1.*

CHAPTER EIGHTEEN

APPROACHES TO OBTAINING PAYMENT IN INJURY CASES

PERSONAL INJURY CASES
  Insurance Cases
LIENS
  Processing the Lien
  Expert Witness Fees,
  Health Professionals Attitudes
  toward Liens
WORKERS' COMPENSATION
  Choosing a Physician
  Filing a Lien for Payment of Bill
  Amended Liens
DEFENSES TO LIENS
  Medical/Legal Objection Letter

WORKERS' COMPENSATION
APPEALS CASE NUMBER
DECLARATION OF READINESS
TO PROCEED
WORKERS' COMPENSATION
APPEALS BOARD HEARING
FEDERAL COMPENSATION
ACT
EXAMPLES/QUESTIONS/
PROJECTS

Key Terms

conjectural   lien   interested party
deductible   legal-lined paper   permanent and stationary

PERSONAL INJURY CASES

Several avenues are open to the allied health professional for securing payment of his or her bill where the patient is being examined or treated for injuries sustained as a result of an accident. First and foremost is "cash up front" payment by the patient at the time the services are rendered. This method of receiving payment is probably the least successful. Often the patient's injuries are severe, which makes extensive treatment necessary, and the bill is higher than the patient can pay at the time. For this reason, other methods of procuring payment are usually necessary.

Insurance cases

The medical assistant or other allied health professional rendering services to the patient should exhaust all sources of insurance coverage that may pay for the treatment. If injury occurred as a result of an automobile collision, the patient should be questioned regarding his or her automobile insurance. There is a strong likelihood that the patient's own insurance company may be obligated to pay for any examinations or treatment under the "medical payment" or "personal injury protection" provisions of the patient's policy. The health professional should obtain the name, address, and telephone number of the patient's insurance agent to ascertain whether or not the patient's insurance policy has such provisions. The policy number and/or claim number should also be obtained in order to submit the bill to the insurance company for payment. The patient's insurance company may be obligated to pay for treatment received by the patient even when the accident did not involve another vehicle.

If the patient was injured while riding as a passenger in someone else's vehicle, information should be obtained regarding the driver's insurance company as well as the patient's insurance company. Most insurance companies are obligated to pay for treatment on behalf of their own insured (or passenger) where their insured's (or passenger's) injuries arise out of an automobile accident.

The patient may also be covered under some group health insurance plan through his or her employment. Where the patient is a minor child, he or she may be covered under one or both of the parents' group policies through their work. Most such insurance policies carry a **deductible**—an amount that the patient must initially pay before the insurance coverage becomes available. For example, a group policy may state that the patient is obligated to pay the first $100 of a bill and that thereafter the insurance company will pay a percentage of any balance for professional services rendered. Most policies will pay 80 percent of the unpaid balance of the bill where the patient is being treated for an illness not related to an accident. In contrast, many policies will pay 100 percent of the patient's bill where the treatment is being rendered for injuries sustained as a result of an accident.

In any event, all pertinent information regarding any possible insurance coverage should be obtained, including the policyholder's name, social security number, group health insurance number, and the name and address of the insurance company. In addition, the patient should be requested to obtain the appropriate insurance forms for billing purposes unless the office or institution already has copies of such forms.

Where the patient is being examined or treated for injuries as a result of an accident, the medical assistant or other allied health professional should obtain all relevant information regarding the accident, including a description of how and where the accident occurred. Obviously, this information is routinely gathered from the patient for purposes of treatment. However, the medical assistant or other professional assistant whose job it is to obtain collection on the patient's bill should be familiar with all potential sources of insurance coverage. In particular, the patient should be questioned regarding the possibility that some other party may become responsible for payment of the patient's bill. A patient will commonly describe how he or she was injured but may fail to state without the prodding of the medical assistant, that he or she was working at the time of the accident. In such cases, the doctor or other professional rendering services could receive payment on the patient's bill under workers' compensation laws.

Similarly, the parent of a minor child may merely state that the child was injured while playing and then go through the elaborate details of how the injury occurred, without stating that the injury occurred at a neighbor's house. The neighbor may have a homeowner's insurance policy that would pay for the examination and treatment of the injured child. In that case, the parents should be told to obtain and provide the office or institution with all pertinent information regarding the neighbor's homeowner's policy. Once this information is obtained, a claim can then be made to the insurance company for payment of the professional's bill.

LIENS

The person providing professional services has another avenue for securing payment of the patient's bill where the patient has obtained the services of an attorney and asserted a claim against another person for causing the patient's injury. This avenue is called a **lien,** which is filed with the patient's attorney. Illustration 18.1 is a sample lien form used in the state of California in personal injury litigation cases.

Processing the lien

Note that the lien is directed to the patient's attorney and must be signed and dated by both the patient and the attorney to be valid. The medical assistant or professional rendering services first obtains the signature of the patient. The

TO: Attorney ___Michael L. Cowdrey___

    1200 N. Main Str.; Suite 910

    Santa Ana, CA 92701

    Re: Medical Reports and Doctor's Lien
  *Patient: Martin Doe

```
Doctor:
James Smith, M.D.
155 N. First Street
Santa Ana, CA 90000
```

AUTHORIZATION AND AGREEMENT TO PAY PHYSICIAN FEES

Date of Injury: Sept. 4, 1981
Date of Consultation: Sept. 5, 1981

I hereby authorize and direct my attorney _Michael L. Cowdrey_
to pay promptly to
from my portion of the proceeds out of any recovery, which may be paid to me,
as a result of the injuries sustained by me, on the date indicated above, the
unpaid balance of any reasonable charges for professional services rendered
by said physician and his associates on my behalf, and professional services
to include those for treatment heretofore or hereafter rendered up to the
time of the settlement or recovery as well as those for medical reports,
consultations, depositions, court appearances and preparations for court
appearances and preparation for court appearances on my behalf. I understand that this does not relieve me of my personal responsibility for all
such charges in the event that there is no recovery, or if the recovery is
insufficient to satisfy such charges; nor does this in any way constitute an
agreement that the above physician will wait for payment of said charges until
settlement of any legal action arising from the injuries sustained on the
above date.

In the event said physician is called upon by me or any attorney to testify in
court, arbitration hearing, deposition or any duly constituted tribunal as a
result of legal action arising from the injuries sustained on the date indicated
above, I further understand and agree I will be responsible for a fee payable
in advance of _$800_ per half day or any portion thereof, and that all rights
under Government Code Section 68092.5 are reserved. The said fee will apply
for appearance of said physician whether for purposes of obtaining medical
opinion, reading medical records or interpretation of medical records or for
any other purpose.

I further authorize said physician to furnish said attorney with any reports
he may request in reference to me.

Dated: _June 4, 1982_ Patient's Signature _Martin Doe_

The undersigned being attorney of record for the above patient does hereby agree
to observe all the terms of the above and agrees to withhold such sums from any
settlement, judgment, or verdict as may be necessary to adequately protect said
doctor above named.

Dated: _June 6, 1982_ Attorney's Signature _Michael L. Cowdrey_

Mr. Attorney: Please date, sign and return one copy to doctor's office at once.

    Keep one copy for your records.

ILLUSTRATION 18.1 SAMPLE LIEN FORM

lien is then sent to the attorney for his or her signature. The attorney then sends the lien back to the doctor or other professional rendering services, and the lien is kept with the patient's chart or other pertinent medical records. The lien ensures that the doctor or other professional institution is paid from any sums received by any settlement or compromise that the patient may obtain from the adversary party. If the attorney fails to pay the patient's bill from any settlement, compromise, or judgment rendered on the litigation, the doctor, clinic, or institution may proceed not only against the patient but also against the attorney for payment of the bill. Strong leverage may be applied to the attorney for payment of the patient's bill by filing a grievance with the state bar association against the attorney for not honoring the lien.

Expert witness fees

As previously discussed, a doctor or other allied health professional may be called to testify at a deposition or in court to give his or her expert opinion. The professional testifying may be compensated in the form of expert witness fees for giving such expert testimony. This right to expert fees is governed by statute in many states, including California. The standard lien form (Illustration 18.1) includes compensation paid to the doctor for such testimony. The amount the doctor or other professional charges for such testimony may vary. The figure cited in the lien is the sum the attorney and the patient agree to pay the doctor in the event he or she is asked to testify as an expert witness in the case.

Health professionals' attitudes toward liens

Physicians, clinics, hospitals and other institutions tend not to accept a lien in lieu of payment. However, this negative attitude is due largely to the fact that professionals and institutional personnel have been misled regarding the meaning and purpose of a lien.

The lien merely acts as a security device to ensure payment from the patient by and through his or her attorney in the event that a settlement is made on the case. The lien does not preclude the doctor or institution from requesting payment from the patient during the course of treatment while the lawsuit is pending. And it does not preclude the physician or institution from receiving payment through other forms of insurance coverage. The only time a lien acts in lieu of payment of a bill is in cases where the attorney is specifically requesting that the hospital, institution, or physician treat the patient and accept the lien in lieu of payment made at the present time.

In cases dealing with workers' compensation litigation, the physician or institution may be precluded from obtaining payment from the patient directly after the case has been concluded unless a lien has been asserted with the workers' compensation appeals board for such payment. But, in cases dealing with matters not covered under workers' compensation laws, the physician or institution providing treatment is not precluded from obtaining payment from the patient directly in the event that the patient is unsuccessful in his or her lawsuit. The patient's bill may even be turned over to a collection agency for collection, or a lawsuit may be brought against the patient for payment of the bill.

For these reasons, the medical assistant, nurse, or practitioner should make every effort to work with the attorney handling the litigation. After all, both the attorney and the professional rendering treatment have a common bond: the patient. No specific rules govern cooperation between the attorney and the allied health professional in a patient's claim for injuries against some other party. Nevertheless, medical assistants, nurses, and other personnel often find it easier to secure payment of the patient's bill when they have a good rapport with the attorney. The attorney can often be helpful in pointing out avenues other than the lawsuit itself for obtaining payment and may even assist the medical assistant in presenting the bill to the patient's insurance company.

WORKERS' COMPENSATION

Each state has a department of industrial relations, a workers' compensation appeals board, an industrial accident commission, or some similar agency where information may be obtained regarding payment of a patient's bills under workers' compensation programs. Every state varies in the procedures required in asserting such claims. The medical assistant, dental assistant, or other allied health professional rendering treatment to patients who have been injured on the job should consult such an agency or a local attorney regarding the steps required to secure payment of the bill. Some states, such as Nevada, tend to follow the federal procedure, in which the patient's bill is sent directly to the agency for payment. The agency then seeks reimbursement from the employer's compensation insurance carrier or from the employer directly.

According to the procedure used in other states, such as California, bills are submitted directly to the insurance company or the employer for payment. Since the procedure for securing payment of the injured patient/employee's bill is more complex in these states, an in-depth discussion is in order. California procedures will be discussed because California provides a variety of avenues for obtaining payment. Remember, however, that states differ in the types of form that must be used to submit a bill or otherwise secure payment.

Choosing a physician

Within thirty days of an injury, an employer in the state of California has the right to pick the physician or institution that will treat the patient. This law saves money for the employer or insurance company because many clinics or physicians contract with insurance companies to provide examinations or treatment of injured employees at discount rates. If the patient does not like the doctor or the treatment he or she receives, the patient may then request the insurance company or employer to provide a list of five other physicians, including at least one chiropractor, if requested, to whom the patient may go for continued treatment. The employer must allow the employee one change of physicians if requested.

One exception to the practice of the employer choosing the physician or institution that will treat the patient exists where, prior to the date of injury, the employee has notified the employer that he or she has a personal physician, in which case the employee shall have the right to be treated by such physician from the date of injury. Once the employee has chosen a physician to treat him or her, the employee or physician must notify the employer of the name and address of the physician. The physician, must submit a report to the employer within five working days of the initial examination and at specific periodic intervals thereafter. The employer is required to pay for the physician's services after receiving the reports. (See Illustration 18.2 for Billing and Statement of Charges for Medical-Legal Reports—to be submitted to the Workers' Compensation Appeals Board.)

After thirty days from the date of the injury, the injured employee is entitled to go to any physician or facility within a reasonable geographic area, for examination and treatment, and the insurance company or employer is obligated to pay the patient's bill if the treatment is necessary. It makes no difference that treatment was not authorized by the insurance company. However, the amount charged by the professional for the examination or treatment must be reasonable. The workers' compensation appeals board may disallow payment for any amount above that normally charged by other professionals or institutions for similar services.

The employer or insurance company has the right to have the patient examined by a physician of its own choosing at any time following the injury. When the employee submits to such an examination, he or she is entitled to receive all reasonable expenses of transportation, meals, and lodging incident to reporting for the examination plus one day of temporary disability payment for each day of wages lost in submitting to such examination. Often disputes arise about whether the patient may return to work or whether further treatment is necessary, and the physician examining the patient on behalf of the insurance company or employer will frequently release the patient to return to work. This physician may indicate that the patient does not need further treatment to cure or relieve him or her of the effects of the injury and may characterize the patient's condition as **permanent and stationary.** The status "permanent and stationary" means that the patient's overall condition will not get any better or any worse. However, the patient's physician may contend that the patient's condition is not "permanent and stationary" and may indicate that further treatment is necessary. At this point, the insurance company routinely sends a letter to the employee and to the treating doctor indicating that it will not pay for any further treatment.

BILLING AND STATEMENT OF CHARGES
For Medical-Legal Reports

This completed form must accompany all initial comprehensive evaluation reports which are filed in a proceeding before the WCAB and are requested to provide a medical opinion on an issue(s) pertaining to an alleged industrial injury. There issues are:

☐ App.
☐ Def.
☐ App. & Def. (AME)
☐ WCAB (IME)

☐ AOE/COE
☐ Apportionment
☐ Voc. Rehab

☐ Type and need for treatment
☐ Extent and duration of disability

WCAB No.

Type of Report (check one): ☐ Supplemental   ☐ Re-evaluation   ☐ Initial Comprehensive

Persons Filing Report with WCAB must complete above, Physician to complete below

DOCTOR'S NAME	IRS No.	PHONE No.	
DOCTOR'S ADDRESS	CITY	STATE	ZIP
PATIENT'S NAME	PATIENT'S ADDRESS		
EMPLOYER	EMPLOYER'S ADDRESS		

1. . . . . Date of Billing _____

2. Check the specialty under which services were rendered.

ORTHOPEDIC SURGERY (a) ☐
PSYCHIATRY (b) ☐
CARDIOLOGY OR INTERNAL MEDICINE (c) ☐
NEUROLOGY (d) ☐
OTHER (Specify) _____ (e) ☐

3. Charge for records review . . . .   (3) $ _____

4. Charge for history and exam . . . .   (4) $ _____

5. Charge for report preparation . . . .   (5) $ _____
(Including dictating, reviewing outside and/or prior laboratory studies, and x-rays, literature review, discussing case with other doctors, etc.)

6. TOTAL CHARGES FOR MEDICAL-LEGAL REPORTS (add Nos. 3, 4, & 5).   (6) $ _____

7. Charges for all other services
(laboratory, x-ray, cardiac or pulmonary function tests, etc.) required to complete your examination, for which you are charging, itemized according to the Official Medical Fee Schedule.

RVS	CHARGE

RVS	CHARGE
_____	$ _____
_____	$ _____
_____	$ _____
_____	$ _____

RVS	CHARGE
_____	$ _____
_____	$ _____
_____	$ _____
_____	$ _____

Total charges for No. 7 $ _____

8. Any other tests or charges not represented in Fee Schedule. (itemize on reverse) $ _____

9. TOTAL CHARGES (Add Nos. 6, 7 & 8) . . . . $ _____

DIA FORM NO. 76 (5/86)

ILLUSTRATION 18.2   BILLING AND STATEMENT OF CHARGES FOR MEDICAL-LEGAL REPORTS

If the patient/employee does indeed need further treatment to cure and relieve him or her of the effects of the injury, the injured employee/patient may still continue treatment at the insurance company's expense. However, payment for any such examination or treatment may be withheld by the insurance company until a judge of the workers' compensation appeals board determines that all such further treatment was and is necessary. Further, the judge may determine from the medical evidence that further treatment may be necessary in the future, for which the insurance company or employer would also be obligated to pay.

Filing a lien for payment of bill

To secure payment of a bill without the insurance company's express authorization or agreement to pay, the physician must file an original lien with the workers' compensation appeals board and serve all interested parties. Illustration 18.3 is a sample of a preprinted workers compensation lien, which may be obtained from any branch office of the workers' compensation appeals board. The various California branch appeals board addresses are listed in the second part of Illustration 18.3. Normally, the medical assistant, secretary, or nurse would merely type in the requested information including the case number. The original of the lien is filed with the workers' compensation appeals board where the case is pending. Copies of the original lien are then mailed to all interested parties in the case, including the applicant's (patient's) attorney, the injured patient's employer, the workers' compensation insurance carrier for the employer, and the patient. In addition, a copy of the lien is kept with the patient's chart or similar billing record. A proof of service form should be attached to the original and copies of the lien to adequately demonstrate to the workers' compensation appeals board that copies of the lien have been sent to all interested parties. Illustration 18.4 is an example of a proof of service form indicating that the lien has been mailed to all persons or companies named. This form may be preprinted with blank spaces to be filled in as the need arises. Verification and proof of service forms may be obtained at most stationery stores at a nominal cost.

As previously discussed in Chapter 13, which deals with workers' compensation benefits in general, an injured employee may be examined by a physician of his or her choice for medical/legal purposes. The purpose of this examination is to obtain a professional diagnostic impression—including the prognosis of the patient's condition and the prognosis for future medical care—to prove a contested claim. As previously noted, a doctor who examines an injured employee on behalf of the insurance company will frequently release the patient to return to work or indicate that no further medical treatment is needed. In this situation, the patient is entitled by law to be examined by a doctor of his or her own choice to legally contradict the opinion of the insurance company's doctor. The patient's doctor is required to file and serve a

WORKERS' COMPENSATION APPEALS BOARD

STATE OF CALIFORNIA

CASE NO._____

NOTICE AND REQUEST FOR ALLOWANCE OF LIEN

_____ VS. LIEN CLAIMANT   _____ ADDRESS

_____ EMPLOYEE   _____ ADDRESS

_____ EMPLOYER   _____ ADDRESS

_____ INSURANCE CARRIER   _____ ADDRESS

The undersigned hereby requests the Workers' Compensation Appeals Board to determine and allow as a lien the sum of

_____ _____Dollars ($_____) against

any amount now due or which may hereafter become payable as compensation to_____
                                                                            EMPLOYEE

on account of injury sustained by him on_____
                                        DATE

This request and claim for lien is for: (Mark appropriate box)

☐ The reasonable expense incurred by or on behalf of said employee for medical treatment to cure or relieve from the effects of said injury; or

☐ The reasonable medical expense incurred to prove a contested claim; or

☐ The reasonable value of living expenses of said employee or of his dependents, subsequent to the injury, or

☐ The reasonable living expenses of the wife or minor children, or both, of said employee, subsequent to the date of injury, where such employee has deserted or is neglecting his family; or

☐ The reasonable fee for interpreter's services performed on_____
                                                             DATE

☐

☐

NOTE: ITEMIZED STATEMENTS MUST BE ATTACHED

The undersigned declares that he delivered or mailed a copy of this lien claim to each of the above-named parties on

_____   _____
ATTORNEY FOR LIEN CLAIMANT   DATE

_____   _____
ADDRESS OF ATTORNEY FOR LIEN CLAIMANT   LIEN CLAIMANT

EMPLOYEE'S CONSENT TO ALLOWANCE OF LIEN

I consent to the requested allowance of a lien against my compensation.

_____   _____
ATTORNEY FOR EMPLOYEE   EMPLOYEE

ILLUSTRATION 18.3 WORKERS' COMPENSATION LIEN

INSTRUCTIONS

1. This declaration must be completed and filed before any case will be set for hearing at the request of any party.

    A hearing includes either a conference hearing or regular hearing. A conference hearing includes **conference pre-trial** to frame issues, record stipulations and join necessary parties and any other setting (such as rating pre-trial and/or standby calendar) for the purpose of assisting the parties in resolving disputes.

    A regular hearing is set for the purpose of receiving evidence.

2. Unless notified otherwise, no witness other than the applicant need attend **conference pre-trial** hearings.

3. The party producing a non-English-speaking witness must arrange for the presence of a certified interpreter.

4. Continuances are not favored and none will be granted after filing of this Declaration without a clear and timely showing of good cause.

5. The Workers' Compensation Appeals Board favors the presentation of medical evidence in the form of written reports.

6. If setting on a priority basis is requested because of hardship or other good cause, a letter should be attached specifying in detail the nature of the hardship and the reason why early setting is requested.

    If setting is requested on any calendar other than the conference pre-trial or regular hearing, a letter should be attached to the Declaration of Readiness specifying in detail just why such setting is requested.

    If a regular hearing is requested, a letter should be attached to the Declaration of Readiness specifying in detail why the matter is not suitable for a conference pre-trial or other setting.

    The Board, upon the receipt of the Declaration of Readiness, may set the case for a type of proceeding other than the one requested (Rule 10417).

WORKERS' COMPENSATION APPEALS BOARD

445 Golden Gate Avenue, San Francisco 94102

DISTRICT OFFICES

BAKERSFIELD	225 Chester Ave (93301)	327-7591
BELL GARDENS	6450 Garfield Ave (90201)	771-8650
EUREKA	619 Second St (95501)	443-4003
FRESNO	2550 Mariposa St (93721)	488-5051
LONG BEACH (Signal Hill)	2828 Junipero Ave (90806)	595-8381
LOS ANGELES	107 S Broadway (90012)	620-2680
OAKLAND	1111 Jackson St (94607)	464-0500
POMONA	300 S Park Ave (91766)	623-4301
REDDING	2115 Akard Ave (96001)	246-6551
SACRAMENTO	1006 Fourth St (95814)	445-9812
SALINAS	21 W Laurel Dr (93906)	443-3060
SAN BERNARDINO	303 W Third St (92401)	383-4341
SAN DIEGO	1350 Front St (92101)	237-7321
SAN FRANCISCO	525 Golden Gate Ave (94102)	557-0680
SAN JOSE	111 N Market St (95113)	277-1246
SANTA ANA	28 Civic Center Pl (92701)	558-4121
SANTA BARBARA	411 E Canon Perdido (93101)	966-1527
SANTA ROSA	750 Mendocino Ave (95401)	542-3146
STOCKTON	31 E Channel St (95202)	948-7757
VAN NUYS (Panorama City)	8155 Van Nuys Blvd (91402)	782-4061
VENTURA	5810 Ralston St (93003)	654-4670
LOS ANGELES (Santa Monica)	11801 W Olympic Blvd (90064)	473-0850

84695-501 11-81 325M CAM Ⓞ D OSP

ILLUSTRATION 18.3 (CONTINUED)

VERIFICATION

STATE OF CALIFORNIA, COUNTY OF

I have read the foregoing_____

_____ and know its contents.

☒ CHECK APPLICABLE PARAGRAPH

☐   I am a party to this action. The matters stated in it are true of my own knowledge except as to those matters which are stated on information and belief, and as to those matters I believe them to be true.

☐   I am ☐ an Officer ☐ a partner_____ ☐ a _____ of_____

a party to this action, and am authorized to make this verification for and on its behalf, and I make this verification for that reason. I have read the foregoing document and know its contents. The matters stated in it are true of my own knowledge except as to those matters which are stated on information and belief, and as to those matters I believe them to be true.

☐   I am one of the attorneys for_____

a party to this action. Such party is absent from the county of aforesaid where such attorneys have their offices, and I make this verification for and on behalf of that party for that reason. I have read the foregoing document and know its contents. I am informed and believe and on that ground allege that the matters stated in it are true.

Executed on_____, 19___, at_____California.

I declare under penalty of perjury under the laws of the State of California that the foregoing is true and correct.

_____
Signature

ACKNOWLEDGMENT OF RECEIPT OF DOCUMENT
(other than summons and complaint)

Received copy of document described as_____

_____

on_____19____.

_____
Signature

PROOF OF SERVICE BY MAIL

STATE OF CALIFORNIA, COUNTY OF

I am employed in the county of_____, State of California.

I am over the age of 18 and not a party to the within action; my business address is:_____

_____

On_____19___, I served the foregoing document described as_____

_____

_____on_____

in this action by placing a true copy thereof enclosed in a sealed envelope with postage thereon fully prepaid in the United States mail at:_____

_____

addressed as follows:

☐   (BY MAIL) I caused such envelope with postage thereon fully prepaid to be placed in the United States mail at_____, California.

☐   (BY PERSONAL SERVICE) I caused such envelope to be delivered by hand to the offices of the addressee.

Executed on_____, 19___ at_____, California.

☐   (State)   I declare under penalty of perjury under the laws of the State of California that the above is true and correct.

☐   (Federal)   I declare that I am employed in the office of a member of the bar of this court at whose direction the service was made.

_____
Signature

STUART'S EXBROOK TIMESAVER (REVISED 7/81)

(May be used in California State or Federal Courts)

ILLUSTRATION 18.4 VERFICATION AND PROOF OF SERVICE (LIEN)

workers' compensation lien (Illustration 18.3) to secure payment of his or her bill, since the insurance company rarely authorizes such an examination. However, a different box than in the first case cited will need to be checked regarding the reason for the lien. Previously, the lien was being asserted for payment for reasonable and necessary expenses incurred regarding treatment. In the case of a medical/legal examination, the lien is being asserted for medical/legal purposes to prove a contested claim. Accordingly, this box on the lien should be checked.

In general, an insurance company is obligated to pay the reasonable medical/legal expenses asserted by liens where the injury to the patient/employee occurred as a result of his or her employment. However, the lien may be disallowed if it is determined that the treatment was not necessary to cure or relieve the injured employee of the effects of the injury. In such instances, the person rendering the treatment may have to seek payment of the bill by some other form of insurance coverage, such as the patient's private group health care insurance company. Generally, the person rendering treatment is not allowed to proceed directly against the patient for payment of the bill when the workers' compensation appeals board disallows the lien. However, the workers' compensation appeals board rarely disallows a lien based on unnecessary treatment, except in extremely obvious situations where treatment is not indicated.

The appeals board may also disallow part of the fees charged by the doctor rendering a medical/legal examination if such fees are unreasonable. Thus, where the physician charges $1,000 for a five-minute examination and provides a two-page narrative report of the examination, the appeals board would undoubtedly disallow all charges above what a similar physician practicing in the local area would charge for the same or a similar examination.

Amended liens

Medical assistants, dental assistants, institutional personnel, and other allied health professionals frequently make mistakes when filing subsequent liens for additional treatment received by a patient. The California Rules of Practice and Procedures require that any subsequent lien filed by the same facility for subsequent treatment on the same injured employee/patient must be filed as an *amended lien* (Illustration 18.5). When the workers' compensation judge reviews a case that has come up for decision, the judge will look at the last lien filed by the doctor or facility. The amount on the lien should reflect the balance owing to the doctor or facility as of the date the lien was signed. The mistake routinely made by medical and dental assistants, front-office personnel, and other professionals in preparing such a lien is to file a new lien setting forth only the patient's most recent charges, those incurred since the prior lien was filed.

For example, patient Kevin's bill for treatment for the month of January is $500, and the medical assistant properly files and serves a lien for that amount.

WORKERS' COMPENSATION APPEALS BOARD
STATE OF CALIFORNIA

CASE NO. _83 ANA 112233_

AMENDED   NOTICE AND REQUEST FOR ALLOWANCE OF LIEN   _AMENDED_

James Smith, M.D.
VS.
LIEN CLAIMANT   _333 E. First St., Anytown, CA 90000_
ADDRESS

John Cowdrey
EMPLOYEE   _345 E. Fir St., Anytown, CA 90000_
ADDRESS

Acme Work Shops, Inc.
EMPLOYER   _112 W. Watson St., Anytown, CA 90000_
ADDRESS

Fly By Night Ins. Co.
INSURANCE CARRIER   _P.O. Box 555, Anytown, CA 90000_
ADDRESS

The undersigned hereby requests the Workers' Compensation Appeals Board to determine and allow as a lien the sum of

Two-Hundred and no/100------------------------- Dollars ($ _200.00_) against

any amount now due or which may hereafter become payable as compensation to _John Cowdrey_
EMPLOYEE

on account of injury sustained by him on _12/5/82_ .
DATE

This request and claim for lien is for: (Mark appropriate box)

☒ The reasonable expense incurred by or on behalf of said employee for medical treatment to cure or relieve from the effects of said injury; or

☐ The reasonable medical expense incurred to prove a contested claim; or

☐ The reasonable value of living expenses of said employee or of his dependents, subsequent to the injury, or

☐ The reasonable living expenses of the wife or minor children, or both, of said employee, subsequent to the date of injury, where such employee has deserted or is neglecting his family; or

☐ The reasonable fee for interpreter's services performed on_____.
DATE

☐

☐

NOTE: ITEMIZED STATEMENTS MUST BE ATTACHED

The undersigned declares that he delivered or mailed a copy of this lien claim to each of the above-named parties on

_____   _March 10, 1983_
ATTORNEY FOR LIEN CLAIMANT   DATE

_____   _James Smith, M.D._
ADDRESS OF ATTORNEY FOR LIEN CLAIMANT   LIEN CLAIMANT

EMPLOYEE'S CONSENT TO ALLOWANCE OF LIEN

I consent to the requested allowance of a lien against my compensation.

(Employee's attorney's signature is helpful, but not necessary)   _(Employee's signature is helpful, but not necessary)_

ATTORNEY FOR EMPLOYEE   EMPLOYEE

DIA WCAB FORM 6 (REV. 8-75)
①o OSP   DEPARTMENT OF INDUSTRIAL RELATIONS
DIVISION OF INDUSTRIAL ACCIDENTS

ILLUSTRATION 18.5 AMENDED LIEN

Kevin then incurs another bill for $250 during the month of February. The mistake commonly made is to file a lien for February's treatment in the amount of $250, when the lien should actually show the total, $750. The actual balance of the patient's account at the time the amended lien is being prepared is the amount that is typed on the lien. Also, the word *amended* should be typed on the new lien below the workers' compensation appeals board case number.

DEFENSES TO LIENS

As previously stated, an insurance company or employer may object to the doctor's or institution's bill. The only two grounds on which an objection may properly be asserted are that the examination or treatment is unnecessary and that the fees charged are unreasonable. To assert these defenses, the defendant must file a formal objection to the lien, called a *medical/legal objection letter*, with the workers' compensation appeals board (see Illustrations 18.6 and 18.7).

Medical/legal objection letter

the lien precludes the physician from requesting payment

The medical/legal objection is sometimes seen with a formal case title on **legal-lined paper.** However, a simple letter format is most commonly used. In either form, the medical/legal objection letter must set forth the grounds on which the defendant, insurance company, or employer is basing its objection—that the bill is unreasonable, that the treatment is unnecessary, or both.

The original medical/legal objection letter is filed with the appropriate appeals board. Copies of the letter are then served on all interested parties, especially the party who filed the lien for professional fees. Most important, the medical/legal objection letter must be filed with the workers' compensation appeals board within sixty days after the original or any subsequent lien is filed. The defendant/employer or insurance company waives any right to object to either the reasonableness of the bill or the necessity of the patient's treatment unless the objection is filed with the board within the sixty-day period. (This period is established by California Labor Code, Section 4622.) Thereafter, the employer or insurance company is obligated to pay the bill based on the lien filed with the appeals board.

The professional rendering services on behalf of the injured employee/patient may be entitled to additional compensation where the sixty-day period has elapsed, payment has not been received, and the employer or insurance company has not filed a medical/legal objection letter. The professional is also entitled to an additional 10 percent of the bill plus interest for the defendant's failure to comply with California Labor Code, Section 4622.

```
                    M. L. COWDREY, ATTORNEY
                       111 E. First Street
                         Anytown, CA.
```

Workers' Compensation Appeals Board
28 Civic Center Plaza
Santa Ana, CA 92701

Re: John Cowdrey
     WCAB Case No. 82 ANA 4444
     Our File No. - 1 W-001

Gentlemen:

Please accept this letter as a formal objection within the meaning of Labor
Code Section 4622.

It is the contention of defendants herein that the charges incurred by the
applicant are neither reasonable nor necessary.

Defendants further object to said lien on the basis that no foundation exists
in evidence to prove the charges of the provider were incurred by applicant and
no order for payment of same can issue without said foundation.

To the extent applicable, defendants respectfully request proof of compliance
with California Labor Code Section 3209.3 and/or 3209.5, as well as an offer
of proof that some benefit was rendered to the applicant herein, which would
allow a finding pursuant to Labor Code Section 4903(b).

We offer this objection to the following lien and request it be placed in
issue at the next appropriate hearing before the WCAB.

     James Smith, M.D. Dated 4-4-82 in the Amount of $175.00.

The payment of said lien will constitute a withdrawal of this objection and in
said event, all parties are asked to disregard this letter.

Very truly yours,

MICHAEL L. COWDREY

Michael L. Cowdrey

ILLUSTRATION 18.6 MEDICAL/LEGAL OBJECTION (ATTORNEY'S LETTER)

```
REPUBLIC INDEMNITY                    WCAB #    :   82 ANA 124719
Company of America                    Injured   :   Lawrence Howorth
16133 Ventura Blvd.                   Employer  :   Sea and Sun Subaru
Encino, CA 91436                      D/Injury  :   8-13-82
Telephone (213) 990-9860             Claim #   :   612421

Norton Hering, M.D.                                  November 23, 1982

1413 N. Broadway

Santa Ana, Ca.  92706
```

The following action is being taken in response to your billing or lien:

☐ In accordance with L/C Sec. 4622 the lien of _____,
dated _____, in the amount of $_____, is being paid in full.
Our check has been sent under separate cover. Please acknowledge payment
by either withdrawing or filing an amended lien.

☒ Defendants raise the issue of REASONABLENESS AND NECESSITY of the lien
of ___Norton Hering, M.D.___ date ___11-15-82___ .
　　　　　　　　　　　　　　　Lien Submitted: $485.00
　　　　　　　　　　　　　　　Amount Paid   : $242.50
　　　　　　　　　　　　　　　Disallowed   : $242.50
Disallowed; ( ) Exam ( ) X-Rays ( ) Laboratory fees ( ) Other

　　Reason: __Balance to be paid by co-defendant -- Insurance Co. of North__

_____America._____

_____

☐ Defendants object to the photocopy lien of _____
as UNREASONABLE AND EXCESSIVE in charges.
　　　　　　　　　　　　　　　Lien Submitted:_____
　　　　　　　　　　　　　　　Amount Paid   :_____
　　　　　　　　　　　　　　　Disallowed   :_____
Our payment is based on a survey of 5 photocopy firms doing business in
Southern California. Average charge for photocopy services is $12.80
(includes service, travel and extra charges) plus $.33 per page.

☐ This is a continuous trauma multi-party case, Republic Indemnity has paid
$_____.
Balance of lien due from co-defendant(s)_____

☐ This is a continuous trauma, this billing should be paid by elected or last
defendant_____.

cc: M.L. Cowdrey   Respectfully submitted
     111 E. First St.
     Anytown, CA   By _Alice Mazmanian_
cc: INA, P.O. Box 1085, Orange CA 92668   Alice Mazmanian: Claims Examiner
```

**ILLUSTRATION 18.7  MEDICAL/LEGAL OBJECTION (INSURANCE COMPANY'S FORM)**
```

WORKERS' COMPENSATION APPEALS CASE NUMBER

We have thus far been discussing how a professional is paid for services rendered on behalf of a patient who has been injured in a work-related accident or exposure. The underlying presumption has been that the patient has filed a grievance, either by himself or through an attorney, with the workers' compensation appeals board for benefits under the labor code. However, sometimes an injured patient does not wish to proceed against his or her employer. Sometimes the insurance company has provided the injured employee (patient) with temporary disability to compensate him or her for lost wages. In some cases, the injured employee has continued working for the employer in a lighter capacity even though he or she is being treated for the injury. There are also cases where the employer or insurance company has made partial payments to the physician or institution rendering service and has disallowed the balance as unreasonable.

Frequently the injured employee/patient has not filed an application for adjudication of claim with the workers' compensation appeals board (see Illustration 18.8). Without the filing of this application, the employee has no worker's compensation appeals board case number on which to file and serve a lien or petition for a judge to issue an order for payment of the bill. In these situations, California allows any **interested party** to file an application for adjudication of claim before the workers' compensation appeals board, together with a declaration (attached to the application) specifying the efforts made by the lien claimant to encourage filing of the claim form by the employee. Therefore, the professional—whether a doctor, dentist, chiropractor, orthodontist, or pharmacist—as well as the institution may file an application on behalf of the injured employee as an interested party. Illustration 18.8 provides an example of a completed application for adjudication of claim.

The application is a preprinted form that may be obtained from any branch of the workers' compensation appeals board of the state of California. The italic typewritten portions of the form illustrate the parts that the medical assistant, nurse, or other health professional associated with the doctor or the institution would complete. Two originals should be filed with the local workers' compensation appeals board, with the request that one original be kept by the board and the other returned to the doctor or institution. This return copy, called a *conformed copy*, will be stamped with a case number by the workers' compensation appeals board.

Photocopies of the conformed application are then made by the medical assistant or personnel of the institution and served on the patient, his or her employer, and the insurance company insuring the employer for workers' compensation (if known). Thereafter, the physician or institution may file and serve medical liens for payment of the patient's bill. Petitions, declarations, and other appropriate documents to obtain payment may also be filed, since there is now a case number to insert on any such documents.

STATE OF CALIFORNIA
DEPARTMENT OF INDUSTRIAL RELATIONS

WORKERS' COMPENSATION APPEALS BOARD

SEE REVERSE SIDE
FOR INSTRUCTIONS

APPLICATION FOR ADJUDICATION OF CLAIM
(PRINT OR TYPE NAMES AND ADDRESSES)

CASE No. _____

Mr. *John Cowdrey* _____   *345 E. Fir Street* _____
                                                                          (INJURED EMPLOYEE'S ADDRESS AND ZIP CODE)

Social Security No.: *222-00-5555* _____   *Anytown, California 90000* _____

James Smith, M.D. _____   *333 E. First St., Anytown, CA 90000* _____
(APPLICANT, IF OTHER THAN INJURED EMPLOYEE)   (APPLICANT'S ADDRESS AND ZIP CODE)

Acme Work Shops, Inc. _____   *112 W. Watson Street, Anytown, CA 90000* _____
(EMPLOYER — STATE IF SELF-INSURED)   vs   (EMPLOYER'S ADDRESS AND ZIP CODE)

Fly By Night Ins. Co. _____   *P.O. Box 555, Anytown, CA 90000* _____
(EMPLOYER'S INSURANCE CARRIER OR, IF SELF-INSURED, ADJUSTING AGENCY)   (INSURANCE CARRIER OR ADJUSTING AGENCY'S ADDRESS)

IT IS CLAIMED THAT:

1. The injured employee, born *3/6/50* _____, while employed as a *Carpenter* _____
                                    (DATE OF BIRTH)   (OCCUPATION AT TIME OF INJURY)

   on *12/5/82* ____ at *112 W. Watson Street, Anytown, CA 90000* ____
        (DATE OF INJURY)   (ADDRESS)   (CITY)   (STATE)   (ZIP CODE)

   By the employer sustained injury arising out of and in the course of employment to

   Low Back, Lower Extremities _____
                                    (STATE WHAT PARTS OF BODY WERE INJURED)

2. The injury occurred as follows: *Lifting box, felt pain in low back and legs* _____
                                          (EXPLAIN WHAT EMPLOYEE WAS DOING AT TIME OF INJURY AND HOW INJURY WAS RECEIVED)

3. Actual earnings at time of injury were: *maximum (or state actual earnings if known. If*
                                          (GIVE WEEKLY OR MONTHLY SALARY OF HOURLY RATE AND NUMBER OF HOURS WORKED PER WEEK)
   unknown, state unknown) _____
   (SEPARATELY STATE VALUE PER WEEK OR MONTH OF TIPS, MEALS, LODGING OR OTHER ADVANTAGES REGULARLY RECEIVED)

4. The injury caused disability as follows: *12/5/82 to 3/1/83*
                                          (SPECIFY LAST DAY OF WORK DUE TO THIS INJURY AND BEGINNING AND ENDING DATES OF ALL PERIODS OFF DUE TO THIS INJURY)

5. Compensation was paid ___*X*___ $_____ $_____ _____
                         (YES)   (NO)   (TOTAL PAID)   (WEEKLY RATE)   (DATE OF LAST PAYMENT)

6. Unemployment insurance or unemployment compensation disability benefits have been received since the date of injury
   __*X*__
   (YES) (NO)

7. Medical treatment was received ___*X*___ *3/10/83* _____ All treatment was furnished by
                                   (YES) (NO)   (DATE OF LAST TREATMENT)
   the Employer or Insurance Company ____ _*X*_ Other treatment was provided or paid for by *self procured*
                                    (YES)   (NO)

   _____ Did Medi-Cal pay for any health care
   related to this claim ___*X*___ doctors not provided or paid for by employer or insurance company who treated or examined
                          (YES) (NO)
   for this injury are *(your doctor) Dr. James Smith, M.D., 333 First St., Anytown, CA*
                       (STATE NAMES AND ADDRESSES OF SUCH DOCTORS AND NAMES OF HOSPITALS TO WHICH SUCH DOCTORS ADMITTED INJURED)

8. Other cases have been filed for industrial injuries by this employee as follows: *unknown*

   _____
   (SPECIFY CASE NUMBER AND CITY WHERE FILED)

9. This application is filed because of a disagreement regarding liability for: Temporary disability indemnity _____

   Permanent disability indemnity _____   Reimbursement for medical expense _*X*_   Medical treatment _*X*_

   Compensation at proper rate _____   Rehabilitation _____   Other (Specify) *Applicant requests a*
                                                                                    AND APPLICANT REQUESTS A HEARING AND AWARD OF
   hearing and award of the same, and for all other appropriate benefits.
   THE SAME, AND FOR ALL OTHER APPROPRIATE BENEFITS PROVIDED BY LAW.

   Dated at *Anytown,* _____ , California, *4/5/83* _____
            (CITY)   (DATE)

   In Pro Per, James Smith, M.D. _____   x *James Smith M.D.* _____
                 (APPLICANT'S ATTORNEY)   (APPLICANT'S SIGNATURE)
   333 E. First St., Anytown, CA 90000 _____
   (ADDRESS AND TELEPHONE NUMBER OF ATTORNEY)

DIA WCAB FORM 1 (REV. 7/81)

ILLUSTRATION 18.8   APPLICATION FOR ADJUDICATION OF CLAIM

INSTRUCTIONS

FILING AND SERVICE OF A DECLARATION OF READINESS (DIA/WCAB Form 9) IS PREREQUISITE TO THE SETTING OF A CASE FOR HEARING.

Effect of Filing Application

Filing of this application begins formal proceedings against the defendants named in your application.

Assistance in Filling Out Application

You may request the assistance of an information and assistance officer of the Division of Industrial Accidents.

Right to Attorney

You may be represented by an attorney or agent, or you may represent yourself. The attorney fee will be set by the Board at the time the case is decided and is ordinarily payable out of your award.

Filling Out Application

All blanks in the application shall be completed. Where the information is unknown, place "unknown" in the blank. If *medical treatment is paid for by Medi-Cal, Medicare, group health insurance or private carrier, please specify*.

Service of Documents

Your attorney or agent will serve all documents in accord with Labor Code Section 5501 and Section 10500 of the Workers' Compensation Appeals Board's Rules of Practice and Procedure.

If you have no attorney or agent, copies of this application will be served by the Workers' Compensation Appeals Board on all parties. If you file any other document, you must mail or deliver a copy of the document to all parties in the case.

IMPORTANT!

If any applicant is under 18 years of age, it will be necessary to file Petition for Appointment of Guardian ad Litem. Forms for this purpose may be obtained at the office of the Workers' Compensation Appeals Board.

CAM ①● OSP

ILLUSTRATION 18.8 (CONTINUED)

DECLARATION OF READINESS TO PROCEED

A declaration of readiness to proceed (Illustration 18.9) is essentially a request made to the workers' compensation appeals board to take some affirmative action on the case. This preprinted document may be obtained from any branch of the appeals board and may be filed by any interested party to the litigation. The document indicates that the party filing the declaration is ready to proceed on a particular issue or issues in the case. As previously indicated, an interested party to the litigation includes the applicant/injured employee,

WORKERS' COMPENSATION APPEALS BOARD
STATE OF CALIFORNIA

Case No. *83 ANA 112233*

James Smith, M.D.
(John Cowdrey, employee)   Applicant

vs.

Acme Work Shops, Inc., Fly By
Night Ins. Co.   Defendants

DECLARATION OF READINESS TO PROCEED

NOTICE: "Any objection to the proceedings requested by a Declaration of Readiness to proceed shall be filed and served within ten (10) days after service of the Declaration.
(Rule 10416)

The [ ] Employee or applicant
    [ ] Defendant
    [X] Lien Claimant

requests that this case be set for hearing at *28 Civic Center Plaza, Rm 400 Santa Ana, CA 90000*
(Place)

and declarant states under penalty of perjury that he or she is presently ready to proceed to hearing on the issues below and has made the following efforts to resolve these issues. *rejected demand by Insurance Carrier for payment of medical bill of Applicant. The parties herein need the Board's assistant to resolve these issues and that of future treatment.*

Declarant requests:

[X] Regular Hearing   [ ] Conference Pre-trial   [ ] Rating Pre-trial

(SEE REVERSE SIDE FOR INSTRUCTIONS)

At the present time the principal issues are—
    [ ] Compensation Rate   [ ] Rehabilitation
    [ ] Temporary Disability   [X] Self-procured Treatment
    [ ] Permanent Disability   [X] Future Medical Treatment
    [X] Other *10% penalty for failure to provide benefits*.

Employee [ ] is (or) [X] is not presently receiving compensation payments.

Employee's condition following injury is permanent and stationary as shown by the report(s) of Doctor(s) _____ Dated _____ ,

filed and served on _____ .

I expect to present *One* witnesses, including *One* medical witnesses, and estimate the time required for the hearing will be *One* hours.

I have completed discovery and all medical reports in my possession or control have been filed and served as required by WCAB Rules of Practices and Procedure.

Adverse parties [ ] have (or) [X] have not served me with medical reports.

Copies of this Declaration have been served this date as shown below.

Name (Print or Type) *James Smith, M.D.*

Declarant's signature *James Smith, M.D.*

Address *333 First St., Anytown, CA 90000*   Phone *(714) 555-5544*

Date *August 15, 1983*

SERVICE

Type or print names and addresses of parties, including attorneys and representatives served with a copy of this Declaration:

Acme Work Shops, Inc.   *112 W. Watson St. Anytown, CA 90000*

Fly By Night Insurance Co.   *P.O. Box 555 Anytown, CA 90000*

(SEE REVERSE SIDE FOR INSTRUCTIONS)

DIA WCAB 9 (REV. 7/80)

ILLUSTRATION 18.9 DECLARATION OF READINESS TO PROCEED

INSTRUCTIONS

1. This declaration must be completed and filed before any case will be set for hearing at the request of any party.

   A hearing includes either a conference hearing or regular hearing. A conference hearing includes **conference pre-trial** to frame issues, record stipulations and join necessary parties and any other setting (such as rating pre-trial and/or standby calendar) for the purpose of assisting the parties in resolving disputes.

   A regular hearing is set for the purpose of receiving evidence.

2. Unless notified otherwise, no witness other than the applicant need attend **conference pre-trial** hearings.

3. The party producing a non-English-speaking witness must arrange for the presence of a certified interpreter.

4. Continuances are not favored and none will be granted after filing of this Declaration without a clear and timely showing of good cause.

5. The Workers' Compensation Appeals Board favors the presentation of medical evidence in the form of written reports.

6. If setting on a priority basis is requested because of hardship or other good cause, a letter should be attached specifying in detail the nature of the hardship and the reason why early setting is requested.

   If setting is requested on any calendar other than the conference pre-trial or regular hearing, a letter should be attached to the Declaration of Readiness specifying in detail just why such setting is requested.

   If a regular hearing is requested, a letter should be attached to the Declaration of Readiness specifying in detail why the matter is not suitable for a conference pre-trial or other setting.

   The Board, upon the receipt of the Declaration of Readiness, may set the case for a type of proceeding other than the one requested (Rule 10417).

WORKERS' COMPENSATION APPEALS BOARD

445 Golden Gate Avenue, San Francisco 94102

DISTRICT OFFICES

BAKERSFIELD	225 Chester Ave (93301)	327-7591	SAN BERNARDINO	303 W Third St (92401)	383-4341
BELL GARDENS	6450 Garfield Ave (90201)	771-8650	SAN DIEGO	1350 Front St (92101)	237-7321
EUREKA	619 Second St (95501)	443-4003	SAN FRANCISCO	525 Golden Gate Ave (94102)	557-0680
FRESNO	2550 Mariposa St (93721)	488-5051	SAN JOSE	111 N Market St (95113)	277-1246
LONG BEACH (Signal Hill)	2828 Junipero Ave (90806)	595-8381	SANTA ANA	28 Civic Center Pl (92701)	558-4121
LOS ANGELES	107 S Broadway (90012)	620-2680	SANTA BARBARA	411 E Canon Perdido (93101)	966-1527
OAKLAND	1111 Jackson St (94607)	464-0500	SANTA ROSA	750 Mendocino Ave (95401)	542-3146
POMONA	300 S Park Ave (91766)	623-4301	STOCKTON	31 E Channel St (95202)	948-7757
REDDING	2115 Akard Ave (96001)	246-6551	VAN NUYS (Panorama City)	8155 Van Nuys Blvd (91402)	782-4061
SACRAMENTO	1006 Fourth St (95814)	445-9812	VENTURA	5810 Ralston St (93003)	654-4670
SALINAS	21 W Laurel Dr (93906)	443-3060	LOS ANGELES (Santa Monica)	11801 W Olympic Blvd (90064)	473-0850

84695-501 11-81 325M CAM Ⓤ D OSP

ILLUSTRATION 18.9 (CONTINUED)

---

the workers' compensation insurance company, the patient's employer, or any other lien claimant. Thus, the professional rendering medical or dental services on behalf of an injured employee may file a declaration of readiness to proceed as an interested party/lien claimant. The lien claimant, by filing the declaration of readiness to proceed, is requesting the appeals board to set the case for a hearing or conference relating to the professional's lien.

In addition, the physician, dentist, pharmacist, or other professional rendering services, as a lien claimant on behalf of the injured employee, may request that a 10 percent penalty be ordered by the appeals board because of the defendant/insurance company's failure to pay the bill on time. Again, the italic typewritten portion of the form represents information that the medical or dental assistant would type on the form.

Once completed, the original declaration of readiness to proceed is filed with the workers' compensation appeals board where the case is pending. Copies of the declaration are served on all other interested parties to the action. A proof of service form does not need to be attached to the declaration, since the preprinted declaration includes this information.

Only two requests may be made regarding the hearing by a lien claimant such as a doctor, dentist, or pharmacist when the declaration of readiness to proceed is being filed: that the appeals board set the matter for a regular hearing or that the board set the matter for a conference pretrial. A conference pretrial is essentially a settlement conference where the parties themselves attempt to resolve certain issues. Little, if any, affirmative action is taken by a workers' compensation appeals board judge at a conference pretrial, other than to make suggestions. Seldom will an appeals board judge make any ruling regarding any asserted lien by the doctor or other lien claimant. More important, the judge seldom issues an order compelling the defendant (insurance company) to pay the doctor's or other lien claimant's bill.

A regular hearing allows a lien claimant, such as a doctor, to present evidence on his or her behalf that the treatment rendered to the injured employee was necessary and that the amount charged was reasonable and customary. It is essentially a trial before the workers' compensation appeals board judge on the limited issue of payment of the medical or dental bill. The defendant (insurance company) is allowed to call witnesses to present evidence either that the treatment was unnecessary or that the amount charged was excessively high as compared to the amount other physicians would charge for the same or similar services. The matter is submitted to the workers' compensation appeals board judge following presentation of the evidence. Thereafter, the judge makes a determination based on the evidence presented and issues an order.

A few suggestions for preparing and filing a declaration of readiness to proceed should be noted at this time. First, an explanation should be made to the appeals board about why the declaration is being filed. For example, the lien claimant (doctor, dentist, and other professional rendering services) would state that all negotiations with the defendant/workers' compensation insurance company regarding the bill have failed, and the parties need the appeals board's assistance in resolving the issues.

Second, note that the time required for the hearing has been estimated at one hour. The estimate also indicates that one witness and one medical witness may be called to testify. The one witness is the injured employee (patient). The medical witness is the doctor, dentist, and other professional who rendered services to the injured employee. Remember, that the issue involved is payment of the bill for these services and not necessarily the entire case.

Many cases take longer than one hour to present to the judge at a hearing. However, the workers' compensation appeals board may schedule the hearing for a later date if the medical or dental assistant preparing the form estimates that the hearing will take more than two hours. Thus, estimating the hearing to be between one and two hours assures that the case will be set for the next available date on the appeals board's calendar. Depending on the worker's compensation appeals board, most cases are scheduled for hearing within two months after the declaration of readiness to proceed has been filed and served on all interested parties.

WORKERS' COMPENSATION APPEALS BOARD HEARING

The workers' compensation appeals board favors the presentation of medical evidence in the form of written reports. However, evidence in the form of witness testimony may be required where the issue before the appeals board is whether the treatment was necessary or whether the amount charged for the services was reasonable. When the lien claimant has filed a declaration of readiness to proceed, it may be advantageous to issue and serve a subpoena on the injured employee (patient) to compel his or her attendance at the hearing. Subpoenas may be obtained from the workers' compensation appeals board for this purpose. The injured employee should be called to testify that the treatment received did help his or her condition, especially any subjective complaints of pain. This would tend to establish that the treatment was necessary to cure or otherwise relieve the employee of the effects of the injury.

Testimony could then be given by the medical or dental assistant on behalf of the doctor, dentist, or other lien claimant regarding the bill. The medical or dental assistant would testify that the amount charged was reasonable compared to the amount other doctors charged for the same or similar services within the community.

Many physicians have used this approach in obtaining payment of their bills. The advantage of having the injured employee testify is that often testimony from the doctor or dentist will then not be required. Accordingly, the medical or other assistant can and often does present the entire case on behalf of his or her employer (the doctor). Illustration 18.10 is a copy of a subpoena that may be obtained from the local branch of the workers' compensation appeals board. Again, the italic typewritten portion of the form represents the information that the medical or dental assistant would type on the form. To be

83 ANA 112233   CASE NO.

James Smith, M.D.   *Acme Work Shops, Inc., Fly By*
                                       Night Insurance Co.
                              vs.

APPLICANT   DEFENDANT

SUBPOENA

The People of the State of California Send Greetings to:

JOHN COWDREY

YOU ARE HEREBY COMMANDED to appear before a Referee of the WORKERS' COMPENSATION
APPEALS BOARD OF THE STATE OF CALIFORNIA at *28 Civic Center Plaza,*
Santa Ana, CA 90000

on the *9th* day of *August* , 19 *83* , at *1:30* o'clock *P.* M.,
to testify in the above-entitled action.

For failure to attend as required, you may be deemed guilty of a contempt and liable to pay to the parties aggrieved
all losses and damages sustained thereby and forfeit one hundred dollars in addition thereto. This subpoena is issued

at request of *James Smith, M.D.* , Telephone No. *(714) 555-5544* .

[SEAL]

WORKERS' COMPENSATION APPEALS BOARD
OF THE STATE OF CALIFORNIA

_____
Secretary, Assistant Secretary, Referee

Date *August 5,* , 19 *83*

This subpoena does not apply to any member of the Highway Patrol, Sheriff's Office or City Police Department
unless accompanied by notice from the Board that deposit of the witness fee has been made in accordance with
Gov't Code 68097.2 et seq.

DIA WACB 30 FORM 30 (REV. 11-74)   △ OSP

ILLUSTRATION 18.10   SUBPOENA TO APPEAR BEFORE THE WORKERS' COMPENSATION APPEALS BOARD

valid, the subpoena must be personally served on any witness called to testify
at the hearing. Proof of personal service is necessary if the witness fails to
appear. An example of a completed preprinted proof of service form is seen in
Illustration 18.11. This form is the back side of the subpoena. A second copy of
the subpoena is served on the witness. The original subpoena is returned to the
appeals board in the event the witness fails to appear at the hearing.

FEDERAL COMPENSATION ACT

The preceding workers' compensation appeals board discussion does not apply to federal government employees who are injured as a result of their
employment. Federal employees are covered for work-related injuries under

PROOF OF SERVICE

STATE OF CALIFORNIA

COUNTY OF_____*Orange*_____ }

I served the foregoing subpoena by showing the original thereof to each of the following named persons, and by delivering a copy thereof to each of said persons, personally, at the date and place set forth opposite each name, to wit:

NAME	PLACE	DATE
John Cowdrey	*345 E. Fir St.* *Anytown, CA 90000*	*August 7, 1983*

Dated_____*August 7,*_____, 19__*83*__

I certify (or declare) under penalty of perjury that the foregoing is true and correct.

_____*Art Eggleston*_____
Signature *Art Eggleston*

ILLUSTRATION 18.11 PROOF OF SERVICE

the Federal Compensation for Work Injuries Act ("Federal Compensation Act"). This act defines a work-related injury and the benefits that the injured federal employee may receive. Certainly, the federal employee most commonly covered by the Federal Compensation Act is the mail carrier. Dog bites, sprained ankles, and sprained shoulders, backs, and necks make up the vast majority of work-related injuries sustained by these individuals.

All employees covered by the Federal Compensation Act are entitled to receive medical, dental, and other health-related services as a result of the work-related injury. Likewise, the physician, dentist, or other professional rendering such services is entitled to payment of his or her bill by the federal government on behalf of the injured employee. The procedure for obtaining payment of the bill is very simple and is uniform throughout the United States.

The following example outlines the procedure for treatment of a mail carrier's injury and payment of the medical bill. The same procedural steps apply to all federal employees who are injured on the job.

Michael is a mailman who has just come into Dr. Gray's office because he was bitten by a dog while delivering mail. The incident occurred approximately thirty minutes before he arrived at the office. He has not informed his immediate supervisor but needs immediate medical attention.

The medical assistant should obtain all standard patient information forms required by the medical facility. In addition, the medical assistant should obtain a detailed description of Michael's injury, including: the time when Michael was bitten; the location where the dog bite occurred; the location of the local post office where Michael works; and the name of the supervisor, safety officer, or postmaster of that post office branch. The medical assistant should then telephone the post office branch to inform Michael's immediate supervisor or safety officer about the dog bite incident. The assistant should request from this person a number to identify the incident. This is called a case number. It is often identified by a capital letter preceding the number. For example, in this case the number assigned is preceded by a captial "A" (such as A-1010) because the incident occurred in California. This number should be put on Michael's chart and billing documents. THIS NUMBER IS CRITICAL IN RECEIVING PAYMENT FOR ANY PROFESSIONAL SERVICES RENDERED to Michael as a result of the dog bite.

Having obtained a case number for the dog bite incident, the medical assistant may then merely send an itemized bill for Michael's treatment to the area administrative office of the U.S. Department of Labor. The identifying case number previously obtained from the local post office MUST be included on the itemized bill. Thereafter, the Department of Labor pays the medical bill directly to the physician for the treatment Michael received.

Michael could have obtained his identifying case number had he notified the safety officer at the office where he worked about the dog bite. He could have given this case number to the medical assistant, in which case the assistant would not have had to contact the local safety officer.

Michael may also have been provided with a form (CA16 or similar form) regarding the claim that is similar to a standard insurance claim form including identifying information about Michael and the dog bite incident.

A section of this form must be completed by the medical assistant on behalf of the doctor or the health professional who rendered services. This section includes the diagnosis, type of treatment rendered, and an itemization of the bill. Michael could have gotten this form from the local safety officer of the post office and given it to the medical assistant to aid in collecting payment from the Department of Labor.

The medical assistant would either complete the form or forward an itemized billing to the Department of Labor located at 450 Golden Gate Avenue, San Francisco, California or other appropriate branch office. REMEMBER, THE CLAIM MUST INCLUDE THE CASE NUMBER, OR PAYMENT WILL NOT BE MADE.

EXAMPLES / QUESTIONS

1. *Obtain and prepare a workers' compensation lien for treatment received by your patient, John Smith, from your boss, Dr. Dean Jones, a chiropractor. The amount of the patient's bill to date is $700. This is the second lien that has been filed on this case. Don't forget to indicate that this really represents an amended lien.*

2. *From the illustration given in this chapter, please prepare a lien for professional services rendered to a patient as a result of an automobile collision (not worker's compensation).*

3. *Obtain and prepare a declaration of readiness to proceed (use Illustration 18.13) according to the lien prepared (and filed with the workers' compensation appeals board) in example 1.*

4. *John and Harry are on a business trip. Harry is driving, and John is riding as a passenger in Harry's car. While they are stopped at a stoplight, their vehicle is rear-ended by a cement truck owned by ABC Cement Co. Sam, an employee of ABC Cement Co., is driving the truck. As a result of the accident, John sustains a back injury and comes into your office for medical treatment.*

   What are all the possible ways to assure collection for any treatment rendered to John by your doctor as a result of the accident? (Hint: there are at least seven possibilities.)

   > **Answer:** Cash up front; workers' compensation with lien; the medical provision of Harry's automobile insurance; any group health insurance that John might have with his employer; payment throught ABC Cement Co.; payment from Sam; payment from ABC's insurance coverage of the cement truck; payment from Sam's own automobile and/or homeowner's insurance company; in the event that a lawsuit is filed, medical liens signed by John and his attorney; in the event that John is married and his wife works, possibly group health insurance coverage throught her employer; in the event that Harry is partly at fault for the accident, Harry's liability insurance coverage on his automobile; and, in the event that all parties are uninsured, possibly John's own automobile insurance company under the uninsured motorists provision of his policy.

5. *Contact your local post office and obtain the proper address of your local regional office of the Department of Labor, where you can submit a bill for treatment of a mail carrier based on a work-related claim.*

Glossary

abrogate (abrogation)   to repeal; to cancel or repeal by authority; to annul.

absolute liability   the state of being bound or obliged by law or justice to do, pay, or make good something that is free from all restrictions or qualifications; unconditional liability.

abstain   to do without voluntarily; to refrain from; to do without some or all food, drink, or other item.

accusation   a formal charge against a person that he or she is guilty of a punishable offense; the charge is laid before a court or magistrate having jurisdiction to inquire into the alleged crime.

actionable   subject to or affording ground for an action—that is, litigation or lawsuit.

ad litem   for purposes of litigation; for example, a guardian ad litem is a person given the power and duty to act in behalf of another, legally incapacitated person for purposes of a lawsuit.

adversary   a litigant; an opponent; the opposite party to a lawsuit.

agency   a relation created either by express or implied contract or by law whereby one person (called the *principal,* or *constituent*) delegates to another person (called the *agent*) the authority to transact some lawful business or to do certain acts for him or her with more or less discretionary power. The agent undertakes to manage the affair and render an accounting thereof. General agency exists when the agent is delegated to do all acts connected with a particular trade, business, or employment.

aggressor   one who engages in aggression; one who initiates an offensive or unprovoked assault or act.

alleged   asserted, claimed, stated, charged.

amenable   responsible, or answerable; accountable, liable to punishment.

apprehension   the seizure, taking, or arrest of a person on a criminal charge; fear; dread; anxiety.

arbitrator   an unofficial person chosen by the parties to a lawsuit who investigates the matter and makes a determination.

Glossary terms are adapted from *Black's Law Dictionary,* 6th Ed., St. Paul, MN: West Publishing Co., 1990.

arrest to seize or take into custody by legal authority; to stop; to check; to catch and hold.

arson the malicious burning of the real or personal property of another. Generally, arson amounts to felonious conduct.

asbestosis lung disease caused by inhaling particles of asbestos.

assault unlawful attempt or threat to commit battery, coupled with the present ability to inflict injury on another person.

assert to state positively; to affirm; to state as true; to put forward or maintain insistently; to put into effect; to thrust oneself forward aggressively.

atrophy the wasting away or the failure to grow of an organ, limb, or other bodily part; to fail to develop.

battery unprivileged, willful, unlawful, and intentional touching of another person.

bona fide literally, "in good faith"; with integrity; honest; sincere; authentic.

burglary the breaking and entering into the dwelling place of another person in the night for the purpose of committing a criminal act (most commonly a felony).

carte blanche complete authority or freedom of action or judgment.

causation (cause) that which produces an effect.

common jury in practice, the ordinary jury by which issues of fact are generally tried; distinguished from a special jury, such as a grand jury; the ordinary jury of twelve men and women for a trial of a civil or criminal action.

compensable damages payment for damages awarded as compensation.

compensate to make suitable or equal return or payment; reimburse; remunerate; make up for; counterbalance; offset; to provide with or to be an equivalent.

complaint the first or initial pleading on the part of the plaintiff in a civil action; the court document that alleges certain misconduct of the defendant and request of redress, compensation, or other relief.

condition precedent a condition that must be fulfilled or an act that must be performed before some right can be gained, some action can be performed, or some agreement can become effective.

conformed copy a copy of a legal document that conforms exactly to that filed with the court, which includes the clerk's filing stamp, the judge's signature, and the date the document is filed or signed by the court or clerk.

conjectural based on or involving conjecture, which is the act of forming an opinion not based on definite evidence or proof; guessing.

consideration the cause, motive, price, or impelling influence that induces a contracting party to enter into a contract; the reason or material cause of a contract; the act or forbearance to act—or the promise to act or forbear—that is afforded by one party to an agreement and accepted by the other as an inducement to that other's act or promise.

consort   acting together, as in a team; one that shares the company of or is associated with another; a spouse.

consortium   the legal right of a husband or wife to the fellowship, company, cooperation, and aid of the other partner.

contract   a promissory agreement between two or more persons that creates, modifies, or destroys a legal relation; an agreement, on sufficient consideration, to do or not to do a particular thing.

credibility   worthiness of belief; the quality in a witness that renders his or her evidence worthy of belief.

deductible   that which may be taken away or subtracted; that portion of an insured loss to be borne by the insured before he or she is entitled to recovery from the insurer.

"deeper pockets" doctrine   the practice whereby a plaintiff who has obtained a judgment against multiple defendants under a theory of joint and several liability seeks to collect his or her damages from the defendant who has the greatest ability to pay the damages awarded.

defendant   a person against whom a civil or a criminal action is brought in a court of law.

deliberate   to weigh, ponder, discuss.

deliberation   the act or process of deliberating; the act of weighing and examining the reasons for and against a contemplated act or course of action; careful consideration with the aim of making a decision.

demean   to lower the dignity or status of; degrade; debase.

derisive   expressing or characterized by words of contempt, mockery, or ridicule.

derivative   coming from another; taken from or owing its existence to something preceding; secondary.

detrimental reliance   any loss or harm suffered by a person based on another person's failure to act as promised; the promise to act may be made by implication.

discovery   in a general sense, the ascertainment of that which was previously unknown through pretrial devices that can be used by one party to obtain facts and information about the case from the other party in order to assist the party's preparation for trial.

disseminate   to scatter widely; to spread abroad; to diffuse.

dissenting opinion   an opinion that disagrees with the majority's view.

doctrine   a rule, principle, theory, or tenet of the law.

duress   constraint or coercion used to force someone to do something.

economist   a specialist in economics, whose area of expertise includes the management of the income and expenditures of a business, community, or person.

emancipate   to free from bondage, control, or restraint; to liberate; to make a legally recognized adult because of marriage, membership in the military or by court order.

emancipation   the act by which one who was unfree or under the power or control of another is rendered free or set at liberty and made his or her own master; principally used with reference to the emancipation of a minor child by the child's parents, involving the entire surrender of the right of the care, custody, and earnings of such child as well as a renunciation of parental duties.

embezzlement   the fraudulent appropriation of property or money by a person to whom it has been entrusted by another person.

employee   one who works for an employer; a person working for salary or wages who is authorized to act on behalf of his or her principal, called the *employer*.

estop   to stop, bar, or impede; to prevent; to preclude.

estoppel   a bar or impediment raised by the law precluding a person from alleging or denying a certain fact or state of affairs because of his or her previous allegation, denial, conduct, or admission or because of a final adjudication (judgment) of the matter in a court of law.

execute   to finish, accomplish, make complete, fulfill, as in executing a judgment or document.

expert witness   person requested by a party to a lawsuit to give an expert opinion regarding some element of the case.

express contract   an actual agreement of the parties, the terms of which are openly stated in distinct and explicit language, either orally or in writing, at the time the contract is made.

extort   to obtain by force, threats, abuse of authority, or other types of oppression; to compel or coerce; to gain by wrongful methods.

failure (omission) to act   tortious (wrongful) conduct associated with the failure to do something that should have been done.

false imprisonment   unlawful imprisonment or detention.

felony   any of several crimes—for example, murder, rape and burglary—designated by statute to be graver than a misdemeanor, commonly punishable in the United States by a minimum penalty of imprisonment in a penitentiary for at least one year and a maximum penalty of death.

formal contract   an agreement by which one person *promises* to do something in exchange for a promise from another person; the promise can be written or verbal.

fortify   to give mental or moral strength to; to give support to; to confirm or corroborate.

fraud   deceitful practice or willful device resorted to with the intent to deprive another person of his or her right or in some manner to cause him or her injury; as distinguished from negligence, it is always intentional and affirmative.

frivolous   of little value or importance; trivial; petty; nonserious; lacking merit.

garnish   to attach or seize (as in attaching a person's wages).

Good Samaritan laws laws that protect from liability a rescuer or one who pities and selflessly helps another or others, as in rendering first aid, unless the rescuer is grossly negligent

grand jury a jury of inquiry summoned to each session of the criminal courts whose duty it is to receive complaints and accusations in criminal cases, hear the evidence adduced on the part of the state, and issue bills of indictment in cases where the jury is satisfied that a trial ought to be held.

guardian a person legally given the power and charged with the duty to manage the property and/or rights of another person who, for some reason, is considered incapable of administering his or her own affairs.

heir a person who succeeds, by descent and right of relationship according to the rules of law, to an estate in land or personal property on the death of an ancestor; primarily, a person related to another by blood who would receive that person's real estate or property at his or her death.

implication that which is logically implied, hinted at, or suggested but not directly expressed.

implied contract an agreement between two or more persons that creates an obligation to do or not do a particular thing that arises by implication. An implied contract is one not created or evidenced by the explicit agreement of the parties but inferred by the law, as a matter of reason and justice from the acts or conduct, the circumstances surrounding the transaction making it a reasonable, or even a necessary, assumption that a contract existed by tacit understanding.

impliedly by implication.

imply to indicate or suggest without direct statement.

incarceration confinement in jail or prison.

incompetent lacking in ability, legal qualification, or fitness to discharge a required duty; used to designate the condition or legal status of persons who are unable or unfit to manage their own affairs by reason of insanity or feeblemindedness and for whom a committee or guardian may be apointed by a court.

indemnification the act of indemnifying; the state of being indemnified.

indemnify to compensate for loss, damage, or expense incurred; to give security against future damage or loss; to insure; especially, to compensate a defendant to a lawsuit.

independent contractor one who, independently employed, contracts to do a piece of work according to his or her own methods and without being subject to the control of his or her employer except as to the result of the work. It is generally held that the right to control the mode of the work contracted is the principal consideration in determining whether one is employed as an independent contractor or as an employee.

indictment an accusation in writing founded and presented by a grand jury charging that the person named therein has committed some act or been guilty of some omission that by law is a public offense.

informant a person who informs or makes an accusation against another person whom he or she suspects to have violated some penal statute; a person who ferrets out crimes and offenses and provides pertinent information to law inforcement authorities to bolster the prosecution, not because of his or her office or any special duty in the matter, but for the sake of the share of the fine or penalty that the law allots to the informer in certain cases.

information an accusation presented against a person for some criminal offense, without indictment.

infraction the breaking or violating of something, such as a law or a rule; infringement; in law, less significant than a misdemeanor.

instrumentality (instrument) the means by or through which something is done or brought about; that which serves or is used for some purpose or means.

intentional infliction of emotional distress tortious (wrong) conduct intended to cause (and does cause) another person emotional distress or psychological injury.

interested party any person or corporation having an interest, a right to, or share in, something; those having a common concern in some industry, cause, or lawsuit.

invasion encroachment on the rights of another person.

invasion of privacy the unwarranted appropriation or exploitation of one's personality; publicizing one's private affairs with which the public has no legitimate concern; wrongful intrusion into one's private activities in such a manner as to cause mental suffering, shame, or humiliation to a person of ordinary sensibilities.

joint and several liability the situation that exists when a plaintiff has the option to sue one or more of the parties to liability separately or all of them together.

judge a public officer, appointed to preside and to administer the law in a court of justice; the chief member of a court, charged with the control of proceedings and the decision of questions of law or discretion.

judgment the official and authentic decision of a court on the respective rights and claims of the parties to an action or suit litigated therein and submitted to its determination; the conclusion of law based on facts found or admitted by the parties or on the default of the parties in the course of the suit.

judgment creditor a person to whom a debt is owed by another person, called the **judgment debtor,** where the debt is based on a judgment rendered in a lawsuit.

judgment debtor a person whose debt to another person has been reduced to or based on that of a judgment following a lawsuit.

judicial abrogation annulment or repeal of a rule of law by the courts.

jurisdiction the power and authority constitutionally conferred on a court or judge to pronounce the sentence of the law or to award the remedies provided by law; the geographic area in which a court has power.

jury a certain number of men and women selected according to law and sworn to inquire into certain matters of fact and declare the truth based on the evidence laid before them.

legal-lined paper stationery that is preprinted with a numbered left margin containing 26 or 28 numbered lines (see Illustration 15.1 as an example).

liability the state of being bound or obliged in law or justice to do, pay, or make reparations for something.

liability in tort the state of being bound or obliged in law or justice to do, pay, or make a person's wrongful or otherwise tortious conduct.

lien a hold or claim by one person on the property of another as a security for some debt or charge; charge on the property for the payment of a debt or duty; in litigation cases, the promise by the patient and his or her attorney to pay the physician from any proceeds received on the case for services rendered on behalf of the patient.

lien creditor one whose debt or claim is secured by a lien on a particular property, as distinguished from a *general creditor*, who has no such security.

litigation a judicial controversy; a contest in a court of justice for the purpose of enforcing a right.

loathsome extremely disgusting; repulsive; offensive.

malfeasance the wrongful or unjust performance of some act that the person has no right to perform or that he or she has stipulated by contract not to perform; the doing of an act that is totally wrongful.

malice the doing of a wrongful act intentionally, without just cause or excuse; the desire to cause injury or pain to another; a condition of the mind and heart that is heedless of social duty and fatally bent on mischief, the existence of which condition is inferred from acts committed or words spoken; in **privileged communications,** malice involves an evil intent or motive arising from spite, personal hatred or illwill, culpable recklessness, or a willful and wanton disregard of the rights and interests of the person defamed.

malicious characterized by, showing, or resulting from **malice.**

malpractice any professional misconduct, unreasonable lack of skill or fidelity in professional or fiduciary duties, evil practice, or illegal or immoral conduct that causes injury to a person.

manslaughter the unlawful killing of another without malice, either express or implied; may be committed voluntarily or involuntarily in a sudden heat of passion, or involuntarily in the commission of an unlawful act or in the commission of a lawful act without due caution and circumspection.

mayhem   the act of unlawfully and maliciously depriving a human being of a member of his or her body or in some way disfiguring that person's body or rendering it useless.

meritorious   worthy of reward or praise; having merit.

misdemeanor   an act committed or omitted in violation of a public law either forbidding or commanding it; under modern statutes, the distinction between **felonies** (major criminal offenses) and misdemeanors is generally the severity of the violation. The grade of the offense is determined by the kind and the extent of punishment that may be inflicted. Misdemeanors characteristically carry a lesser degree of punishment.

misfeasance   a misdeed or trespass; improper performance of some lawful act.

moral turpitude   an act or behavior that gravely violates moral sentiment or accepted moral standards of community and is a morally culpable quality held to be present in some criminal offenses as distinguished from others.

murder   a crime in which a person of sound mind and discretion kills another person without any warrant, justification, or excuse in law, with malice— that is, with the deliberate purpose or design formed in the mind before the commission of the act.

negligence   the failure to do something that a reasonable person would do when guided by those considerations that ordinarily regulate human affairs; the doing of something that a reasonable and prudent person would not do; the failure to use ordinary care; the failure to do something that results in an injury; carelessness, thoughtlessness, disregard, inattention, inadvertence, and oversight.

neurosis   a functional mental disorder characterized by varying combinations of anxieties, compulsions, obsessions, phobias, depression, and other problematic psychological states.

nonfeasance   the neglect or failure of a person to do some act that he or she ought to do; not generally used to denote a breach of contract but rather the failure to perform a duty toward the public whereby some individual sustains special damages.

notary public   a public officer whose function is to administer oaths and to attest to and certify, by his or her hand or official seal, certain classes of documents to give them credit and authenticity.

ostensible agency (agent)   a principal/agent relationship established by implication that the agent is authorized to act on behalf of the principal; for example, an ostensible agent is an employee who by his or her position alone gives another person the impression that he or she has the granted authority to act on behalf of the employer.

peers   equals; others who are of a person's rank and station; thus, "a trial by a jury of one's peers" means a trial by a jury of citizens.

penalty of perjury the penalty for knowingly and willfully giving false testimony, which may be incarceration.

percentage-of-fault culpability in causing injury that is apportioned among two or more persons; that amount of negligent conduct assessed against one of multiple defendants that caused a person's injury.

percipient witness a person with knowledge of the facts and circumstances of a litigation *not* being called as an expert witness.

perjury giving willful, knowing, and false testimony when one is under an oath to tell the truth.

permanent and stationary terminology used when a patient's permanent injury has become stationary, or stabilized—that is, it will not get better or worse.

permanent disability a disability that causes impairment of earning capacity, impairment of normal use of a bodily part, or handicap of competitive ability in the open labor market.

per quod words "actionable per quod" are words not actionable per se on their face but are actionable only in consequence of intrinsic facts showing that the circumstances under which the words were said resulted in damages to a slandered party.

per se by himself, herself, or itself; in itself; taken alone; inherently; in isolation; unconnected with other matters—in other words, in the absence of other circumstances.

plaintiff the party in a civil lawsuit who brings the action into a court of law.

precedence the act or state of going before; adjustment; the right to be placed first in a certain order.

premeditated the degree of forethought sufficient to show intent to commit an act.

prima facie sufficient to establish a fact or facts unless rebutted or contradicted; at first sight; before further investigation. A litigating party is said to have a prima facie case when the evidence in its favor is sufficiently strong that its opponent is called on to answer it.

privacy the right of individuals (or corporations) to withhold themselves and their property from public scrutiny, if they so choose.

privileged communications certain kinds of communication passing between persons who stand in a confidential relationship to each other and who, on account of their situation, are bound by a rule of secrecy; the law will not permit these communications to be divulged or allow them to be inquired into in a court of law (for example, communication between a physician and his or her patient or between an attorney and his or her client).

propensity a natural inclination or tendency.

propound to put forward for consideration; to set forth; to propose.

proximately directly or immediately; pertaining to that which in an ordinary, natural sequence produces a specific result.

publication   the act of publishing, making public, offering to public notice, or rendering accessible to public scrutiny.

punitive damages   damages awarded to a plaintiff against the defendant for the sake of example and as a form of punishment imposed on the defendant.

quantum merit   literally, "as much as he or she deserves;" an implied promise on the part of the defendant to pay the plaintiff as much as he or she reasonably deserves for his or her labor.

rape   unlawful sexual intercourse with another person without his or her consent.

recitation   the formal statement or setting forth of some matter of fact (as to recite).

republication   the reexecution or reestablishment by a second publication.

rescission   the act of cancelling or abrogating; withdrawal.

responding party   the person to whom a request or question is directed for a response.

restatement of torts   a set of definitions regarding types of conduct that are considered tortious

restitution   the act or restoring something that has been lost or taken away; compensation for loss of damage; reparation.

robbery   the deprivation of a person of his or her property through force and violence.

sanction   (v.) to impose a penalty of punishment on a person as a means of enforcing obedience to a law.

sanctions   (n.) penalties or punishments provided as a means of enforcing obedience to a law.

semantics   the twisting of meaning to mislead or confuse; the branch of linguistics dealing with meanings given to words and the changes that occur in those meanings over time.

standard of care   that degree of care and skill associated with a particular profession as a whole in rendering examinations and/or treatment for a particular illness.

statute of limitations   a statute prescribing limitations to the right of an action on certain described causes of action or criminal prosecution—that is, declaring that no suit shall be maintained on such cause of action, nor any criminal charge be made, unless brought within a specified period of time after the right accrued.

statutory   introduced or governed by statute (a law passed by the legislature) as opposed to common law.

temporary disability   compensation paid to an injured employee for lost earnings while the patient/employee's injury is healing or otherwise not considered permanent and stationary.

theory   idea or ideas that explain a group of facts or phenomena; assumption or guess based on evidence; formulation assumed to be true but based on certain principles not completely certified; abstract reasoning; speculation.

toll   to suspend or stop temporarily; usually refers to the temporary suspension of a statute of limitations while a plaintiff is a minor, or in prison, or unable, for some other reason permitted by statute, to maintain a lawsuit.

tort   wrong; injury; the opposite of right; legal wrong committed on a person or property independent of contract; the violation of some private obligation by which damages accrue to the individual; civil as opposed to criminal wrong.

tort law   that area of the law based on a private or civil wrong or injury, other than a breach of contract, for which the court will provide a remedy in the form of an action for damages. The elements of every tort action are: existence of a legal duty from defendant to plaintiff, breach of duty, and damages as a proximate result.

tortious   wrongful; of the nature of a tort.

trespass   an unlawful interference with the person, property, or rights of another person.

tribunal   the whole body of judges who compose a jurisdiction; where a case is tried before multiple judges in lieu of a jury. Alternatively, a panel empowered to hear and decide certain controversies (see, for example, medical malpractice tribunals discussed in Chapter 14).

trust   a right of real or personal property held by one party for the benefit of another party.

ultimate facts   specific facts; particular facts relating to someone's conduct.

unconscionable   bargain or contract that no person in his or her senses and not under delusion would make and that no fair and honest person would accept.

unprivileged   not privileged; not consented to.

verification   the examination of a writing for the purpose of ascertaining its truth; a certificate or affidavit that such writing is true.

vicarious   performed or experienced in place of another.

vindicate   to prove (someone) innocent of suspicion of wrongdoing; to maintain or defend (a right or claim) against opposition; to justify.

writ   a written precept issued from a court of justice, sealed with its seal, and addressed to a sheriff or other officer of the law or directed to the person whose action the court desires to command: requires the performance of a specified act or gives authority and commission to have it done.

Bibliography/
Suggested readings

Barry, V., *Moral Aspects of Health Care.* Belmont, Calif.: Wadsworth, 1982.

Bayles, M. D., *Professional Ethics.* Belmont, Calif.: Wadsworth, 1982.

Black, H. C., *Black's Law Dictionary,* 6th ed. St. Paul, Minn.: West Publishing Co., 1990.

Brosnahan J. J., *Trial Handbook for California Lawyers.* San Francisco: Bancroft-Whitney, 1974.

Conway, P. R., *Outline of the Law of Contracts,* 3rd ed. Irvington-on-Hudson, N.Y.: American Legal Publications, 1968.

Hanna, W. L., *California Law of Employee Injuries and Workmen's Compensation,* vol. 2, 2nd ed. San Francisco and New York: Matthew Bender, 1983.

Herlick, S. D., *California Workers' Compensation Law Handbook,* vol. 1, 2nd ed. Los Angeles: Parker & Son, 1978.

James, F., Jr., *Civil Procedure.* Boston and Toronto: Little, Brown, 1965.

Keeton, W. P., et al., *Prosser and Keeton on The Law of Torts,* 5th Ed., St. Paul, MN, West Publishing Co., 1984

Kennedy, R. D., *California Expert Witness Guide.* Berkeley, Calif.: California Continuing Education of the Bar, 1983.

King, J. H., Jr., *The Law of Medical Malpractice In A Nutshell,* 2nd Ed., St. Paul, MN, West Publishing Co., 1986.

Lewis, M. A. and Tamparo, C. D., [*Medical Law, Ethics, & Bioethics in the Medical Office*], 3rd Ed., Philadelphia, F. A. Davis Co., 1993

Mason, L. R., *California Civil Procedure Handbook.* Los Angeles: Parker & Son, 1983.

Mastoris, J. F., 1981–1982 *Summary of California Workers' Compensation Law.* Los Angeles: Conference of California Workers' Compensation Judges, 1982.

McConnell, T. C., *Moral Issues in Health Care: An Introduction to Medical Ethics,* Belmont, Calif.: Wadsworth, 1982.

Munson, R., *Intervention and Reflection: Basic Issues in Medical Ethics,* 2nd ed. Belmont, Calif.: Wadsworth, 1983.

Nolan, J. R. and Sartorio, L. J., *Tort Law, Massachusetts Practice Series,* vols. 37 & 37A, 2nd Ed., St. Paul, MN, West Publishing Co., 1989 & 1994 Supplements.

O'Brien, D. W., *California Employer-Employee Benefits Handbook,* 6th ed. Covina, Calif.: Winter Brook, 1981.

Stein, J. A., *Damages and Recovery: Personal Injury and Death Actions.* Rochester, N.Y. and San Francisco: The Lawyers Co-Operative Publishing Co., and Bancroft-Whitney, 1972.

Werchick, J., *California Preparation and Trial,* 3rd ed. Los Angeles: Parker & Son, 1981.

Witkin, B. E., *California Procedure,* 2nd ed. San Francisco: Bancroft-Whitney, 1970.

Witkin, B. E., *Summary of California Law,* 8th ed. San Francisco: Bancroft-Whitney, 1973.

INDEX

Boldface numbers indicate pages on which glossary terms are introduced.